Revise
AS&A2

F

History

Modern British & European History

Contents

Specification lists 6

AS/A2 Level History courses 11

Different types of questions 13

Exam technique 15

Chapter 1 From Pitt to Peel, 1783–1846

1.1 Pitt the Younger, 1783–1801 17

1.2 Lord Liverpool and the Tories, 1815–30 18

1.3 The Great Reform Act, 1832 21

1.4 The Whigs, 1830–41 23

1.5 Chartism 24

1.6 Peel 25

Sample question and model answer 28

Chapter 2 England, 1846–86

2.1 Mid-Victorian Britain, 1846–68 29

2.2 Gladstone 32

2.3 Gladstone and Ireland 34

2.4 Disraeli 37

Sample question and model answer 40

Chapter 3 Nineteenth century Britain: protest and reform

3.1 Parliamentary reform 41

3.2 Chartism 43

3.3 The Poor Law 47

3.4 Public health 48

3.5 Factory legislation 50

3.6 Education 51

Exam practice questions 52

Chapter 4 Foreign affairs, 1815–1914

4.1 Castlereagh, Canning and Palmerston 54

4.2 The Eastern Question 58

4.3 The expansion of the Empire 60

4.4 British foreign policy, 1890–1914 62

4.5 The experience of war 66

Exam practice questions 68

Chapter 5 The Edwardian age

5.1 The Conservatives, 1900–5	69
5.2 The Liberals, 1905–15	70
5.3 Votes for women	75
5.4 The rise of the Labour Party	78
5.5 The First World War, politics and society	80
Sample question and model answer	82

Chapter 6 Britain and Ireland, 1798–1922

6.1 Irish Nationalism	84
6.2 Support for the Union	88
6.3 British policies towards Ireland	89
6.4 The Irish economy	90
Sample question and model answer	93

Chapter 7 Britain in peace and war, 1918–45

7.1 Politics, 1918–24	94
7.2 The Conservative government of 1924–9	96
7.3 Britain in the 1930s	98
7.4 Churchill, 1920–45	103
Sample question and model answer	108

Chapter 8 Appeasement and World War, 1919-45

8.1 British foreign policy in the 1920s	110
8.2 Appeasement	112
8.3 The Second World War	115
Exam practice questions	119

Chapter 9 Post-war Britain, 1945–2007

9.1 The Labour governments, 1945–51	120
9.2 The Conservatives, 1951–64	123
9.3 Conservative and Labour governments, 1964–79	125
9.4 Mrs Thatcher, 1979–90	130
9.5 Major and Blair, 1990–2007	133
9.6 Northern Ireland, 1968–98	135
Exam practice questions	137

Chapter 10 The development of democracy in Britain, 1868–1997

10.1 The electoral system	138
10.2 Politics and parties, 1868–1918	141
10.3 Politics and parties, 1918–45	142
10.4 Political parties and government, 1945-97	144
10.5 Government, Parliament and people	147
10.6 The influence of trade unions and the media	148
Exam practice questions	152

Contents

Chapter 11 France, 1814–71

11.1 The restored Bourbons and the Orleans Monarchy	153
11.2 Napoleon III	156
11.3 The Third Republic	160
Exam practice questions	162

Chapter 12 Russia, 1855–1917

12.1 Tsarist Russia, 1855–94	163
12.2 Nicholas II, 1894–1917	165
12.3 The 1917 revolutions	170
Sample question and model answer	172

Chapter 13 The unification of Italy

13.1 Nationalism and the 1848–9 revolutions	173
13.2 The forging of the Italian nation	175
Sample question and model answer	178

Chapter 14 The unification of Germany

14.1 Germany, 1815–62	179
14.2 Bismarck and unification, 1862–71	182
14.3 Bismarck's Germany, 1871–90	186
14.4 The Kaiserreich, 1890–1914	188
Exam practice questions	192

Chapter 15 Italy, 1896–1945

15.1 Italy, 1896–1915: a troubled nation	193
15.2 The rise of Fascism	194
15.3 The Fascist dictatorship	196
15.4 Mussolini's Italy	198
15.5 Foreign affairs	201
Exam practice questions	205

Chapter 16 Germany, 1918–45

16.1 The Weimar Republic	206
16.2 The rise of Hitler, 1930–3	210
16.3 Nazi Germany, 1933–9	214
16.4 Nazi Germany at war	221
Exam practice questions	223

Chapter 17 Soviet Russia, 1917–41

17.1 Lenin, 1917–24	224
17.2 Stalin's dictatorship, 1924–41	228
Sample question and model answer	234

Chapter 18 International relations, 1879–1941

18.1 Causes of the First World War	235
18.2 The First World War	239
18.3 The Versailles settlement	241
18.4 The League of Nations and international diplomacy in the 1920s	244
18.5 The Versailles settlement challenged, 1931–7	247
18.6 The outbreak of the Second World War, 1937–41	249
Exam practice questions	252

Chapter 19 Germany 1945–90: from defeat to unification

19.1 From occupation to division, 1945–9	253
19.2 The Federal Republic of Germany, 1949–63	256
19.3 The German Democratic Republic, 1949–71	259
19.4 The two Germanies, 1961–89	260
19.5 Reunification, 1989–91	262
Sample question and model answer	264

Chapter 20 The USSR, 1941–90

20.1 Stalin, 1941–53: the Second World War and after	265
20.2 Khrushchev and destalinisation	268
20.3 The Brezhnev era, 1964–82	270
20.4 The end of the Soviet Union, 1982–91	272
Sample question and model answer	275

Chapter 21 The Cold War, 1945–90

21.1 The outbreak of the Cold War, 1945–53	276
21.2 Peaceful co-existence and détente, 1953–82	280
21.3 Eastern Europe, 1953–85	283
21.4 The end of the Cold War	285
Exam practice questions	289

Exam practice answers	290
Index	302

Specification lists

AQA AS

Unit	Specification topic	Chapter reference
Unit 1: Change and Consolidation	Britain, 1815–1865 (B)	1.2–1.6, 2.1, 3.2, 4.1
	Tsarist Russia, 1855–1917	12.1–12.3
	The development of Germany, 1871–1925	14.3, 14.4, 16.1
	Russia and Germany, 1871–1914	12.1, 12.2, 14.3, 14.4, 18.1
	Britain, 1906–1951 (B)	5.1–5.3, 5.5, 7.1–7.3, 9.1
	Totalitarian ideology in theory and practice, c.1848–c.1941	15.2–15.4, 16.2, 16.3, 17.2
Unit 2: Historical Issues: Periods of Change	The forging of the Italian nation, 1848–1871	13.1, 13.2
	Britain, 1902–1918: the impact of New Liberalism (B)	4.4, 5.1–5.5
	Britain and appeasement, 1919–1940 (B)	8.1, 8.2
	A new Roman Empire? Mussolini's Italy, 1922–1945	15.2–15.5
	The impact of Stalin's leadership in the USSR, 1924–1941	17.2
	Life in Nazi Germany, 1933–1945	16.2–16.4
	Anti-semitism, Hitler and the German people, 1919–1942	16.2–16.4

Examination analysis

British History options are marked (B). Candidates may not combine a British History Unit 1 option with a British History Unit 2 option. Candidates may take a non-British option in both Units, but if they progress to A2 they must then take a British option in Unit 3.

Unit 1: Change and Consolidation

Three two-part structured questions from which candidates choose two. The first part of Unit 1 (12 marks) will focus on a narrow issue. The second part (24 marks) will test understanding of links between a narrow issue and the wider context. **1 hr 15 min exam** **50% of AS**

Unit 2: Historical Issues: Periods of Change

Candidates must answer one compulsory two-part source-based question and one two-part structured question from a choice of two. The source-based question will be based on three sources (around 300 words). The first sub-question (12 marks) will require comparison between two sources. The second question (24 marks) will require candidates to use the sources and their own knowledge to answer a general question.

In the first part of the structured question (12 marks) candidates will be asked to use their knowledge to make a judgment on a historical issue. The second part (24 marks) will require them to assess a judgment contained within a quotation. **1 hr 30 min exam** **50% of AS**

AQA A2

Unit	Specification topic	Chapter reference
Unit 3: The State and the People: Change and Continuity	British State and People, 1865–1915 (B)	2.1–2.4, 4.2–4.4, 5.1–5.4, 6.1, 6.3
	Monarchies and Republics in France, 1815–1875	11.1–11.3
	The State and people: Britain, 1918–1964 (B)	7.1–7.4, 9.1, 9.2
	Triumph and collapse: Russia and the USSR, 1941–1991	20.1–20.4
	From defeat to unity: Germany, 1945–1991	19.1–19.5
	The making of modern Britain, 1951–2007 (B)	9.2–9.5
	Aspects of international relations, 1945–2004	21.1, 21.2, 21.4
Unit 4: Historical Enquiry	Coursework unit	

Examination analysis

Unit 3: The State and the People: Change and Continuity

Candidates answer two essay questions from a choice of three. Each question carries 45 marks. The questions test candidates' understanding of change and development either in key critical periods or over the period as a whole. **1 hr 30 min exam** **60% of A2**

Unit 4: Historical Enquiry

Coursework unit. Internally assessed. Candidates must submit an essay of approximately 3500 words, based on the investigation of a historical issue. The topic chosen must arise from, and be placed in the context of, 100 years. This enables candidates to demonstrate synoptic understanding. **40% of A2**

6

OCR AS

Unit	Specification topic	Chapter reference
Unit 1: Period Studies	British History: • From Pitt to Peel 1783–1846 • Liberals and Conservatives 1846–95 • Foreign and imperial policies 1856–1914 • Domestic issues 1918–51 • Post-war Britain 1951–94	1.1–1.4, 1.6 2.1–2.4 4.2–4.4 7.1–7.3, 9.1 9.2–9.4, 9.6
	European History: • Monarchy, Republic and Empire: France 1814–70 • Peace and war: international relations c.1890–1941 • From autocracy to communism: Russia 1894–1941 • Democracy and dictatorship: Italy 1896–1943 • Democracy and dictatorship in Germany 1919–63 • The Cold War in Europe from 1945 to the 1990s	11.1, 11.2 18.1–18.6 12.2, 12.3, 17.1, 17.2 15.1–15.5 16.1–16.4, 19.1–19.3 21.1–21.4
Unit 2: Enquiries	British History: • The condition of England 1815–53 • The age of Gladstone and Disraeli 1865–86 • England and a new century 1900–24 • Churchill 1920–45	3.1–3.6 2.1–2.4, 4.2 5.1–5.5, 7.1 7.4
	European History: • The unification of Italy 1815–70 • Dictatorship and democracy in Germany 1933–63	13.1, 13.2 16.2–16.4, 19.1–19.3

OCR A2

Unit	Specification topic	Chapter reference
Unit 3: Historical Interpretations and Investigations	This is a coursework unit	
Unit 4: Historical Themes	The challenge of German Nationalism 1789–1919	14.1–14.4, 16.1, 18.3
	Britain and Ireland 1798–1921	2.3, 6.1–6.4
	Russia and its rulers 1855–1964	12.1–12.3, 17.1, 17.2, 20.1, 20.2
	The development of democracy in Britain 1868–1997	10.1–10.6

Examination analysis

Unit 3: Historical Interpretations and Investigations

Two extended essays of up to 2000 words each. One essay focuses on historical interpretations and the other on historical investigations. The unit allows candidates the opportunity to investigate critically a particular historical problem of their own choice. Each essay is worth a maximum of 40 marks. Internally assessed. **40% of A2**

Unit 4: Historical Themes

Three essay questions are set for each topic. Candidates answer two questions, either two from one topic or one question from each of two topics. Unit 4 is a synoptic part of the specification. The topics are based on Key Themes covering an extended period of at least one hundred years with an emphasis on continuity, development and change within the topic. Each question is worth a maximum of 60 marks.

2 hr exam **60% of A2**

Examination analysis

Candidates must combine either a British History option from Unit 1 with a European History option from Unit 2, or a European History option from Unit 1 with a British History option from Unit 2.

Unit 1: Period Studies

Three essay questions are set for each topic. Candidates answer two questions, either two from one topic or one from each of two topics. Each question is worth a maximum of 50 marks. **1 hr 30 min exam** **50% of AS**

Unit 2: Enquiries

One two-part source-based question. For the Unit 2 question, four or five sources are provided (maximum 500 words in total). Sources are mainly primary, but one may be secondary. The first sub-question (30 marks) requires comparison of two sources. The second question (70 marks) requires candidates to test an assertion against all the sources and their own knowledge.

1 hr 30 min exam **50% of AS**

Edexcel AS

Unit	Specification topic	Chapter reference
Unit 1: Historical Themes in Breadth	Russia in revolution, 1881–1924: From autocracy to dictatorship	12.1–12.3, 17.1
	Stalin's Russia, 1924–53	17.2, 20.1
	The road to unification: Italy, c.1815–70	13.1, 13.2
	The unification of Germany, 1848–90	14.1–14.3
	The collapse of the liberal state and the triumph of Fascism in Italy, 1896–1943	15.1–15.5
	Germany divided and reunited, 1945–91	19.1–19.5
	From Second Reich to Third Reich: Germany, 1918–45	16.1–16.4
Unit 2: British History Depth Studies	Britain, 1830–85: representation and reform	1.3, 2.1, 3.1, 3.2, 10.1
	Poverty, public health and the growth of government in Britain, 1830–75	3.3, 3.4
	The experience of warfare in Britain: Crimea, Boer and the First World War, 1854–1929	4.5, 5.5
	Britain, c.1860–1930: the changing position of women and the Suffrage Question	5.3, 10.1
	Britain and Ireland, 1867–1922	2.3, 5.2, 6.1–6.4, 7.1
	British political history, 1945–90: consensus and conflict	9.1–9.4

Examination analysis

Unit 1: Historical Themes in Breadth

Candidates answer two essay questions, one on each of two topics. There is a choice of two questions for each option. 30 marks for each question; total for the paper is 60 marks. **1 hr 20 min exam** **50% of AS**

Unit 2: British History Depth Studies

Candidates answer one two-part source-based question. Five sources (approximately 550 words in total), are provided. Part (a) focuses on analysis and evaluation of sources. In part (b) candidates are asked to assess a historical view using sources and their own knowledge. Part (a) carries 20 marks; part (b) carries 40 marks. Total for the paper is 60 marks.

1 hr 20 min exam **50% of AS**

Edexcel A2

Unit	Specification topic	Chapter reference
Unit 3: Depth Studies and Associated Historical Controversies	From Kaiser to Führer: Germany, 1900–45	14.4, 16.1–16.4, 18.1
	Britain and the challenge of fascism: saving Europe at a cost? c.1925–60	8.2, 8.3, 9.1
	The world in crisis, 1879–1941	18.1, 18.3–18.6
	A world divided: superpower relations, 1944–90	21.1–21.4
Unit 4: Historical Enquiry	Coursework unit	

Examination analysis

Unit 3: Depth Studies and Associated Historical Controversies

Candidates answer two questions on their chosen option:

(a) An essay question with an analytical focus (30 marks)

(b) A source-based question (40 marks) – three secondary sources (approximately 350–400 words) are provided for use in conjunction with candidates' own knowledge to reach a judgment on a historical controversy.

2 hr exam **60% of A2**

Unit 4: Historical Enquiry

Candidates complete an assignment in two parts: maximum length 4000 words; approximately 2000 words for each part. In Part A candidates must assess the short-term significance of the chosen individual or event. In Part B, candidates must assess the significance of the chosen event or individual in the long term (at least 100 years). Internally assessed. **40% of A2**

Both of these units allow candidates to demonstrate synoptic understanding.

WJEC AS

Unit	Specification topic	Chapter reference
Unit 1: Period Study	Wales & England, c.1780–1886: • Politics & government, c. 1780–1832 • Economic & social change and popular protest, c.1815–1848 • Foreign policy, c.1793–1841	1.1, 1.2, 1.3 3.2, 3.3 4.1
	Wales & England, c.1880–1980: • Wales & England in transition, c.1880–1929 • British foreign policy, c.1902–1939 • Party politics, c.1900–1940	5.2, 5.4, 5.5, 7.2 4.4, 8.1, 8.2 5.1, 5.2, 7.1–7.3, 10.2, 10.3
	Europe, c.1815–1917 • Italy, c.1830–1871 • Germany, c.1830–1871	13.1, 13.2 14.1, 14.2
	Europe, c.1878–1939 • International relations, c.1878–1920 • Italy, c.1918–1944 • The Communist Revolution in Russia, c.1917–1941	18.1, 18.3 15.2–15.5 12.3, 17.1, 17.2
Unit 2: In-Depth Study	Reform and protest in Wales and England, c.1830–1848	1.3, 3.2–3.6
	Britain c.1929–1939	7.3
	Nazi Germany, c.1933–1945	16.2, 16.3, 18.5, 18.6

Examination analysis

Candidates who choose a period study based on aspects of the history of Wales and England/Britain must choose a European history in-depth study, and vice versa.

Unit 1: Period Study

Two structured questions, from a choice of three. There are three nominated areas within each Period Study. One question is set on each. Part (a) focuses on explanation (24 marks) and part (b) on assessment (36 marks). 60 marks in total.　　　**1 hr 30 min exam**　　　**60% of AS**

Unit 2: In-Depth Study

One set of questions, based on the evaluation of historical sources and interpretations, from a choice of two. Five sources are set. There are five sub-questions, focusing on explanation, comparison, reliability and usefulness. 80 marks in total.　　　**1 hr 30 min exam**　　　**40% of AS**

WJEC A2

Unit	Specification topic	Chapter reference
Unit 3: In-Depth Study	Coursework: Historical Investigation arising from the In-Depth Study	
Unit 4: Period Study and In-Depth Study	Wales and England, c.1780–1886 • The Conservatives in the age of Peel & Disraeli, 1834–1880 • The development of Liberalism, 1846–1886 • Social Reform, c.1780–1886 • Parliamentary Reform, c.1780–1886	1.6, 2.1, 2.4 2.1–2.3 2.2, 2.4, 3.3–3.6 3.1, 3.2, 10.1
	Wales and England, c.1880–1980 • Depression and austerity, 1929–1951 • Social reform, c.1880–1980 • Britain and Europe, c.1880–1980	7.3, 8.3, 9.1 5.2, 7.3, 8.3, 9.1, 9.3 4.4, 8.1, 8.2
	Europe, c.1815–1917 • France, 1848–1870 • Russia, c.1881–1917 • Germany, c.1815–1914	11.2 12.1–12.3 14.1–14.4
	Europe, c.1878–1989 • International relations, c.1918–1945 • International relations, c.1945–1989 • Germany, c.1878–1989 • Russia, c.1881–1989	18.3–18.6 21.1–21.4 14.3, 14.4, 16.1–16.3, 19.1–19.5 12.1–12.3, 17.1, 17.2, 20.1–20.4
	Reform and protest in Wales and England, c.1830–1848	1.6
	Britain c.1929–1939	7.3, 8.2
	Nazi Germany c.1933–1945	16.2–16.4

Examination analysis

For A2, candidates revisit the Period Study and In-Depth Study chosen for AS.

Unit 3: Historical Investigation

An essay of 3000–4000 words, focusing on a historical problem or issue arising from the In-Depth study. Candidates are required to investigate a particular historical issue arising from within the in-depth study, using a range of sources, both contemporary and later sources and historical interpretations. Internally assessed.　　　**40% of A2**

Unit 4: Topics and themes relating to both the Period Study AND the In-Depth Study

Candidates answer three questions:
- One essay question from a choice of two, arising from the Period Study
- One synoptic essay question, from a choice of two, arising from the Period Study
- One essay question from a choice of two, arising from the In-Depth Study.

The Unit 4 exam is in two parts. 1 hr 40 min is allowed to answer the two questions on the Period Study. These questions are worth 40 marks each. 50 min is allowed for the question on the In-Depth Study, which is worth 40 marks. Total marks for the exam is 120.　　　**2 hrs 30 min exam**　　　**60% of A2**

Specification lists

CCEA AS

Unit	Specification topic	Chapter reference
AS 1: Historical Investigations and Historical Interpretations	England 1815–1868	1.1–1.6, 2.1, 3.2
	Unification of Italy and Germany 1815–1871	13.1, 13.2, 14.1, 14.2
	Germany 1918–1945	16.1–16.4
AS 2: Conflict and Change in Europe	Challenge and crisis in Ireland 1812–1867	6.1, 6.4
	France 1815–1871	11.1, 11.2
	Russia 1903–1941	12.2, 12.3, 17.1, 17.2
	Italy 1914–1943	15.1–15.5

Examination analysis

AS 1: Historical Investigations and Historical Interpretations

Two questions, one involving a short response and one two-part source-based question. The short response question is worth 12 marks. For the second question three sources are provided. The first sub-question focuses on usefulness (13 marks). For the second sub-question (35 marks), candidates are required to use the sources and their own knowledge to assess a historical issue. Total mark for the paper 60.

1 hr 30 min exam   50% of AS

AS 2: Conflict and Change in Europe

Two two-part questions from a choice of four on the chosen option. The first part focuses on explanation (8 marks). The second part (22 marks) requires candidates to assess a judgment on a historical issue. Total mark for the paper 30.

1 hr 30 min exam   50% of AS

CCEA A2

Unit	Specification topic	Chapter reference
A2 1: Change Over Time	Liberalism and Nationalism in Europe 1815–1914	13.1, 13.2, 14.1, 14.2, 18.1
	Unionism and Nationalism in Ireland 1800–1900	6.1–6.3
	Clash of ideologies 1900–2000	17.2, 21.1–21.4
A2 2: Historical Investigations and Historical Interpretations	Partition of Ireland 1900–1925	6.1, 6.2

Examination analysis

A2 1: Change Over Time

One essay question from a choice of two on the chosen option. Questions test synoptic understanding over a period of 100 years. There are 50 marks for this paper.

1 hr 15 min exam   20% of A2

A2 2: Historical Investigations and Interpretations

One question involving source evaluation and analysis and one essay question from a choice of two on historical interpretation. For the first question three sources are provided, one of which may be from a modern historian. The first sub-question (15 marks) focuses on the usefulness of the sources in assessing a particular historical issue. The second (20 marks) asks candidates to use the sources and their own knowledge to assess a historical judgment. The essay question carries 35 marks. Total mark for the paper 70.

2 hr exam   30% of A2

AS/A2 Level History courses

AS and A2

All A Level qualifications comprise two units of AS assessment and two units of A2 assessment. This offers History students the opportunity to complete a freestanding AS course or to complete their historical education and to develop ideas, themes and concepts into a full A Level course via the more demanding and challenging A2 course.

How will you be tested?

Assessment units

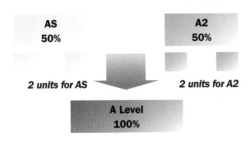

For AS History, you will be tested by two assessment units. For the full A Level, you will take a further two units.

Each unit can normally be taken in either January or June. Alternatively, you can study the whole course before taking any of the unit tests. There is a lot of flexibility about when exams can be taken and the diagram below shows just some of the ways that the assessment units may be taken for AS and A2 Level History.

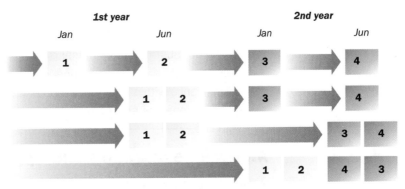

Remember that the combinations shown here might not be the route chosen by your school to go through the examination. There are other possible combinations.

If you are disappointed with a module result, you can re-sit each module taken and most exam boards will offer papers in both January and June. The higher mark always counts.

A2 and synoptic assessment

After having studied AS History, hopefully you will want to continue studying History to A2 Level. For this you will need to take two further units of History. Similar assessment arrangements apply except that some units draw together different parts of the course in a 'synoptic' assessment.

Coursework

Coursework is an integral part of the A2 History course for all boards except CCEA. The detailed requirements vary from board to board, so it is important to follow closely the advice given by your teacher. Coursework allows candidates to undertake a substantial piece of work in which they can develop and practise the skills of the historian for themselves. Credit is given for appropriate use of source material and discussion of the views of historians. Coursework for AQA and Edexcel requires students to address a chosen issue over a period of at least 100 years in order to develop their understanding of the process of change. OCR coursework focuses on interpretations and investigations, while WJEC requires candidates to investigate an issue arising from their In-Depth Study.

Key skills

AS and A2 History specifications identify opportunities for the development of the Key Skills of Communication, Information Technology, Working with Others, Improving Own Learning and Performance, and Problem Solving. History may also offer some opportunities for developing Application of Number skills, but these depend on the specific options chosen.

What skills will I need?

For AS and A2 History, you will be tested by assessment objectives: these are the skills and abilities that you should have acquired by studying the course. The assessment objectives for AS History are shown below.

Knowledge and understanding

- Recall, select and deploy historical knowledge appropriately, and communicate knowledge and understanding of history in a clear and effective manner.
- Demonstrate understanding of the past through explanation, analysis and arriving at substantiated judgments of:
  – key concepts such as causation, consequence, continuity, change and significance within a historical context
  – the relationships between key features and characteristics of the periods studied.

Analysis, evaluation and application

- As part of a historical enquiry, analyse and evaluate a range of appropriate source material with discrimination.
- Analyse and evaluate, in relation to the historical context, how aspects of the past have been interpreted and represented in different ways.

Assessment of your work will also take into account the quality of your written communication, including clarity of expression, structure of arguments, presentation of ideas, spelling, grammar and punctuation.

Stretch and Challenge

Stretch and Challenge refers to the new provision by the exam boards to add extension material for the top candidates at A Level. In History it will be introduced within the A2 Units through essay questions which test understanding in both breadth and depth. It will also be provided through the coursework units which test either understanding over a 100-year period or skill in assessing historical interpretations.

Different types of questions

In AS and A2 History examinations, three main types of question are used to assess your abilities and skills: source-based questions, structured questions and essay questions.

Source-based questions

Source-based questions are mainly used in AS units. The types of question you may encounter are:

- **Comprehension and explanation of words or phrases in the sources** – This type of question is only used by WJEC at AS level and requires only a sentence or two in response.
- **Extraction of information from the sources** – This type of question is only used by WJEC at AS level and requires a short paragraph in response.
- **Evaluation of the reliability or usefulness of one or more of the sources** – Use all the information available to you: the content of the source; the information given to you about it by the examiners; comparison with the other sources and your own knowledge, in order to decide what use a historian could make of it.
- **Comparison between two sources** – The question will always ask you to compare the sources in relation to a particular issue. Make sure you focus on the issue rather than providing a general comparison between the sources. Look for points of similarity and points of difference. Difference means not only disagreement but also relevant points in one source that are missing from the other. Compare not only the content of the sources but, where relevant, their reliability, usefulness and provenance (who wrote them). Here are two examples, worded differently:
  - Q. Compare Sources A and B as evidence for Disraeli's motives in the reform crisis of 1867.
  - Q. Explain how far the views in Source A differ from those in Source B in relation to Mussolini's 'march on Rome'.
- **Use of sources and own knowledge as evidence to answer a broader question**, for example to construct an explanation, discuss an interpretation or assess a judgment. This is always the most heavily weighted part of a source-based question and needs to be answered at some length. It requires you to use your own knowledge as well as the sources. Make sure you refer to both: failure to do so is one of the most common mistakes made by candidates. But do not extract evidence from the sources and then bolt on your own knowledge. Evidence from the sources and own knowledge should be integrated to support each point in your argument. Here is an example:
  - Q. From Source A and from your own knowledge, explain why Ulster was such an important consideration in the Home Rule question in 1886.

Structured questions

Structured questions are only used at AS level. They are in two parts, which are usually related to a common issue. The second part is more demanding than the first. Typically, the first part of a two-part question will ask for identification or explanation of key issues and the second part will ask for analysis of causation or assessment of the significance of an issue. The mark allocation in the example below indicates that you should spend about one-third of the time allowed on part (a) and two-thirds on part (b). You will be expected to write up to a page for part (a) and between one and two pages for part (b). Here is an example:

Q. (a) Explain why a Labour government came into office in 1924. [12]

(b) 'Ramsay MacDonald betrayed the Labour Party out of personal ambition in 1931'. Explain why you agree or disagree with this verdict. [24]

Essay questions

The A2 examinations consist almost entirely of essay questions. There are two main types:

- **Questions focusing on causation** – These may require an analysis of the causes of an historical event or process, or may suggest a cause for discussion. In either case you should aim to consider a range of causes and to make a judgment about their relative importance. If the question suggests a cause, make sure you give it proper consideration before going on to discuss other possible causes. You may decide that other causes are more important. You should aim to reach a reasoned conclusion about the relative importance of the causes you have identified and how they relate to each other. Here are two examples, formulated in different ways, but both about causation:

    Q. Why did Britain's relations with Germany deteriorate in the period from 1898 to 1914?

    Q. 'Increasing affluence was the main reason why the Conservatives held office continuously from 1951 to 1964.' How far do you agree or disagree with this view?

- **Questions requiring you to make or evaluate a judgment** – Often such questions take the form of a quotation, which you are required to discuss. Here are some examples:

    Q. How successful were Stalin's economic policies in the Soviet Union in the years 1928–41?

    Q. 'The domestic reforms of Gladstone's First Ministry alienated more people than they pleased.' How far do you agree?

Thematic questions

All specifications include a requirement to study a theme over a period of at least 100 years. Questions focus on understanding of continuity, change, trends and turning points. You are not expected to demonstrate detailed knowledge of the whole of the period but you will need to know the main developments and turning points. It is important to ensure that you draw material for your answer from the whole of the period.

Synoptic questions

Synoptic assessment concerns your understanding of the connections between the essential characteristics of historical study. Synoptic questions test your knowledge and understanding, your ability to explain and evaluate interpretations of historical events and issues, and your capacity to present historical explanations and arrive at substantiated judgments. Questions require you to address an issue, formulate an argument and reach a conclusion. You are also required to make connections between historical perspectives relevant to the question set (for example political, social, economic and cultural factors). It is essential to adopt an analytical approach and to consider alternative views or interpretations.

Exam technique

AS and on to A2

AS History builds on the knowledge, understanding and skills established by GCSE History, but does not depend on them. If you have not studied History for some time, you should still be able to learn AS History from this text.

It is, of course, necessary to have studied History to AS Level to move on to A2! A2 builds on AS by drawing on more sophisticated content and evidence. It develops a more complex understanding of historical concepts and the ability to produce more analytical responses and more effectively substantiated judgments. To get the most out of A2 History you will need an enquiring mind, an interest in the past and its relevance to current affairs and an ability to communicate ideas effectively.

It is important to remember that History is not a subject that can be learnt from a single text. This Study Guide will provide you with the essential knowledge and ideas you need to understand the topics you study, but you will need to build on this by incorporating the wider reading suggested by your teacher.

What examiners are looking for

The most common types of question are those which require an analysis of **cause** and **consequence**, and those which require an **assessment** or **judgment**. Examiners are not looking for a pre-determined 'correct' answer but they expect you to address the question set and use your knowledge to support your argument. They indicate the type of answer they expect by command words in the questions (see below).

Explain, Examine, In what ways?
Instructions such as 'Explain...', 'Examine...' and 'In what ways...' call for a piece of analytical writing. Be sure to focus on the issue or event required, for example, aims, factors, policies or results.

Why? For what reasons?
Question words such as 'Why...' and 'For what reasons...' ask for an analysis of causes. Make sure you do not leave out important causes and that you consider long-term causes as well as short-term ones. A good answer will consider the relative importance of causes and how they are linked together.

Assess, How far?, To what extent?
Instructions and question words such as 'Assess...', 'How far...' and 'To what extent...' require you to make a judgment. The examiners expect you to set out the main arguments on opposite sides and then balance them in your conclusion. For example, you might assess the success of a statesman by explaining his successes and then his failures. Most questions which begin with the word 'how' (e.g. 'How valid...', 'How serious...', 'How important...') are of this type. Another way of setting this type of question is to offer you a judgment for assessment and ask you to explain why you agree or disagree.

Compare
If you are asked to compare two sources, look for similarities and differences. You should explain in turn each point of similarity or difference for both sources. Avoid the temptation to paraphrase the first source and then the second.

Some dos and don'ts

Dos

- *Do* answer the question

  No credit can be given for good History that is irrelevant to the question. Read the questions carefully. The command words indicate the type of answer expected and the rest of the question specifies the issue to be addressed. Take particular note of any date limits specified.

- *Do* be sure to refer to source material if the question requires it

  You will lose marks if you ignore this. You will also lose marks if you answer entirely from the sources when a question asks you to use own knowledge as well as the sources.

- *Do* spend some time planning your answers

  This is especially important for questions requiring extended writing. It will ensure that your argument is coherent and that you avoid omissions.

- *Do* pay attention to correct spelling, grammar and punctuation

  Quality of written communication is taken into account in all assessment units.

- *Do* write legibly

  An examiner cannot give marks if the answer cannot be read.

Don'ts

- *Don't* produce undirected narrative

  Most questions require you to use your knowledge to follow the instructions given in the command words of the question.

- *Don't* introduce irrelevant material

  You will get no credit for it. A common fault is an 'all I know' response to a trigger in the question.

- *Don't* waste time on lengthy introductions

  The ideal introduction sets outs briefly the line of argument you intend to pursue. It follows from this that before you start writing you should have made up your mind about the conclusion you intend to reach. And this takes you back to the need to plan.

What grade do you want?

Your final grade depends on the extent to which you meet the assessment objectives. To gain the best possible mark you will have to work hard throughout the course and be highly motivated.

To achieve a grade A or A* you will need to:
- show relevant, accurate and detailed historical knowledge
- demonstrate understanding of key concepts such as causation, continuity, change and significance
- demonstrate understanding of the relationship between key features of the historical period
- show critical understanding of the use of source material and interpretations of the past
- be able to organise an argument and communicate it effectively.

1 From Pitt to Peel, 1783–1846

The following topics are covered in this chapter:

- Pitt the Younger, 1783–1801
- Lord Liverpool and the Tories, 1815–30
- The Great Reform Act, 1832
- The Whigs, 1830–41
- Chartism
- Peel

1.1 Pitt the Younger, 1783–1801

LEARNING SUMMARY	After studying this section you should be able to understand:
	- how Pitt achieved political dominance
	- Pitt's record as Prime Minister in peacetime
	- the impact of the French Revolution on politics in the 1790s

Pitt's ministry in peacetime, 1783–93

OCR **U1** WJEC **U1**

The election of 1784

- Defeat in the American War of Independence led to the fall of Lord North's government in 1782.
- King George III had to accept the Fox–North coalition in 1783, but he was bitterly opposed to Fox. The coalition fell in December 1783.
- Pitt was appointed Prime Minister with the King's backing. He survived several defeats in the Commons before calling an election.
- In the election of March 1784 Pitt gained a comfortable majority.

> **KEY POINT**
>
> The support of the King was crucial, but Pitt also had the support of the City and the movement for parliamentary reform.

Reform of finance and administration

> The National Debt had ballooned during the War of American Independence.

Pitt's **budgets** of 1784–7 achieved financial stability and economic revival after the defeat in the American War of Independence.

- Customs duties were simplified and reduced on consumer goods, the most important being tea. This reduced smuggling.
- Waste was reduced, e.g. misuse of parliamentary post by MPs.
- A commercial treaty was signed with France in 1786.

However, an attempt to introduce freer trade between Britain and Ireland failed. The sinking fund for the National Debt helped to restore confidence in the short-term, but was a failure in the longer-term.

Pitt disappointed the radicals over parliamentary reform. Demands for reform of an unrepresentative Parliament and the elimination of corruption had reached their height with the Association movement (1779–80). Pitt introduced a reform bill in 1785, but backed down in the face of opposition in the Commons. He also backed down over the abolition of the slave trade.

> **KEY POINT**
>
> Pitt's reforms enabled Britain to finance the wars against France from 1793 to 1815.

The impact of the French Revolution

OCR **U1**   WJEC **U1**

Attitudes towards reform were completely changed by the outbreak of the French Revolution. At first, many saw events in France as a move towards a limited monarchy similar to Britain's. As the revolution progressed, the upper classes feared that its ideas threatened them. **Burke** argued in *Reflections on the Revolution in France* that revolution was a threat to the stability of society. In reply, the leading radical **Thomas Paine**, in *The Rights of Man*, argued that the revolution stood for liberty. Pitt came to share Burke's view. After the outbreak of war with France in 1793, the government saw the radicals as not only dangerous but unpatriotic and introduced a series of **repressive measures** to clamp down on radical opinion.

- *Habeas Corpus* was suspended.
- Radical leaders were prosecuted.
- The Treason and Sedition Acts clamped down on political meetings.
- Correspondence Societies were suppressed.
- The Combination Acts made trade unions illegal.

The overall effect of these measures was to drive radicalism underground. Most MPs – both Whigs and Tories – supported Pitt, but a small minority of the Whigs, led by Fox, continued to support the revolution. Although he had little support, Fox kept alive a tradition of respect for the liberty of the individual and a belief in the need for reform.

> **KEY POINT**
>
> The cause of parliamentary reform was effectively dead until after 1815.

1.2 Lord Liverpool and the Tories, 1815–30

LEARNING SUMMARY

After studying this section you should be able to understand:
- the discontent in the post-war years, 1815–22
- the response of Liverpool's ministry to discontent
- whether these policies can be described as repressive
- the reforms carried out by the Liberal Tories, 1822–30
- the split in the Tory party over Catholic emancipation

The post-war years, 1815–22

AQA	U1	WJEC	U1
OCR	U1	CCEA	AS1

Distress and discontent

See also page 41.

In the period after the end of the Napoleonic Wars there was widespread discontent. There were Luddite outbreaks (machine breaking) in some industrial areas from 1811 onwards. The main disturbances were the Spa Fields Riots in London, 1816; the Derbyshire Rising, 1817; the March of the Blanketeers, 1817; Peterloo, 1819; and the Cato Street Conspiracy, 1820.

One of the main causes of discontent was **unemployment**, which was particularly high after 1815 because of the end of wartime contracts for industry and the demobilisation of soldiers. The industrial revolution made some workers (e.g. many hand-loom weavers) redundant. Living and working conditions in the new industrial towns were very poor.

Conditions in the countryside were often even worse. Some rural workers responded to enclosure and population pressure by moving to the towns. Those who stayed were badly paid. In much of southern England, their wages were so low that they had to be supplemented by the Poor Law under the **Speenhamland System**.

Government policies added to discontent. The **Corn Laws** (1815) kept the price of bread high. When income tax was abolished in 1816, indirect taxes were raised, adding to the burden on the poor.

The Government's response to discontent

AQA	U1	WJEC	U1
OCR	U1	CCEA	AS1

Lord Liverpool and his ministers feared a revolutionary outbreak like that in France in 1789. They also believed it was the first duty of government to maintain law and order. So they followed a policy of **repression**.

- *Habeas Corpus* was suspended and the Seditious Meetings Act was passed in 1817.
- Spies, e.g. Oliver, were sent into the industrial areas where discontent was greatest.
- Troops were used to disperse crowds, e.g. at Peterloo.
- The Six Acts were passed in 1819, giving magistrates increased powers of search and the power to try political cases without a jury. The stamp duty on journals was increased with the aim of making Cobbett's *Political Register* too expensive for working men to buy.

The government did nothing to remedy the causes of discontent. The Tories were firmly opposed to parliamentary reform (one of the main demands of the Radicals). Ministers believed in *laissez faire*, i.e. that intervention in the economy was undesirable. Therefore, they failed to introduce social or political reforms.

Assessment

Examiners will look for a balanced assessment, with evidence on both sides of the argument. The government had some justification for its attitude.

Liverpool's government may have exaggerated the danger of revolution. Discontent was at its highest when economic conditions were worst and when they improved in 1818, and again in 1820, the disturbances died down. Some of the government's policies actually increased the discontent. The Corn Laws and the tax changes were highly unpopular and government spies sometimes became **agents provocateurs**. This seems to have been the role of Oliver in the Derbyshire Rising. On the other hand, the government was undoubtedly faced by disorder and it had no effective police force. Could it have done less in the circumstances? It is worth noting also that the powers taken by the government were used sparingly.

The Liberal Tories, 1822–30

AQA	U1	WJEC	U1
OCR	U1	CCEA	AS1

> Reform was easier after 1822 as disturbances died down.

The suicide in 1822 of the Foreign Secretary, Castlereagh, led to the entry of Canning, Peel, Huskisson and Robinson into the Cabinet. These Liberal Tories were responsible for some important reforms.

- **Peel** (Home Secretary) reformed the administration of justice. The penal code was reformed and conditions in the bigger gaols were improved. He also established the Metropolitan Police (1829).
- **Huskisson** (President of the Board of Trade) introduced free trade measures including reduction of import duties, relaxation of the Navigation Acts, reciprocity agreements and preferential duties for the colonies. He also modified the Corn Laws in 1828 by the introduction of a sliding scale.
- The **Combination Acts** were repealed in 1824. This made the formation of trade unions legal, but an Amending Act (1825) made it difficult to organise strikes and stay within the law.

Catholic emancipation and the Tories

AQA	U1	WJEC	U1
OCR	U1	CCEA	AS1

> You will need to be able to explain why Catholic emancipation was a turning point in politics.

In 1827 Liverpool resigned after a stroke. His great merit was his ability to hold together the differing wings of the Tory party. His successors as Prime Minister – Canning, Goderich and Wellington – were unable to do this. Nevertheless, two further important reforms were passed.

- The **Test and Corporation Acts,** which excluded nonconformists from public office, were repealed in 1828. In practice they had not been enforced for many years. Roman Catholics were still excluded, but –
- In 1829 the **Catholic Relief Act** (Catholic emancipation) was passed. Wellington (Prime Minister) and Peel (Home Secretary) believed this was necessary to avert civil war in Ireland after the election of Daniel O'Connell in the County Clare by-election, even though they had previously opposed it. But it split the Tory party.

The High Tories accused Wellington and Peel of betrayal. Wellington's ministry survived the general election of 1830, but fell later that year.

You should be able to explain the significance of each of these dates.

KEY DATES

1812–27	Lord Liverpool was Prime Minister
1815	End of Napoleonic Wars; Corn Laws passed
1816	Spa Fields Riots
1819	Peterloo 'massacre', followed by the Six Acts
1822	Entry of 'Liberal Tories' into the ministry
1824	Repeal of the Combination Acts
1827–8	Ministries of Canning and Goderich
1828–30	Wellington ministry
1828	Repeal of Test and Corporation Acts; County Clare by-election
1829	Catholic emancipation

1.3 The Great Reform Act, 1832

LEARNING SUMMARY

After studying this section you should be able to understand:

- why there was a demand for reform of parliament
- the Reform Bill crisis of 1830–2
- the impact of the Reform Act

The demand for reform

AQA	**U1**	WJEC	**U1, 2**
OCR	**U1**	CCEA	**AS1**
Edexcel	**U2**		

The unreformed parliament had many defects.

- Qualifications for voting were outdated, arbitrary and illogical. In the counties, forty shilling freeholders had the vote, but in the boroughs there was a wide variety of different qualifications. In some of the corporation boroughs there were fewer than fifty voters.
- The electorate was tiny – less than half a million.
- The distribution of seats did not match the distribution of population. The South of England was over-represented and the North and Scotland were under-represented.
- There were many rotten and pocket boroughs. Notorious examples were Old Sarum, Dunwich and Gatton.
- Growing industrial towns, such as Manchester, were unrepresented.
- There was no secret ballot, leading to bribery and intimidation of voters.

The movement for reform dated back to the eighteenth century. Pitt tried to bring about some limited reforms in 1785, but dropped the idea after the outbreak of the French Revolution. The Tories, after the Napoleonic Wars, were strongly opposed to parliamentary reform.

The split in the Tory Party over Catholic emancipation opened the way for the Whigs to come to power on the fall of Wellington in 1830. Grey, who had long favoured limited reform, led the new Whig government.

The Reform Bill crisis

AQA	U1	WJEC	U1, 2
OCR	U1	CCEA	AS1
Edexcel	U2		

Examiners will expect you to understand that the opponents were not acting purely out of self-interest.

There was fierce opposition to reform from Tories in the Commons and from the Lords. Some of the opposition came from people who would lose out by reform, e.g. members of the House of Lords who were able to nominate MPs for pocket boroughs. But there were also genuine arguments against reform. Some argued that the present system worked perfectly well and did not need to be changed. Pocket boroughs, they said, enabled promising young men to be brought into parliament (e.g. Pitt, who became an MP at 21 and Prime Minister at 24). They argued that all the important 'interests' in the country, e.g. landowners, merchants and the professions, were represented. Peel argued (correctly) that this would not be the end of reform as the Whigs claimed: one reform would lead eventually to another.

Three Bills had to be introduced before the Reform Act was finally passed. A general election in 1831 strengthened the supporters of reform. Fear of revolution, strengthened by the 1830 revolution in France and widespread disturbances in England in 1831–2, helped the Whigs to overcome the opposition. In 1832 Grey resigned when the House of Lords rejected the third version of the Bill. Wellington tried to form a government, but failed, and Grey returned to office with a promise from the King to create enough peers to force it through if necessary. The House of Lords then gave way and the Bill was passed.

The **terms of the Reform Act** were that:
- the vote was given to £10 householders in the boroughs
- in the counties the 40 shilling freeholders retained the right to vote and the vote was also given to £50 leaseholders and £10 copyholders. Over 140 seats were redistributed from rotten and pocket boroughs to growing towns and the larger counties.

The impact of the Reform Act

AQA	U1	WJEC	U1, 2
OCR	U1	CCEA	AS1
Edexcel	U2		

In many respects the results of the Reform Act were limited.
- The electorate was still only about 800 000. Constituencies still varied greatly in size and open voting and bribery continued. Consequently, voters, especially in the counties, still followed the lead of local landowners.
- The redistribution of seats gave greater representation to the industrial north and midlands, but the agricultural south was still over-represented.
- MPs were still largely drawn from the landowning class, though a few businessmen and industrialists joined them. Governments therefore were still overwhelmingly aristocratic.
- The working classes were disappointed. They had played an important part in the agitation for reform in 1831–2, but the Reform Act denied them any share in political power. This resulted in the rise of the Chartist movement in the years 1838–48.

Be sure you can explain why the Reform Act was a crucial step towards democracy, even though it was so limited.

Nevertheless, the Reform Act was a turning point in British political history. The main effect of the changes in the franchise was to give the vote to the **middle classes** in the boroughs. Therefore, as the Whigs intended, the Act restored the balance of the constitution by giving proper representation to a class which had previously been under-represented.

Although the landed classes remained politically dominant, the political parties became more responsive to the needs of the middle classes. The Whig reforms of the 1830s and Peel's Tamworth Manifesto of 1834, which aimed to adapt the Tory party to the needs of the new electorate, both show this. The outstanding example of the importance of the shifting political balance between the landed classes and the industrial middle class was the repeal of the Corn Laws in 1846.

> **KEY POINT**
>
> The Reform Act set a precedent for changing the constitution and opened the way for future reforms of parliament.

1.4 The Whigs, 1830–41

LEARNING SUMMARY	After studying this section you should be able to understand:
	• the importance of the main Whig reforms

The Whigs in power, 1830–41

AQA	U1	CCEA	AS1
OCR	U1		

The most important of the Whig reforms were:

- The abolition of slavery in the British Empire, 1833.
- The **Factory Act** (1833), which restricted child labour in textile factories (except for silk mills). Children under 9 were not permitted to work. Those aged 9–13 were only allowed to work for eight hours a day and they had to receive two hours' schooling. Young people aged 14–18 were limited to twelve hours a day. For the first time, inspectors were appointed to enforce the law, but there were only four of them. Nevertheless, this was the first effective Factory Act.

There had been previous Factory Acts but they had not been enforced.

- The **first government grant for education** (1833) provided £20 000 divided between two religious societies that provided elementary schools (the National Society and the British and Foreign School Society). The grant was increased to £30 000 in 1839.
- The **Poor Law Amendment Act** of 1834 abolished outdoor relief (the payment of money to the poor) except for the sick and aged. This meant the end of the Speenhamland system. For the able-bodied poor, relief was to be provided in workhouses, which were to be run on the principle of 'less eligibility'. This meant that life in the workhouse should be as unattractive as possible – less attractive than the condition of the poorest labourer outside it. This would ensure that the poor would only come to the workhouse as a last resort. Administration of the Poor Law was completely reformed. Parishes were grouped into Poor Law Unions run by elected Boards of Guardians. A central Board of Commissioners was appointed to supervise the whole system.

The Poor Law is dealt with more fully in Chapter 3.

- The **Municipal Corporations Act** of 1835 reformed local government in the boroughs. Councils were to be elected by ratepayers. They were obliged to set up a police force and were allowed to provide other services such as drainage and street cleaning. Because such services would be a burden on the rates, many boroughs did not use these powers at first. Nevertheless, the Act laid the foundations for later improvements in the administration of urban areas.
- Registration of births, marriages and deaths (1836).
- Church reforms: the Marriage Act permitted marriages in nonconformist chapels and Roman Catholic churches and the Tithe Commutation Act replaced the tithe with a money payment.

These reforms were intended to satisfy the demands of the new middle class electors and to tackle the problems of an emerging industrial society. They were much influenced by pressure from radicals (following the ideas of Bentham) and humanitarians. But they were limited and the most important of them, the Poor Law Amendment Act, was immensely unpopular with the working classes.

> **KEY POINT**
>
> The Whig reforms were a major step in adjusting central and local government to the needs of an industrialising society. But they were bitterly disappointing to the working classes, many of whom turned to Chartism in the late 1830s. Moreover, the Whigs were faced in the late 1830s with a growing demand from the industrial middle classes for the repeal of the Corn Laws.

1.5 Chartism

> **LEARNING SUMMARY**
>
> After studying this section you should be able to understand:
> - why the Chartists gained so much support and account for their failure

The Chartist movement

AQA **U1**   CCEA **AS1**

There is a fuller account of Chartism in Chapter 3.

The aim of Chartism was a democratic parliament to be achieved by the Six Points of the **People's Charter**. The years of greatest Chartist activity were 1839, 1842 and 1848, in each of which a petition was presented to parliament. All three petitions were rejected and after 1848 support dwindled.

Chartism was a movement of the industrial working class, protesting against their living and working conditions. It arose as a response to the economic depression of the late 1830s and 1840s. These were years of high unemployment – hence the description of Chartism as a 'knife and fork question'. The Chartists sought political reform as the first step to a better society. It can therefore be seen as reflecting working class disappointment with the 1832 Reform Act. It also reflected working class anger at the Poor Law Amendment Act and the collapse of Owen's Grand National Consolidated Trade Union. It was a movement with much local diversity and only loosely held together by its leaders, its organisation and its press.

Reasons for the failure of Chartism

- Poor leadership – Lovett, Attwood and O'Connor all had their differing faults.
- Divisions over tactics – moral force vs. physical force.
- Lack of co-ordination, reflecting the local nature of much Chartist activity.
- Improving economic conditions from the mid 1840s (except in 1848).
- Firm action by the government.
- Lack of middle class support; in this respect it was at a great disadvantage compared with the Anti-Corn Law League.

> **KEY POINT**
>
> The Six Points of the Charter were unacceptable to the middle classes, who had just gained the vote by the Reform Act. Without their support the Chartists were almost bound to fail.

Be sure to consider why Chartism was important even though it failed in the short-term.

Although the Chartist movement failed, it was not insignificant. It drew attention to working class grievances. Some historians would see it as an important step on the road to organising an effective working class movement in the Labour Party.

1.6 Peel

<table>
<tr><td rowspan="4">LEARNING SUMMARY</td><td>After studying this section you should be able to understand:</td></tr>
<tr><td>• how Peel rebuilt the Tory party after the split of the late 1820s and the passing of the Reform Act</td></tr>
<tr><td>• the reforms of Peel's Second Ministry</td></tr>
<tr><td>• the achievements of Peel</td></tr>
</table>

Peel and the Tory party, 1812–41

| AQA | U1 | WJEC | U4 |
| OCR | U1 | CCEA | AS1 |

These are examples of Peel's 'betrayal' of the Tory Party, which represented the landowners and the Church.

Peel first gained prominence as Chief Secretary for Ireland from 1812–18. In 1819 he was Chairman of the Bullion Committee, which recommended a return to the gold standard. This upset landowners, who blamed this decision for a sharp fall in agricultural prices. From 1822–7 and 1828–30, as one of the Liberal Tories, Peel was Home Secretary. In 1829 he played a crucial role, with Wellington, in bringing about Catholic emancipation, even though he was a staunch Anglican who had previously opposed it. Many Tories attacked him for betraying the Church.

Peel opposed the 1832 Reform Act, but then went on to re-shape the Tory party to appeal to the new electorate. In the election of 1834 he issued the **Tamworth Manifesto**. This set out two basic principles for the Tory Party, which was renamed the Conservative Party.
- It accepted that the Reform Act could not be reversed.
- It would reform proven abuses, while preserving what was good about the British system of government.

Peel was briefly Prime Minister in 1834–5. Despite the Tamworth Manifesto, the Whigs returned to power after the 1835 election, but Peel won a convincing victory in the election of 1841. By then he had won the confidence of the new electorate. The Whigs had lost their reforming impetus after 1835 and they had failed to balance the budget.

KEY POINT

The Tamworth Manifesto saved the Tory Party from being marginalised.

Peel's Second Ministry, 1841–6

| AQA | U1 | WJEC | U4 |
| OCR | U1 | CCEA | AS1 |

Reforms

Make sure you understand the arguments for free trade. Remember that Britain was the leading industrial nation at this time.

Peel's **budgets of 1842 and 1845** were a major step towards **free trade**. Peel believed that free trade would make imports cheaper and boost exports, industry would benefit and the cost of living would be reduced. Thus, free trade would make Britain 'a cheap country for living'. The case for free trade was based on the work of Adam Smith. Huskisson had made some progress in this direction in the 1820s. By removing duties on over 600 articles, and reducing many others,

Peel's budgets helped to bring about a trade revival. To make up for the revenue lost, he reintroduced income tax – for three years at first, but it was then renewed and has never been abolished.

Two other Acts were important for the economy.
- The **Bank Charter Act** (1844) stabilised the banking system and the currency under the control of the Bank of England.
- The **Companies Act** (1844) established better regulation of companies.

There were two social reforms.
- The **Mines Act** (1842) prohibited the underground employment of women, girls and boys under the age of ten. This resulted from the report of a Royal Commission which shocked public opinion.
- The **Factory Act** (1844) lowered the age at which children could be employed in textile factories to eight years, but also reduced hours of work for children aged up to 13 to six and a half hours.

Ireland

Peel had played a major role in bringing about Catholic emancipation in 1829 because he feared civil war would result if O'Connell was not allowed to take his seat after the County Clare election. By 1843 O'Connell's leadership was challenged by a new Irish organisation, 'Young Ireland'. O'Connell tried to re-establish his authority by holding a series of meetings to demand repeal of the Act of Union, culminating in a mass meeting at Clontarf in 1843. Peel banned the meeting, rightly judging that there was no real danger that the agitation would develop into rebellion. At the same time he appointed the Devon Commission to investigate problems of Irish land tenure, but was unable to act on its report before the fall of his ministry. More controversially, he increased the government grant to Maynooth College, a training college for Catholic priests, in the face of opposition from some of his own party, including Gladstone. In 1845 a more serious problem arose in Ireland – the potato famine.

> Remember that the Tory Party was the party of the Church of England.

The Repeal of the Corn Laws

The **Irish potato famine** brought a new urgency to the issue of the repeal of the Corn Laws. Throughout Peel's ministry the **Anti-Corn Law League** had been campaigning for repeal. The League was formed in Manchester in 1839 and its sole aim was the repeal of the Corn Laws, which were the last main obstacle to free trade. It had middle class leadership (Cobden and Bright, both of whom became MPs), and gained support from both the middle and working classes. It ran a highly organised campaign, making good use of the press.

Its arguments were that free trade would:
- reduce the price of bread and thus improve living standards
- enable British manufacturers to expand exports, thus increasing employment
- make agriculture more efficient by exposing it to foreign competition
- promote international peace through trade.

Repeal was opposed by the landed interest, which dominated the Conservative Party. They argued that repeal would lead to an influx of cheap foreign corn, ruining farmers and causing unemployment in the countryside.

The campaign against the Corn Laws, therefore, had a political as well as an economic significance – it was a struggle by the industrial middle classes against the continuing influence of the landed aristocracy.

Although the Anti-Corn Law League's campaign was highly effective, it was Peel himself who played the decisive role in bringing about repeal. He was already committed to free trade, but knew that repeal of the Corn Laws would split the Conservative Party. The Irish potato famine made him decide to act. The Repeal Bill was passed with the support of the Whigs and a minority of Conservatives. Peel was accused by Disraeli of betraying his party. Shortly afterwards his ministry was defeated and Peel was forced to resign.

The Repeal of the Corn Laws was a turning point in British politics. It was disastrous for the Conservatives, who subsequently held office for only three short periods between 1846 and 1874. Peel's followers, the Peelites, led by Gladstone, eventually joined the Whigs to form the Liberal Party. The Whigs held office for most of the next twenty years. British agriculture, contrary to the landowners' fears, entered a period of prosperity until the depression of the 1870s.

> **KEY POINT**
>
> The Repeal of the Corn Laws was a key event both politically and economically. Politically, it prompted a realignment of the parties. Economically, it was the decisive step in Britain's development into a free trade country.

Assessment of Peel

There are two main points of view about Peel.

- Some historians argue that he was a great statesman because he put the national interest before the Conservative Party. They claim that his free trade policies and the repeal of the Corn Laws brought economic prosperity and probably saved the country from revolution in 1848.
- Others emphasise that he was a poor party leader, failing to win support for his policies and accused of betraying the party on the issues of corn, cash and Catholics.

You might consider whether this is a distinction between a politician and a statesman.

> Examiners will expect you to be able to assess the importance of the potato famine among the factors which influenced Peel.

> Examiners will also expect you to understand the political, as well as the economic, importance of 1846 – particularly for Gladstone and Disraeli.

> You should be able to explain the significance of each of these dates.

KEY DATES	
1830	Whigs come to power
1832	Reform Act
1834	Poor Law Amendment Act; Tamworth Manifesto
1839	People's Charter published; Anti-Corn-Law League founded
1841–6	Peel's Second Ministry
1842	Free trade budget; Second Chartist Petition
1845	Irish potato famine
1846	Repeal of the Corn Laws

Sample question and model answer

The keyword in this question is 'liberal'.

How far do the domestic policies of the Tory government of 1822–30 justify the description 'Liberal Tories'?

[50]

Undoubtedly the `Liberal Tories´ were liberal by contrast with their immediate predecessors. The post-war Tory ministry, faced with distress and discontent, had followed a policy of repression, symbolised by Peterloo and the Six Acts. By 1822, trade was recovering and the fear of revolution was receding. It was possible for the Liberal Tories to adopt a policy of moderate reform, which is their chief claim to be called liberal.

The next three paragraphs offer a lot of relevant factual information to support the label 'Liberal Tories'. But the examiner is still waiting for a counter-argument.

Peel, the Home Secretary, reformed the penal code and the prisons. The savage criminal code was moderated, so that the death penalty was abolished for over 100 offences. This had the beneficial effect of making juries more willing to convict offenders for lesser offences. By the Gaols Act (1823) a number of urgently needed improvements in prison conditions were introduced, e.g. women officers for women prisoners, wages for jailers instead of fees and regular visits by doctors and chaplains. The reforms were, however, limited to the larger gaols - conditions in many smaller prisons remained terrible. Finally, in 1829, Peel set up the Metropolitan Police Force. This was limited to London, but its success led to the formation of similar forces throughout the country in the following twenty years. The overall effect of Peel's reforms was the establishment of a more humane and more efficient system for the administration and enforcement of the criminal law. Much of this work was based on the ideas of humanitarian reformers such as Sir Samuel Romilly and Elizabeth Fry.

Peel's acceptance of their ideas may be regarded as liberal by the standards of his time. So too may Huskisson's move towards free trade. Working with Robinson at the Exchequer, he reduced import duties, relaxed the Navigation Laws and secured the passing of the Reciprocity of Duties Act. He also modified the Corn Laws by the introduction of a Sliding Scale in 1828, though there was, of course, no thought of repealing them.

Three other important reforms provide further evidence of the liberalism of the Liberal Tories. In 1824 the Combination Acts, which had made the formation of trade unions illegal since 1799, were repealed. In 1828 the Test and Corporation Acts, which prevented nonconformists from holding public office, were repealed and in 1829 Catholic emancipation was achieved by the Catholic Relief Act.

In the last two paragraphs the candidate puts the case against the label 'liberal' and thus shows the critical skill needed to make a balanced judgement in the conclusion.

This is an impressive catalogue of reform, particularly by contrast with the preceding decade. This is not, however, the whole story. The repeal of the Combination Acts was followed in 1825 by an Amending Act, which effectively deprived trade unions of the power to strike. The repeal of the Test and Corporation Acts merely made permanent rights which the nonconformists had for long been granted by annual indemnity acts. Catholic emancipation was accepted by Wellington (who was Prime Minister at the time) and Peel, not as a matter of principle, but reluctantly because of the threat of civil war in Ireland. Moreover, it split the Tory party and led to the fall of the Tory government in 1830. This, in turn, paved the way for the one major reform which the Tories were unwilling even to contemplate - parliamentary reform.

The opposition of the Liberal Tories to Parliamentary reform and, until their hand was forced, to Catholic emancipation, is proof that they were not liberals in the modern sense. On the other hand, the work of Peel and Huskisson shows willingness to reform which distinguishes them from the ministers of 1812-22. In many ways, the modern overtones of the word `liberal´ are misleading. Perhaps the alternative term `enlightened Tories´ is a better description of them.

2 England, 1846–86

The following topics are covered in this chapter:

- Mid-Victorian Britain, 1846–68
- Gladstone
- Gladstone and Ireland
- Disraeli

2.1 Mid-Victorian Britain, 1846–68

LEARNING SUMMARY

After studying this section you should be able to understand:

- the changes in the Liberal and Conservative Parties, 1846–68
- the prosperity of mid-Victorian Britain
- the Second Reform Act of 1867 and its significance

Liberals and Conservatives, 1846–68

AQA	**U1**	WJEC	**U4**
OCR	**U1**	CCEA	**AS1**
Edexcel	**U2**		

The Whigs/Liberals

The crisis over the **repeal** of the Corn Laws in 1846 cast its shadow over the politics of the next twenty years. The split in the Conservative Party produced a confused situation, in which no party won an overall majority in the elections of 1847 and 1852. Technically, the Conservatives did have an overall majority of 6, but the party was divided between Protectionists and Peelites. Because of the weakness of the Conservatives, the Whigs dominated politics and were in office for most of the period 1846–68.

Palmerston was the outstanding figure. He held office, as either Foreign Secretary or Prime Minister, for most of the period 1846–1865. His willingness to stand up for British interests made him popular and helps to explain the political dominance of the Whigs. Palmerston had little interest in domestic affairs and saw little need for reform. He opposed the renewed demand for parliamentary reform in the 1860s.

By the end of the period, however, the Whig Party had evolved into the Liberal Party. The **Peelites** – those Conservatives who had supported Peel over the repeal of the Corn Laws – gradually moved towards the Whigs. In 1852–5 they joined a coalition with the Whigs, with the Peelite Aberdeen as Prime Minister.

> Religion was always very important to Gladstone.

The outstanding figure among the Peelites was **Gladstone**. Gladstone had entered Parliament in 1832 as a Tory and had soon become noted for his strong views on the role of the Church of England in national life. From 1843–5 he was President of the Board of Trade under Peel and this gave him his interest in financial and economic affairs. In 1846 he supported Peel over the repeal of the Corn Laws. His decision to accept office as Chancellor of the Exchequer under Palmerston in 1859 was the turning point in the evolution of the Liberal Party. From this point it is customary to describe the Whig-Peelite-Radical alliance as the Liberals.

KEY POINT

The emergence of the Liberal Party was the most important development in the political parties in this period.

29

Gladstone's Budgets

Gladstone was Chancellor of the Exchequer from 1852–5 and 1859–65. His main aim was to continue the move to free trade.

- His budgets of 1853 and 1860 abolished nearly all remaining duties.
- The Cobden Treaty with France (1860) boosted Anglo-French trade.
- He lowered income tax to 4d in the £, though he was unable to achieve his aim of abolishing it.

These were popular moves. Food became cheaper and the cost of living was reduced. **Free trade** became one of the fundamental principles of the Liberal Party and Gladstone's stature grew considerably. In 1867, he became leader of the Liberal Party on the retirement of Russell.

The Conservatives

As a result of the split in 1846, the Conservatives did not win a general election until 1874. There were three short Conservative ministries under Lord Derby, all of them minority governments. It was during this period that Disraeli, who led the attack on Peel by Protectionist Conservatives over the repeal of the Corn Laws, came to the fore.

Although **Disraeli** was the dominant figure in the Conservative Party over the next twenty years, he was mistrusted. This was partly because of his background. Disraeli came from a Jewish family which had converted to Christianity and he lacked influential connections, but he was also regarded as eccentric, ambitious and unscrupulous. He had good reason to describe his rise to be leader of the Conservative Party as 'climbing the greasy pole'. In the three Derby ministries he was Chancellor of the Exchequer. He was largely responsible for the 1867 Reform Act (see page 31). On the retirement of Derby in 1868 he became Prime Minister, but was defeated in the election at the end of the year.

> **KEY POINT**
>
> The split in the Conservative Party in 1846 led to a realignment of the political parties by 1868.

Mid-Victorian prosperity in Britain

AQA   U1

From the mid 1840s to 1873 Britain enjoyed great prosperity. Industrial exports surged and real wages for industrial workers rose by about 30%. Agriculture also enjoyed a period of prosperity, contrary to the fears expressed at the time of the repeal of the Corn Laws. The Great Exhibition of 1851 was a symbol of this prosperity.

Free trade played an important part in this. Britain's position as the first industrial nation had not yet been challenged. This meant that free trade was to its advantage. Peel's free trade budgets of 1842 and 1845, and the repeal of the Corn Laws, thus provided favourable trading conditions for Britain.

The Second Reform Act, 1867

AQA	**U3**	OCR	**U2**
OCR	**U1**	WJEC	**U4**
Edexcel	**U2**		

Pressure for further parliamentary reform built up in the 1860s. The Radicals, led by Bright, campaigned vigorously both in and out of Parliament. In 1864 Gladstone was converted to the idea. The death of Palmerston in 1865 removed an obstacle. Eventually, Disraeli concluded that reform was inevitable and aimed to see that the Conservatives got the credit.

Both parties were divided on the issue. A Liberal reform bill was defeated in 1866 when Liberal opponents of reform voted against it. The Conservatives came to office. Public pressure for reform was growing – there was a massive demonstration in Hyde Park. Disraeli introduced a more far-reaching bill in the hope of winning support for the Conservatives and a series of amendments made the final Act still more radical.

The terms of the Act were:

> This meant working class men.

- in the boroughs the vote was extended to male householders with one year's residence and £10 lodgers
- in the counties the vote was extended to £12 leaseholders
- seats were redistributed from small boroughs to large counties and growing towns.

As a result of the Act the electorate doubled to 2.5 million. Since most of the new voters were from the urban working class, it was an important step towards democracy. The Act also marked an important stage in the development of political parties because in the larger boroughs the electorate was too big to bribe. It was therefore necessary to have an efficient local organisation. Although Disraeli was mainly responsible for this Act, Gladstone won the 1868 election, primarily because he and Bright conducted a nationwide campaign to win the support of the new voters.

KEY POINT

- The 1867 Reform Act was 'a leap in the dark' – a major step towards democracy, though still far short of full democracy.
- It was Disraeli's greatest parliamentary triumph, but the immediate benefit went to Gladstone.

KEY DATES

> You should be able to explain the significance of each of these dates.

1846	Repeal of the Corn Laws; split in the Conservative Party
1846–52	Russell's first ministry (Whig)
1851–2	First Derby-Disraeli ministry (Conservative)
1852–5	Aberdeen ministry; Gladstone Chancellor of the Exchequer
1855–8	Palmerston's first ministry (Whig)
1858–9	Second Derby-Disraeli ministry (Conservative)
1859–65	Palmerston's second ministry (Liberal); Gladstone accepts office as Chancellor of the Exchequer
1867	Second Reform Act
1868	Liberal election victory; formation of Gladstone's first ministry

2.2 Gladstone

LEARNING SUMMARY

After studying this section you should be able to understand:

- Gladstonian liberalism
- reforms of Gladstone's first ministry
- the domestic policies of Gladstone's second ministry
- Gladstone's foreign and imperial policies

Gladstonian liberalism

AQA **U3** WJEC **U4**
OCR **U1, 2**

> Try to link these principles to the phrase 'peace, retrenchment and reform'.

The chief characteristics of the Liberal Party under Gladstone were:

- commitment to free trade
- *laissez faire* – the view that the government should not intervene in the economy
- strict economy in government finance, which meant a restricted role for government and a high degree of efficiency
- equality of opportunity and hostility to privilege; this meant an emphasis on institutional reform rather than social reform
- a peaceful foreign policy based on respect for other countries.

The Gladstonian Liberal Party was an uneasy alliance of Whig landowners, former Peelites, Benthamite radicals and nonconformists. Gladstone added a strongly moralistic flavour, derived from his strong religious beliefs. This is shown, for example, in his opposition to Disraeli's policy on the Balkans and his growing obsession with the Irish problem.

Religion played an important part in Gladstone's political outlook. As a young man he believed that the Church of England, supported by the state, could be the means of bringing religious unity to the country. Later, he came to accept that this was not practical and he came to a belief in religious tolerance, which made it possible for him to lead the party of nonconformity, even though he was himself a devout Anglican. He shared with the nonconformists a belief in the importance of morality in politics, which was an essential element in both his foreign policy and domestic affairs. It was this moralistic aspect of Gladstone's politics which attracted most hostility from Disraeli and the Conservatives. Disraeli found Gladstone's habit of claiming that he was doing the will of God hard to stomach.

Gladstone's first ministry, 1868–74

AQA **U3** WJEC **U4**
OCR **U1, 2**

As well as two Acts concerning Ireland (see pages 34–7), Gladstone's first ministry was responsible for an important series of domestic reforms.

- **Forster's Education Act** (1870) provided for elementary schools to be established wherever the existing provision by the two religious societies was inadequate. Local School Boards, elected by ratepayers, were to provide Board Schools funded from the rates. These were to provide non-denominational religious education (which angered the nonconformists). Attendance was not to be compulsory or free, though the Boards had the power to pay the fees for poor children.
- The **University Tests Act** (1871) opened teaching posts at Oxford and Cambridge to nonconformists.

- The **civil service reforms** (1871) provided that posts were to be filled by competitive examination rather than by recommendation by an MP or a peer.
- The **Trade Union Act** (1871) gave unions legal recognition, allowing them to protect their funds in the courts, but the **Criminal Law Amendment Act** (1871) made picketing – even peaceful picketing – illegal. This made strikes almost impossible to organise and antagonised union members.
- The **Ballot Act** (1872) instituted secret ballot in elections, thus reducing bribery and intimidation.
- **Cardwell's army reforms** reorganised the regiments and the administration of the army, abolished flogging and the purchase of commissions and reduced the length of service to six years overseas and six years in the reserves.
- The **Licensing Act** (1872) gave magistrates the power to reduce the number of pubs and imposed closing times.
- The Judicature Act (1872) reorganised the law courts.

> Think about these reforms. Which promoted equality of opportunity? Which reflected the views of nonconformists? Which aroused opposition, and from whom?

This added up to a remarkable record of reform. Gladstone's first ministry did a great deal to reduce privilege and to make Britain a more efficiently run country. Many of the reforms, however, provoked opposition, especially the Education Act, the Criminal Law Amendment Act and the Licensing Act. Moreover, to the disappointment of the working classes, Gladstone failed to bring in social reforms in areas such as public health (the Public Health Act of 1872 was a failure). As a result, Gladstone lost the election of 1874.

> **KEY POINT**
>
> Gladstone's first ministry was a great reforming ministry, but failed to tackle social reform. Many of its reforms created enemies.

Gladstone's second ministry, 1880–5

AQA **U3** WJEC **U4**
OCR **U1, 2**

Gladstone had retired from the leadership of the Liberal party after his defeat in 1874, but created a great stir in 1878 with his pamphlet *The Bulgarian Horrors*, which was, in effect, an attack on Disraeli's support for Turkey in the Balkan crisis. In 1880 he attacked Disraeli's imperial policies in the **Midlothian Campaign**, which not only played a great part in the Liberal victory in the 1880 election but was also the first occasion when a party leader appealed directly to the electorate.

There was comparatively little reform in Gladstone's second ministry. The Married Women's Property Act (1882) and the Corrupt Practices Act (1883) are worth noting. There was, however, one important achievement – a further instalment of parliamentary reform in the **Reform and Redistribution Acts** (1884–5). These Acts gave the vote to all male householders in the counties and redistributed 147 seats from smaller boroughs to more populous areas. They marked an important step towards full democracy, but all women, and about 40% of men (mainly those who were not householders), were still without the vote.

> This brought the franchise in the counties into line with the boroughs.

> Look back to the section on Gladstonian liberalism to explain why Gladstone was unenthusiastic.

The sparse record of the ministry in reforms was partly because of Gladstone's involvement with the Irish problem and partly because the Liberal Party was divided about the need for social reform. The Radicals were keen on this, as shown by Joseph Chamberlain's Unauthorised Programme (1885), but the aristocratic Whigs opposed it and Gladstone was unenthusiastic.

Gladstone's foreign and imperial policies

| AQA | U3 | WJEC | U4 |
| OCR | U1, 2 | | |

Gladstone's attitude to foreign affairs was based on his moralistic outlook. He sought to preserve peace through working with other powers. This attitude led to policies which the public thought were weak. In the first ministry, two episodes brought him unpopularity.

- Gladstone was unable to do anything when Russia renounced the **Black Sea clauses** of the Treaty of Paris of 1856.
- In 1872 Gladstone agreed to pay compensation to the USA for the damage caused to shipping in the American Civil War by the *Alabama*, a warship built in Britain.

In the second ministry the main problems were in imperial affairs and were the legacy of Disraeli.

- In South Africa, the Zulus were defeated, but this led to problems with Transvaal, which, freed from the Zulu threat, declared itself independent. The First Boer War resulted in a British defeat at Majuba Hill and the recognition of Transvaal's virtual independence.
- Britain became involved in the internal affairs of Egypt as a result of Disraeli's purchase of Suez Canal shares. Growing disorder in Egypt led Gladstone to order its occupation in 1882. This led Gladstone into difficulties in the Sudan, which was nominally ruled by Egypt, but in a state of rebellion. Gladstone decided to abandon it, but in the course of withdrawing the Anglo-Egyptian garrisons, General Gordon was besieged and killed in Khartoum. Prompter action by Gladstone could have saved him and public opinion was outraged.

KEY DATES

1868–74	Gladstone's first ministry
1870	Forster's Education Act
1871	Trade Union Act; Criminal Law Amendment Act
1872	Ballot Act; Licensing Act
1874	General election; Gladstone defeated
1880–5	Gladstone's second ministry
1884	Third Reform Act

You should be able to explain the significance of each of these dates.

2.3 Gladstone and Ireland

LEARNING SUMMARY

After studying this section you should be able to understand:

- Gladstone's attempts to settle Irish grievances in his first ministry
- how Gladstone responded to Parnell in his second ministry
- the reasons for the failure of the Home Rule Bills of 1886 and 1893.

Pacifying Ireland: Gladstone's first ministry

AQA	U3
OCR	U1, 2, 4
Edexcel	U2
WJEC	U4

Irish grievances

The Irish had three main grievances in the 1860s.

- The established church, to which tithes had to be paid, was the Protestant Church of Ireland. The majority of the Irish were Roman Catholics.

Ireland had little industry, so most people lived by farming.

- Much of the land was divided into small plots, which the Irish rented from absentee English landlords. They had no security of tenure and no incentive to improve their holdings. If they did, their rents would be raised and they would receive no compensation if they were evicted. There were frequent outbreaks of agrarian violence.
- The Act of Union (1800) had abolished Ireland's parliament. The Irish felt that Ireland was being ruled from London by an unsympathetic English government. Hence, a demand arose for Home Rule. In 1873 Isaac Butt founded the Home Rule League.

The Irish Home Rule League grew out of the Irish Home Government Association founded in 1870.

In 1867 the **Fenian** brotherhood, a revolutionary Irish-American organisation, was responsible for a number of terrorist outrages in Britain. This drew attention to the grievances of Ireland.

Gladstone's remedies

English politicians were generally ignorant about Ireland. It was unusual to give it such a high priority.

When Gladstone came to power in 1868, he announced, 'My mission is to pacify Ireland'. He aimed to do this by tackling the first two grievances. In 1869 the Irish Church Act **disestablished** the Church of Ireland. In 1870 the **First Irish Land Act** was passed: evicted tenants were to be compensated for improvements, unless evicted for non-payment of rent. The Act failed to stop evictions because there was no effective provision to stop landlords raising rents to unaffordable levels.

Later, in the 1870s the situation in Ireland deteriorated. In 1873 an agricultural depression began. Evictions increased as landlords sought to consolidate small farms into larger, more efficient units. In 1877 **Parnell**, who was willing to use more militant tactics than Butt, took over leadership of the Home Rule League. In 1879 Michael Davitt founded the **Irish Land League**. The Home Rule League, the Land League and the Fenians came together in the New Departure – using militant tactics to pressurise the government into giving way to nationalist demands.

> **KEY POINT**
>
> Despite the Irish reforms of Gladstone's first ministry, by 1880 the situation in Ireland was worse.

Gladstone and Parnell

AQA	**U3**	Edexcel	**U2**
OCR	**U1**	WJEC	**U4**
OCR	**U2, 4**		

Compare this with the First Land Act and consider the charge that Gladstone's policy offered Ireland 'too little, too late'.

When Gladstone returned to power in 1880, the Land League was carrying out a campaign of rent strikes and boycotts of anyone who took over a farm from which a previous tenant had been evicted. Outbreaks of violence were becoming more frequent. In Parliament Parnell's 60 Irish Nationalist MPs were mounting a campaign of deliberate obstruction. Gladstone's response was the **Second Irish Land Act** (1881). This granted Irish tenants the three Fs: fair rents, fixity of tenure and free sale of the lease. At the same time a Coercion Act was passed to control the violence.

Parnell hoped that, if he kept up the pressure, Gladstone would grant Home Rule. The Land League therefore organised a campaign of non-payment of rent. Gladstone then ordered the arrest of Parnell, but after six months made an agreement with him, the **Kilmainham Treaty** (1882). Parnell called off the rent strike and Gladstone promised an Arrears Bill. Four days later the **Phoenix Park murders** took place. This act of terrorism convinced many people in England that the Irish were not fit to govern themselves. A more severe Coercion Act was passed. Gladstone, however, reached a different conclusion – that only Home Rule would pacify Ireland. He also realised that he would need to move cautiously to win support and to avoid a split in the Liberal Party.

The Home Rule Bills of 1886 and 1893

AQA	U3	Edexcel	U2
OCR	U1	WJEC	U4
OCR	U2, 4		

The First Home Rule Bill, 1886

The 1885 general election gave Parnell's Irish Home Rule party the balance of power in the House of Commons. Gladstone's son then revealed his father's conversion to Home Rule. Parnell, therefore, gave the support of the Irish MPs to Gladstone, who formed his third ministry in 1886 and introduced the **First Home Rule Bill**. This proposed a parliament in Dublin to deal with Irish domestic affairs and that there would be no Irish MPs at Westminster.

> Don't confuse this with the Second Home Rule Bill. The First Home Rule Bill never reached the Lords.

The Home Rule Bill split the Liberal party: 93 Liberals, led by **Joseph Chamberlain** and Hartington, voted against it and it was defeated in the Commons. The split in the Liberal party ushered in twenty years of largely Conservative government, during which time the Liberal Unionists (those Liberals who had voted against Home Rule) moved over to become allies of the Conservatives.

> This was a crucial moment in the development of the parties. By 1895 a realignment had taken place.

The Second Home Rule Bill, 1893

In 1892 Gladstone, with Irish support, formed his fourth ministry. The **Second Home Rule Bill** (1893) differed from the first in that it proposed that there should be Irish MPs at Westminster. The Bill passed the Commons, but was heavily defeated in the Lords, where there was a Conservative majority. Gladstone then retired.

Ireland in the 1890s

Despite the failure of Gladstone's Home Rule Bills, Ireland in 1894 was relatively quiet. The Conservatives had introduced a scheme to help Irish tenants to buy their land (Ashbourne's Land Purchase Act, 1885). This, together with Gladstone's Second Land Act, took some of the heat out of the land question. Balfour, as Irish Secretary, had introduced in 1887 a Crimes Act which succeeded in suppressing some of the violence in Ireland.

> Look back over Parnell's career to assess what he had achieved for Ireland.

Perhaps more importantly, Parnell's authority was undermined by the **O'Shea** divorce case (1890) where Parnell was named as co-respondent. Immediately before this, he was at the peak of his power after it was revealed that letters alleged to incriminate him in the Phoenix Park murders had been forged by Pigott. His downfall and his death a year later left the Irish nationalists divided and weak.

Why did Gladstone fail to achieve Home Rule for Ireland?

* The Liberal Party split over the issue.
* The House of Lords, dominated by landowners, many with land in Ireland, was overwhelmingly opposed.
* There was opposition in Ulster (though this was probably not as strong at this time as some Conservatives claimed, or as it was to be later).
* Many people, e.g. Chamberlain, believed that Home Rule would stir up demands for independence in other territories in the British Empire.
* The Irish Nationalists were weakened by the downfall of Parnell.

KEY DATES

1800	Act of Union
1869	Disestablishment of the Irish Church
1870	First Irish Land Act
1877	Parnell leader of the Home Rule League
1879	Foundation of Irish Land League
1881	Second Irish Land Act
1882	Kilmainham Treaty; Phoenix Park murders
1886	First Home Rule Bill
1890	O'Shea divorce case – Parnell named as co-respondent
1891	Death of Parnell
1893	Second Home Rule Bill

> You should be able to explain the significance of each of these dates.

2.4 Disraeli

LEARNING SUMMARY

After studying this section you should be able to understand:

- the nature of 'Tory democracy'
- the success and popularity of Disraeli's second ministry, 1874–80

Tory democracy

AQA **U3**   WJEC **U4**
OCR **U1, 2**

> Disraeli realised that the Conservatives needed working class support.

'**Tory democracy**' is the phrase used to describe Disraeli's political philosophy. It was developed from the ideas he put forward in his novels *Coningsby* and *Sybil* in the 1840s. Disraeli set out his ideas in his **Crystal Palace** and Manchester speeches in 1872. Tory democracy was intended to appeal to the new electorate created by the 1867 Reform Act. It helped Disraeli to win a handsome victory in the 1874 election. The main ideas were as follows.

- Disraeli stressed the central role of the monarchy, the aristocracy and the church in national life.
- A Conservative government would pursue a policy of social reform on the paternalist ground that the rich should help the poor. This would strengthen the loyalty of the unprivileged to the monarchy and the aristocracy.
- The Conservative Party would develop the Empire (imperialism).

Some historians claim that what Disraeli actually said in these speeches was vaguer than was subsequently claimed. It has also been argued that he took up social reform simply to win votes. But it does seem to have won some working class support – in 1874 the Conservatives won 18 out of 25 seats in Lancashire. Equally important in making the Conservatives a national party was the electoral organisation created by Gorst, stretching from the Carlton Club at the centre to the constituencies.

KEY POINT

> Disraeli realised that after the 1867 Reform Act the Conservative Party needed to win working class support.

Disraeli's second ministry, 1874–80

| AQA | U3 | WJEC | U4 |
| OCR | U1, 2 | | |

Domestic reforms

Tory democracy can be seen in action in the reforms passed in Disraeli's second ministry.

- The **Public Health Act** (1875) imposed a range of duties on local authorities, e.g. the supply of clean water, sewage and the removal of nuisances.
- The **Artisans' Dwellings Act** (1875) gave local authorities the power to clear slums, though they were not compelled to do so.
- The **Factory Act** (1874) reduced the working day to ten hours and raised the minimum age for the employment of children to ten.
- The **Conspiracy and Protection of Property Act** (1875) made peaceful picketing legal.
- The **Employers and Workmen Act** made breach of contract by a worker a civil offence, as it was for an employer.
- The **Education Act** (1876) set up School Attendance Committees to encourage attendance, though it was still not compulsory.
- Other reforms were the Sale of Food and Drugs Act, the Rivers Pollution Act and the Merchant Shipping Act.

> **KEY POINT**
>
> Disraeli's second ministry produced a substantial record of social reform, much of which was the work of the Home Secretary, Cross. The weakness was that many of the Acts were permissive i.e. local authorities were allowed, but not required to enforce them.

Foreign and imperial affairs

The Balkan crises is explained more fully on pages 59–60.

Public opinion played an important part, first supporting Gladstone, then Disraeli.

In foreign affairs, the ministry was dominated by the **Balkan crisis** of 1875–8. Disraeli wished to follow the traditional British policy of supporting Turkey as a bulwark against Russian expansion. Turkish brutality, which provoked a savage denunciation by Gladstone, made this difficult. But when Russia intervened and threatened Constantinople, Disraeli sent the British fleet and threatened war. In the end he was able, in co-operation with Bismarck, to put pressure on Russia to agree to the **Congress of Berlin**. This was a triumph for Disraeli. The settlement which Russia had imposed on Turkey was considerably modified and Britain gained Cyprus.

Disraeli was also very active in imperial affairs. His policies were popular at first. In 1875 he purchased the **Suez Canal shares** and in 1876 he created the title **Empress of India** for Queen Victoria. But, in 1878–9 his 'forward' policies led to the outbreak of the Afghan and Zulu Wars.

- The Boer republics of Transvaal and the Orange Free State, facing a serious threat from the Zulus, in 1877 accepted the status of a British protectorate. War broke out with the **Zulus** in 1879. This was really the responsibility of Frere, Disraeli's High Commissioner in South Africa, rather than Disraeli himself. The British force was defeated at Isandlwana, though the Zulus were eventually defeated in 1880.
- The Afghan War was caused by concern about Russian influence, which could be a threat to British India. After a short war, the Amir accepted a British mission in Kabul, but its members were massacred in 1878. A further war followed.

Public opinion began to see Disraeli's imperialism as dangerous and this contributed to his defeat in 1880. An attack on 'Beaconsfieldism', the name coined to describe Disraeli's imperial policies, was a major feature of Gladstone's Midlothian Campaign.

KEY POINT

Disraeli made imperialism a distinctive feature of the Conservative Party.

You should be able to explain the significance of each of these dates.

KEY DATES

1872	Crystal Palace speech
1874–80	Disraeli's second ministry
1875	Public Health Act; Artisans Dwellings Act; Conspiracy and Protection of Property Act; Purchase of Suez Canal Shares
1876	Queen Victoria, Empress of India
1878	Congress of Berlin; Afghan War
1879	Zulu War

Sample question and model answer

This question is really about differences of principle and it covers all aspects of policy – domestic, foreign and imperial.

Were there significant differences of principle dividing Gladstone and Disraeli or were they simply rivals for power? **[50]**

There were significant differences of principle between Gladstone and Disraeli, as well as some underlying similarities of outlook which probably neither would willingly have acknowledged.

In domestic affairs, both Gladstone and Disraeli headed reforming ministries. In this sense there was little difference between them. But the philosophy underpinning their domestic policies was different and so was the emphasis of their reforms. `Gladstonian liberalism´ was derived from Gladstone's commitment to individualism. It advocated civil and religious liberty, a minimal state, free trade, low taxes and equality of opportunity. In his ministry of 1868-74, many of Gladstone's reforms were directed towards removing privileges and creating conditions in which individualism could flourish. This added up to a considerable volume of reform, but it was administrative and legal rather than social reform. Indeed, it was not Gladstone's wish to change society, as was shown by his lack of interest in Chamberlain's radical reform programme in the 1880s.

At this point, give some details, e.g. civil service and army reforms, education, secret ballot, etc.

Disraeli's political philosophy is known as `Tory democracy´. Disraeli was not a rigorous political thinker and Tory democracy (a term not used by Disraeli himself) is not very easy to pin down. In essence, it amounts to a belief in an aristocratic, paternalist government protecting the poor through social reforms in an attempt to bring together the `two nations´ Disraeli had identified in his early writing. As set out in his Crystal Palace speech, it was intended to win the support of the recently enfranchised working class for the Conservatives. It was also an attack on the individualism of Gladstonian liberalism. In practical terms, this led to much more social reform than in Gladstone's first ministry.

Here give details.

This discussion of political philosophy and its practical outcome in domestic affairs is promising. It sets out the main differences and assesses their significance.

In practice, however, the difference between the two in domestic reform was smaller than a description of their political philosophies would suggest. Although they were both involved in the extension of the franchise in the 1867 Reform Act, and both sought to win the new electorate for their parties, neither was truly a democrat in the modern sense. They accepted the basic class framework of Victorian society. It was Gladstone, not Disraeli, who said, `I am a firm believer in the aristocratic principle´. Although Disraeli's ministry achieved more social reform, it was Cross, rather than Disraeli, who was responsible and in any case the impact was much reduced by the permissive nature of much of the legislation.

There was also a clear difference of outlook between the two men on foreign policy. Gladstone based his policy on his strong moral sense and so Gladstonian liberalism stood for peace. This explains Gladstone's controversial decision to pay compensation to the USA for the Alabama affair, for which Disraeli attacked him.

Hence, too, Gladstone's outrage over the Bulgarian atrocities. Gladstone's campaign on this was regarded by Disraeli as undermining Britain's true interest, which was to prevent Russia exploiting the situation. Gladstone's moral indignation was again directed against Disraeli in the Midlothian campaign in 1879, this time against his imperial policies which led to the Zulu and Afghan Wars. Disraeli's Crystal Palace speech placed great emphasis on patriotism and pride in the empire and these became hallmarks of Disraelian conservatism. All this suggests an important difference of principle between the two men. In practice, however, the differences were smaller. Disraeli's `forward´ policy in Afghanistan and South Africa, over which Gladstone attacked him, was as much the work of the men on the spot, as of Disraeli himself. Furthermore, for all the vehemence of his attacks on Disraeli's imperialism, Gladstone's behaviour in Egypt was little different from what Disraeli would have done, except perhaps that Disraeli would have made more effort to rescue Gordon.

Factual evidence is used selectively to underpin the argument rather than for description. Similarities are referred to as well as differences.

Thus there does seem to be real differences of principle between the two men. Gladstone's emphasis on individualism, self-help and the role of morality in politics were alien to Disraeli. Some would argue that Disraeli had no real principles and that his sole aim in politics was to reach the `top of the greasy pole´. Even if this were so, Gladstone was undoubtedly motivated by political principles and Disraeli's opposition to them was in itself a difference of principle.

3 Nineteenth century Britain: protest and reform

The following topics are covered in this chapter:

- Parliamentary reform
- Chartism
- The Poor Law
- Public health
- Factory legislation
- Education

3.1 Parliamentary reform

LEARNING SUMMARY	After studying this section you should be able to understand:
	- the development of radical ideas in the early nineteenth century
	- the legislation to reform parliament between 1832 and 1885
	- the effects of these reforms

Pre-Chartist radicals

Edexcel	**U2**	OCR	**U2**
WJEC	**U4**		

The demand for political reform had its roots in a radical tradition dating back to the late eighteenth century. Major Cartwright's *Take Your Choice*, published in 1776, argued for annual parliaments and 'equal representation'. **Thomas Paine** was influential in publicising the ideas of the American and French revolutions in England. In the 1790s, following the French Revolution, radicals were largely driven underground by Pitt's repressive measures.

After 1815 the radical tradition resurfaced. There was widespread discontent, caused primarily by economic conditions. This accounts for the Luddite outbreaks (machine breaking) in some industrial areas from 1811 onwards. Radical leaders channelled the unrest into demands for parliamentary reform. Prominent among radical leaders were William Cobbett, Henry Hunt, Joseph Hume and Francis Place. Henry Hunt's fiery oratory made him, in the eyes of the government, a feared rabble-rouser. The methods employed varied from petitions and mass meetings to attempted insurrection.

- Journalism – Cobbett's *Political Register* was particularly influential.
- Petitions – the March of the Blanketeers (1817) was intended to carry a petition to the Prince Regent.
- Mass meetings – the most notorious being Peterloo (1819).

There were also on the fringes some who were prepared to resort to violence. The Pentridge (Derbyshire) Rising (1817) was an armed insurrection, betrayed by the government spy Oliver, who was really an *agent provocateur*. The Cato Street Conspiracy (1820) was a plot to blow up the cabinet.

> **KEY POINT**
>
> After the French Revolution the governing classes feared that concessions to the radicals would lead to revolution.

Reform Acts, 1832–1885

Edexcel **U2** WJEC **U4**

In the early nineteenth century Britain had a parliamentary system of government, but it was not democratic. There were fewer than 500 000 voters out of a population of 24 million. The geographical distribution of seats in the House of Commons bore no relation to population. There was no secret ballot, so bribery and other corrupt practices were common features of elections. Between 1832 and 1885 a series of reforms brought about a significant shift towards democracy.

- **The Great Reform Act (1832)** increased the number of voters to over 800 000. In the counties £10 copyholders and £50 leaseholders were given the vote. In the boroughs the old qualifications were replaced by a uniform £10 householder qualification. In total 87 small boroughs in England and Wales lost one or both MPs, 65 seats were re-allocated to larger counties, 65 to newly created boroughs, 8 to Scotland and 5 to Ireland. Electoral registers were introduced.
- **The Second Reform Act (1867)** added £12 ratepayers (£14 in Scotland) to the county franchise, but the major change was in the boroughs, where the vote was given to all male householders and £10 lodgers. The electorate increased to nearly 2.5 million out of a population of 30 million. 52 borough seats were abolished and 25 of them were re-allocated to counties, 19 to existing or newly created boroughs and 6 to Scotland. An important feature was that Birmingham, Leeds, Liverpool and Manchester became three-member boroughs.
- **The Secret Ballot Act (1872)** ended the system of voting in public and reduced bribery and intimidation in elections.
- **The Corrupt Practices Act (1883)** laid down limits for election expenses and prescribed penalties for bribery and corruption in elections.
- **The Reform and Redistribution Acts (1884–5)** introduced a uniform franchise for counties and boroughs – male householders and £10 lodgers. The electorate was increased to 5.7 million, but about 40% of men were still excluded by this definition. There was a major redistribution of seats, resulting in single-member constituencies except in big cities.

The effects of the Reform Acts

Edexcel **U2** WJEC **U4**

The effects of the changes in the franchise can be summed up:
- The 1832 Great Reform Act gave the vote to the middle classes in the boroughs.
- The 1867 Second Reform Act gave the vote to the urban working class.
- The 1884–5 Reform and Redistribution Acts gave the vote to the rural working class.

But only men were allowed to vote and working class men who were not householders (about 40% altogether) were not given the vote. So, by 1885 Britain was still only part of the way to democracy.

The Reform Acts had a significant impact on the political parties. The 1832 Act made it necessary to appeal to the new middle class voters. The Whig reforms of the 1830s followed the example of the Reform Act itself in responding to pressures for reform. Peel's Tamworth Manifesto of 1834 had the clear aim of adapting the Tory party to the needs of the new electorate – hence the adoption of the name 'Conservative Party'.

In 1846, again partly in response to the needs of the industrial middle class, Peel repealed the Corn Laws and the effect was to split the Conservatives. The Peelites – those who supported the repeal – were eventually led by Gladstone into an alliance with the Whigs to form the Liberal Party. The 1867 Act meant that both parties had to make a further shift in their appeal to a new electorate. In the 1868 election the new voters elected a Liberal government, but by 1874 Disraeli had broadened the appeal of the Conservatives to the new working class voters with his vision of Tory Democracy. By this time both parties had made significant progress in developing party organisations, both centrally and in the constituencies.

> **KEY POINT**
>
> By 1885 Britain had made significant progress towards democracy, but still only about 60% of men could vote – and no women.

3.2 Chartism

LEARNING SUMMARY

After studying this section you should be able to understand:
- the early history of trade unionism
- the causes of Chartism
- interpretations of the reasons for the failure of Chartism

Early history of trade unionism

OCR   U2

In the early nineteenth century trade unions were feared by governments and by employers, both in industry and agriculture, as potentially revolutionary. Pitt made them illegal by the Combination Acts of 1799 and 1800. A campaign by Francis Place and Joseph Hume secured their repeal in 1824, though a year later an Amending Act placed some restrictions on union activities. Many small local unions of skilled workers sprang up.

In 1834 the **Grand National Consolidated Trades Union** was founded by Robert Owen and John Doherty. It aimed to unite skilled and unskilled workers in a single organisation. It proved to be over ambitious and collapsed within a year. In the same year the case of the **Tolpuddle Martyrs** vividly illustrated the hostility towards trade unions among employers. The sentence of seven years' transportation on six agricultural labourers for administering an illegal oath was backed by the government.

The causes of Chartism

AQA   U1
Edexcel U2
OCR   U2
WJEC   U1, U2, U4
CCEA   AS1

Chartism was a movement of the industrial working class demanding a democratic parliament, to be achieved by the Six Points of the People's Charter.
- Universal male suffrage.
- Vote by secret ballot.
- Equal electoral districts.
- Payment for MPs.
- Abolition of the property qualification for MPs.
- Annual parliaments.

The years of greatest Chartist activity were 1839, 1842 and 1848, in each of which a petition was presented to Parliament. All three petitions were rejected and after 1848 support dwindled.

Political causes

The main demand of the Chartists was reform of Parliament. Many Chartists may have seen this as the means by which society could be reformed and social justice achieved for the working classes, but what gave the movement its distinctive character was its concentration on political reform. In this respect it differed from other movements which sought to improve conditions for the working classes, such as the Ten Hours Movement.

There is a direct link between the 1832 Reform Act and the emergence of Chartism. Politically aware members of the working classes were disappointed by their exclusion from the reformed franchise, especially as they believed that working class pressure had helped the Whigs to force the Act through. After 1832 the Whig governments created further political grievances.

- They passed the Poor Law Amendment Act in 1834.
- They helped to bring about the collapse of the Grand National Consolidated Trades Union by encouraging magistrates to impose heavy penalties on trade unionists, culminating in the affair of the Tolpuddle Martyrs.
- They tried to suppress the unstamped press by reducing the stamp duty, but enforcing it more vigorously.

> Radical newspapers were cheap enough for the working classes to buy because they evaded the stamp duty.

It was in these circumstances that William Lovett founded the **London Working Men's Association** (LWMA) in 1837. Its aim was 'equal political and social rights' for 'all classes of society'.

Working class disillusion with the Whig governments was shared by middle class radicals. The Birmingham Political Union, founded by Thomas Attwood in 1830 and prominent in the struggle for the Reform Act, was revived in 1838. It worked with the LWMA in drawing up the Charter. Attwood himself presented the first Chartist petition to Parliament in 1839. However, the violence of the language used by some Chartists, especially O'Connor, and the development of the split between the advocates of moral force and physical force soon alienated many of the middle class supporters. Chartism thus became an almost exclusively working class movement.

> **KEY POINT**
>
> The distinctive feature of Chartism was its focus on political demands.

Economic causes

The years of maximum Chartist activity coincided with economic hardship. After a period of relative prosperity, an economic depression began in 1837 and reached its lowest point in 1842. The economy revived after 1843 and support for Chartism declined. A further economic downturn in 1847–8, when there were two bad harvests and a financial crisis resulting from the bursting of the railway boom, coincided with the final outburst of Chartist activity.

> Relative prosperity between 1843 and 1846 coincided with Peel's free trade budgets and 'railway mania'.

> **KEY POINT**
>
> For most of its supporters Chartism was a 'knife and fork question', even though its leaders saw their aims as political.

An examination of the geography of Chartist activity shows that it was primarily a phenomenon of the newly industrialised areas of the country. In that sense it was a product of the Industrial Revolution. Among its causes must be included poor conditions in factories and in industrial towns. But these were not in themselves sufficient to cause strong support for Chartism except in years of exceptional hardship or in association with particular local problems.

Chartist activity was particularly strong in Lancashire, Yorkshire and the East Midlands.

Support for Chartism

It is important in considering the causes of Chartism to note that it encompassed many groups with other aims beyond parliamentary reform, e.g. the Anti-Poor Law Movement. This diversity was a source both of strength (it drew together a variety of discontents in a single movement) and of weakness (it lacked unity of purpose).

There was also strong female involvement in the early years of the movement.

There was much local diversity. Support for Chartism was strongest where industrial change produced local grievances, e.g. handloom weavers displaced by power looms were consistent supporters of Chartism in Lancashire and Yorkshire. Other groups which were prominent in the Chartist movement in their own areas included nail-makers in the Black Country, potters in Staffordshire, framework knitters in Nottingham and miners in South Wales and the north east.

Reasons for the failure of Chartism

AQA	**U1**
Edexcel	**U2**
OCR	**U2**
WJEC	**U1, U2, U4**
CCEA	**AS1**

Robert Owen, the New Lanark mill owner, advocated producers' and consumers' co-operatives.

Leadership

The leaders of the Chartist movement were divided over aims and tactics. This was partly a matter of temperament and background.

- **William Lovett**, who founded the London Working Men's Association (LWMA), was a self-taught craftsman who had been involved in attempts to put into practice Owen's co-operative ideas. He was a moderate who believed that Chartism could attain its aims by moral force, i.e. by persuasion through meetings and pamphlets.
- **Thomas Attwood** was a Birmingham banker and radical MP who had been prominent in the agitation for the Reform Bill in 1831–2. Like Lovett, he believed in moral force. As leader of the Birmingham Political Union he was in a strong position at first, but later was alienated by the violent language of O'Connor.
- **O'Connor**, however, became the dominant figure. He alienated the other leaders by his advocacy of physical force.

Divisions within the movement

The divisions within the movement are clearly illustrated by the story of the National Convention in 1839. Within a few weeks many of the delegates had withdrawn for one reason or another. Divisions over whether to use 'ulterior measures' were barely kept in check. The Convention decided on a 'sacred month' and then went back on it.

A general strike.

The localism of much Chartist activity accentuated the problem of divisions within the movement. Since the grievances which drew men to Chartism often arose from conditions in local industries, the level of Chartist activity varied from district to district.

A further source of division was the existence within the movement of pressure groups with their own agendas. Attwood's advocacy of currency reform is an example of this. Others are the Temperance Chartists and the Christian Chartists, some of whom set up Chartist churches.

The role of O'Connor

Lack of middle class support is often seen as a reason why the Chartist movement failed, but the Anti-Corn Law League succeeded.

Many historians see O'Connor as a liability to the Chartist movement, alienating the middle classes by the violence of his language and by his refusal to co-operate with Joseph Sturge's Complete Suffrage Union or the Anti-Corn Law League. Some critics regard him as more interested in self-advertisement than in the aims of the Chartist movement. He is blamed for bringing the movement into ridicule in 1848 when his proposed procession to Parliament to present a petition after a mass meeting at Kennington was banned. The petition was eventually delivered by O'Connor and a handful of supporters and was found to contain many forged signatures. His Chartist Land Society represented a diversion of the movement from its original political aims and in any case collapsed in a financial muddle after only three years.

Government measures

The government took effective steps to deal with the Chartist threat. In 1839 it increased the size of the army in the north of England and appointed General Napier to command it. Napier was sympathetic to working class grievances, but made it clear that, if the Chartists used force, he would respond with force. The main outbreak of violence, the Newport Rising, was quickly suppressed by the magistrates, who knew in advance what was planned. In 1848 Wellington stationed troops at key points and 150 000 special constables were enrolled. The government made effective use of the newly invented electric telegraph and the newly constructed railways.

Economic prosperity

Because Chartism was a working class movement, support for it depended on the depth of working class discontent. Thus when economic prosperity increased, support for Chartism dropped. From about 1850 Britain entered a long period of prosperity and Chartism lost much of its appeal.

Probably the fundamental reason for the failure of Chartism was that it was ahead of its time. In the words of Asa Briggs, 'It is difficult to see how, given the nature of English society and government in the Chartist period, the Chartists could have succeeded in the way that O'Connor's critics claim that it might have done. The cards were too heavily stacked against them.'

> **KEY POINT**
>
> With the aristocracy and middle class united in opposing the demands of the Charter, only revolution could have achieved success and there was no sign that the working class were in revolutionary mood.

3.3 The Poor Law

LEARNING SUMMARY

After studying this section you should be able to understand:

● the origins and terms of the Poor Law Amendment Act, 1834
● how it was implemented and modified to 1865

The Poor Law Amendment Act, 1834

Edexcel **U2**
OCR **U2**
WJEC **U1, U4, U2**

Provision for the Poor in 1830

● Each parish was responsible for its own poor. To this end a parish rate was levied by the Overseers of the Poor.
● The poor were classified into the impotent poor (the sick, the old and children), the able-bodied poor (the unemployed) and the idle poor (those who refused to work).
● In many parishes workhouses were set up to provide for the poor, but this was by no means universal.
● In much of southern England the Speenhamland System had been adopted after 1795. This meant that outdoor relief (money payments) was given to poor labourers whose wages were inadequate. The payments depended on the size of the labourer's family and the price of bread.

By 1830 the old Poor Law was under fire for three main reasons.
● The total cost of poor relief in 1830 was estimated at £8 million.
● Outdoor relief under the Speenhamland System was alleged to encourage idleness, since labourers knew their wages would be supplemented. It also encouraged employers to pay less than a living wage, which meant that other ratepayers were in effect subsidising them.
● There was much variation between parishes, which offended utilitarians with their passion for efficiency.

A utilitarian, **Edwin Chadwick**, was the most influential member of a commission which was appointed in 1832 to investigate the Poor Law. It recommended a complete overhaul of the Poor Law, based on three principles.
● Encouraging the poor to look for work and not to rely on the Poor Law.
● Value for money – cheap, efficient and uniform administration.
● Central supervision of the system.

The Amendment Act, 1834

These principles were embodied in the Poor Law Amendment Act of 1834. The central feature was the **workhouse**. Outdoor relief could still be given to the sick and aged in some cases, but otherwise poor relief would only be provided in workhouses. Parishes were to be grouped into Poor Law Unions and a central Board of Commissioners, with Chadwick as its Secretary, was to supervise the system. The underlying view seemed to be that poverty was an avoidable misfortune and that the poor needed to be discouraged from seeking relief. Hence, workhouses were to be run on the principle of 'less eligibility', which also had the convenient result of making them cheaper to run.

'Less eligibility' meant that life in the workhouse should be less attractive than the condition of the poorest labourer outside it.

The operation of the Poor Law

OCR	U2	Edexcel U2
WJEC	U2	

The New Poor Law was popular with ratepayers (largely middle class) because the overall national cost of poor relief was immediately cut by 40%. By 1838 almost 90% of the parishes of England and Wales had been grouped into Unions and workhouses were rapidly established.

> Hence the nickname 'Poor Law Bastilles'.

It was highly unpopular with the working classes and played a part in the rise of the Chartist movement. It seemed that poverty was being treated as a crime and there was undoubtedly a punitive element in the workhouse regime. Husbands, wives and children were kept separate. Meals had to be eaten in silence and the food was poor. The work was hard – tasks, such as stone breaking and bone grinding, were similar to those in prison.

KEY POINT

The Poor Law Amendment Act achieved its aims of cutting costs and deterring the poor. Fear of the workhouse was ingrained in working class attitudes for the remainder of the century.

But there was a cost. Class divisions were accentuated, as shown by the growth of an Anti-Poor Law movement in the north, which merged into the Chartist movement at the end of the 1830s. In the south, where wages of agricultural labourers remained pitifully low, there was great hardship.

> Cyclical unemployment arose because there were alternate periods of high demand and slack demand.

The New Poor Law never operated fully in the way Chadwick had envisaged. It proved too expensive for each Union to provide separate workhouses for the unemployed, the sick, the aged and the workshy. In industrial areas, cyclical unemployment made it impossible to abolish outdoor relief, since there were sometimes too many out of work at the same time to accommodate them in workhouses. This failure to take account of the nature of unemployment in industrial areas was one of the great weaknesses of the Act, which had been framed more to cope with conditions in the agricultural south.

The harshness of the New Poor Law was somewhat mitigated by reforms from the 1840s. In 1842 separation of husbands and wives and of parents and children was ended. In 1847 the Poor Law Commission was replaced by the Poor Law Board. Poor Law schools were set up. Poor Law infirmaries gradually improved. Outbreaks of dangerous diseases between 1863 and 1865 led to parliamentary debates which resulted in the provision of better medical care.

KEY POINT

In spite of these improvements, working class families which fell on hard times would endure considerable hardship rather than go into the workhouse.

3.4 Public health

LEARNING SUMMARY	After studying this section you should be able to understand:
	• the development of public health legislation to 1875

Chadwick and public health

OCR **U2**
WJEC **U4, U2**
Edexcel **U2**

There were no planning laws, so builders tried to cram in as many houses as possible.

In 1842 Chadwick published his *Report on the Sanitary Condition of the Labouring Population of Great Britain*. It revealed a series of problems arising mainly from the rapid growth of industrial towns.

- Overcrowding and bad housing.
- Lack of sanitation – working class houses relied on outside privies connected to cesspits.
- Lack of pure water. Only the rich had water piped to their house – everybody else had to rely on stand-pipes or pumps in the street. The water often came from polluted rivers.
- Health hazards arising from overcrowded burial grounds.
- Serious outbreaks of infectious diseases, e.g. the cholera outbreak of 1831–2 which caused 30 000 deaths in England, Wales and Scotland. The result was a rising death rate (20% higher in 1849 than in 1831).

Chadwick's interest in public health arose from his position as Secretary to the Poor Law Commission. He argued that sickness caused people to become paupers and that therefore it would, in the long run, save money to tackle the problem. One of the reasons for the state of affairs he described was that measures to tackle public health problems depended on local initiative. Many towns had set up Improvement Committees, but their powers and efficiency varied enormously. He proposed a centralised national system to improve public health, rather like the New Poor Law. He found less support for this, however, than for the reform of the Poor Law because, while the latter was designed to save money, the provision of adequate sanitation and water supplies was likely to be expensive.

Public Health Acts, 1848–75

The **Public Health Act of 1848** was therefore a compromise. It created a General Board of Health, headed by Chadwick, with powers to set up local Boards of Health in areas where the death rate was high or where there was a local petition for one. However, progress was slow. By 1854 only just over 10% of the population was covered by local boards, many of which were slow to act.

Many towns were provided with sewage and water supplies, for which the engineers deserve great credit.

Over the next twenty years many local acts were passed, but public health provision was piecemeal. Moreover, it was not until 1854 that John Snow demonstrated that cholera was spread through polluted water and even then the government and local authorities were slow to take the necessary action. In 1866 the Sanitation Act compelled local authorities to appoint sanitary inspectors and in 1872 the Public Health Act divided the country into districts which were to set up health boards with a Medical Officer and staff. It did not impose clear duties on them, however.

The **Public Health Act of 1875**, the work of R. A. Cross, compelled local authorities to ensure that there was adequate water supply, drainage and sewage disposal. Regulations were laid down for removal of nuisances, burials, destruction of contaminated food and notification of infectious diseases.

> **KEY POINT**
>
> For the first time the Public Health Act of 1875 ensured an effective system of public health throughout the country. It has been described as the single most important Act of Parliament of the century.

3.5 Factory legislation

Factory and Mines Acts, 1833–1850

OCR **U2**
WJEC **U2, U4**

At the beginning of the nineteenth century working conditions in factories and mines were unregulated. Consequently many were dangerous and unhealthy. Hours of work were excessive, especially for children, who were commonly employed from the age of seven and sometimes earlier.

> Ashley later became Lord Shaftesbury, the name by which he is better known.

Pressure for government action came from the humanitarians, many of whom, such as Ashley, were members of the Evangelical movement in the Church of England. In the prevailing climate of *laissez faire*, however, many of the upper and middle classes opposed government intervention on principle. Moreover, factory owners claimed that shorter hours would push up costs and make British exports uncompetitive.

Textile mills

In 1830 a Yorkshire Evangelical, Richard Oastler, founded the Ten Hours Movement. With the help of Lord Ashley the movement succeeded in getting Parliament to accept the **Factory Act of 1833**. There had been previous Factory Acts, but this was the first one to be effective, because it provided for four inspectors to be appointed to enforce it. The Act prohibited the employment of children under the age of nine. Children aged 9–13 were limited to eight hours' work a day and young people aged 14–18 to twelve hours a day. But the Act was a disappointment to the Ten Hours Movement. By using a relay system for child labour, factory owners were still able to require adults to work twelve hours or more.

The Ten Hours Movement therefore continued and achieved most of its aims in three Acts passed between 1844 and 1850.

- **The Factory Act of 1844** imposed a twelve-hour limit on women's work. The age at which children could work in the mills was lowered to 8, but hours of work for those aged 8–13 were reduced to 1½. Mill owners were also required to fence dangerous machinery.

> The prime mover for this Act was John Fielden, a Lancashire millowner.

- The **Factory Act of 1847** brought in a ten-hour day for women and young people aged 14–18. The Ten Hours Movement appeared to have achieved its goal. Some mill owners, however, got round the Act by using a relay system for women and children and requiring men to work for twelve hours or more.
- The **Factory Act of 1850** limited the opening hours of textile mills to twelve hours a day, of which 1½ hours had to be for meals. Women and young people were only allowed to work for 10½ hours a day and were to have a Saturday half-holiday. The effect was that the working day for men was also limited to 10½ hours.

Coal mines

Ashley also spearheaded a campaign to improve conditions in mines. The report of a Royal Commission on the Employment of Women and Children in Mines in

1842 shocked public opinion and resulted in the Mines Act, which prohibited the employment of females underground in mines and also of boys under the age of ten. One inspector was appointed to enforce the Act.

> **KEY POINT**
>
> The Factory Acts established the principle of regulation of working conditions by law. They were the foundation of modern health and safety law.

3.6 Education

LEARNING SUMMARY	After studying this section you should be able to understand: • the provision for elementary education in England in the first half of the nineteenth century

Schools for the children of the poor

OCR   U2
WJEC   U4, U2

In the early nineteenth century about 60% of English children went to a school of some sort at some time, but only 10% were at schools of a reasonable educational standard. Few attended school regularly. In the industrial areas the great majority of children gained what education they had from Sunday Schools. There was a good deal of prejudice against educational reform and even more indifference.

The impetus for the development of education for the poor came first from the churches and especially the Evangelicals, who saw it as a duty to educate children in the principles of religion. Schools were provided mainly by two religious societies, the **National Society** (a Church of England Society founded in 1811) and the **British and Foreign School Society** (founded in 1814). Both placed more emphasis on religious instruction than general education and used the monitorial system.

The older children (monitors) were used to help the schoolmaster teach the younger ones.

> **KEY POINT**
>
> Because education for the working classes was first provided by religious societies, the development of elementary education in the later nineteenth century was bedevilled by denominational rivalry and disputes about the place of church schools in the state system of education.

By 1830 it was clear that the religious societies did not have the funds to provide for more than a minority of children. Moreover, the Factory Act of 1833 required that factory children should have two hours of schooling a day. In order to make this possible the first government grant for education was made in 1833. Thus the principle of state responsibility for education had been established, though in a very small way – £20 000 a year at first. In 1839 this was increased to £30 000 and a committee of the Privy Council was set up to supervise the way it was spent. The secretary of the committee, Sir James Kay-Shuttleworth, sent inspectors into the schools. They found the monitorial system to be very inefficient. A new system was therefore set up by which able pupils were selected to work as pupil teachers for five years, after which they were sent to training colleges.

Exam practice questions

1 How far do you agree that the principal reason for the rise of the Chartist movement was economic distress? **[50]**

2 Study Sources A to E. Answer parts (a) and (b).

  (a) Study Sources A, B and C.

    How far do Sources B and C support the view expressed in Source A about the true purpose of the Reform Act?

    Explain your answer using the evidence of Sources A, B and C. **[20]**

  (b) Use Sources D and E and your own knowledge.

    Do you agree with the view that the passage of the Reform Act defused a revolutionary situation?

    Explain your answer, using sources D and E and your own knowledge. **[40]**

Source A: From an editorial in *The Poor Man's Guardian*. It was addressed to those attending a working class meeting in Birmingham in October 1832.

Do not flatter yourselves that the Whig Bill will do you any good. The Bill was never intended to do you one particle of good. The object of the promoters was not to change that 'glorious constitution' which has caused you so much misery, but to make it immortal. The Whigs know that the old system could not last, and desiring to establish another as like it as possible and also to keep their places, they framed the Bill in the hope of drawing to the feudal aristocrats and county gentry a large reinforcement of the middle class. The Bill was in effect an invitation to the shopkeepers of the enfranchised towns to join the Whig aristocrats of the country and make common cause with them in keeping down the people and thereby to quell the rising spirit of democracy in England.

Source B: From a speech in the House of Commons, in March 1831, by Lord John Russell who was introducing the first version of the Reform Bill on behalf of the government. Russell was a prominent Whig who had helped draw up the Bill.

The measure will add to the electors of the House of Commons about half a million persons, all of them connected with the property of the country and having a valuable stake amongst us. These are the persons on whom we can depend in any future struggle in which this country may be engaged and who will maintain and support parliament and the monarchy in carrying that struggle to a successful termination. I think that the measure will produce a future benefit to the people by the great incitement which it will give to hard work and good conduct. For when a man finds that by industrious exertion he will entitle himself to a place on a list of voters, he will have an additional motive to improve his circumstances. I think therefore that we are providing for the moral as well as the political improvement of the country.

Source C: From a speech by Thomas Macaulay in the debate in the House of Commons on the Reform Bill, March 1831. Macaulay was a Whig MP and a well-known writer on political matters.

I hold it to be clearly necessary that in a country like this the right of suffrage should depend on a financial qualification. Every argument which would persuade me to oppose universal suffrage, persuades me to support the measure which is now before us. I oppose universal suffrage because I think it would produce a destructive revolution. I support this measure because I am sure it is our best security against revolution. The voice of great events is proclaiming to us, Reform that you may preserve.

Exam practice questions

Source D: From a letter dated 18 May 1832 from Francis Place to J.T. Hobhouse, a minister in the Whig government, which had resigned because the House of Lords tried to water down the Bill. The Duke of Wellington had been asked to form a Tory government, which radicals, such as Place, were determined to prevent.

Lists containing the names of all persons likely to be useful in resisting have been made. Addresses and proclamations to the people have been sketched and printed copies will, if need be, be sent to every such person. Means have been devised to placard towns and villages, to circulate handbills and to assemble the people. If the Duke comes into power now, we shall be unable to hold the laws; break them we must, be the consequences what they may. Towns will be barricaded and the first town which is barricaded shuts up all the banks. 'Go for gold', it is said, will produce dreadful evils. We know it will, but it will prevent other evils being added to them. It will stop the Duke.

Source E: From E. J. Evans, *The Great Reform Act of 1832*, published in 1994.

The Act was passed as the climax to a two-year period of high political tension and excitement both within parliament and outside. Many MPs believed that, unless a measure of parliamentary reform was passed no later than the spring of 1832, a violent revolution would sweep away all established institutions. The Reform Act was not a piece of timeless constitution-making, the product of a full and dispassionate consideration of the nation's needs. It was a compromise stitched together during a crisis. It dissatisfied a substantial majority of those who had most strenuously urged the need for parliamentary reform. Yet, from the government's point of view, it served its major purpose: it removed the immediate threat to the security of the state.

4 Foreign affairs, 1815–1914

The following topics are covered in this chapter:

- Castlereagh, Canning and Palmerston
- The Eastern Question
- The expansion of the Empire
- British foreign policy, 1890–1914
- The experience of war

4.1 Castlereagh, Canning and Palmerston

LEARNING SUMMARY

After studying this section you should be able to understand:

- the success of Castlereagh as both an international statesman and British Foreign Secretary
- how effectively Canning and Palmerston secured British interests between 1822 and 1841
- Aberdeen's foreign policy between 1841 and 1846

Castlereagh

AQA **U1**   WJEC   **U1**

> Understanding these principles is crucial for a study of foreign policy.

The aim of foreign policy is to protect the national interest. For Castlereagh this meant, firstly, promoting trade, which in turn depended on a powerful navy. Secondly, it meant maintaining the balance of power in Europe. This would preserve peace, which was beneficial to trade. Thirdly, it meant keeping a close watch on Russia and France, which Castlereagh saw as the main threats to the balance of power. The principles followed by Castlereagh became the basis for British foreign policy in the nineteenth century.

> Don't forget the period 1812–5 when assessing Castlereagh.

Castlereagh became Foreign Secretary in 1812, so his first task was to build up and hold together the Fourth Coalition, which overthrew Napoleon in 1814. When Napoleon escaped from exile, Castlereagh played a big part in reviving the coalition. This brought about Napoleon's final defeat at Waterloo. Castlereagh also ended the war of 1812–4 with the USA, which had been caused by the British navy's enforcement of the Orders in Council.

The Vienna Settlement

> The treaty confirmed Britain's naval supremacy.

Castlereagh played a leading role in shaping the **Peace of Vienna** (1815). His aim was a peace that would last. It was largely because of him that the peace embodied three important principles.

- France was treated firmly, but not vindictively.
- A balance of power in Europe was maintained.
- Buffer states were built up around France to guard against future aggression.

At the same time he did not neglect Britain's national interest. Britain's gains were colonies which were valuable for trade or as naval bases: Heligoland, Malta, Mauritius, Trinidad, Tobago, St. Lucia, the Cape of Good Hope and Ceylon.

The Congress System

To ensure lasting peace Castlereagh and Metternich, the Austrian Chancellor, wanted to set up a permanent system of consultation between the great powers – a Concert of Europe. In the **Quadruple Alliance** of 1815 Britain, Austria, Prussia and Russia agreed to meet regularly to discuss threats to peace. These meetings were known as the Congress System, though some historians dispute whether 'system' is an appropriate word. The aims of the Congress System were muddled by the creation by Tsar Alexander I of Russia of the Holy Alliance, the members of which were supposed to guarantee the existing frontiers and monarchs. Castlereagh disapproved of this, describing it as 'a piece of sublime mysticism and nonsense' and King George III did not sign it.

There were four congresses.

- The first, at **Aix-la-Chapelle** in 1818, was successful. France was admitted to the Quintuple Alliance and the army of occupation was withdrawn.
- The **Congress of Troppau** (1820), however, revealed an important difference of outlook between Britain and the continental powers. Revolutions had broken out in Spain, Portugal, Naples and Piedmont. The continental powers issued the **Troppau Protocol** asserting their right to intervene. Castlereagh in his **State Paper** of 1820 opposed intervention in the internal affairs of other countries. He was particularly suspicious of the motives of the Tsar, who was keen to march the Russian armies across Europe to suppress the revolution in Spain.

> An example of Castlereagh's fear that Russia would upset the balance of power.

- Castlereagh was so worried by this turn of events that he only sent an observer to the **Congress of Laibach** in 1821. Despite British opposition, Austrian troops were sent to suppress the revolts in Naples and Piedmont.
- The fourth Congress (1822) was held at **Verona** after Castlereagh's death (see below).

> **KEY POINT**
>
> By the time Castlereagh died in 1822 Britain was on the verge of dropping out of the Congress System.

Foreign policy 1822–41

AQA **U1**   WJEC **U1**

Canning

Canning succeeded Castlereagh in 1822. He shared many of Castlereagh's aims, but his style was different. Both aimed to promote British trade and to maintain a European balance of power. Both were wary of the motives of France and Russia. But Canning appeared more favourable to liberal movements and he was better at winning public support for his policies. Like Castlereagh, he disapproved of intervention in the internal affairs of other countries. Unlike him, he did not have a founder member's desire to make the Congress System work. Nevertheless, in distancing Britain from it, he was only following the policy set out by Castlereagh in his State Paper.

> **KEY POINT**
>
> Canning followed the same principles in foreign policy as Castlereagh, but his style was different.

The last Congress, which met at **Verona** in 1822, gave its approval to a French invasion of Spain to support the king against the liberals. Wellington, the British delegate, therefore withdrew. The French invasion nevertheless went ahead in 1823. But Canning did prevent Spanish intervention in Portugal by sending a naval squadron to help the Portuguese liberals to win control. This reinforced the impression that he followed a liberal foreign policy. He also stopped France and Spain reasserting Spanish authority over the former Spanish colonies in South America. In 1825 Canning recognised the independence of Mexico, Colombia and Argentina. The Monroe Doctrine, issued by the USA, also helped bring about this result. A prime motive behind Canning's policy was the importance of this area for British trade.

> Canning claimed, 'I called the New World into existence to redress the balance of the old.'

Canning's biggest problem was the **Greek Revolt**, which broke out in 1821. The Greeks sought independence from Turkey. Canning wanted to uphold Turkey as a bulwark against Russian expansion into the Mediterranean area, but there was much sympathy for the Greeks in Britain. In 1825 Turkey called in help from Mehmet Ali, the ruler of Egypt. It seemed likely that Russia would help the Greeks, which Canning thought would be dangerous to British interests. To prevent Russia acting alone, he acted jointly with Russia and France with the aim of forcing Turkey to grant self-rule to Greece. In 1827 an allied fleet sank the Turkish and Egyptian fleets at Navarino.

> Consider whether Canning's motive was to promote liberalism or to promote British trading interests.

Unfortunately, after Canning's death in 1827, Wellington failed to continue joint action with Russia. Russia declared war on Turkey and forced it to grant full independence to Greece. Russia's influence in the Balkans was substantially increased, which was what Canning had tried to prevent.

> **KEY POINT**
>
> Castlereagh was pulling out of the Congress System when he died. Canning was happy to drop out of the Congress System.

> You should be able to explain the significance of each of these dates.

> **KEY DATES**
>
> | | |
> |---|---|
> | 1815 | Peace of Vienna |
> | 1818 | Congress of Aix-la-Chapelle |
> | 1820 | Congress of Troppau; Castlereagh's State Paper |
> | 1821 | Congress of Laibach; Outbreak of Greek Revolt |
> | 1822 | Death of Castlereagh; Canning Foreign Secretary; Congress of Verona |
> | 1824–5 | Independence of former Spanish colonies in South America recognised |
> | 1827 | Death of Canning; Battle of Navarino |
> | 1830 | Greek Independence |

Palmerston's Foreign Policy, 1830–41

AQA   **U1**   WJEC   **U1**

Palmerston's main aims in foreign policy were similar to those of Castlereagh and Canning – to protect Britain's trading interests and to maintain the balance of power. Like Canning, he was prepared to support liberal and national movements, unless they conflicted with British interests. He was very conscious of the need to uphold British prestige. To other European statesmen his conduct of diplomacy often seemed blunt, even high-handed. He wanted to maintain peace by diplomacy if possible, but was prepared to use force if necessary. In this respect Britain's naval supremacy was a great aid to his diplomacy. His outlook on foreign affairs was coloured by suspicion of Russia, especially in the Eastern Mediterranean area, and of France.

Palmerston dealt with four main issues as Foreign Secretary between 1830 and 1841.

Note how these issues can be used to illustrate Palmerston's suspicion of France and Russia.

- In **Belgium**, where there was a revolt in 1830, Palmerston's aim was to prevent France gaining too much influence. Working with Louis Philippe, he ensured that Belgium would be genuinely independent and neutral. He had to threaten war on two occasions – once when the Belgians invited Louis Philippe's second son to be their king and once when French troops invaded Belgium to counter a Dutch invasion in 1831. On both occasions Louis Philippe climbed down. Leopold of Saxe-Coburg, Queen Victoria's uncle, became King. In 1839 the **Treaty of London** guaranteed Belgium's neutrality.
- In **Spain and Portugal**, there were disputes between rival claimants to the throne. In both cases constitutional governments faced absolutist pretenders. Palmerston, fearing that France might intervene, arranged the **Quadruple Alliance** of Britain, France, Spain and Portugal. By this means he succeeded in preserving constitutional governments in Spain and Portugal, while preventing France from gaining too much influence.
- In the **Near East** Palmerston feared the growth of Russian power at the expense of a weak Turkey. This would endanger Britain's trading interests in the Eastern Mediterranean and threaten its route to India. The **Treaty of Unkiar Skelessi** (1833) particularly worried him, because it gave Russia control over the Dardanelles and excessive influence in Turkey. Palmerston was unable to do anything until 1839, when a war broke out between the Sultan of Turkey and Mehmet Ali, the ruler of Egypt. The Sultan looked to Russia for help, while Mehmet Ali was backed by France. These were the two powers Palmerston regarded with most suspicion. By working together with Russia, Austria and Prussia and threatening France with war, he resolved the situation in Britain's interests. French ambitions in the Eastern Mediterranean were checked. Russian influence over Turkey was curbed by the **Straits Convention** (1841), by which the Dardanelles was closed to warships of all nations in peacetime.
- In **China**, Palmerston took advantage of a dispute over the import of opium into China to provoke the **Opium War**. The British fleet bombarded Canton. By the Treaty of Nanking, signed in 1842 after the Whigs had fallen from power, five Chinese ports were opened to British trade and Hong Kong was ceded to Britain.

> **KEY POINT**
>
> Palmerston pursued British national interests and prestige and asserted Britain's influence in Europe with great success. But his high-handed methods won him enemies among the statesmen of Europe.

> **KEY POINT**
>
> Palmerston has been described as a master of improvisation, i.e. he reacted to situations as they arose.

Aberdeen, 1841–6

AQA   U1

Aberdeen was Foreign Secretary in Peel's ministry of 1841–6. His style of negotiation was more conciliatory than Palmerston's. This enabled him to improve relations with France, where Guizot also sought to reduce tensions. He managed to prevent an unsatisfactory outcome to the most difficult issue between the two countries, the question of the Spanish marriages. The matter had not, however, been resolved when Peel's ministry was overthrown in 1846. Aberdeen also resolved two outstanding problems with the USA: the Ashburton Treaty of 1842 settled the eastern border between the USA and Canada and the Oregon Treaty of 1846 settled the western border, leaving Vancouver Island in Canada.

1822–46: an overview

The issues described above can also be viewed thematically.

- France was viewed with suspicion for most of the period. Canning worked to prevent France taking advantage of revolts in Spain and the Spanish colonies in the 1820s. Palmerston took the same line over disputes between rival claimants in Spain and Portugal in the 1830s. Fear of French ambitions motivated his attitude towards the Belgian Revolt in 1830 and to the problems presented by Mehmet Ali. Only when Aberdeen took over as Foreign Secretary did relations with France ease.
- Russia was similarly viewed with suspicion, as shown in Canning's policy towards the Greek Revolt and Palmerston's handling of the problems in the near east in the 1830s.
- The USA was seen by Canning as having a common interest with Britain in resisting Spanish attempts with French backing to recover their South American colonies, but the border with Canada remained a matter of dispute until the 1840s.

You should be able to explain the significance of each of these dates.

KEY DATES	
1830–9	Belgian Independence issue, ending with Treaty of London
1833	Treaty of Unkiar Skelessi
1834	Quadruple Alliance of Britain, France, Spain and Portugal
1839–42	Chinese Opium War
1841	Straits Convention

4.2 The Eastern Question

LEARNING SUMMARY

After studying this section you should be able to understand:

- the significance of the 'Eastern Question'
- the development of the Balkan Crisis of 1875–8

Britain and the Eastern Question to 1856

OCR   U1

The Eastern Question was perhaps the most important international issue in the nineteenth century and was eventually to spark off the First World War. It arose from the decline of the Turkish (or Ottoman) Empire, which in 1815 still ruled

Greece, Bulgaria, Romania, Serbia, Bosnia and Albania. If it collapsed, the balance of power would be upset. Consequently, all the great powers had an interest in events in the Balkans. Most of them also had their own specific interests.

Britain's concern arose from its suspicion of Russian ambitions. Russia not only had racial (Slav) and religious (Orthodox) sympathies with the peoples of the Balkans, but also wanted access to the Mediterranean from the Black Sea for its fleet. But, if Russia gained control of the Balkans, this would endanger Britain's trading interests in the Eastern Mediterranean and could even make Russia a threat to Britain's Indian Empire.

The domestic consequences of the Crimean War are discussed on page 66.

The Eastern Question had already caused problems for Canning and Wellington in the 1820s and for Palmerston in the 1830s. It was the underlying cause of the **Crimean War** of 1854–6. Palmerston returned to office as Prime Minister in 1855 in the middle of the Crimean War, which he brought to a successful end for Britain. By the Treaty of Paris, the Black Sea was neutralised, which meant that Russia was not allowed to have a navy there.

Disraeli and the Balkan Crisis, 1875–8

AQA **U3**
OCR **U1, 2**

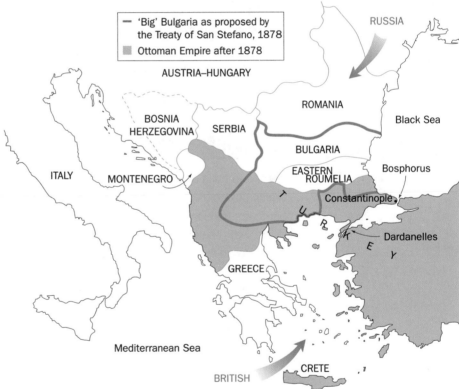

The Balkans in 1878

Be clear about the difference between Gladstone and Disraeli. For Disraeli the key issue was preventing Russian expansion, even if it meant ignoring Turkish brutality.

Turkey's failure to carry out reforms, as it had promised after the Crimean War, caused revolts in Bosnia, Herzegovina and Bulgaria in 1875–6. Disraeli, suspicious of Russian and Austrian ambitions, wished to support Turkey, but Turkish brutality in suppressing the revolts made this difficult. Gladstone's savage denunciation of the Turks in his pamphlet *The Bulgarian Horrors* turned public opinion against the Turks. This may have played a part in encouraging Tsar Alexander II to declare war on Turkey (1877).

When Russian troops approached Constantinople, however, the traditional British fear of Russian expansion into the Mediterranean was aroused and Disraeli sent

> Disraeli and Bismarck agreed that 'big' Bulgaria would upset the balance of power.

a fleet to Constantinople. Russia then made peace with Turkey (the **Treaty of San Stefano**). This set up a 'big' Bulgaria, which Disraeli feared would be under Russian control. Working with Bismarck, he put pressure on Russia to agree to the **Congress of Berlin**, as a result of which Bulgaria was reduced in size. An area known as Eastern Roumelia was given autonomy within the Turkish Empire and Macedonia was returned to Turkey. Britain gained Cyprus.

KEY POINT

The Congress of Berlin was regarded as a triumph for Disraeli. He had checked Russian ambitions without a war and had bolstered Turkey.

In 1885 Eastern Roumelia declared itself united with Bulgaria. Since 1878 Bulgaria had shown itself to be independent of Russia. Salisbury therefore supported Austria and Germany in opposing Russian demands for Eastern Roumelia to be returned. Two years later he negotiated the Mediterranean Agreements with Italy and Austria by which the three powers agreed to maintain the status quo in the Mediterranean.

4.3 The expansion of the Empire

LEARNING SUMMARY

After studying this section you should be able to understand:
- the reasons for, and the nature of, imperialism in Britain
- the part Britain played in the 'scramble for Africa'
- the reasons for the outbreak of the Second Boer War

Imperialism

AQA **U3** OCR **U1**

> Don't be cynical about imperialism: it must be understood in the context of its time.

The desire to build up an empire was a marked feature of the policies of the European powers in the late nineteenth century. The expansion of European empires was nothing new. By 1850 the British Empire comprised India, Canada, Australia, New Zealand, islands in the Caribbean, and Cape Colony and Natal in South Africa. In the late nineteenth century there was a new enthusiasm for the acquisition of colonies. There was a sense of mission and theories were developed to justify imperialism. The literature of the period encouraged imperialist ideas, notably the work of Kipling, who coined the phrase 'The white man's burden'. The newly emerging popular press played an important part in arousing enthusiasm for the empire. Expansion of the empire, it was claimed, would:
- help the economy by providing markets for exports, outlets for investment and sources of raw materials for industry
- protect the route to India
- help to reduce over-population by emigration
- bring the benefits of civilisation to 'backward' peoples
- spread Christianity.

KEY POINT

The motives behind imperialism were mixed: economic self-interest, rivalry with other European powers and a genuine belief in a mission to spread European civilisation and religion.

There was also a strategic dimension. The imperial ambitions of Britain and other European powers in the last quarter of the nineteenth century focused above all on Africa. The 'scramble for Africa' which developed added an important competitive motive for imperialism. National prestige demanded that each major imperial power should not allow its rivals to gain more than it did itself. Some historians argue that the 'scramble for Africa' was essentially the means by which European powers worked out their rivalries without going to war in Europe.

The two British statesmen most involved with imperialism were Disraeli and Chamberlain.

- **Disraeli** made the development of the empire a key part of 'Tory democracy'. In 1875 he purchased Suez Canal shares and in 1876 he created the title Empress of India for Queen Victoria. In 1878–9 his 'forward' policies led to the outbreak of the Afghan and Zulu Wars, in both of which British troops suffered defeats before they were eventually successful.

> Chamberlain was worried about Britain's economic decline: his solution was this vision of the empire.

- **Chamberlain** deliberately took the post of Colonial Secretary in preference to any other in Salisbury's second ministry in 1895, because he regarded it as so important. In this office he played a key role in the events leading to the Boer War, which are explained below. He encouraged investment in the colonies such as in the development of railways. He wanted to develop the empire into a single economic and political unit. At the Colonial Conference of 1897 he put forward ideas for an imperial customs union, but was unable to bring it about. He later incorporated this idea into his tariff reform campaign. He envisaged a system of imperial preference, as well as protective duties on imports into Britain.

Another important figure was **Cecil Rhodes**. In 1885 he set up a British protectorate over Bechuanaland and in 1889 he formed the British South Africa Company to develop colonies in Rhodesia (modern Zimbabwe and Zambia). Rhodes envisaged British colonies from southern Africa to Egypt (the Cape to Cairo Railway). His activities aroused deep suspicion among the Boers and played a big part in bringing about the Second Boer War.

The 'scramble for Africa'

AQA **U3** OCR **U1**

Egypt and the Sudan

Britain's involvement in Egypt resulted from Disraeli's purchase of seven-sixteenths of the Suez Canal shares for the British government in 1875. Growing disorder in Egypt culminating in a revolt against the Khedive led Gladstone to order its occupation in 1882. Egypt became effectively a British colony, although it was not annexed.

Sudan, which was nominally ruled by Egypt, was in a state of rebellion. Gladstone decided to abandon it, but in the course of withdrawing the Anglo-Egyptian garrisons, General Gordon was besieged and killed in Khartoum. In 1896, Chamberlain sent an expedition under Kitchener to reconquer it. His victory at **Omdurman** (1898) brought the Sudan under British control, but led to a confrontation with the French at **Fashoda**. In the end the French withdrew and in 1904 they recognised Egypt and the Sudan as a British sphere of influence.

The **Berlin Conference** of 1884–5 gave the green light for Africa to be carved up. Between 1884 and 1896 Britain acquired Somaliland, Nigeria, the interior of the Gold Coast, Kenya, Uganda, Bechuanaland, Nyasaland and Rhodesia.

> **KEY POINT**
>
> Britain acquired extensive colonial territories in the 'scramble for Africa'.

The Second Boer War 1899–1902

AQA **U3** OCR **U1**

Causes of the Second Boer War, 1899–1902

The discovery of gold in the Transvaal in 1886 attracted thousands of foreigners, mainly British. By 1895 these 'uitlanders' outnumbered the Boers, but they had no political rights and were heavily taxed. They had genuine grievances which the Boers, who resented their presence, did little to meet. At the same time the activities of Rhodes, who became Prime Minister of Cape Colony in 1890, left the Boer republics almost encircled.

> This was a provocative attack to exploit 'uitlander' grievances.

Tensions between the British and the Boers were heightened by the **Jameson Raid** (1895), for which Rhodes was responsible. Chamberlain was suspected, probably wrongly, of being involved in the background. Talks between Milner, the British High Commissioner, who completely mistrusted the Boers, and Kruger, the President of Transvaal, on the 'uitlander' question in 1899 broke down. War broke out when the Boers attacked Natal.

The War

After initial setbacks the British gained military superiority by 1900, but it took two more years to wear down resistance by Boer guerilla groups. One of the methods used by the British in this phase of the war was the establishment of concentration camps.

> The domestic consequences of the Second Boer War are discussed on page 67.

By the Treaty of Vereeniging (1902) Transvaal and the Orange Free State were annexed, but were promised eventual self-government, which was granted in 1906. In 1910 they were joined with Cape Colony and Natal in the Union of South Africa.

> **KEY POINT**
>
> The war exposed Britain's diplomatic isolation. All the other great powers sympathised with the Boers.

4.4 British foreign policy, 1890–1914

LEARNING SUMMARY

After studying this section you should be able to understand:

- Britain's emergence from 'splendid isolation'
- the making of the Ententes
- the effect of the naval race on relations with Germany
- Grey's policies towards the crises between 1908 and 1914
- differing interpretations of the reasons for Britain's entry into the First World War

'Splendid isolation'

AQA **U3**
OCR **U1**
WJEC **U1, U4**

Lord Salisbury, who conducted Britain's foreign policy for most of the period 1886–1902, regarded war as 'the final and supreme evil' and therefore aimed to protect Britain's interests by diplomacy. He saw France and Russia as the main threats to Britain's interests.

From 1894, the other great powers were grouped into two alliances: the Triple Alliance (Germany, Austria–Hungary and Italy) and the Dual Alliance (France and

Russia). Britain was isolated in the sense that it was in neither alliance. Since Britain was a trading nation with a worldwide empire, its major interest lay in protecting its trade routes. For this it relied on its navy, which was the most powerful in the world, rather than on alliances with European powers.

The phrase 'splendid isolation' is, however, misleading. Salisbury was anxious to avoid any alliance which might commit Britain to war in support of another power, but he was quite prepared to make agreements with other countries, such as with Germany, Italy and Portugal over African colonies in 1890 and with Germany over European trade with China in 1900 (the Yangtze Agreement).

Britain moves away from isolation

In the late 1890s, however, isolation began to seem increasingly uncomfortable. Relations with Germany began to deteriorate in 1896, when the German Emperor William II congratulated Kruger, the President of Transvaal, on repelling the Jameson Raid. Pro-Boer attitudes in Germany during the Boer War made matters worse. Even more important, however, was the fact that Germany embarked upon the expansion of its navy with the Naval Laws of 1898 and 1900. This was a threat to Britain's naval supremacy, the basis of its foreign policy.

> The German Emperor was over-confident that Britain would ultimately ally with Germany on his terms.

The Boer War and the **Fashoda incident** provided further evidence of the dangers of 'splendid isolation'. Britain began to seek allies. Joseph Chamberlain made three attempts to secure an alliance with Germany in 1898, 1899 and 1901. On each occasion the Germans rebuffed him.

In 1902, however, Britain secured an ally in **Japan**, which provided a safeguard against Russian expansion in the Far East. The background to this was Russia's occupation of Manchuria in 1900, which posed a threat to the highly important British export market in China. Britain was no longer isolated, but it still had no ally among the European great powers.

> **KEY POINT**
>
> By 1900 isolation had come to seem dangerous rather than splendid.

The Ententes

AQA **U2, 3**
OCR **U1**
WJEC **U1, U4**

On the face of it it seemed unlikely that Britain should gain a friend (though not yet an ally) in France. Anglo-French relations had been strained ever since Britain occupied Egypt in 1882. During the 1880s and 1890s there had been tensions arising from the colonial ambitions of the two powers in Africa, culminating in the Fashoda Incident in 1898. This arose out of the British conquest of the Sudan between 1896 and 1898. A simultaneous French expedition from West Africa reached the Upper Nile at Fashoda and the resulting confrontation nearly led to war. Moreover, the French press was violently anti-British during the Boer War.

> German policies pushed Britain towards an understanding with France.

The French government, however, regarded the Germans as their main enemy and the Foreign Minister, Delcassé, worked to improve relations with Britain. In 1902 Chamberlain opened negotiations to settle colonial disputes with France. The growing threat of a war between Russia and Japan, which might draw in France and Britain on opposite sides, made a settlement more urgent. The highly successful visit of King Edward VII to France in 1903 won over French public opinion.

In 1904, Britain and France signed the **Entente Cordiale**. It was simply a settlement of disputes: France recognised British control in Egypt, while Britain accepted France's ambitions in Morocco. It was not an alliance, nor was it intended to be anti-German. But the behaviour of the German Emperor drew Britain and France closer together. In 1905 he tried to undermine the Entente by a personal visit to Tangier, during which he declared a German interest in the future of Morocco. In the ensuing conference on Morocco at **Algeciras** in 1906, Britain supported France. The growing friendship between the two powers was shown by the opening of military conversations.

The policy of settling colonial disputes was taken a stage further in 1907 when an agreement was made with Russia to settle differences over Persia (Iran), Afghanistan and Tibet. Like the Entente Cordiale, this was an agreement, not an alliance. Nevertheless, since France and Russia were allies, it created a **Triple Entente**, which aligned Britain with them against the Triple Alliance.

> **KEY POINT**
>
> The Entente Cordiale marked a turning point in British foreign policy, but did not commit it to an alliance or to an anti-German policy.

The naval race

AQA	**U2, 3**
OCR	**U1**
WJEC	**U1, U4**

The **naval race**, which began with the German Naval Laws of 1898 and 1900, played an important part in the deterioration of relations between Britain and Germany and in cementing the Anglo-French Entente. Tirpitz claimed that Germany needed an expanded navy to make it a world power and to compete with Britain. From the British point of view, this was a threat to the naval supremacy on which the defence of Britain and its overseas empire depended. The race intensified after 1906 when, as a result of the Cawdor-Fisher naval reforms, the **Dreadnought** was launched. Germany responded by starting its own programme of building similar battleships. In 1909 public opinion in Britain, alarmed by the growth of the German navy, demanded that eight Dreadnoughts should be built.

This brought Britain and France close to being allies who would be obliged to help each other in a war.

The race continued unabated up to the outbreak of the war. Haldane's mission to Berlin in 1912, to propose a cut in the naval building programme, was unsuccessful and Churchill's suggestion of a 'naval holiday' in 1913 was also rejected. As a result Britain made the 1912 **Anglo-French Naval Agreement**; Britain was to concentrate its naval strength in the North Sea and France in the Mediterranean.

> **KEY POINT**
>
> The naval race played a key role in souring Anglo-German relations.

Grey's foreign policy 1908–14

AQA	**U2, 3**
OCR	**U1**
WJEC	**U1, U4**

The Kaiser claimed to have refused to join a coalition against Britain in the Boer War.

In 1908 Austria annexed Bosnia and Herzegovina (the **Bosnian crisis**). This outraged Serbia, which turned to Russia for help. William II, however, made it clear that Germany would support Austria in the event of war and Russia had to back down. The crisis convinced the Foreign Secretary, Grey, that Germany's intentions were aggressive, an impression confirmed by the Kaiser's *Daily Telegraph* interview in October 1908 and the discovery that Tirpitz had accelerated Germany's naval building programme.

The **second Morocco crisis** (1911), when the German gunboat *Panther* was sent to Agadir, provoked Britain to threaten war (Lloyd George's Mansion House speech). Germany backed down, though it gained some 'compensation' in the Congo. The crisis strengthened the Anglo-French Entente and led to the Anglo-French Naval Agreement. It also caused a wave of anti-British feeling in Germany.

Nevertheless, Grey worked towards improving relations with Germany and had some success in co-operating over the **Balkan Wars** (1912–3). His over-riding aim was to broker a peace settlement, since if Austria and Russia were drawn in, France and Germany would become involved and Britain might then be unable to stand aside. Grey therefore called a conference in London which met from December 1912 to May 1913. In this he worked with Germany to restrain Austria from taking advantage of the situation. Right up to June 1914 Grey was negotiating with Germany over issues such as British and German interests in Africa and in the Persian Gulf. As the crisis sparked off by the assassinations at **Sarajevo** developed, drawing in Russia and France, it still seemed possible that Britain would remain neutral.

> **KEY POINT**
>
> In 1914 Britain was still not firmly committed to an alliance with France and Russia and was trying to maintain good relations with Germany. The German invasion of Belgium tipped the balance.

Why did Britain enter the First World War?

AQA	U2, 3
OCR	U1
WJEC	U1, U4

The official reason for Britain's entry into the war was 'to defend gallant Belgium'. The German invasion of Belgium broke the Treaty of London (1839) which guaranteed the neutrality of Belgium. Moreover, it had long been a major aim of British foreign policy to ensure that Belgium was not under the control of the strongest continental power. These were reasons for British intervention which Liberal MPs and the British public could understand, whereas a continental war arising out of a dispute in the Balkans did not seem to require British participation.

It can also be argued that Britain had a moral obligation to support France. Ever since the signing of the Entente Cordiale Britain had given France diplomatic support and relations between the two countries had grown closer. The 1912 Naval Convention came close to an alliance.

> **KEY POINT**
>
> Probably the underlying reason why Britain entered the war was that a German victory would mean German domination of Europe, which would upset the balance of power and threaten Britain's trading interests.

Could Britain have prevented the war? Some critics argue that Grey should have made it clear sooner that Britain would intervene if Germany violated Belgian neutrality. But it was only when Germany invaded Belgium that Grey was able to get the support of the majority of his Cabinet colleagues in declaring war. Until then the Cabinet was divided and most members believed that Britain should stay out. In any case, it is doubtful if Germany would have acted differently at this stage, whatever Grey had done. Grey tried throughout the period 1906–14 to avert war and in the end failed. His efforts to conciliate Germany only served to convince the Kaiser that in the end Britain would not support France in war.

You should be able to explain the significance of each of these dates.

KEY DATES	
1896	William II's telegram to Kruger after the Jameson Raid
1898	First German Naval Law; Fashoda Incident
1902	Anglo-Japanese Alliance
1904	Entente Cordiale
1905–6	First Moroccan Crisis; Algeciras Conference
1907	Anglo-Russian Entente – Triple Entente
1911	Second Moroccan Crisis
1912	Anglo-French Naval Convention; Outbreak of Balkan Wars
1914	German invasion of Belgium; Outbreak of war

4.5 The experience of war

LEARNING SUMMARY

After studying this section you should be able to understand:

- how the Crimean and Second Boer Wars led to changes in the army, politics, medicine and social policies

The impact of the Crimean and Second Boer Wars

Edexcel **U2**

Wars always have an impact beyond the battlefield. Two wars in this period had important effects.

The Crimean War

- The Crimean War highlighted the weaknesses of the army. Poor administration led to lack of supplies, including medical supplies. The generals, Lords Raglan and Cardigan, who had bought their commissions, were incompetent. The war showed the need for reform. Cardwell's army reforms in Gladstone's first ministry reorganised the regiments and the administration of the army, abolished flogging and the purchase of commissions and reduced the length of service to six years overseas and six years in the reserves.

It was also the first war which was photographed (by Roger Fenton).

- It was the first war in which **the press** played a significant role, both in whipping up anti-Russian feeling and in reporting the weaknesses of the army's administration. **William Howard Russell**, who reported the war for *The Times* newspaper, was in a sense the first modern war reporter. Most of his reports took three weeks to reach London, but some were sent over the newly invented telegraph. The notoriety of the Charge of the Light Brigade is due to his report. He not only provided the material for Tennyson's poem glorifying the charge, but also the evidence that the generals were incompetent.

- Russell's reports of the appalling treatment of sick and wounded soldiers were partly responsible for **Florence Nightingale's** determination to take a party of nurses out to the military hospital at Scutari. Horrified by what she found there, she used her influence and her energy to improve conditions. She used her experience to set up a training school for nurses on her return and spent the rest of her life campaigning on public health issues. The work of Mary Seacole should also be noted.

The Crimean War led to significant reforms in the army and in nursing.

The Second Boer War

- Public opinion, swayed by the press, was strongly in favour of the Boer War. This was a period when there was strong support for imperialism. After early reverses, the British army gained military superiority in 1900. The Conservative government, headed by Salisbury, capitalised on this by calling an election in 1900, the **Khaki election**, in which the Conservatives gained a large majority.
- Public opinion changed in the later stages of the war. Unable to defeat Boer guerrilla tactics, Kitchener set up concentration camps. Conditions in the camps were appalling and this generated much adverse publicity.
- The war divided opinion in the Liberal party. The **Liberal Imperialists**, including Rosebery, Asquith and Grey, supported the war, but they faced strong opposition from a pro-Boer group led by Lloyd George. The party was reunited in support of free trade when Joseph Chamberlain began his campaign to convert the Conservatives to tariff reform, but the division was symptomatic of a fundamental difference over the meaning of Liberalism, which contributed to the eventual decline of the Liberal Party.
- The war was a major factor in the rise of the **National Efficiency** movement. About one in three recruits for the army had to be turned down as medically unfit. The evidence of the extent of urban poverty had been revealed by the social surveys of Booth in London and Rowntree in York, but it was the Boer War which really drew it to public attention. The New Liberals argued that the situation could only be remedied by state intervention. By 1906 they had won over the majority of the Liberal Party. The Liberal ministry of 1906–15 enacted a series of reforms to tackle the problem.
- The war showed that the formation of the Royal Army Medical Corps in 1898 had brought about improvements in care for the battlefield wounded. More soldiers died from illness, especially typhoid fever, than from wounds.

The war was a catalyst for social reform.

Exam practice questions

1 **(a)** Why did Castlereagh issue the State Paper of 1820? [12]

(b) How successful was Canning in promoting British interests between 1822 and 1827? [24]

2 **(a)** Why did Canning recognise the independence of the former Spanish colonies in South America? [12]

(b) How far was suspicion of France the main influence on the foreign policy of Palmerston between 1830 and 1841? [24]

3 To what extent were economic considerations the main reason for British involvement in Africa between 1875 and 1902? [50]

4 Why did Britain's relations with Germany deteriorate in the period between 1898 to 1914? [50]

5 The Edwardian age

The following topics are covered in this chapter:

- The Conservatives, 1900–5
- The Liberals, 1905–15
- Votes for women
- The rise of the Labour Party
- The First World War, politics and society

5.1 The Conservatives, 1900–5

LEARNING SUMMARY	After studying this section you should be able to understand:
	- the achievements of Balfour's ministry, 1902–05 - the reasons for the Liberal victory of 1906

Balfour's Ministry, 1902–05

AQA   U1, 2, 3
OCR   U2
WJEC   U1

The 'Khaki' election and the retirement of Salisbury

The **Boer War** (1899–1902) aroused patriotic fervour in Britain, which the Unionist (Conservative) Prime Minister, Salisbury, exploited to win the 'Khaki' election of 1900. The war had two other important effects.

- It exposed Britain's diplomatic isolation.
- It drew attention to the condition of the urban poor, as a high proportion of volunteers for the army were rejected as unfit.

Foreign affairs in the Salisbury and Balfour ministries are explained on pages 62–4.

Balfour's ministry, 1902–05

Salisbury retired in 1902 and was succeeded as Prime Minister by his nephew Balfour. Like his uncle, Balfour had little interest in social reform, but his ministry did produce one major domestic reform: the **Education Act of 1902**. This transferred responsibility for the Board Schools to County Councils and County Boroughs. The voluntary schools – mostly church schools – were brought under the control of the local authorities in return for financial assistance from the rates. The local authorities were also to set up fee-paying secondary schools (state grammar schools). Nonconformists were outraged that money from the rates was to go to church schools.

A major step in the development of state education, comparable with 1870 and 1944.

The dominant political issue in Balfour's ministry was Chamberlain's **tariff reform** campaign. Chamberlain was very much aware of the challenge to British industry and trade from Germany and the USA, both of which protected their industries with tariffs. He wanted Britain to abandon free trade and impose protective duties. He also envisaged linking this with a system of imperial preference. In 1903 he resigned from the government to conduct a campaign for the introduction of tariffs. This split the Conservative Party. Balfour's attempts to produce a compromise were ineffective.

The reasons for the Liberal victory of 1906

This split was the main reason for the downfall of the Conservatives. In December 1905 Balfour resigned. Campbell-Bannerman formed a Liberal government and in the general election of January 1906 the Liberals won a landslide victory. The centrepiece of the Liberal campaign was an attack on tariff reform on the grounds that it would lead to dearer food. But there were several other reasons for the Liberal victory.

- There was a growing demand for social reform, which the Conservatives had failed to meet. The investigations of Charles Booth and Seebohm Rowntree had shown that there was serious poverty among the urban population.
- There was a reaction after the Boer War, especially when the public became aware of the conditions in the concentration camps.
- The **Taff Vale case** alienated trade unionists (see page 78).
- Nonconformists were angry about the 1902 Education Act.
- There was public indignation about the Chinese labour scandal. Balfour allowed a scheme for Chinese labourers to be brought into the Transvaal to work in the gold mines on terms which made them virtually slaves.
- The weakness of the Conservatives encouraged the Liberals to unite around the principle of free trade.

> Booth carried out a survey of the London poor. Rowntree investigated York. Both estimated that one third of the working class were in serious poverty.

KEY POINT

Chamberlain's tariff reform campaign was probably the crucial reason for the defeat of the Conservatives. He is the only politician to have split two major parties (the Liberals in 1886 over Irish Home Rule, the Conservatives in 1903 over tariff reform).

KEY DATES

1902–5	Balfour's ministry
1902	Balfour's Education Act
1903	Tariff Reform Campaign begins
1906	General election; Liberal landslide victory

> You should be able to explain the significance of each of these dates.

5.2 The Liberals, 1905–15

LEARNING SUMMARY

After studying this section you should be able to understand:

- the meaning of 'New Liberalism' and how it was put into practice
- how far the Liberal reforms created a modern welfare state
- the struggle with the Lords and its outcome
- the development of the Irish problem 1910–4
- why Britain became involved in war against Germany in 1914

New Liberalism

AQA	U1, 2, 3
OCR	U2
WJEC	U1

The policies of the Liberal ministries were much influenced by '**New Liberalism**'. Gladstonian Liberalism placed great emphasis on individual liberty and self-help. It took a *laissez faire* view of the role of the state and sought to make government as cheap and efficient as possible by limiting its activities. New Liberalism advocated social reform, financed by higher taxes on the wealthy. The social surveys of Booth and Rowntree had revealed the extent of poverty. The New Liberals argued that individual liberty had little meaning for the very poor, since

Be sure you can explain 'collectivist' and 'individualist' and relate them to the rise of New Liberalism.

their poverty restricted what they could do and self-help could not lift them out of poverty. State intervention was necessary in the interests of both national efficiency and social justice. Their political outlook was thus collectivist rather than individualist. There was also a political motive: the New Liberals saw social reform as the way to attract working class votes and to avoid being outflanked by the recently formed Labour Party.

By 1905 the New Liberals had probably won over the majority of the party, but there was still a minority which stood for Gladstonian Liberalism. This was to be a source of weakness later, but between 1906 and 1914 New Liberal policies were pursued. The outstanding New Liberal ministers were Lloyd George and Churchill.

KEY POINT

'New Liberalism' advocated collectivist solutions to social problems. This was the basic difference from Gladstonian Liberalism, which was individualist.

The Liberal reforms and their impact

AQA   U1, 2, 3
OCR   U2
WJEC   U1, 4

The Liberals were responsible for a notable series of social reforms.

Note how the principles of New Liberalism were carried out in these reforms. The reforms helped vulnerable groups in society.

- There were two measures affecting **trade unions**. The Trade Disputes Act (1906) reversed the Taff Vale judgment and freed unions from liability to pay damages for employers' losses in a strike. The Trade Union Act (1913) gave them the right to add a 'political levy' to their members' subscriptions, though members were allowed to 'contract out'.
- The so-called **Children's Charter** comprised several measures to help the children of the poor. There were to be compulsory medical inspections in schools and local authorities were allowed to provide free medical treatment and free school meals for poor children. Juvenile courts and special corrective schools (borstals) were set up in order to keep child offenders out of adult law courts and prisons. Free places were provided at fee-paying grammar schools.
- A number of measures were introduced to help working people. In 1909 Churchill set up employment exchanges to help the unemployed find jobs. The Trade Boards Act of the same year set up boards to fix minimum wages in the 'sweated' industries where there were no trade unions. Acts were also passed to regulate hours of work and wages in the coal mines and to give shop assistants a weekly half-holiday.
- The **Old Age Pensions Act** (1908) provided pensions of 5 shillings a week at 70, but only for the very poorest old people – those whose income was below £21 p.a. The pensions were financed out of taxation. The measure was very popular, as it kept old people out of the workhouse. Lloyd George gained great credit for it.
- The most important reform was the **National Insurance Act** of 1911. This provided insurance against sickness for all workers earning less than £160 p.a., though not for their wives or families. It was a contributory scheme, financed by payments from workers, employers and the state. Lloyd George claimed that workers got 'nine pence for four pence'. There was also an unemployment insurance scheme, financed in the same way, for workers in certain industries such as building, shipbuilding and engineering (the industries where demand for labour fluctuated most).

Assessment

The problem is defining a welfare state. One answer is to call the outcome of the Liberal reforms a social service state.

Some historians claim that, taken together, these measures laid the foundations of the welfare state. Undoubtedly they relieved the worst effects of poverty. Equally they involved an increased role for the state. But they also fell short of a comprehensive system of social security. This had to wait until after the Second World War.

Two important criticisms have to be made. Firstly, some of the Liberal reforms were limited in scope. The old age pensions were very small and paid to only the very poorest. Unemployment insurance covered only a small proportion of the workforce. Secondly, nothing was done about the Poor Law. Balfour had set up a Royal Commission on the Poor Law in 1905. Because of disagreements between its members, it did not report until 1909, and then it produced two reports. The Majority Report proposed reform of the Poor Law, the Minority Report abolition. Neither was acted upon and the Poor Law survived until 1929, alongside the pension and insurance schemes of the Liberals.

> **KEY POINT**
>
> These reforms were a great step forward in social welfare. The Liberals tried to make sure that the state provided minimum standards of social services and thus laid the foundations for the welfare state.

The struggle with the Lords

AQA   **U1, 2, 3**
OCR   **U2**

This is why the Lords were accused of being 'Mr. Balfour's poodle'.

Apart from the law lords and the bishops, the House of Lords consisted entirely of hereditary peers, two-thirds of whom were Conservatives. The Lords rejected Gladstone's Second Home Rule Bill in 1893, but did not interfere with any bills during the Conservative ministries of 1895–1905. After the Liberal victory in 1906 Balfour used the built-in Conservative majority in the Lords to obstruct Liberal government policies. Several important bills were rejected between 1906 and 1908. The hereditary House was thus thwarting the will of the electorate. Matters came to a head with Lloyd George's 1909 budget.

The 1909 Budget

The budget was 'redistributive' – taxing the rich to pay old age pensions to the poor.

Lloyd George had to raise revenue to pay for pensions and for building eight Dreadnought-type battleships. As a New Liberal, he proposed to tax the wealthy by raising income tax and imposing a supertax on high incomes. He also proposed a tax on land values. This was particularly objectionable to the House of Lords, most of whose members were landowners. Some historians believe Lloyd George intended to provoke a quarrel with the Lords, but there is no clear evidence for this. The Lords rejected the budget. This was unprecedented, as it had always been accepted that they did not reject finance bills. Their action raised the question of the power of the hereditary house to overrule the elected house and thus caused a constitutional crisis.

The 1910 elections and the Parliament Act

After a general election in January 1910, which returned the Liberals to power with the support of the Labour and Irish MPs, the Lords were forced to accept the budget. But the Liberals were now determined to limit the powers of the Lords. The problem was that, for a Bill to this effect to become law, the Lords would themselves would have to pass it. Matters were further complicated by the death of King Edward VII in the middle of the crisis. A second general election was held in December 1910 on the specific issue of limiting the powers of the Lords. It produced an almost identical result to the first. The Lords then accepted the **Parliament Act**, though only because King George V promised to create up to five hundred new peers if necessary. The Act had three main provisions.

- The Lords were no longer able to reject a money bill.
- Their power to reject other bills was reduced to a two-year delaying power.
- The interval between general elections was reduced to five years.

> **KEY POINT**
>
> The Parliament Act was a triumph for democracy. It ensured that in the end the will of the elected House of Parliament would prevail over the hereditary House.

Ireland 1910–14

AQA   **U2, 3**   CCEA   **A2.2**
OCR   **U2**   Edexcel **U2**

Gladstone's Home Rule Bill of 1893 had been rejected by the House of Lords. The Parliament Act removed that obstacle to Home Rule. The Irish Nationalists supported the Parliament Act in the expectation that Home Rule would be their reward. Moreover, the elections of 1910 gave them the balance of power between Liberals and Conservatives. A Home Rule Bill was introduced in 1912 and became law in 1914 under the Parliament Act despite the opposition of the Lords.

Ireland, however, had changed since 1893. Its sense of nationhood had been enhanced by the Irish cultural revival. Linked with this was the foundation in 1905 of **Sinn Fein**, which aimed for an independent Irish republic rather than Home Rule. It was as yet relatively obscure, but its existence made it more difficult for **Redmond**, the leader of the Irish Nationalists, to compromise. Of more immediate importance was the rise of a militant **Ulster Unionist** movement under the leadership of Carson. In 1912 he set up the Ulster Volunteers to prepare for armed resistance to Home Rule. The nationalists responded by forming the Irish Volunteers. The '**Curragh Mutiny**' in March 1914 (actually a threat of mutiny rather than an actual mutiny) showed that the government could not rely on the army to enforce Home Rule. Both sides smuggled arms into Ireland in the spring and summer of 1914. Ireland seemed on the verge of civil war. The outbreak of the First World War enabled the government to escape from the problem for the time being by suspending the Act.

> The Unionists believed that Home Rule would put Ulster Protestants under a Catholic government in Dublin.

Many historians blame Asquith for mishandling the Irish problem. He adopted a policy of 'wait and see'. He should have been firmer in banning private armies and arms imports. He put forward a plan for partition in 1914 which, if he had proposed it earlier, it might have succeeded.

The Conservative leader, Bonar Law, must also be blamed for the situation in 1914. He openly encouraged Ulster Unionist preparations for armed resistance.

> **KEY POINT**
>
> By 1914, Home Rule could only be enforced at the cost of civil war in Ireland. Home Rule might have solved the Irish problem in Gladstone's time; by 1914, the problem had changed.

You should be able to explain the significance of each of these dates.

KEY DATES

1905	Resignation of Balfour; Campbell-Bannerman Prime Minister
1906	General election: Overwhelming Liberal victory
1908	Asquith Prime Minister; Old Age Pensions Act
1909	Lloyd George's 'People's Budget'
1910	Two general elections
1911	Parliament Act; National Insurance Act
1912	Third Home Rule Bill rejected by the Lords
1914	Third Home Rule Bill becomes law but its operation was immediately suspended; Curragh Mutiny; outbreak of war

Britain and the outbreak of war in 1914

AQA   U2, 3

The Triple Entente

There is a fuller explanation of foreign affairs, 1900–14, on pages 62–6.

Sir Edward Grey, the Foreign Secretary, built on the agreements made with Japan and France by the Conservatives. In 1905 the German Emperor tried to undermine the Anglo-French Entente by declaring an interest in the future of Morocco. In the ensuing conference on Morocco at **Algeciras** in 1906, Britain supported France. Germany's clumsy diplomacy had strengthened the Anglo-French Entente. In 1907 an agreement was made with Russia to settle differences over Persia, Afghanistan and Tibet. This created the **Triple Entente**, which aligned Britain with France and Russia against the Triple Alliance, but it did not commit Britain to go to war as an ally of France and Russia.

The naval race

Relations with Germany continued to deteriorate. The naval race intensified as both Britain and Germany built Dreadnought-type battleships. In 1909 public opinion in Britain demanded that eight should be built. Haldane's mission to Berlin in 1912 to propose a cut in the naval building programme was unsuccessful and Churchill's suggestion in 1913 of a '**naval holiday**' was also rejected.

The countdown to war, 1911–4

The **second Morocco crisis** (1911), when the German gunboat *Panther* was sent to Agadir, provoked Britain to threaten war (Lloyd George's Mansion House speech). Germany backed down, though with some 'compensation' in the Congo. The crisis strengthened the Anglo-French Entente and led to the **Anglo-French Naval Agreement** (1912). Britain was to concentrate its naval strength in the North Sea and France in the Mediterranean. At the same time, however, Grey continued to try to improve relations with Germany and had some success in co-operating over the Balkan Wars (1912–3).

Perhaps a clearer indication of Britain's intentions would have deterred Germany.

In 1914 Britain was still not firmly committed to an alliance with France and Russia. As the crisis sparked off by the assassinations at Sarajevo developed, drawing in Russia and France, it still seemed possible that Britain would remain neutral. The German invasion of Belgium tipped the balance.

You should be able to explain the significance of each of these dates.

KEY DATES

1906	Algeciras Conference; First Dreadnought launched
1907	Triple Entente
1911	Second Morocco (Agadir) crisis
1912	Anglo-French Naval Agreement
1913	Churchill's 'naval holiday' proposal rejected by Germany
1914	German invasion of Belgium; War declared

5.3 Votes for women

LEARNING SUMMARY

After studying this section you should be able to understand:

- the development of the movement to improve the status of women
- the contribution of the suffragettes to gaining the vote for women

The changing position of women and the suffrage question

AQA **U1, 2, 3**
OCR **U2**
Edexcel **U2**

The status of women in the late nineteenth century

The status of women in the mid nineteenth century was that of second-class citizens. Working class women often worked long hours for low wages, e.g. in textile mills or domestic service. Middle class women were not expected to have careers, but to preside over the house as wives and mothers. Women were barred from the universities and the professions. When they married, their property passed to their husbands. They were not allowed to vote or to become MPs.

In the second half of the century things began very slowly to improve. Girls' schools and women's colleges at Oxford and Cambridge were founded. In 1878 London University allowed women to take degrees on the same terms as men, but at Oxford and Cambridge the inferior status of women was indicated by the fact that, although they could sit the examinations, they were not allowed to take degrees. Florence Nightingale's work established nursing as a recognised career. Increasing numbers of women went into teaching as a career. A few began to qualify as doctors, e.g. Elizabeth Garrett Anderson.

The Matrimonial Causes Act (1858) made it possible for women to divorce their husbands, though the grounds for divorce were more restricted for women than men. In any case, the cost of divorce proceedings meant that divorce was only for the better off. The **Married Women's Property Act** (1882) gave them the legal right to own their own property. In 1886 women were given the right to claim custody of the children if the marriage broke up. In 1870 women were allowed to vote for School Boards and in 1894 stand as candidates in local elections.

Suffragists and suffragettes

The question of votes for women was raised during the debates on the 1867 Reform Act by John Stuart Mill, who also wrote a treatise *On the Subjection Of Women*. During the 1860s a number of women's suffrage societies were formed in various parts of the country. The members were mainly middle class women and their aim was that women should have the vote on the same terms as men. In 1897 Millicent Fawcett formed the **National Union of Women's Suffrage Societies** (NUWSS) to co-ordinate their work. The NUWSS used moderate methods, e.g. leaflets, meetings and petitions, with the aim of winning over public opinion. It won much support, but failed to persuade the Conservative governments of Salisbury and Balfour to take action. The members of the NUWSS were known as **suffragists**.

It is easy to confuse the suffragists and the suffragettes. Make sure you know which is which.

In 1903 Mrs Emily Pankhurst, together with her daughters Christabel and Sylvia, founded the **Women's Social and Political Union (suffragettes)**. Mrs Pankhurst had long been associated with the suffrage movement in Manchester. She was also associated with the Independent Labour Party, which was sympathetic to the cause of votes for women. The Pankhursts, impatient with the failure of the suffragists to achieve results, advocated more militant tactics to draw attention to their demands.

Attitudes of the political parties

Both political parties were divided on the issue. Among the Liberals Lloyd George favoured women's suffrage, but Asquith opposed it. The Liberals were, however, generally more sympathetic than the Conservatives. The question was made complicated by the fact that only 60% of men had the vote because they had to be householders living in the constituency for one year to qualify. If the vote was given to all women, they would outnumber men. The solution of giving the vote to all men and women was too radical for most Liberal and Labour MPs. On the other hand giving the vote only to women who owned property might benefit the Conservatives.

Male voting rights were also an issue – one which is often forgotten.

The militant suffragette campaign

Several attempts were made between 1907 and 1912 to get a Bill through the House of Commons, but without government backing none succeeded. The suffragettes became increasingly militant. They progressed from disrupting political meetings to breaking windows and chaining themselves to the railings of Buckingham Palace. In 1913 they began a campaign of arson and physical attacks on ministers. Emily Davison threw herself under the King's horse at the Derby. When imprisoned, suffragettes went on hunger strike. If the government let them die, it would lose public support – which was of course the aim of the hunger strikers. At first they released them, but then they were force-fed – a most unpleasant process.

The suffragettes' tactics had some success at first. They gained much publicity and ensured that the issue had to be faced. By 1912 even Asquith accepted that women must be given the vote. The extremism of 1912–3, however, made the cabinet reluctant to proceed because they did not want to be seen to give in to violence. They countered the suffragettes' violence with the **Cat and Mouse Act**, which allowed the authorities to release women who went on hunger strike and then re-arrest them.

> **KEY POINT**
>
> The suffragettes' campaign won valuable publicity for the issue of votes for women, but in the end their militancy was probably counter-productive.

The impact of the war

When war broke out both the suffragettes and the suffragists called off their campaigns. Mrs Pankhurst urged women to join in the war effort. Women worked in factories, farms, offices, transport and as nurses. Some 16 000 women joined the Women's Land Army (WLA). Women's contribution to the war effort changed many people's ideas about their role in society and played a vital part in winning votes for women in 1918. The **1918 Representation of the People Act** allowed women over 30 to vote and to stand for elections as MPs. The first woman MP, Lady Astor, was elected in 1919.

But at the same time, the vote was given to all men over the age of 21.

The position of women by 1930

The 1918 Act was the decisive point in the campaign for the vote, but they still did not have it on the same terms as men. This was rectified in 1928 when women over the age of 21 gained the vote. In 1929 the first woman cabinet minister was appointed. The war had not only proved decisive in the suffrage campaign, but also more generally changed the role of women in society. But not all the gains were sustained. After the war women lost many of the jobs which they had taken on during the war. This was particularly the case for working class women. Middle class women were still expected to stop work when they married.

> **KEY POINT**
>
> The war was probably decisive in winning the vote, but the campaigns of the suffragists and the suffragettes prepared public opinion.

You should be able to explain the significance of each of these dates.

KEY DATES	
1882	Married Women's Property Act
1897	National Union of Women's Suffrage Societies founded by Millicent Fawcett
1903	Women's Social and Political Union founded by Mrs Pankhurst
1918	Women over 30 gain the vote
1928	Women have the vote on the same terms as men

5.4 The rise of the Labour Party

LEARNING SUMMARY

After studying this section you should be able to understand:

- the origins and development of the Labour Party (to 1918)

Formation of the Labour Party

AQA	U2, 3
OCR	U2
WJEC	U1

The origins and development of the Labour Party

> A socialist/working class party was slow to emerge in Britain compared with continental Europe.

The Labour Party has its origins in the social and economic changes of the nineteenth century. By the second half of the century Britain had a large and growing industrial working class. Like the middle classes, skilled workers enjoyed a rising standard of living during the nineteenth century. But social surveys showed that around 30% of the working class were living in severe poverty. Agricultural workers often received starvation level wages. Awareness of these inequalities fuelled a demand among both the working classes and middle class intellectuals for social reform. At the same time socialist ideas, such as those of Karl Marx, who spent half his life in London, had their impact.

In 1884 two socialist societies, the **Social Democratic Federation (SDF)** and the **Fabian Society**, were founded. Their members were largely middle class. Another important organisation, the **Independent Labour Party (ILP)**, was formed in 1893 by Keir Hardie with the aim of securing the election of MPs who would represent the interests of 'labour', i.e. the working classes. He aimed for a group of working class MPs who were not tied to the Liberals and would press for social reform. Hardie was elected MP for West Ham in 1892, but lost his seat in 1895. The 1867 and 1884 Reform Acts enfranchised many working class voters and a few working class men had been elected as 'Liberal-Labour' MPs. The lack of social reform from both Gladstone's second ministry and Salisbury's ministries disappointed many working class electors.

The formation of the Labour Representation Committee

> The 'New' unions were trade unions for unskilled workers.

> The TUC was founded in 1868 to co-ordinate the work of the various trade unions.

In the 1890s trade union interest in political action began to develop. Many of the leaders of the 'New' unions were socialists and wanted political action to improve the condition of the poor. The failure of the engineers' strike in 1897–8 and the *Lyons v. Wilkins* case in 1899 convinced the **Trades Union Congress (TUC)** of the need for MPs to represent them in Parliament. In 1900 the TUC called a meeting in London which was attended by the SDF, the Fabians and the ILP. They agreed to set up the **Labour Representation Committee** (LRC). Its secretary was Ramsay Macdonald. Keir Hardie was one of two LRC candidates elected to Parliament in 1900.

At first many trade union leaders were unenthusiastic, but the **Taff Vale case** changed their minds. In 1901 the Amalgamated Society of Railway Servants was ordered to pay £23 000 damages, plus costs, to the Taff Vale Railway Company for losses suffered as a result of a strike. This ruling meant that strike action became virtually impossible, since it would bankrupt the union.

Macdonald made an electoral pact with the Liberals in 1903 as a result of which 29 Labour MPs were elected in 1906. In that year the name Labour Party was adopted.

> **KEY POINT**
>
> The Taff Vale Case highlighted the need for parliamentary representation.

The development of the Labour Party, 1906–18

Labour supported the Liberal government which came into office in 1905 and succeeded in persuading it to reverse the Taff Vale judgement by the **Trade Disputes Act** of 1906. This enabled the party to win further support from the unions, including in 1909 the mineworkers.

The **Osborne Judgment** (1909), which ruled that it was illegal for trade unions to charge a political levy, was a setback. The political levy was a compulsory contribution by union members to the union's political funds, which were used to support the Labour Party. Labour MPs depended on this since MPs were not paid. In 1911, however, payment for MPs was introduced and by the Trade Union Act of 1913 unions were allowed to charge a political levy, though members were allowed to contract out.

Ramsay Macdonald, the Labour leader, opposed Britain's entry into the First World War and resigned the leadership. The new leader, Henderson, was a member of Asquith's coalition (1915–6) and Lloyd George's War Cabinet (1916). He resigned in 1917 as a protest against Lloyd George's dictatorial methods. Up to this point many people saw Labour as a radical group on the left wing of the Liberals. To emphasise its distinctive nature Henderson gave Sidney Webb the task of producing a **Labour Manifesto**, which included the commitment to nationalisation (Clause 4).

> You should be able to explain the significance of each of these dates.

KEY DATES	
1884	Foundation of Social Democratic Federation and Fabian Society
1893	Foundation of the Independent Labour Party
1900	Labour Representation Committee
1901	Taff Vale case
1906	29 Labour MPs elected; Trade Disputes Act
1909	Osborne Judgment
1918	Labour Manifesto including Clause 4

5.5 The First World War, politics and society

LEARNING SUMMARY

After studying this section you should be able to understand:

- how and why the First World War changed the political parties and the role of the state in Britain
- how far the First World War caused or accelerated social and economic change

The effects of the First World War on politics

AQA   **U1, 2**
OCR   **U2**
Edexcel **U2**

The political parties

The war had important effects on the political parties. It was a major factor in the decline of the Liberals. In 1915 Asquith bowed to criticism of his conduct of the war by forming a coalition, including some leading Conservatives and the Labour leader, Henderson. Lloyd George, as Minister of Munitions, was the outstanding member: his energy contrasted markedly with Asquith's detachment. In December 1916, with Conservative support, he forced Asquith to resign and became Prime Minister. The Liberal Party remained split between supporters of Lloyd George and of Asquith until 1923, by which time Labour had overtaken it as the main opposition to the Conservatives. Meanwhile, the Conservatives revived, entering the government in 1915, and Labour began to create a distinctive image after Henderson broke away from Lloyd George's war cabinet. An important development affecting all the parties was the Representation of the People Act (1918), by which voting rights were extended to all men over 21 and women over 30.

> **KEY POINT**
>
> The split between Asquith and Lloyd George was a crucial moment in the decline of the Liberal Party and therefore in the post-war rise of the Labour Party.

The government

In 1914 the **Defence of the Realm Act** (DORA) was introduced to give the government additional powers to enable it to fight the war effectively. This allowed it to censor the press and to take over any factories or land it needed. A War Propaganda Bureau was set up. Government controls were set up over merchant shipping, farming and factories and the coal mines were put under direct government management.

When Lloyd George became Prime Minister he reorganised the government and gave it unprecedented powers.

- He set up a small war cabinet of five men.
- He set up the Cabinet Secretariat to co-ordinate the different departments.
- Food was rationed in 1918 and wages and prices were controlled.

> The wartime government accustomed people to the idea of a bigger role for the state – one of the big changes between the nineteenth and twentieth centuries.

The social and economic consequences of the First World War

AQA   **U1, 2**
WJEC   **U1**
Edexcel **U2**

The war had important social and economic effects.

- The status of women advanced; women of all classes took jobs.
- The Fisher Education Act (1918) raised the school leaving age to 14.
- The living standards of the aristocracy and the middle classes declined while those of the working classes rose.
- The British economy suffered: export markets were lost and huge debts incurred, mainly to the USA.
- There was a loss of respect for authority.
- There was a decline in church attendance.

The army

Edexcel **U2**

The British Expeditionary Force (BEF) was sent to France in August 1914. By November the western front had settled into **trench warfare** on a line from Switzerland to the North Sea. The BEF, originally six divisions, was expanded to an army which reached a maximum size of two million men. Life in the trenches was extremely unpleasant. Attempts to break the stalemate involved crossing No-Man's Land and casualty rates were extremely high. At the **Battle of the Somme** (1916) there were nearly 60 000 casualties on the first day including 19 000 killed. Nevertheless, it did help to relieve pressure on Verdun, as was intended, and German losses were also very heavy. At the **Third Battle of Ypres** (1917) casualties again ran into the hundreds of thousands, but German losses were even greater. The Germans were unable to replace their losses whereas the Allies were about to be reinforced by the Americans. The British Army played a leading role in the final offensive against the Germans in 1918.

Recruitment on the scale needed was not a problem at first. Men volunteered in large numbers. Government propaganda in the form of recruitment posters was very successful, as was the idea of getting men to join up in Pals Brigades from a town or a company. There was pressure from public opinion on men who had not volunteered to join up. Even so, the scale of the losses was such that in 1916 **conscription** had to be introduced. Provision was made for conscientious objectors, but they met with little sympathy.

Treatment of large numbers of severely wounded men led to advances in medicine. The use of X-rays, blood transfusions and skin grafts saved lives. Doctors began to recognise shell-shock, but officers accused sufferers of cowardice and sent them back into the line. Some deserted and were then court-martialled and shot.

Sample question and model answer

Study the six sources on the suffragettes and then answer **both** sub-questions.

(a) Study Sources A, B and C.

How far do Sources B and C challenge Source A in its views about giving women the vote?

Explain your answer, using the evidence of Sources A, B and C. **[20]**

(b) Use Sources D, E and F and your own knowledge.

Do you agree with the view that the campaign of the militant suffragettes held back the cause of votes for women? **[40]**

Source A: He thought the view of all really sensible men who had considered the subject was that they did not think it fitting that women should come down into the arena of politics. They thought that women had their own honourable position in life and that their proper sphere was the home, where they might exercise their good and noble influence in the sacred circle of the family.

From a speech in the House of Commons by Mr S. Evans, a Liberal MP, on 25 April 1906.

Source B: The test he would apply to this was simply, 'Is it right?' and he held that few men could say from their conscience that it was not right to give the vote to women. The disfranchisement of women was unconstitutional, inexpedient, mischievous, and unjust. Women were excluded from the learned professions, and were ineligible to serve on juries or to become magistrates. Give them the vote and the injustice would be to a certain extent remedied.

From a speech in the House of Commons by Mr J. Slack, a Liberal MP, on 12 May 1905.

Source C: It is useless to declaim upon the equal or superior worth of women, so long as men exercise their power to exclude them from any sphere of activity which they may desire to enter. It is useless to declare that they are willing to admit women into everything except politics. Any person who is not fit to take part in English politics will inevitably encounter all the consequences of subjection in education, in professional and industrial employments, and in social relations.

From W. L. Blease, The Emancipation of Women, *published 1910. Blease was an active member of the Liberal Party.*

Source D: The women are winning again. What they lost by window-smashing has been restored to them and multiplied a hundred fold by the Government's Cat and Mouse Act. That, by God, we can't stand. Forcible, Feeble, Wait-and-See Asquith has tried obstinacy, promises, trickery, bullying and cowardly cruelty. The women have opposed with persistence, wit, indomitable pluck and endurance. Their combined skill and courage have beaten him.

From The Clarion, *a Labour weekly newspaper, published 6 June 1913. Here it is commenting on the Cat and Mouse Act.*

Source E: The contention of the old-fashioned suffragists has always been that an educated public opinion will ultimately give votes to women without any force being exerted. In the year 1906 there was an immensely large public opinion in

Sample question and model answer

favour of woman suffrage. But what good did that do the cause? We have tried every means – processions and meetings – which were of no avail. We have tried demonstrations, and now at last we have to break windows. I wish I had broken more. I am not in the least repentant.

From Emmeline Pankhurst, My Own Story, *published 1914.*

Source F: The activities of the militant suffragettes had now reached the stage at which nothing was safe from their attacks. Churches were burnt, public buildings and private residences were destroyed, bombs were exploded, the police and individuals were assaulted, meetings broken up. The feeling in the House, caused by the extravagant and lawless action of the militants, hardened the opposition to their demands.

From Viscount Ullswater, A Speaker's Commentaries, *published in 1925.*
Here he recalls suffragette activities when he was Speaker
of the House of Commons in 1913.

(a) Study Sources A, B and C. How far do Sources B and C challenge the views in Source A about giving women the vote?

Source A makes two claims: that women should not take part in politics and that they have equal worth but in their own sphere. Source C attacks both, arguing that exclusion from politics means that women are denied equal worth. It also argues that the consequence of exclusion from politics is discrimination in education, employment and social relations. The implication of Source A, on the other hand, is that women are no more suited for employment than for politics since their sphere is the home. Source B agrees with Source C that women are discriminated against in the professions and argues that giving them the vote would 'to some extent remedy the injustice'. But it bases its argument on a fundamental question not addressed in either of the other sources: is it right? Thus Sources B and C completely reject the views expressed in Source A. Note that all three sources are by Liberals, showing how divided opinion was.

(b) Use Sources D, E and F and your own knowledge. Do you agree with the view that the campaign of the militant suffragettes held back the cause of votes for women?

Source D thinks the militant campaign is succeeding. It notes that smashing windows lost the women support but claims that the Cat and Mouse Act more than compensated. Feelings were running high at the time and the language of this source indicates strong support for the women. It may therefore exaggerate their success. Source F, in more measured language, suggests that militancy was counter-productive. Since it was written in 1925, the writer will have had time to reflect - in contrast to Source D. By this time the issue had been resolved by the 1918 Act, so Ullswater could afford to be more measured. As Speaker, he was probably well-informed about 'feeling in the House'. But his tone suggests lack of sympathy for the suffragettes. For obvious reasons Source E justifies militancy. It points out the failure of the suffragist approach, suggesting that militancy, so far from holding back the cause, was the only way forward. Suffragette activities did, however, play a part in the failure of the Conciliation Bill in 1911-12. Their increased violence in 1912-3 presented a dilemma for the government, since it did not want to be seen to give in to violence. Another problem was that forced feeding and the Cat and Mouse Act won public sympathy for the women. Arguably the suffragettes' tactics were unwise. They polarised public opinion, winning support from some but antagonising others. It is possible that but for the violence the Liberals would have given women the vote before the war broke out - certainly Asquith's attitude had softened.

These answers are summaries of the main points.

Use quotations to illustrate the point about language.

The answer first analyses the sources, amplifying them from own knowledge, then goes on to discuss the issues from own knowledge.

Britain and Ireland, 1798–1922

The following topics are covered in this chapter:

- Irish Nationalism
- Support for the Union
- British policies towards Ireland
- The Irish economy

6.1 Irish Nationalism

LEARNING SUMMARY

After studying this section you should be able to understand:

- the importance of the United Irishmen, O'Connell, 'Young Ireland' and the Fenians in arousing opposition to the Union
- the rise and decline of the Home Rule (Irish Nationalist) Party
- the Easter Rising, the rise of Sinn Fein and establishment of the Irish Free State in 1922

Ireland at the end of the eighteenth century

OCR   U4

Politically Ireland was subordinate to the British government in London. It had its own Parliament, but until 1782 the laws it passed had to be approved by the British Parliament. Even after 1782 the British government still appointed the Viceroy and his officials.

In **religion** Ireland was divided between Protestants and Catholics. The majority of the Irish were Roman Catholics and as such were denied many of the rights of citizenship, including the right to be MPs. It was only in 1793 that they were given the right to vote. The established church, the Church of Ireland, to which the greater part of the aristocracy and gentry belonged, was to all intents and purposes a branch of the Church of England. The one part of Ireland where Protestantism predominated was Ulster.

> But most Ulster protestants were Presbyterians of Scottish descent, not members of the Church of Ireland.

The United Irishmen, the Rebellion of 1798 and the Act of Union

OCR   U4

> The rising was particularly dangerous because it was supported by revolutionary France, with which Britain was at war.

The Society of United Irishmen was formed in 1791 to demand reform of the corrupt Irish Parliament and full civic rights for Catholics, i.e. Catholic emancipation. An Ulster Protestant, **Wolfe Tone**, rapidly became its leading member. Rebellion broke out in 1798, but the British had little difficulty in suppressing it. The most dangerous rebel force was defeated at Vinegar Hill. Protestants portrayed the rebellion as a Catholic uprising, though the Society was originally supported by both Protestants and Catholics.

Pitt's solution to the danger from Ireland was to propose the union of Ireland with Britain and at the same time to grant Catholic emancipation. By the **Act of Union** the Irish Parliament was abolished. Ireland was to return 100 MPs to the British Parliament at Westminster. Unfortunately George III blocked the second part of the plan, Catholic emancipation. He claimed it was against his coronation oath, when he swore to protect the Protestant religion.

- Nationalists looked back to 1798 as a heroic rising against oppression and Wolfe Tone as a martyr to the Irish cause.
- The failure to grant emancipation left Catholics feeling cheated.

O'Connell

OCR **U4**
CCEA **AS2, A2.1**

In the twenty years after, the Union Catholics made no progress with the demand for emancipation because of opposition from the Tories. In 1823 **Daniel O'Connell** founded the **Catholic Association** to press their claims. From 1824 money was raised by the 'Catholic rent' of a penny a month. This produced considerable sums and also gained mass support for the movement. The repeal of the Test and Corporation Acts in 1828, removing the disabilities imposed on Protestant nonconformists, made the case for Catholic emancipation more difficult to resist. The crucial moment was the election of O'Connell as MP for County Clare in a by-election in 1828. The law did not prevent him from standing for election, but as a Catholic he would be unable to take his seat. Wellington and Peel realised there was a danger of civil war in Ireland unless concessions were made and in 1829 the **Catholic Relief Act** was passed.

> The Catholic Relief Act allowed Catholics to hold all but a very few public offices.

> In the Lichfield House Compact (1835) he agreed to support the Whigs in return for reforms in Ireland.

O'Connell's long-term aim was repeal of the Union. After the success of the campaign for emancipation he led a group of Irish MPs who stood for repeal, but used his position to bring pressure on the Whigs to introduce Irish reforms. In 1840 he founded the **Repeal Association**, but was soon challenged by 'Young Ireland'. In response O'Connell stepped up the pressure for repeal by holding a series of mass meetings. The climax of the campaign was to be a meeting at Clontarf in 1843, but when Peel banned it, O'Connell called it off. He died in 1847.

'Young Ireland'

OCR **U4**
CCEA **AS2, A2.1**

The members of '**Young Ireland**' wanted to see a revival of Irish culture and the development of a sense of Irish nationhood. They were impatient of O'Connell's methods and advocated more violent measures. The movement was, however, overtaken by the Great Famine. In the excitement of the revolutions of 1848 in Europe they attempted to start a rebellion in Ireland, led by Smith O'Brien, but it was quickly suppressed. The leaders were transported to Australia and the movement faded out.

Although 'Young Ireland' was a failure, it played an important part in the development of nationalist ideas.

The Fenians

AQA **U3**   CCEA **AS2, A2.1**
OCR **U4**
Edexcel **U2**

> The name refers to the warriors of ancient Ireland.

Fenianism emerged in the late 1850s, developing from revolutionary groups formed among Irish immigrants in New York. In 1858 James Stephens founded a revolutionary society in Dublin with financial backing from the USA. This later became known as the Irish Republican Brotherhood. It quickly gained adherents in Ireland itself and among Irish immigrants in the USA and Britain. It was strongly nationalist and anti-English and its methods were conspiratorial and revolutionary.

The Fenians were involved in 1867 in a series of terrorist outrages. They tried to seize Chester. In Manchester a policeman was shot during an attempt to rescue Fenian prisoners from a police van. Another Fenian rescue attempt, this time at Clerkenwell prison, caused an explosion in which 12 people were killed. These actions achieved little in themselves, but drew attention to the Irish question.

> **KEY POINT**
>
> The American connection marked an important step in the growth of Irish-American political and financial support for Irish nationalist movements.

The Home Rule Party

AQA	U3	Edexcel	U2
OCR	U4	CCEA	A2.1

> Home Rule meant a separate Parliament and government for Ireland, i.e. devolution.

> There was a considerable rise in evictions.

The **Home Rule League** was founded in 1870 by **Isaac Butt**. In the 1874 election the Home Rule Party won 59 seats. In the late 1870s it came under the influence of **Parnell**, who became leader of the Home Rule Party in parliament in 1880. The party gained publicity for its aims by pursuing obstructionist tactics in Parliament.

The development of the party was profoundly affected by the agricultural depression of the late 1870s, which led in 1879 to the formation of the **Land League**. The moving force in this, Michael Davitt, persuaded Parnell to become its President, thus bringing together the agitation for land reform and for self-government. This '**new departure**' was also supported by some Fenians, particularly the Irish-American John Devoy. The Home Rule Party (Irish Nationalist Party) was thus closely linked with the militant tactics of the Land League in the 'land war' of 1879–82.

In the 1885 general election the Irish Nationalists won 86 seats, which gave them the balance of power in the House of Commons. Parnell gave his support to Gladstone when it became known that he had become converted to Home Rule. The **First Home Rule Bill**, however, split the Liberal Party and was defeated in the Commons. The subsequent general election produced a Conservative government, though the Nationalists again won most of the Irish seats.

> In 1882 the Chief Secretary for Ireland, Lord Frederick Cavendish, and the Under-Secretary, T. H. Burke, were murdered in Phoenix Park, Dublin, by the Invincibles, an extremist organisation.

Parnell's policy was now to await a shift in electoral fortunes which would bring the Liberals to power. An attempt to discredit him by *The Times*, which published letters allegedly implicating him in the **Phoenix Park murders**, backfired when it was proved that the letters were forged. Parnell was at the peak of his power, but a year later his authority was undermined by the O'Shea divorce. His fight to retain control over the Irish Nationalist Party in the face of the disapproval of the Catholic bishops split it and left it weakened on his death in 1891.

With the failure of Gladstone's two Home Rule Bills and the splits in the Nationalist Party, the movement for Home Rule lost its momentum. However, the Nationalist Party was reunited in 1900 under **Redmond**, but it was not until 1910 that Home Rule again became a serious possibility. The crisis over the House of Lords made the votes of the Irish Nationalists vital to the Liberal government and Redmond demanded Home Rule as the price of Irish Nationalist support. As a result the **Third Home Rule Bill** was passed by the House of Commons in 1912 and became law, under the provisions of the Parliament Act, in 1914. Because of the outbreak of war, however, it was suspended.

Sinn Fein and the Easter Rising

OCR **U4** CCEA **A2.2**
Edexcel **U2**

Sinn Fein means 'Ourselves Alone'.

The origins of **Sinn Fein** lie in the Irish cultural renaissance of the 1890s. The Gaelic League, founded in 1893, aimed to revive the Irish language as a means of building up a sense of nationhood. This emphasis on the special cultural identity of Ireland led several writers to advocate the separation of Ireland from Britain. Arthur Griffith, who founded Sinn Fein in 1905, argued for a dual monarchy of Britain and Ireland under the British crown. Sinn Fein remained a relatively small organisation on the nationalist fringe until after the **Easter Rising**.

The Irish Republican Brotherhood developed from the Fenians.

The Easter Rising was the work of a small group of extremists, most of whom were members of the Irish Republican Brotherhood. On Easter Monday 1916, 1500 rebels occupied the General Post Office and other buildings in Dublin. Patrick Pearse declared a new Irish Republic. The rebels gained little support and within a week the rising had been crushed – 450 rebels and over a hundred soldiers and policemen were killed.

The only one not executed, because he had American nationality, was de Valera, the future President of Ireland.

The harsh response of the British authorities turned the rebels into martyrs. Martial law was declared throughout Ireland, thousands were arrested and fifteen of the leaders of the rising were executed. Irish opinion swung decisively away from Redmond's Irish Nationalist Party to Sinn Fein, which was taken over by the republicans. In the 1918 election Sinn Fein swept the board in southern Ireland, winning 73 seats. The Nationalist Party was almost wiped out.

> **KEY POINT**
>
> The Easter Rising was a turning point. Thereafter, Home Rule was no longer enough to satisfy majority opinion in Ireland outside Ulster.

The Anglo-Irish War 1919–21

OCR **U4** CCEA **A2.2**
Edexcel **U2**

The Irish Volunteers had been formed in 1914 in opposition to the Ulster Volunteers.

The Sinn Fein MPs elected in 1918 refused to take their seats at Westminster and instead constituted themselves as the Dail, or Parliament, of Ireland. The Irish Republican Army (successor to the Irish Volunteers) conducted a campaign of violence, particularly against the police. The overwhelming victory of Sinn Fein in southern Ireland in the 1921 elections held under the Government of Ireland Act (1920), showed that, for the majority of Irish people outside Ulster, Home Rule was no longer enough. At the end of 1921 Lloyd George made an agreement (the **Anglo-Irish Treaty**) by which most of Ireland became the Irish Free State, with dominion status, in 1922. Northern Ireland remained in the United Kingdom. The Irish Free State comprised 26 counties – all of Ireland, except six counties in the north-east.

> **KEY POINT**
>
> The Sinn Fein leaders had to accept partition as the price for independence for southern Ireland, but the result was civil war between supporters and opponents of the Treaty.

6.2 Support for the Union

LEARNING SUMMARY	After studying this section you should be able to understand:
	• the importance of the Protestant Ascendancy and its decline after 1870
	• the importance of Ulster Unionism in shaping Irish history from the 1880s to 1921

The Protestant Ascendancy

OCR | U4 | CCEA | A2.1

In the eighteenth century, government and society in Ireland were dominated by a landowning class which was Protestant (Church of Ireland) and Anglo-Irish. This constituted the **Protestant Ascendancy**. For much of the nineteenth century, it continued to dominate Ireland. Tenants voted as the landowners decided and most Irish MPs at Westminster thus represented the Ascendancy.

> Voting by secret ballot allowed Irish tenants to vote for Home Rule candidates without fear of eviction.

The power of the Ascendancy declined as a result of the disestablishment of the Church of Ireland in 1869 and changes in the land law by which Irish tenants gained more security and eventually became owner-occupiers. Moreover the Ballot Act (1872) deprived the landowners of their electoral power and led to the rise of the Home Rule Party.

The Orange Order and Ulster Unionism

OCR | U4 | CCEA | A2.1

> 'Orange' in memory of William of Orange (William III), who preserved British supremacy in Ireland against the Catholic James II in the seventeenth century.

The **Orange Order** was founded in 1796 after a clash between Protestants and Catholics in County Armagh. Its members swore to defend the King 'as long as he supports the Protestant Ascendancy'. The Order opposed the Union at first, but became fiercely pro-Union in response to O'Connell's Repeal Association. It had members throughout Ireland, but was heavily concentrated in the north. With the growth of Belfast it gained strength among the working classes there. From the 1870s onwards, in opposition to the Home Rule movement, it was at the heart of Ulster Unionist opposition to Home Rule.

The rise of **Ulster Unionism** was a direct response to the Home Rule movement. Up to 1880 Ulster elections were fought mainly between the Liberals and the Conservatives. But when Gladstone declared for Home Rule in 1886, alarm bells rang. Ulster politics were reshaped along sectarian lines. Demonstrations and rallies were organised by the Orange Order. At a mass meeting in Belfast, Lord Randolph Churchill, a leading English Conservative, played 'the Orange card', threatening 'Ulster will fight and Ulster will be right'. In the 1886 election, 17 Unionists were elected in Ulster. In the rest of Ireland Nationalists swept the board. Two main factors lay behind this development.

- Religion. Protestants were a majority in Ulster, but a minority in Ireland, as a whole. 'Home Rule', they believed, would be 'Rome rule'.

> They also believed the Union was vital for the prosperity of Belfast.

- The economic development of the north-east of Ireland, and especially the growth of Belfast, placed the industrial wealth of Ulster behind Unionism. Ulster's business leaders were overwhelmingly Protestant.

The crisis of 1912–4

OCR **U4** Edexcel **U2**
CCEA **A2.2**

Ulster Unionists threatened armed resistance to Home Rule. When the House of Commons passed the Third Home Rule Bill in 1912, drilling of volunteers began and in 1913 the **Ulster Volunteer Force** (UVF) was formed. In 1914 the UVF successfully landed a large cargo of arms and ammunition at Larne (the Larne gun-running). Meanwhile, the Unionists' leaders, Carson and Craig, organised a 'Solemn League and Covenant', which attracted just under half a million signatures. The signatories pledged to use 'all necessary means' to defeat Home Rule. Sympathy for Ulster Unionism in the army led to the so-called 'Curragh Mutiny', in which a number of cavalry officers said they would rather resign than fight in Ulster to enforce Home Rule. Unionist preparations for armed resistance naturally led to similar preparations by the Nationalists. The realisation that civil war would result from any future attempt to enforce Home Rule on Ulster explains why Ireland was partitioned in the settlement of 1921.

> **KEY POINT**
>
> By 1914 Ulster Unionist resistance to Home Rule had brought Ireland to the verge of civil war.

> You should be able to explain the significance of each of these dates.

> **KEY DATES**
>
> | | |
> |---|---|
> | 1798 | Rebellion of United Irishmen |
> | 1800 | Act of Union |
> | 1829 | Catholic emancipation |
> | 1845–9 | Great Famine |
> | 1869–70 | Irish Church Disestablishment and First Land Act |
> | 1879 | 'New Departure' |
> | 1886 | First Home Rule Bill |
> | 1912–4 | Third Home Rule Bill brings Ireland to the verge of civil war |
> | 1916 | Easter Rising |
> | 1919–21 | Anglo-Irish War |
> | 1922 | Partition |

6.3 British policies towards Ireland

> **LEARNING SUMMARY**
>
> After studying this section you should be able to understand:
> - the policies of British governments towards Ireland, 1829–1922

Irish reforms, 1829–81

OCR **U4** CCEA **A2.1**

The most important Irish reform in the first half of the nineteenth century was **Catholic emancipation**, which was finally passed in 1829 under pressure from O'Connell's Catholic Association. Peel, who had previously affirmed his opposition, agreed with the Prime Minster, Wellington, that the alternative was civil war in Ireland.

> There was a 'tithe war' in 1830–3 which involved violent protests against paying tithes to the (Protestant) Church of Ireland.

In the 1830s the Whigs tried to win Catholic support for the Union by reforming tithes and introducing a national system of elementary education into Ireland. **Peel** (Prime Minister 1841–6) also tried to win Irish support for the Union by increasing the grant for Maynooth College and establishing three new non-sectarian university colleges (the Queen's Colleges) at Belfast, Galway and Cork. At the same time he acted firmly against O'Connell's Repeal Association, banning the Clontarf meeting in 1843. His measures to deal with the Great Famine are discussed below.

In his first two ministries (1868–74 and 1880–5) Gladstone tried to 'pacify Ireland' by dis-establishing the Irish Church (1869) and tackling the land problem (First Land Act, 1870 and Second Land Act, 1881).

Home Rule and partition, 1886–1922

AQA	U3	Edexcel U2
OCR	U4	

In 1895 most of the liberals followed Chamberlain into alliance with the Conservatives, which became the Unionist Party.

By 1885 Gladstone had come to the view that the only solution to the Irish problem was **Home Rule**, but his first Home Rule Bill (1886) split the Liberal Party and was defeated in the Commons. Ninety-three Liberals, led by Chamberlain and Hartington, voted against the Bill. The second Home Rule Bill was passed in the Commons, but was overwhelmingly defeated in the Lords.

> **KEY POINT**
>
> Gladstone's efforts to solve the Irish problem became almost obsessive, but it can be argued that he failed because he offered 'too little too late'.

The Conservative ministries of 1886–92 and 1895–1905 followed a policy of '**constructive Unionism**', or 'killing Home Rule with kindness'. The centrepiece of this was land purchase, which they encouraged in a series of Acts culminating in Wyndham's Land Purchase Act of 1903. This was not the whole story, however. Faced by the 'Plan of Campaign' (1886–91), Balfour as Chief Secretary for Ireland employed coercion and was nicknamed 'Bloody Balfour'.

The Liberals returned to office in 1905, but it was not until after the 1910 elections, which gave the Irish Nationalists the balance of power in the House of Commons, that they introduced a third Home Rule Bill. Under the Parliament Act this would have come into force in 1914, but was suspended on the outbreak of war. At this point Ireland was on the verge of civil war. The Conservatives backed Ulster Unionist opposition to the implementation of Home Rule and their leader, Bonar Law, came dangerously close to encouraging armed rebellion.

At the end of the war Irish opinion had shifted because of the Easter Rising. Faced by armed rebellion in 1919, Lloyd George sent in troops and ex-soldiers (the Auxiliaries and the Black and Tans). Home Rule was clearly no longer practical and the eventual settlement achieved by Lloyd George involved acceptance of **partition** with Home Rule for the six counties of Northern Ireland and a separate state, with dominion status, in southern Ireland.

6.4 The Irish economy

LEARNING SUMMARY

After studying this section you should be able to understand:

- the main features of the Irish economy in the nineteenth century
- the reasons for and consequences of the Great Famine, 1845–9
- the Irish land problem and how it was resolved in the late nineteenth and early twentieth centuries

The Irish economy in the nineteenth century

OCR **U4** CCEA **AS2**

This was in spite of emigration, which was already significant before the Great Famine of 1845–9.

Early nineteenth century Ireland was poor and economically backward. There were three key reasons for this.

- Rapid population growth. Between 1791 and 1841 the population almost doubled from 4.7 million to 8.2 million.
- Lack of industrial development, except in the north-east.
- The land tenure system.

Most land in Ireland was owned by members of the Protestant Ascendancy. Many landowners, especially the wealthiest, managed their estates through land agents.

Because of the lack of industry, it was only possible to escape from rural poverty by emigration.

Most **Irish tenant farmers** held their land on short leases. From the early nineteenth century it was increasingly common for them to hold annual tenancies, which meant that rents could be raised each year. Except in Ulster they were not entitled to compensation for improvements at the end of the lease or tenancy. Consequently, it was not worth their while to invest in improvements. As the population grew and pressure on the land increased, farms were sub-divided into smaller and smaller holdings. This in turn led many farmers to depend on potato growing.

The system was extremely inefficient. Much of the Irish rural population was living at subsistence level. The right of the landlords to raise rents and evict tenants led to much unrest and at times serious disorder. This in turn made it difficult for landlords to consolidate holdings into bigger farms which would permit the introduction of improved agricultural techniques. Agriculture therefore remained backward. Landlords themselves were often in debt.

> **KEY POINT**
>
> The land tenure system meant that the ability of Irish agriculture to feed the growing population was increasingly precarious. If the potato crop failed, there would be widespread hunger.

The Great Famine, 1845–9

OCR **U4** CCEA **AS2**

Diseases, especially typhus and relapsing fever, spread rapidly in a population weakened by malnutrition.

In 1845, 1846 and 1848 **potato blight** virtually wiped out the crop. Because the potato was the staple diet of so much of the population, this was disastrous.

- Between 1845 and 1851 it is estimated that over a million people died from starvation or disease. Large numbers emigrated to Britain, Canada or the USA. The population declined by one-fifth.
- The British government responded in various ways. Peel brought in maize from America and inaugurated a programme of public works. The Whig government, which came to power in 1846, expanded this and set up kitchens to supply meals throughout the country. But it refused to intervene to stop export of agricultural produce from Ireland.
- Landlords lost income from rents and faced high rates to pay for poor relief. Many were already indebted and the Encumbered Estates Act (1849) enabled them to sell up. By 1857, 3000 estates had been sold. Nevertheless the bulk of the land remained in the possession of the old landed families.
- Evictions increased greatly. Many small farms disappeared as holdings were consolidated into larger farms. There was, however, still a substantial number

of small farms and most tenants, whatever the size of their farms, were still faced by the problems of short leases, high rents and evictions without compensation.

- There was a sharp fall in the number of agricultural labourers after the Famine. High mortality among this class was followed by heavy emigration.
- Irish opinion, especially among the Irish who emigrated to America, blamed the British for the famine. This helps to explain the support of the Irish-American community for Irish nationalism, beginning with the foundation of the Fenian Society.

KEY ISSUE

Could the British government have done more? Some would argue that in the context of the *laissez faire* ideas of the time, it did as much as could be expected. Others claim that it would have acted differently if a famine of such proportions had occurred in England.

The Land and Land Purchase Acts

OCR **U4** Edexcel **U2**

Gladstone identified the land problem as one of the main sources of Irish unrest in the 1860s. He attempted to solve it by the **Irish Land Act** of 1870, which provided for tenants to be compensated for improvements and for disturbance if evicted other than for non-payment of rent. The weakness of the Act lay in the fact that there was no effective provision to prevent landlords raising rents and then evicting tenants. The agricultural depression which began in 1877 led to a big increase in evictions and the Land War of 1879–82.

Gladstone's **Second Land Act** (1881) granted Irish tenants the three Fs – fixity of tenure, free sale of the lease and fair rents. This went a long way to solving the problems of Irish land law. What Irish tenants really wanted, however, was to own their land. A series of Land Purchase Acts – Ashbourne's Act (1885), Balfour's Act (1891) and Wyndham's Act (1903) – facilitated this.

Wyndham's Act provided cheap loans for tenants to buy their land and generous cash payments to landlords for releasing land for sale to tenants.

KEY POINT

By 1909 over half of Ireland's tenant farmers had become owner-occupiers, thus effectively solving the land problem.

Sample question and model answer

The key word is change, so a chronological approach is appropriate. But, it is important to note the need to explain why changes took place.

Note the explanation of the reasons for O'Connell's changed approach.

All three strands need explaining in some detail.

You should also point out the effect of land purchase in changing the nature of Irish rural society.

This answer is a summary of main points. Look over it to make sure you can explain them all.

In what ways, and why, did the aims of Catholic and nationalist movements in Ireland change between 1798 and 1921? **[50]**

In the early nineteenth century Catholic opinion was divided about the Union itself, but united in demanding emancipation. O'Connell's Catholic Association and his victory in the County Clare election achieved this in 1829. In the 1830s O'Connell's approach was pragmatic - he aimed for repeal, but used his position as leader of a group of Irish MPs to put pressure on the Whigs for reforms. In the 1840s O'Connell stepped up the pressure for repeal. This was partly because of the rise of Young Ireland. He was not prepared to resort to violent methods and acquiesced when Peel banned a meeting at Clontarf in 1843.

Young Ireland aimed to revive a sense of Irish nationhood and criticised O'Connell's reluctance to use force to oppose the Union. But, it failed to gain mass support and its 1848 rising was a fiasco.

After the Famine, and the collapse of Young Ireland, Catholic and nationalist demands were comparatively muted. But in the 1860s and 1870s three new strands emerged. The Fenians aimed to break away from Britain. They blamed England for Ireland's ills, especially the Famine, and their methods were revolutionary. They did much to raise Irish consciousness of grievances. The Home Rule Association sought to modify the Union by giving Ireland self-government in domestic affairs, while the Land League arose as a result of the agricultural depression.

In 1879 these three strands came together in the New Departure. As a result, Parnell became the leader of nationalist opinion. The Land League campaign secured the 1881 Land Act, after which Parnell focused nationalist aims on Home Rule. By 1886, the strength of the support for Home Rule in Ireland convinced Gladstone that this was the right policy. Parnell allied with the Gladstonian Liberals. The achievement of Home Rule, by Act of Parliament, remained the aim of the Irish Nationalist Party through nearly thirty years of disappointment - the failure of Gladstone's Home Rule Bills, the divisions in the party after the fall of Parnell and the long period of Conservative government. When the Third Home Rule Bill finally became law, in 1914, opposition in Ulster brought Ireland to the verge of civil war. The failure to achieve Home Rule helps to explain the swing of Irish opinion away from the Nationalist Party.

The Easter Rising of 1916 was a turning point. The rising was the work of a small group of extreme nationalists who rejected the policy of co-operating with the British government in the First World War. They had comparatively little support at first, but after the execution of the leaders nationalist opinion swung dramatically to Sinn Fein, which aimed to make Ireland an independent republic. It also aimed for a united Ireland rather than partition, whereas partition came to be the aim of the Ulster Unionists.

7 Britain in peace and war, 1918–45

The following topics are covered in this chapter:

- Politics, 1918–24
- The Conservative government of 1924–9
- Britain in the 1930s
- Churchill, 1920–45

7.1 Politics, 1918–24

LEARNING SUMMARY

After studying this section you should be able to understand:

- why Lloyd George won an overwhelming victory in the 1918 election
- the achievements and failings of the coalition government, 1918–22
- Lloyd George's handling of the Irish problem
- why the Conservatives gained and then lost power in 1922–23
- the work of the first Labour government

The 'coupon election', 1918

AQA	U1, 3
OCR	U1, 2
WJEC	U1

Think about why this arrangement suited both Lloyd George and the Conservatives.

The election of 1918 was not fought on normal party lines. The coalition which Lloyd George had formed in 1916 fought the election as a coalition. Its supporters – the majority of the Conservative Party and the Lloyd George Liberals – were identified by a '**coupon**' or letter from their party leader. Opponents of the coalition were the Asquith Liberals, the Labour Party and a few Conservatives. Since Lloyd George was popular as the man who had led Britain to victory, the coalition won an overwhelming victory. But he was dependent on the Conservatives, who formed two-thirds of the coalition MPs.

In continuing the coalition Lloyd George was pursuing his own vision of a National, or Centre, party dedicated to reconstruction and the pursuit of national efficiency – led, of course, by himself. But the post-war coalition failed to realise his vision. It suited the Conservatives because they benefited from Lloyd George's popularity as the man who won the war, but by 1922 they regarded him as a liability and dropped him.

The Lloyd George coalition, 1918–22

AQA	U1, 3
OCR	U1, 2
WJEC	U1

The coalition tried to honour the promise that post-war Britain would be 'a land fit for heroes to live in' by Addison's housing drive, extending the National Insurance scheme to most working men earning less than £250 a year (the Unemployment Insurance Act, 1920) and an increase in old age pensions. Before long, however, the coalition faced serious economic difficulties. After a brief post-war boom, there was a slump in 1921. Unemployment rose to nearly 2 million and as a result public expenditure rose. The government's response was to make expenditure cuts (the Geddes Axe). The cuts affected mainly the armed forces, education and housing (Addison's housing drive was abandoned).

There were also serious industrial troubles, especially in the coal industry. The issue was whether the mines, which had been put under government control during the war, should be nationalised or returned to private ownership. The Sankey Commission was appointed in 1919 to investigate the problem, but failed to reach agreement. In 1921, because of the slump, the government decided to hand the mines back to the owners, who immediately proposed wage cuts. The miners went on strike, but were defeated after the collapse of the Triple Alliance (**Black Friday**).

> Remember 'Black Friday' when you come to study the General Strike.

The fall of the coalition

In 1922 Lloyd George was overthrown when the Conservatives decided to withdraw from the coalition (**Carlton Club meeting**).

- They had become increasingly unhappy with Lloyd George as Prime Minister because he was a Liberal at the head of a mainly Conservative coalition.
- Lloyd George was criticised for selling honours to finance the Liberal party.
- The Conservatives disliked the Irish treaty which broke up the Union.
- They thought Lloyd George had handled the Chanak crisis badly.
- Because of these controversial actions, many Conservatives feared that Lloyd George would split the Conservative Party, as he had split the Liberal Party.

> **KEY POINT**
>
> Lloyd George held office after 1918 courtesy of the Conservatives, who used his popularity as the man who won the war to their own advantage and then cast him off when he no longer served their purpose.

Ireland, 1916–22

AQA	U3	Edexcel	U2
OCR	U1	CCEA	A2.2

> You need to understand what happened in Ireland in 1912–4 as background. See page 73.

The most serious domestic problem facing Lloyd George was Ireland. The Easter Rising (1916) had strengthened support for Sinn Fein, which triumphed in Ireland in the 1918 general election and set up an (illegal) Irish Parliament in Dublin. A rebellion broke out, which the government tried to suppress with the 'Black and Tans'. Finally, a 'treaty' was made with Sinn Fein in 1921. As a result of this treaty most of Ireland was given dominion status, but the six counties of Northern Ireland remained part of the United Kingdom, with a Parliament for local affairs. This solution came into effect with the establishment of the **Irish Free State** in 1922, although there was then a civil war in Ireland itself.

Bonar Law, Baldwin and the Conservatives, 1922–3

AQA	U1, 3
OCR	U1, 2
WJEC	U1

The split in the Liberal Party between Asquith and Lloyd George meant that the Conservatives were the majority party after the 1918 election. After the fall of the coalition Bonar Law became Prime Minister and he called an election in which the Conservatives won a substantial majority. However, he had to resign through ill health after only seven months and Baldwin succeeded him as Prime Minister. Baldwin called another election at the end of 1923, because he wanted to introduce tariff reform and saw this as an issue of such importance that it needed electoral approval. The result gave the Conservatives the most seats, but short of an absolute majority. Baldwin's government was defeated in a vote of no confidence and he resigned to allow the formation of a Labour government. He believed that this would strengthen the 'responsible' elements in the Labour Party, led by MacDonald.

The first Labour ministry, 1924

AQA	U1, 3
OCR	U1, 2
WJEC	U1

Why do you think the Liberal Party declined so rapidly?

Labour's rise to power was very rapid – partly because of the split in the Liberal Party. In the 1922 election Labour gained more seats than the Liberals and became the official opposition. A year later, in the 1923 election, it made further gains. The Conservatives, who had called the election to seek the voters' approval for tariff reform, lost their overall majority. MacDonald, as leader of the next largest party, was asked to form a minority government.

The main domestic achievements of the first Labour ministry were the Wheatley Housing Act and increases in unemployment benefits and old age pensions. In foreign affairs MacDonald restored diplomatic relations with Russia and played an important role in negotiating the Dawes Plan and the Geneva Protocol (see page 111). However, the ministry depended on Liberal support, which it lost over the Campbell case. The subsequent general election was heavily influenced by the **Zinoviev letter**, which contained instructions from the Russian President of the Communist International to British communists about the organisation of revolutionary activities. It was a forgery, but it caused great alarm. The Conservatives won a big majority.

You need to consider whether Labour would have lost the election anyway.

KEY POINT

A Labour minority government was not likely to last long, but it was important to prove that the Labour Party was capable of governing.

7.2 The Conservative government of 1924–9

LEARNING SUMMARY	**After studying this section you should be able to understand:**
	• the domestic policies of Baldwin's second ministry
	• the causes and consequences of the General Strike

Baldwin's second ministry

AQA	U1, 3
OCR	U1
WJEC	U1

Baldwin took pains to present himself as an 'ordinary' man. His political skill won the middle ground of politics for the Conservatives. Under his leadership they rejected the notion of class war and accepted the need for government to engage in social reform and management of the economy. They had a solid core of support from the upper and middle classes, who supplied money and leadership. Middle class fear of socialism benefited them in the 1924 election. They also had the support of around a third of working class voters.

Baldwin's ministry made some valuable reforms.
- The old age pension scheme was extended to cover widows (1925).
- The Local Government Act (1929) transferred the functions of the Poor Law Guardians to local authorities. Credit for this must go to Neville Chamberlain.
- The BBC became a public corporation (1926).
- The vote was extended to women aged between 21 and 30 (1928).

The most controversial aspects of the ministry were the return to the gold standard and Baldwin's handling of the General Strike.

The return to the gold standard, 1925

Churchill, as Chancellor of the Exchequer, took the decision to return to the gold standard at the 1913 parity on the advice of the Governor of the Bank of England and other leading figures in the financial establishment. They regarded it as an important symbol of a return to normality after the war and the post-war period of readjustment and they believed it would be good for the City. The decision was criticised by **Keynes** in *The Economic Consequences of Mr Churchill*, and his view has generally been upheld by historians. He argued that to return to gold at the pre-1914 rate would over-value the pound. It would make exports expensive, hindering recovery and creating unemployment, while it would also cause deflation through cheaper import prices. It certainly damaged coal exports and was one of the causes of the General Strike.

Assessment

Despite the General Strike, the ministry succeeded in preserving stability. Its main achievements in home affairs were the work not of Baldwin, but of Neville Chamberlain. It failed, however, to come up with any new ideas for dealing with unemployment. Baldwin's election slogan in 1929, 'Safety First', summed up his outlook, but failed to fire the electorate.

The General Strike, 1926

AQA   **U1, 3**   WJEC   **U1**
OCR   **U1**

> The coal owners, the mineworkers' union leaders, the Trades Union Congress (TUC) and the government were all partly responsible. Consider the aims and behaviour of each.

> Not to be confused with 'Black Friday', 1921.

Causes of the General Strike

The **General Strike** had its origins in the problems of the coal industry, which was inefficient and in need of modernisation. The miners believed this could only be achieved by nationalisation, which the government rejected. The mines were put under government control during the First World War, but in 1921 Lloyd George handed them back to the owners. The problems of the industry worsened in the 1920s. In 1925, following the return to the gold standard and the ending of the Ruhr crisis, coal exports dropped. The coal owners proposed a wage cut, which the mine workers rejected. The government averted a strike by providing a subsidy and appointing the Samuel Commission to investigate the problems of the industry. This was '**Red Friday**' – an apparent victory for the miners.

When the commission reported, both sides rejected its proposals. The TUC tried to bring about a negotiated settlement, but on 1 May the miners were locked out by the owners. When negotiations finally broke down, the TUC ordered a general strike on 3 May.

The government was well prepared and the TUC half-hearted. After ten days the strike was called off. The miners were eventually defeated.

The failure of the strike

The General Strike failed because:
- the government had prepared emergency plans to safeguard food supplies, transport and to maintain order
- the TUC had embarked on the strike without proper preparations and without a clear idea how far they were prepared to go
- moderate leaders in the TUC began to fear that the strike might lead to violence and that they would lose control of it
- the TUC also realised that their funds were likely to run out before the government gave way.

Consequences

As a result of the General Strike, trade union membership dropped because workers were disillusioned with industrial action. Instead they looked to Parliament for improvements – hence the increase in Labour votes in the 1929 general election. The coal industry was not modernised and continued to decline. The government made general or sympathetic strikes illegal in the **Trade Disputes Act** (1927). This Act also hit Labour Party funding by making the political levy subject to contracting in.

Baldwin and the General Strike

There are differing views on Baldwin's handling of the General Strike.

- Some historians say he broke off negotiations with the TUC too soon and thus provoked the strike. They claim that he had given in to the more right-wing members of the cabinet who wanted a showdown and that he failed to restrain them during the strike itself.
- Other historians argue that he genuinely believed that the real issue was a constitutional one (the authority of the government) and that he was playing a waiting game, knowing that the TUC was not prepared to risk the revolutionary possibilities of a prolonged strike.

It does seem, however, that he gave way to right-wing pressure in bringing forward the vindictive Trade Disputes Act.

> Be sure you understand the distinction between 'contracting out' and 'contracting in'. Contracting in hit Labour Party funds and Labour considered the Act vindictive and unfair.

KEY POINTS

- The failure of the General Strike brought to an end a period of trade union militancy stretching back to the strike wave of 1910–4.
- The government feared the revolutionary implications of a general strike and the TUC came to think it had been playing with fire. Both were probably wrong about the risks of revolution.

7.3 Britain in the 1930s

After studying this section you should be able to understand:

- Britain's economic problems and the impact of the Great Depression on them
- the impact of the economic crisis on the second Labour ministry and the subsequent fortunes of Labour
- the National Government's economic policies and its responses to unemployment between the wars
- the importance of the responses of the extreme right and left in Britain to the Depression
- the importance of the abdication crisis
- the formation and composition of the wartime coalition

LEARNING SUMMARY

Britain's economic problems and the Great Depression

AQA	U1, 3
OCR	U1
WJEC	U2, 4

Unemployment never fell below one million between 1921 and 1939 and reached over three million in 1932–3. The underlying cause of this was Britain's long-term economic decline, dating back to the 1870s, which was exacerbated by the First World War. The older export industries – coal, textiles, shipbuilding, iron and steel – faced increasing competition from foreign countries where more modern machinery resulted in greater efficiency. In the areas where these industries were concentrated – the north of England, South Wales and Scotland – there was high unemployment throughout the period.

The **Great Depression**, which began in the USA with the **Wall Street Crash** in 1929, made the problem much worse. As world trade shrank, demand for British goods dropped. Exports in 1932 were one-third less than in 1928. In that year 23% of the insured workforce was unemployed. In shipbuilding the figure was 59.5%.

Governments of the period took the view that there was little they could do about Britain's economic problems and generally adopted a policy of deflation. Some alternatives were suggested, but not adopted. J.M. Keynes argued that, instead of cutting expenditure and wages, the government should spend its way out of depression through a programme of public works. This would create jobs. The workers would then spend what they earned and this would stimulate economic activity. In 1935 a group of young Conservative MPs led by Harold Macmillan suggested a programme of public works. Sir Oswald Mosley, a minister in the 1929–31 Labour government, proposed cutting unemployment by raising the school leaving age to 15 and lowering the pension age to 60. The Labour cabinet was, however, too cautious to adopt his ideas.

KEY POINTS

- Britain's long-term economic decline was made worse in the inter-war period by the economic effects of the First World War and the Great Depression.
- The most serious effects were felt in the old staple industries in which Britain had led the world in the nineteenth century.

The second Labour ministry, 1929–31

AQA **U1, 2** WJEC **U1, 2**
OCR **U1**

In the general election of 1929 Labour emerged for the first time as the biggest party, though still without an overall majority and therefore dependent on the Liberals. It had achieved little apart from a new Housing Act and the Coal Miners Act (1930) before it was overtaken by a financial crisis resulting from the Great Depression. By 1931 unemployment had risen to 2.75 million. As a result, expenditure on benefits went up, while the tax yield went down. The **May Committee**, appointed to find ways of balancing the budget, produced an alarming report in July 1931, which led to a run on the pound. The Chancellor of the Exchequer, Snowden, wanted to cut unemployment benefit to save the pound, as proposed by the May Committee, but the Cabinet could not agree on this and the Labour government resigned.

Consider why this would be unacceptable to a Labour cabinet.

To the surprise of his colleagues, MacDonald then accepted office as Prime Minister of a **National Government** to deal with the crisis. He was supported by the Conservatives and most of the Liberals, but only a handful of Labour MPs followed him. In the 1931 general election the National Government won an

Consider the case for and against MacDonald. A lot depends on assessment of his personality.

overwhelming victory; Labour was reduced to 52 seats. The majority of the Labour Party condemned MacDonald. They claimed that he had betrayed the party in the pursuit of personal ambition.

> **KEY POINTS**
>
> - The Labour government was overwhelmed by the economic crisis.
> - MacDonald's critics accuse him of betraying the Labour Party, but he may well have believed that an all-party government was needed in the national interest to restore confidence.

The impact of the 1931 economic crisis on the Labour party

Labour swung to the left after the disaster of 1931. The new leader, Lansbury, was an idealistic socialist. There was much debate in the party, in which young left-wing intellectuals played a prominent part. Many of them looked to Stalin's Russia as an example of socialist planning in action. Some, such as Cripps, wanted Labour to join with the Communists in a common front. There was also much debate about defence and rearmament and it was over this that Lansbury, who was a pacifist, resigned the leadership in 1935. He was succeeded by Attlee. In the 1935 election Labour won 154 seats – back to the position of 1924, but still a long way from gaining office.

You should be able to explain the significance of each of these dates.

> **KEY DATES**
>
> | | |
> |---|---|
> | 1918 | Coupon election |
> | 1921 | Black Friday – collapse of the Triple Alliance |
> | 1922 | Establishment of the Irish Free State; Partition of Ireland; Fall of the Lloyd George coalition |
> | 1924 | First Labour Ministry |
> | 1924–9 | Baldwin's second ministry |
> | 1926 | General Strike |
> | 1929–31 | Second Labour ministry |
> | 1929 | Wall Street Crash |
> | 1931 | Resignation of Labour Ministry; MacDonald Prime Minister of National Government |

The National Government

AQA **U1, 3**
OCR **U1**
WJEC **U1, 2, 4**

The National Government remained in office until the outbreak of war in 1940. MacDonald remained as Prime Minister until 1935, but with over 400 Conservative MPs, Baldwin as Lord President of the Council and Chamberlain as Chancellor of the Exchequer, the government was in all but name a Conservative one. When Macdonald resigned in 1935, Baldwin took over, to be succeeded in turn by Chamberlain in 1937.

Economic policies

The immediate financial crisis was tackled by orthodox deflationary methods, e.g. 10% cuts in public sector pay and unemployment benefit. The government was nevertheless forced to abandon the gold standard in 1931. Although great efforts had been made to avoid this, it actually benefited British exports. In 1932

> Make sure you understand why abandoning the gold standard would help. Tip: it was equivalent to devaluation.

free trade was abandoned and protective tariffs were introduced. This increased the domestic market for British goods and brought in increased revenue to the government. An attempt to set up a scheme of imperial preference at the Ottawa Conference of 1932, however, met with only limited success. The bank rate was cut to 2%. An attempt was made to tackle the problem of the decline of the older industrial areas by the Special Areas Act (1934). Marketing boards were set up for agricultural products such as milk.

By 1933 economic recovery was under way. This was more due to a housing boom, stimulated by the reduction in the bank rate and the revival of world trade, than to government policies. By 1937 unemployment had fallen to 1.4 million, though much of this was concentrated in the older industrial areas, where it remained a serious problem and a source of much bitterness. In the south and the midlands, by contrast, the second half of the 1930s was a time of growing prosperity. New industries, such as car manufacturing, were expanding and sales of consumer goods, such as radios, electric cookers and vacuum cleaners, were increasing rapidly. The number of private cars doubled in ten years and annual holidays at the seaside were becoming usual.

The depressed areas were another world. In 1934 in Jarrow 68% of the workforce was unemployed compared with 3% in High Wycombe. Why did the unemployed not migrate from the depressed areas to the prosperous ones? Many did, but others, especially men with families, could not afford to move long distances to low-paid jobs in areas where housing was expensive.

> **KEY POINT**
>
> There was a growing contrast between the relatively prosperous south and midlands and the depressed areas of the north and Scotland. The National Government failed to reduce unemployment below 1.4 million.

The unemployed and the 'dole'

Governments in the 1920s had responded to the problem of long-term unemployment by firstly extending the original 1911 National Insurance scheme to most workers with incomes below £250 a year and secondly instituting 'uncovenanted' benefits (i.e. benefits not covered by the worker's insurance contributions). This became known as the dole and from 1927 it was available for an indefinite period if the unemployed man was genuinely seeking work.

> This meant that in effect the distinction between 'covenanted' and 'uncovenanted' benefits was abolished.

In 1931, because of the financial crisis, benefits were cut by 10% and means testing was imposed for all those unemployed for more than six months. The 10% cut was restored in 1934 when the Unemployment Assistance Board was set up to take over administration of the dole. These measures, together with the abolition of the Poor Law in 1929, meant that the state had taken responsibility for supporting the unemployed. But the benefits left the long-term unemployed living in poverty. Moreover the means test, which was applied to payments of the dole, was greatly resented.

> The means test took into account all family income, so unemployed men could be dependent on the wages of their wives or unmarried children.

> **KEY POINTS**
>
> - The most bitterly resented aspect of the benefit system was the means test. It came to be regarded as a symbol of the plight of the unemployed.
> - Memories of the plight of the unemployed in the 1930s played a large part in the Labour victory in 1945.

Extremist responses to the Depression

AQA   **U1, 3**
WJEC   **U2, 4**

Throughout Europe extremist parties of the right and the left gained support as a result of the Great Depression. This also happened in Britain but it was never a real threat to British democracy.

- On the left, the **Communist Party**, founded in 1920, won sympathy among left-wing intellectuals. The National Government took a tough line with demonstrations and in 1934 passed the Incitement to Disaffection Act, though little use was made of it. The National Unemployed Workers' Movement, led by the Communist Wal Hannington, made some impact by organising hunger marches which aroused the conscience of the middle classes.
- On the right, **Sir Oswald Mosley**, a former Labour minister, founded the British Union of Fascists (BUF) in 1932 after his New Party had done very badly in the 1931 election. It was based on Mosley's admiration for Mussolini. Like the Italian fascists, its members wore a blackshirt uniform and relied on marches and violence. It was anti-Semitic. The BUF gained some 20 000 members at its peak, with particular strength in the East End of London, but never gained any seats in Parliament. It was virtually killed by the Public Order Act of 1936, which forbade the wearing of uniforms for political purposes and gave the police the right to ban marches which might cause serious disorder. Its biggest handicap was that the communist threat, which it existed to fight, never became serious in Britain.

> **KEY POINT**
>
> Extremists caused alarm, but never gained widespread support.

The abdication crisis, 1936

AQA   **U3**

In 1936 Edward VIII became King. His relationship with Mrs Simpson, an American who was going through her second divorce, posed constitutional questions which alarmed Baldwin, who advised the King to abdicate. He had the support of the Church of England, most MPs and public opinion. Edward accepted the inevitable and abdicated in December 1936. There were fears that the episode might damage the monarchy, but these proved to be unfounded. A few months later Baldwin retired with his reputation at its height. The ministry of Chamberlain, who replaced him, was dominated by the European crisis.

Chamberlain's foreign policy is discussed in Chapter 8.

The wartime coalition

AQA   **U1, 3**   WJEC   **U1**
OCR   **U2**

Because of the war, there was no general election between 1935 and 1945.

In May 1940 Chamberlain lost the support of a substantial number of Conservative MPs and resigned. Churchill became Prime Minister and formed a wartime coalition government. Attlee, the leader of the Labour Party, was a member of the Cabinet and later Deputy Prime Minister. Other Labour leaders who were ministers during the war included Cripps, Morrison and Dalton. Bevin, the Secretary of the Transport and General Workers' Union, was a highly successful Minister of Labour. When Labour came to power in 1945, all these men had experience in government, unlike the members of the first Labour ministry in 1924. Churchill also brought in the newspaper proprietor, Lord Beaverbrook, as Minister of Aircraft Production. The coalition was a genuinely national government.

> **KEY POINT**
>
> The formation of a coalition helped to keep the nation united in the war effort.

7.4 Churchill, 1920–45

LEARNING SUMMARY

After studying this section you should be able to understand:

- Churchill's career in the 1920s
- Churchill's political fortunes out of office in the 1930s
- Churchill's record as wartime Prime Minister

Churchill and post-war Britain, 1920-9

OCR U2

Fear of communism

Churchill regarded communism as extremely dangerous. After the 1917 revolution in Russia he supported British intervention to support the Whites in the Russian Civil War. As Secretary for War (1919–21) in Lloyd George's coalition government he prolonged this despite lack of support in Parliament or public opinion. He also feared that a Labour government would be a step down the same road – hence his opposition to Asquith's decision as Liberal leader to allow Labour to form a minority government after the 1923 election. This in turn led him to move back to the Conservatives in 1924. He had previously (1904) crossed from the Conservatives to the Liberals. This is why many Conservatives mistrusted him.

The return to the gold standard, 1925

> Make sure you understand why it was a mistake. It is explained on page 97.

In 1924 Churchill became Chancellor of the Exchequer in Baldwin's second ministry. The return to the gold standard at the pre-war parity was the most important decision he took and it has generally been regarded as a serious mistake.

The General Strike, 1926

Churchill was not opposed to trade unions, but he saw a general strike as a threat to the social order with potentially revolutionary implications. He pursued a moderate line towards the miners' demands before and after the General Strike. In 1925, he was instrumental in setting up the Samuel Commission to enquire into the problems of the coal industry and, as Chancellor, provided a subsidy to the coal industry pending its report. When the proposed strike was called off, Churchill tried unsuccessfully to mediate between the coal owners and the miners.

But when the strike broke out in May 1926 he was foremost in advocating tough action. Baldwin restrained him and diverted him into running the government news-sheet, the *British Gazette*, in which he denounced the strikers as 'the enemy'. His attitude during the General Strike confirmed the hostility of Labour supporters dating from his intervention in the Russian Civil War.

Churchill in the political wilderness, 1929–39

OCR   U2

The Conservatives were defeated at the general election of 1929. When the National Government was formed in 1931, Churchill was not offered a post. In 1930–1 he had alienated Baldwin at a time when Baldwin's leadership of the Conservative party was under threat from a campaign spearheaded by the press barons Beaverbrook and Rothermere. There were two issues: protection and India. Churchill, who had always been a free trader, threatened in October 1930 to resign from the shadow cabinet over Baldwin's proposal of a limited scheme of protection. He actually resigned in January 1931 over India (see below). Baldwin did not trust him thereafter. He remained out of office until 1939.

- The majority of Conservative MPs thought that his judgment was erratic and that, having changed parties twice, he was not a true Conservative. His behaviour in 1931 reinforced this feeling. Many also suspected his loyalty and felt that his aim was to oust Baldwin from the leadership.

- From 1931–5 he continued to fight government policy towards India – an issue which aligned him with a right-wing minority in the Conservative party with which he had otherwise little in common.

- After 1935 he was the leading critic of government policies over rearmament and appeasement – the central issue of the day. On this issue he was no longer associated with the right-wing fringe, but still relatively isolated within the party.

- His reputation suffered a further blow when he supported Edward VIII during the **abdication crisis**. He was shouted down in the House of Commons. It was a serious blow to his credibility, but had little long-term effect on his career.

> **KEY POINT**
>
> By 1931 Churchill had separated himself from the majority of the Conservative Party. He was too big a figure to ignore completely, but was regarded as a maverick.

India

He was involved in the conquest of the Sudan in 1898 and was a war correspondent in the Second Boer War.

Churchill's views about the empire were essentially those of a Victorian imperialist. He believed in the civilising mission of the empire and was sceptical about colonial peoples governing themselves. His views were by today's standards often racist. He also saw the empire as vital for British exports.

Baldwin advocated a policy of gradual advance towards self-rule for India. In 1931 Churchill resigned from the shadow cabinet and threw himself into a passionate campaign against Baldwin's policy.

- He attacked Gandhi in violent racist terms. (Gandhi had initiated a campaign of civil disobedience, culminating in the Salt March in 1930.)
- He was a founder of the India Defence League.
- He refused to join the Joint Select Committee on India in 1933.
- He opposed the Government of India Act (1935) tooth and nail, speaking 68 times on the report stage.

> **KEY POINT**
>
> Churchill's attack on Baldwin's policy towards India excluded him from office in the 1930s.

Rearmament and appeasement

Churchill was one of the first to sound the alarm about the rise of Hitler. In April 1933 he spoke of 'odious conditions in Nazi Germany' and at the same time drew attention to the weakness of Britain's defences, particularly the air force. At the time anti-war sentiment was strong, as shown by the East Fulham by-election (1933) and the Oxford Union motion not to fight 'for King and Country', so Churchill was relatively isolated. In 1936 the government finally embarked on a programme of rearmament, but Churchill continued to attack Baldwin for not starting it sooner.

> The Labour victory at East Fulham, overturning a large Conservative majority, was generally interpreted as a vote for pacifism.

He was unwavering in warning of the danger posed by Hitler. He opposed the Anglo-German Naval Treaty (1935) and attacked appeasement. During the Czech crisis he advised standing firm behind the integrity of Czechoslovakia and seeking the collaboration of Russia. He condemned the Munich agreement and correctly predicted the dismemberment of Czechoslovakia. In 1939 he continued to urge an agreement with the USSR, but it was too late: Stalin made the German-Soviet Pact in August.

> For a discussion of the events leading up to Munich see pages 113–114.

Wartime Prime Minister

AQA **U3** OCR **U2**

On the outbreak of war, Chamberlain appointed Churchill as First Lord of the Admiralty. He set about his work with his usual energy in contrast to the lack of vigour in the government as a whole. The 'phoney war' came to an end in April 1940 when the Germans invaded Denmark and Norway. British forces were sent to defend Norway, but had to be withdrawn. As a result on 10 May Chamberlain resigned. He wanted Halifax to succeed him, but he wisely declined. Churchill, who alone commanded the support from all three parties in a war against Hitler, became Prime Minister.

> But many MPs, especially among the Conservatives, were uneasy about his appointment

Churchill immediately committed himself and the nation to all-out war. His aim was total victory. He rejected the idea of a negotiated peace which was put forward by Halifax after the fall of France in May 1940. He contributed enormously to lifting the morale of the British people in the dark days of 1940. He communicated the will to win through his speeches, especially his effective use of the radio. His stirring speeches in Parliament and radio broadcasts hardened public support for the war effort.

> See also page 115 for the events of 1940.

> **KEY POINT**
>
> Churchill made a vital contribution to maintaining national morale.

Churchill's leadership style was crucial.
- He was Minister of Defence, as well as Prime Minister, so that he was directly in charge of the conduct of the war.
- He took the lead in diplomacy, especially relations with the other leaders of the Grand Alliance.
- At the centre of government was the war cabinet. Initially there were five members, including the Labour leader Attlee. The number fluctuated, but it was always small so as to enable speedy decision-making.
- Although the government had very extensive powers, Parliament was not neglected. Rather Churchill saw it as a way of maintaining public support.

> **KEY POINT**
>
> Churchill was directly involved in all aspects of running the war.

Conduct of the war

Churchill saw himself as a military expert and insisted that his own ideas about strategy should be exhaustively considered. The generals, who were the professionals, were often irritated or frustrated by his interference. Since he was in charge of overall strategy, he made the final decisions and sometimes they were impractical. Also, Churchill was the one who had to consider the political implications of military decisions. He never hesitated to replace a general he thought was not acting with sufficient vigour. He was probably right that some of the generals were too cautious.

> Churchill replaced Wavell in Egypt with Auchinleck in 1941 and Auchinleck with Alexander in 1942.

Churchill's impact on strategic decisions was important.

- He was responsible for the primacy given to the Mediterranean campaigns, beginning with the decision to send reinforcements to Egypt in July 1940. He pressed Wavell to send troops to Greece in 1941 and then, with disastrous results, to Crete. In 1943 he argued that the assault on Germany should be through Italy and, if possible, the Balkans. Sicily and then Italy were invaded from North Africa in 1943, but Churchill was unable to persuade the Americans to concentrate on this campaign rather than the invasion of France. Whether his ideas would have worked remains a matter of debate.
- How far Churchill was responsible for the strategic bombing of German cities is controversial. It was Churchill who appointed Harris, the great advocate of strategic bombing, to Bomber Command in 1942. The thousand bomber raids on Cologne, Hamburg, Berlin and finally Dresden between 1942 and 1945 were designed to destroy civilian morale. Both the effectiveness and the morality of these raids are matters of debate.
- Churchill's insistence on postponing the invasion of Normandy until 1944 allowed time for the careful preparations which made a success of what could have been a disastrous gamble. He failed, however, to persuade the Americans to drop the idea of a landing in the south of France, which, as he predicted, diverted resources from the Italian campaign. He also failed to persuade Roosevelt to press as far as possible into Germany in the final campaign.

Reconstruction

Some important preparations for the post-war world were made during the war, notably the Beveridge Report. But Churchill regarded this as a distraction from the winning of the war and showed little enthusiasm – a factor in the outcome of the 1945 election.

The Grand Alliance and the wartime conferences

In 1940–1, when Britain stood alone against Germany, Churchill recognised the importance of cultivating good relations with **Roosevelt**. Britain's war effort depended heavily on buying goods from the US. In 1941 Roosevelt set up the **Lend-Lease** scheme: American goods would be supplied on credit. In the same year Churchill met Roosevelt and agreed the 'Atlantic Charter', the basis of the United Nations.

By the end of 1941, as a result of Hitler's invasion of Russia and the Japanese attack on Pearl Harbour, Britain was no longer alone. From 1942 Hitler faced the Grand Alliance, of which Britain was a member. Churchill's personal relationship with Roosevelt and Stalin was important for the co-ordination of the war effort.

The main meetings of the Grand Alliance were:

- **Washington** (December 1941): Churchill and Roosevelt agreed that Germany was the main enemy, not Japan.
- **Moscow** (August 1942): Churchill persuaded Stalin that Britain and the US should mount an attack on North Africa. This meant postponing an invasion of north-west Europe. The timing of this was the main bone of contention between the three leaders in 1942–3.
- **Casablanca** (January 1943): Churchill and Roosevelt agreed on the invasion of Italy, which again meant postponing the invasion of France.
- **Quebec** (August 1943) and Cairo (November 1943): Churchill and Roosevelt discussed the strategy for the war against Japan.
- **Tehran** (November 1943): The three leaders agreed on the invasion of France in 1944.
- **Yalta** (February 1945): The three leaders agreed on the division of Germany into zones of occupation and the organisation of a conference to set up the United Nations. By this time Churchill was suspicious of Stalin's intentions in Eastern Europe, but Roosevelt did not share his doubts.

> They also agreed to require the 'unconditional' surrender of the Axis powers.

As a result of the 1945 general election Churchill was replaced by Attlee during the final meeting of the big three at **Potsdam** in July–August 1945.

Another important relationship was with de Gaulle, the head of the Free French Movement. De Gaulle was prickly and difficult to deal with, but Churchill recognised that he was a vital link to the French resistance.

KEY POINT

Churchill's relationship with Roosevelt was vital to the outcome of the war.

The 1945 general election

After the surrender of Germany in May 1945, Churchill called a general election. There had not been a general election since 1935 and the Labour Party was unwilling to prolong the coalition beyond October. Churchill was confident of victory – after all, he was generally regarded as the man who had won the war. But to his surprise – and that of most observers – Labour won and Attlee became Prime Minister in July.

KEY POINT

The election was more a verdict on the National governments of the 1930s than on Churchill.

KEY DATES

> You should be able to explain the significance of each of these dates.

1924–9	Churchill, Chancellor of the Exchequer
1925	Return to the gold standard
1929–39	Churchill out of office
1935	Government of India Act
1938	Munich agreement
1939	Outbreak of war; Churchill appointed First Lord of the Admiralty
1940	Fall of Chamberlain; Churchill forms wartime coalition; Dunkirk; Battle of Britain
1941	German invasion of Russia; Pearl Harbour
1945	Yalta and Potsdam conferences; General election

Sample question and model answer

This is not just a → question about the Conservative Party.

How far do you agree that the main reason for the dominance of the Conservative Party in British politics between 1922 and 1939 was the weakness of the other parties?

[50]

The Conservatives were in office, either as the governing party or as the dominant party in a coalition for the whole of the inter-war period, except for the brief interval of the two Labour ministries. Clearly this must, in part, be because of their popularity with the electors. For a full explanation of their domination, however, we must also consider the condition of the Labour and Liberal parties at this time.

The electoral success of the Conservatives was, in large measure, due to the personality of Stanley Baldwin, their leader between 1923 and 1937. Baldwin's image of pipe-smoking unflappability was reassuring. His attraction was his apparent ordinariness, though he was in reality a shrewd and skilful political tactician. True, on occasions the image he projected worked against the Conservatives, as in 1929 when his slogan, `Safety First' failed to catch the mood of the country. But on the whole, and especially in times of crisis, for example the General Strike, the 1931 financial crisis and the abdication crisis, he was trusted. Under him the Conservative party seemed a party of moderation, financial orthodoxy and administrative competence, all of which reassured the middle classes. It seems likely also that on the whole the Conservatives benefited from the extension of the vote to women.

Nevertheless, equally important in explaining the dominance of the Conservatives in this period was the weakness of their opponents. The elections of the 1920s were three-cornered contests, with the anti-Conservative vote split between Labour and the Liberals. The Liberals, divided by the quarrel between Lloyd George and Asquith in 1916, came third to Labour in the 1922 general election and never recovered, even though the split was healed in 1923. The decline of the Liberals benefited the Conservatives in two ways. Firstly, many former Liberals turned to the Conservatives in order to keep out Labour. Secondly, Liberal support remained strong enough to prevent Labour winning an overall majority in a general election.

Labour, too, had handicaps which worked to the Conservatives' advantage. In the 1920s it was a relatively new party, still establishing its claim to be the main alternative to the Conservatives. Its success in doing this was remarkable enough - in 1929 it emerged from the general election as the biggest single party, though without an overall majority. It had a solid base in the working classes and the backing of the trade unions, but this was a disadvantage as well as an advantage, for it frightened some Liberals who saw it as a class party. Moreover, many voters distrusted Labour because of its socialist aims and because of its leaders' lack of experience of high office. To many voters Labour seemed a gamble, while Baldwin by contrast offered reassurance.

Note the clear → structure of the essay: after the introduction, there are paragraphs about the Conservatives, the Liberals, Labour in the 1920s and Labour after 1931 – and they all focus on analysis rather than description.

In the 1930s Labour suffered a new handicap as a result of the crisis of 1931. The `betrayal' of MacDonald gave it the appearance of disunity, though in reality only a small minority of the party followed him. The collapse of the second Labour ministry in the face of the financial crisis convinced many that it was not fit for government. Labour then refused to join the National government in circumstances which a majority of electors thought required a coalition. The National government was therefore Conservative dominated and won an overwhelming majority for a `doctor's mandate' in the 1931 election. Labour was almost wiped out, though it recovered somewhat in 1935.

Sample question and model answer

This answer demonstrates a grasp of the interaction of the various factors and draws them together to produce a fully developed explanation.

Political circumstances worked to the Conservatives' advantage, most obviously in 1931, but also in the 1920s. In 1922 they (and the Labour Party) profited from the split in the Liberals between Asquith and Lloyd George. The Conservatives lost the election of 1923. However MacDonald's minority Labour government only lasted a year. In the 1924 election, MacDonald's reopening of relations with Russia, followed by the Zinoviev letter, helped Baldwin to a convincing victory which put the Conservatives in office for five years. Conservative gains were mainly from the Liberals, many of whom turned to the Conservatives to keep Labour out.

Thus the transitional state of British politics in the 1920s, with the rise of Labour and the decline of the Liberals, explains the dominance of the Conservatives in the first half of the period under discussion, while in the 1930s they benefited from the political fall-out from the Great Depression. In retrospect we can see how lucky the Conservatives were to lose the 1929 election. Their financial orthodoxy and air of calm competence were what the electorate wanted in the 1930s.

8 Appeasement and World War, 1919–45

The following topics are covered in this chapter:

- British foreign policy in the 1920s
- Appeasement
- The Second World War

8.1 British foreign policy in the 1920s

LEARNING SUMMARY

After studying this section you should be able to understand:

- the aims of foreign policy and the constraints on action
- Britain's role in the Versailles settlement
- British attitudes to the League of Nations
- Britain's approach to the German question
- Britain's attitude to disarmament

Foreign policy

AQA   **U2**
WJEC **U1, 4**

The main aims of British foreign policy in the inter–war years were:

- avoiding/preventing war
- maintaining a balance of power
- protecting the empire.

Britain's economic problems were an important constraint, as they led to cuts in defence spending. Public opinion, horrified by the thought of another war after the experience of the Great War, was another constraint.

Britain's role in the Versailles settlement

AQA   **U2**
WJEC **U1, 4**

The Paris peace conference in 1919 was dominated by Lloyd George, Georges Clemenceau and Woodrow Wilson. Lloyd George's role was influenced by anti-German public opinion. In the election campaign of December 1918 (the 'coupon election') he urged that Germany should be made to pay for the war 'to the limit of her capacity'. But he also realised that an excessively harsh settlement would leave Germany embittered and therefore opposed the more extreme French demands. The surrender of the German navy ensured Britain's security. Britain had no territorial claims in Europe, but Lloyd George aimed to secure Germany's colonies in Africa (as well as some Turkish territories in the Middle East). He shared Wilson's desire for an international organisation to preserve peace and the Covenant of the League was largely the work of the British Foreign Office (FO).

The details of the settlement are set out in Chapter 18, pages 242–4.

How far the final settlement was the work of Lloyd George is a matter of debate. Some historians claim that he was its principal architect because he occupied a position midway between Clemenceau's demand for a punitive treaty and Wilson's opposition to such a treaty. Others argue that Lloyd George was the main opponent of French demands and so Wilson was the arbiter.

The League of Nations

AQA   U2
WJEC   U1, 4

British public opinion, especially on the left, was enthusiastic about the League as a means of ensuring peace. It was in this spirit of enthusiasm for the League that MacDonald in 1924 proposed the **Geneva Protocol** which would have strengthened it by making arbitration compulsory. The Labour government fell from office, however, before it was ratified and the Conservatives, whose support for the League was more lukewarm, abandoned it. The Locarno Treaties signalled that the Conservatives preferred treaties between the powers to collective security.

The German question

AQA   U2
WJEC   U1, 4

In Germany the peace settlement aroused great bitterness. The Germans called it a *diktat* – a treaty forced on them rather than negotiated. They regarded the War Guilt Clause as humiliating and unfair and claimed that the treaty deprived Germany of territories which were rightly hers, disarmed her and imposed a crippling burden in reparations. In this latter claim they were supported by the English economist J. M. Keynes who argued in *The Economic Consequences of the Peace* that the amount demanded in reparations was far beyond Germany's ability to pay. World trade would be distorted because Germany would need a massive increase in exports, which would not be balanced by imports.

Nevertheless, the French insisted on strict enforcement of the Treaty. In 1922 Lloyd George called a conference at Genoa, hoping to settle the whole issue of reparations and war debts. It was a failure. The French refused to compromise and the Americans did not attend. In 1923, the French sent troops into the Ruhr after the Germans had defaulted on reparations. The German government responded by ordering passive resistance. The British Prime Minister, Ramsay MacDonald, played a key role in resolving the crisis by persuading the French and Germans to accept the **Dawes Plan**. This involved rescheduling Germany's reparations and thus amounted to a revision of the peace settlement.

> Named after an American banker, Charles Dawes, who chaired the committee which drew it up.

> Unlike the Treaty of Versailles, which was dictated to the Germans, the Locarno Treaties were negotiated with them.

This was followed by the most important attempt to resolve the German question, the **Locarno Treaties** of 1925.
- Germany, France and Belgium accepted as final the boundaries laid down at Versailles. Britain and Italy guaranteed these boundaries.
- Germany agreed that its frontiers with Poland and Czechoslovakia could only be altered by arbitration.

The British Foreign Secretary, Austen Chamberlain, played a key role in negotiating these agreements, which were regarded as a triumph at the time and were followed by a period of much greater harmony known as the 'Locarno honeymoon'. Germany was admitted to the League of Nations in 1926 and to the Kellogg–Briand Pact in 1928. In 1929 a further modification of reparations was agreed in the Young Plan. Relations between France and Germany were much more harmonious. But many historians criticise Locarno.
- No guarantees were given for Germany's eastern frontiers, thus suggesting that they were open to change.
- Britain had no plans to back the guarantees. No military talks were held with France because Locarno was as much a guarantee to Germany as to France.

Disarmament

AQA	U2
WJEC	U1, 4

Many people believed that one of the main causes of the First World War had been the arms race. One way of ensuring that such a war could never happen again, therefore, was to reduce armaments. British governments reduced armaments because public opinion favoured it and because economic problems required cuts in public expenditure. In 1919 Lloyd George told the armed forces to assume there was no threat of war for at least ten years and this Ten Year Rule was applied until 1932. The army was cut back to a size sufficient to maintain control in the empire. The **Washington Naval Treaty** (1922) made it possible to cut naval construction at the price of abandoning naval supremacy. Preparations were made for a World Disarmament Conference, but progress was slow. It did not meet until 1932 and in 1933, with Hitler in power, Germany withdrew.

> The British and American navies were to have equal numbers of battleships.

In the meantime, a different approach to the prevention of war was made in the **Kellogg–Briand Pact** of 1928. This prohibited the use of war 'as an instrument of national policy', except in self-defence. Britain signed this, along with the USA, Russia, Germany, Japan and over 50 other nations. Since this prohibition was already enshrined in the Covenant, it indicated a lack of faith in the League and it had little effect. At the time, however, it was seen as another step towards a more peaceful world and one in which, unlike the League, the USA took part.

> **KEY POINT**
>
> At the end of the 1920s the 'Locarno honeymoon' raised hopes for international stability, but there were signs that the League of Nations could not be relied upon and that general disarmament was unlikely.

8.2 Appeasement

LEARNING SUMMARY	**After studying this section you should be able to understand:**
	• why Britain followed a policy of appeasement
	• responses to the aggressive actions of Japan, Germany and Italy, 1931–6
	• the policy of appeasement as followed by Chamberlain

Why Britain followed a policy of appeasement

AQA	U2
Edexcel	U3
WJEC	U1,4

In the 1930s the world faced new and greater dangers from the aggressive nationalism of Japan, Italy and Germany. The response of British foreign policy was appeasement. This meant accepting the demands of the aggressors as reasonable and thus avoiding war. There were many reasons for this.

- Appeasement was very much in tune with public opinion. The British public wished above all to avoid war, as was demonstrated by the Peace Ballot in 1935. The slaughter of the First World War was a fresh memory and people were aware that a new war was likely to be even more devastating. The Spanish Civil War showed that in a new war the civilian population would be exposed to aerial bombing.
- There was also a widespread feeling that Germany had genuine grievances. Hitler was able to play on this by claiming that Germans outside Germany had the right of self-determination. Appeasement, it was believed, would remove grievances and thus promote Anglo–German friendship.

- Many people, especially Conservatives, thought this was particularly important because they saw Germany as a bulwark against Communist Russia, which they regarded as a greater threat than Nazi Germany.
- There is a strong case for the view that there was no alternative to appeasement. Britain was militarily not prepared for full-scale war. Public opinion did not favour rearmament and governments were keen to keep public expenditure as low as possible because of the economic situation. The Ten Year Rule, which was only abandoned in 1932, meant that, even when Britain began to rearm in the late 1930s, it was trailing behind Germany.
- Moreover, Britain had a worldwide Empire to defend and there was a risk that war with Germany would lead to war against Italy and Japan as well. In such a war Britain's main ally would probably be France, which was weak and divided. The USA was committed to isolation. It was likely, therefore, that Britain would find itself fighting alone, as indeed happened in 1940. The policy of appeasement did at least provide the opportunity for Britain to rearm from 1936 onwards.
- Baldwin and Chamberlain both believed that Hitler and Mussolini were rational statesmen like themselves and that appeasement was the rational policy towards them. Outstanding among the few prominent politicians who took the opposite view was Churchill.

> **KEY POINT**
>
> It is easy with hindsight to judge that appeasement was the wrong policy. At the time there were strong arguments for it.

Challenges to peace, 1931–6

AQA **U2**
Edexcel **U3**
WJEC **U1, 4**

The Japanese invasion of Manchuria, 1931

The Lytton Commission, appointed by the League of Nations, criticised Japan's action and proposed that Manchuria should be self-governing under China. The League accepted this, but Japan rejected it. Britain and France, the leading members of the League, took no action and Japan established a puppet regime in Manchuria. At the time there was probably nothing else that Britain or France could do.

> This episode seemed to show that the League's decisions could be ignored.

German rearmament, March 1935

Hitler introduced conscription in defiance of the Versailles Treaty. Britain, France and Italy condemned this and agreed to resist any further breaches of the treaty (the **Stresa Front**). But the British government then undermined the Stresa Front by making the **Anglo-German Naval Agreement**, which it saw as a way of limiting German rearmament and preserving British naval superiority.

> This implied that the Versailles settlement could be re-negotiated.

The Italian invasion of Abyssinia, October 1935

The League declared Italy an aggressor and imposed sanctions, but coal, steel and – most importantly – oil were excluded. The sanctions therefore had little effect on Italy's war effort. The failure to impose effective sanctions was largely because Britain and France were not prepared for war and were anxious to maintain good relations with Italy. They even proposed, in the **Hoare-Laval Pact**, to allow Mussolini to keep two-thirds of Abyssinia (modern Ethiopia), but public outrage in Britain and France forced the withdrawal of this plan.

> This confirmed the ineffectiveness of the League.

The reoccupation of the Rhineland, 1936

Baldwin judged that public opinion would not support military action since the Rhineland was German territory.

Baldwin's handling of these problems was criticised later as weak and therefore encouraging the aggressive policies of the dictators. He believed that Hitler and Mussolini were rational statesmen like himself. He was also criticised for his failure to embark on rearmament sooner. He defended himself, with some justice, on the grounds that public opinion was not ready for rearmament.

Chamberlain and appeasement, 1937–40

AQA **U2**
Edexcel **U3**
WJEC **U1, 4**

Chamberlain believed that Hitler's aims were limited and that he merely wanted to right the wrongs done to Germany at the Treaty of Versailles. He saw Hitler as a reasonable man with whom he could do business. He was also acutely aware of Britain's weaknesses: war in Europe would endanger the economy and the empire. To Chamberlain, negotiation with Hitler was the only rational policy.

The development, and then abandonment, of appeasement is seen in his response to the successive demands made by Hitler in 1938–9.

- The **Anschluss, March 1938**: when Hitler took over Austria, Chamberlain accepted it on the grounds that Austria was racially German.
- The **Sudetenland, September 1938**: Hitler demanded this area which was in Czechoslovakia. Chamberlain flew to Germany three times to negotiate with him. Finally, at the **Munich Conference** he agreed to Hitler's demands. Chamberlain's claim that it brought 'peace in our time' marked the apparent triumph of appeasement.
- **Czechoslovakia, March 1939**: Chamberlain's belief that Hitler had no more territorial demands was shattered in March 1939 when German troops occupied the rest of Czechoslovakia. For the first time Hitler had taken over a country which was not German-speaking. Chamberlain changed his policy and offered guarantees to Poland, which seemed likely to be Hitler's next victim.
- **Poland, April 1939**: Hitler demanded Danzig and a road and railway across the Polish Corridor. The Poles, fearing that this was a prelude to a German invasion, as in Czechoslovakia, refused. The key to the situation was the attitude of Russia. Chamberlain began negotiations, but progress was slow. Stalin decided that Russia's security would be better served by doing a deal with Hitler and signed the **Nazi–Soviet Pact** in August.

> This undermined the argument that Hitler was simply aiming to bring all Germans into an enlarged Germany.

Hitler believed that with Russia neutral the British government would revert to its policy of appeasement, but he was wrong. Hitler invaded Poland on 1 September and on 3 September Britain declared war.

Assessment

Appeasement failed to avert war and Chamberlain has therefore been blamed for pursuing a mistaken policy. Critics allege that he allowed Hitler to dupe him by false promises. They point out that he had little experience of foreign affairs and it does seem that he was outmanoeuvred by Hitler at Munich. He could probably have held out for better terms and he should have sought the support of Russia, which obviously had a strong interest in events in Eastern Europe. In this, Chamberlain allowed his fear of communism to outweigh his fear of Hitler. The result of his mistakes was that Czechoslovakia was sacrificed and the stage was set for the Nazi–Soviet Pact a year later. On the other hand, Munich averted war and allowed Britain a year to rearm. Chamberlain, more than anyone, was responsible for the acceleration in Britain's rearmament in 1938–9. Britain was better prepared for war in 1939, though of course Germany's armed strength also increased in the year after Munich. He was suspicious about Hitler's ambitions and did not trust him, but he thought he had little alternative but to negotiate with him.

Churchill attacked Chamberlain strongly over Munich and was proved right in his view that concessions only encouraged further demands. But Chamberlain rejected Churchill's view on the grounds that he exaggerated Britain's ability to stop Hitler.

> You should be able to explain the significance of each of these dates.

KEY DATES

1931	Japanese invasion of Manchuria
1935	Hitler announces German rearmament; Stresa Front; Anglo–German Naval Agreement; Italian invasion of Abyssinia
1936	Remilitarisation of the Rhineland
1938	Anschluss between Germany and Austria; Munich Conference
1939	German occupation of Bohemia and Moravia; Nazi–Soviet Pact; German invasion of Poland and outbreak of war

8.3 The Second World War

LEARNING SUMMARY

After studying this section you should be able to understand:

- how Britain survived after the fall of France in 1940
- how the formation of the Grand Alliance led to eventual victory
- developments on the home front

Defeat and survival, 1939–41

Edexcel **U3**

Dunkirk and the fall of France

Within a month of the outbreak of war, Poland had been conquered by Germany and Russia, but then nothing happened for several months. This period was known as the 'phoney war'. In April 1940, the Germans invaded Denmark and Norway to protect their access route to Swedish iron ore. The failure of British forces to prevent this led to Chamberlain's resignation and Churchill became Prime Minister. On the same day, the German army invaded Holland and Belgium and then swept into France. The British Expeditionary Force (BEF), which had joined the French in defending the Franco–Belgian border, was cut off. Some 340 000 British and French troops were rescued from **Dunkirk**. The Germans then swept across France. A new French Prime Minister, Marshal Pétain, made an armistice, leaving northern France under German occupation and setting up a nominally independent government of southern France at Vichy.

> Remember that Dunkirk was not a victory, but a lucky escape.

KEY POINT

By June 1940 Britain was alone against Hitler and Mussolini.

The Battle of Britain

Hitler now planned to invade Britain. First, he had to gain control of the air. In the Battle of Britain (July–September 1940) the RAF inflicted heavy losses on the German Luftwaffe. Hitler changed his tactics to bombing London and other large cities (the Blitz).

> Hitler's decision was a mistake. The RAF was also nearly exhausted.

> **KEY POINT**
>
> The Battle of Britain was Hitler's first defeat.

North Africa

Meanwhile, the war had spread to Greece and North Africa as a result of the entry of Italy into the war. An attempt by Britain to save Greece and Crete from German occupation in 1941 failed with serious losses. An Italian advance from Libya into Egypt threatened the Suez Canal. Churchill regarded this as a vital link to India and to the Gulf oilfields, so British troops were sent to Egypt. They drove the Italians back into Libya, forcing Hitler to rescue the Italians by sending German forces under the command of Rommel.

By June 1942, Rommel's army was only sixty miles from Alexandria and the British position in Egypt was seriously threatened. The decisive victory of Montgomery's Eighth Army over Rommel at **El Alamein** (1942) was the turning point in the North Africa campaign. The German forces were driven back through Libya to the border of Tunisia. Meanwhile, Allied troops landed in Algeria and advanced east to meet up with Montgomery. In 1943 the Allies invaded Sicily from North Africa and then advanced steadily north through Italy in 1943–5.

The Grand Alliance and victory

Edexcel **U3**

The character of the war changed completely in 1941.

- On 22 June Hitler invaded Russia. By the end of the year German armies had advanced deep into Russia.
- On 7 December the Japanese attacked the US Pacific fleet at Pearl Harbour. The USA and Britain declared war on Japan and Japan's allies, Germany and Italy, declared war on the USA.

For the rest of the war Britain, the USA and Russia formed the Grand Alliance, co-ordinating their war efforts. Churchill and Roosevelt agreed to concentrate their main effort against Germany, while containing the Japanese offensive in the Pacific. Churchill then persuaded Stalin (with some difficulty) that Britain and the USA should gain complete control of North Africa before invading north-west Europe. Meanwhile, the Russians forced the German army at **Stalingrad** to surrender in January 1943. This was the turning point of the war in the east and from that point on the Russian armies gradually pushed the Germans back. By the end of the war in 1945 they had reached Berlin.

The Battle of the Atlantic

> Churchill wrote later that the U-boat campaign was the only thing that really frightened him.

Britain's war effort depended heavily on supplies from the USA and was seriously threatened by the German U-boat campaign. In 1942 losses of merchant shipping were heavy. During 1943, however, Allied losses were more than halved by various measures: convoys of merchant ships were escorted by warships and aircraft, radar was used to locate U-boats and German secret codes were broken, enabling the Allies to follow the movements of U-boats.

The bomber offensive

In 1942 the RAF launched its first thousand bomber attack on Cologne. The bomber offensive continued for the rest of the war, with Hamburg, Berlin and, notoriously, Dresden sustaining massive damage. The stated aim was to destroy Germany's industrial and transport infrastructure, but it was also intended to destroy civilian morale. Whether the latter aim was justified, or achieved, remains a matter of controversy.

D-Day, 6 June 1944

Meticulous planning prepared the way for the successful invasion of Normandy. By the end of August Paris had been liberated. A last ditch attack by Hitler (the Ardennes offensive) in December was halted and driven back. In March, the Allied armies crossed the Rhine and at the end of April American and Russian forces met on the river Elbe. Hitler committed suicide. Germany surrendered on 8 May 1945.

The home front

Edexcel **U3**   WJEC   **U4**

Unlike in previous wars, civilians were in the front line because of the development of aerial warfare. The government made plans for this by distributing air raid shelters (Anderson shelters) and gas masks. A 'black-out' was enforced to hide lights in people's homes. In 1939 about 1½ million people (mainly schoolchildren and mothers with infants) were evacuated from cities to country areas. Because of the phoney war many returned – just in time for the Blitz! The Blitz itself made 1.4 million people homeless.

Morale, however, remained high. The Blitz reinforced people's determination not to give in. Churchill's wartime speeches, broadcast on the radio, played a crucial part in maintaining morale. Up to 1½ million men joined the Home Guard and others volunteered as air raid wardens and auxiliary fire-fighters.

The government took new powers to fight the war. The **Defence of the Realm Act**, originally introduced in 1914, was renewed and the Emergency Powers Acts increased government controls still further. The government took control of industry and transport. Ministries of Food and Supply were set up and food and clothes rationing were introduced. The government was empowered to direct labour to where it was most needed – a power which was used to great effect by Bevin.

> Bevin was a trade union leader who was brought into the government by Churchill to organise the workforce for the war effort.

The war had a significant impact on the **role of women**. They played a crucial part in the war effort. From 1941 all women aged 18–60 had to register so that they could be directed into appropriate war work. They worked as nurses, in factories, on the buses and in a wide variety of other occupations. The Women's Land Army was revived. The Women's Voluntary Service, with over a million members, helped with tasks such as organising evacuation and running mobile canteens. Women's branches of the armed services were formed – WRNS (navy), WAAF (air force), ATS (army).

> **KEY POINT**
>
> Although not all the gains were maintained in the short term, the war opened doors for women and was an important step in their emancipation.

The war also had an impact on the **class system**. Service in the armed forces or in war work threw together people of different classes. There was a long-term effect in the decline of deference.

In time of war it was natural to look forward to better times when it was over. There was a growing expectation that the government would plan for this while the war was continuing and the result was the **Beveridge Report** (1942), which laid plans to overcome the five evils it identified: want, ignorance, disease, idleness and squalor. This was the basis for the welfare state set up by the post-war Labour government. The **Butler Education Act** (1944) was also important as it promised secondary education for all.

The war had a profound effect on the British economy. It had been financed by massive borrowing and sales of overseas investments. Exports had fallen by over a half. Merchant shipping was down by 30%, and industry and transport, overstretched by wartime demands, were in great need of investment. Britain would pay the price in the post-war world.

> **KEY POINTS**
>
> - Britain's war effort depended heavily on the USA. The post-war relationship between the two reflected this. Britain was to be clearly the junior partner.
> - Britain's economy was severely stretched by the war. It emerged from the war greatly weakened.

Exam practice questions

1 **(a)** Explain why J. M. Keynes regarded the Versailles settlement as unwise. **[12]**

(b) 'The principal aim of British foreign policy in the 1920s was to strengthen the post-war settlement.'

Explain why you agree or disagree with this statement. **[24]**

2 'Until 1936 appeasement was a sensible policy for Britain; after 1936 it was not.'

How far do you agree with this view? **[50]**

9 Post-war Britain, 1945–2007

The following topics are covered in this chapter:

- The Labour governments, 1945–51
- The Conservatives, 1951–64
- Conservative and Labour governments, 1964–79
- Mrs Thatcher, 1979–90
- Major and Blair, 1990–2007
- Northern Ireland, 1968–98

9.1 The Labour governments, 1945–51

LEARNING SUMMARY	After studying this section you should be able to understand:
	- why Labour won a decisive election victory in 1945
	- the significance of the Labour government's welfare reforms
	- Labour's economic policies in this period
	- Labour's defeat in the 1951 election

The 1945 Election

AQA   U1, 3
OCR   U1
Edexcel U2, 3

In the 1945 general election Labour won an overall majority of 146 – the first time it had won an outright majority in an election. This was in spite of the popularity of Churchill as the man who had won the war.

> The result was a verdict on the National Governments of the 1930s rather than Churchill.

- The Conservatives were blamed for inadequate social policies and failures in foreign policy in the 1930s.
- Labour caught the mood of the time with its manifesto 'Let Us Face the Future'. After the sacrifices of the war, there was a general desire for a government committed to building a better future. Labour offered a more wholehearted commitment to social reform, promising full employment, a housing drive and a national health service.
- The role of the Labour leaders in the wartime coalition ensured that they could not be accused of inexperience.
- Churchill misjudged the campaign, fighting as a partisan Conservative rather than a national leader. His charge that socialist government would require 'some sort of Gestapo' to quell discontent was a bad mistake.

The Welfare State

AQA   U1, 3
OCR   U1
Edexcel U2, 3
WJEC   U4

Labour's social reforms, which set up the Welfare State, were based on the **Beveridge Report** (1942). Beveridge had identified five evils to be overcome: want, ignorance, disease, idleness and squalor. The main reforms were:

> This was the great achievement of Bevan.

- The **National Health Service Act** (1946) provided free medical care for the whole population. It was to be financed partly from National Insurance contributions, but mainly from taxation. All hospitals, including voluntary ones, were taken into the National Health Service (NHS). Opposition from doctors was overcome by paying them fees based on the number of patients on their lists rather than a salary. The NHS was inaugurated in 1948.

- The **National Insurance Act** (1946) covered all adults and provided increased sickness and unemployment benefit, old age pensions, widows' and orphans' pensions, maternity allowances and death grants.
- The **National Assistance Act** (1948) provided benefits for those not covered by National Insurance, e.g. old people receiving pensions under the scheme set up in 1908. It also required local authorities to provide welfare services for the elderly and handicapped.
- The **National Insurance Industrial Injuries Act** provided compensation for injuries and pensions for the disabled.
- In education the **Butler Act** (1944) was carried out. Secondary education was provided for all children and the school leaving age was raised to 15 from 1947.
- Over a million **houses were built** (though because of demographic changes there was still a serious shortage in 1951). Many were pre-fabricated and were at first intended to be temporary.
- The **New Towns Act** aimed to create towns which were healthy and pleasant. By 1951 fourteen New Town Corporations had been set up.
- The **Town and Country Planning Act** (1946) made county councils responsible for planning.
- The **Trade Disputes Act** (1946), though not strictly a welfare measure, may also be mentioned. This reversed the Act of 1927, which Labour supporters had always regarded as a vindictive measure designed to cripple Labour Party funds. Trade unions were now able to levy a contribution for political purposes provided members were allowed to contract out of it.

> **KEY POINT**
>
> Labour's greatest achievement was to set up the Welfare State it had promised.

The economy

AQA	U1, 3
OCR	U1
Edexcel	U2, 3
WJEC	U4

At the end of the war Britain had lost two-thirds of its export trade, faced a huge balance of payments deficit and had incurred massive debts, mainly to the USA. Moreover, the need to modernise industry was even greater than in the 1930s. Labour attempted to solve these problems by a planned economy.

Nationalisation

A key part of this was **nationalisation**. Labour believed that the most important industries should be owned by the state and run in the public interest, with the profits going to the treasury. Between 1945 and 1951 Labour nationalised the Bank of England, air transport, Cable and Wireless, the coal mines, the railways, docks, canals, road haulage, electricity and gas. It also nationalised iron and steel, but only after a struggle with the House of Lords, which rejected the proposal. The government reduced the delaying powers of the Lords to one year by the Parliament Act of 1949. It then completed the nationalisation of iron and steel, but the Conservatives denationalised the industry in 1953.

Government controls were another key feature of Labour's economic policy. Food rationing continued – indeed, some allowances were even lower than during the war. In the harsh winter of 1946–7 there were power cuts and fuel rationing. Rents, profits, interest rates and foreign exchange were all controlled. There were strict building restrictions. Britain was helped through its immediate post-war difficulties by an American loan in 1946. This was given on condition that the pound sterling was made convertible, but when this was put into effect in 1947 it led to a balance of payments crisis.

Cripps and austerity

The Marshall Plan is explained on page 278.

Immediately after this Cripps became Chancellor of the Exchequer. He believed that austerity was the solution to Britain's economic problems. Import controls were imposed to direct economic activity towards exports and there was a wage freeze between 1948 and 1950, even though prices were rising. Together with the **Marshall Plan**, Cripps's measures achieved some success in this. By 1950 exports were 75% above the 1938 level. Even so, the balance of payments continued to be a problem and it was necessary in 1949 to devalue the pound. This made imports dearer and exports cheaper, which helped the balance of payments.

> **KEY POINTS**
>
> - Labour carried out its promises on nationalisation, maintained full employment and led Britain to recovery after the war.
> - The performance of the economy remained a long-term problem. In the short-term, continuing austerity produced growing disillusionment.

Why did Labour lose the 1951 election?

AQA **U1, 3**
OCR **U1**
Edexcel **U2, 3**

- Despite what had been achieved in the setting up of the Welfare State and the revival of the economy, people were tired of rationing, austerity, controls and the continuing housing shortage. The Conservative manifesto offered to end all of these.
- Despite the success of the export drive, the balance of payments deficit worsened in 1950–1 because the **Korean War** caused a sharp rise in the price of imported raw materials.
- The Korean War also made it necessary to increase the period of National Service to two years, which was unpopular.
- The government faced financial problems resulting from the unexpectedly high cost of the NHS and the cost of the Korean War. The Chancellor, Gaitskell, tackled them by making expenditure cuts and introducing charges for spectacles and dental treatment. This in turn led to the resignation of Bevan and Wilson from the government and a split in the party.
- The government seemed tired, especially in the period between the 1950 and 1951 elections when it had a very small majority.
- The Conservative Party had overhauled its organisation and its election campaign was much more effective.
- The Liberal Party had very little money for a second election in less than two years and put up very few candidates. This benefited the Conservatives.

Despite all this, Labour only lost by a narrow margin (295 seats to the Conservatives' 321).

You should be able to explain the significance of each of these dates.

KEY DATES

1945–51	Labour government; Attlee Prime Minister
1948	National Health Service inaugurated
1949	Devaluation of the pound
1950	General election – narrow Labour victory
1950–3	Korean War
1951	Labour defeated in general election

9.2 The Conservatives, 1951–64

LEARNING SUMMARY

After studying this section you should be able to understand:

- the record of Eden and Macmillan as Prime Ministers
- the economic policies of the Conservatives
- the defeat of the Conservatives in 1964

Eden and Macmillan

AQA	**U3**	Edexcel **U2**
OCR	**U1**	

Of the four Conservative Prime Ministers in this period, Harold Macmillan requires most attention. Churchill was 77 in 1951 and left much of the work to the foreign Secretary, Eden, who succeeded him as Prime Minister in 1955. **Eden** had a distinguished record as an opponent of appeasement before the war and Foreign Secretary in Churchill's War Cabinet. He was popular and led the Conservatives to a convincing victory in the 1955 election. His ministry, however, was cut short by illness. It was notable chiefly for the disastrous **Suez campaign** (1956), when Britain and France, in co-operation with Israel, attacked Egypt and occupied the Suez Canal Zone. American opposition to this forced Britain and France to withdraw. The episode demonstrated Britain's dependence on the USA and ruined Eden's reputation for statesmanship.

Macmillan (1957–63) was a 'one nation Tory', believing in social reform in the tradition of Disraeli's Tory democracy. Something of a showman and a natural leader, he restored the Conservatives' confidence after Suez and led them to a third successive election victory in 1959. His ministry was marked by prosperity and rising standards of living, but the underlying economic problems remained unsolved. It was also a period when Britain began to come to terms with its reduced influence in a world dominated by the superpowers, the USA and the USSR, and with the need to dismantle its empire. Macmillan talked of a 'wind of change' blowing through Africa. Many of Britain's African colonies gained independence during his ministry.

Economic and social changes

AQA   U3   Edexcel U2
OCR   U1

> Note the contrast with the austerity of the Labour government.

Living standards improved markedly in the 1950s. This was the period of the 'affluent society'. Food rationing and building restrictions were ended and controls swept away. Wages rose faster than prices and people were able to afford more consumer goods such as cars, refrigerators and TVs. A vigorous 'national housing crusade' by Macmillan as Minister of Housing (1951–4) produced a 50% increase in the number of new houses. Further subsidies to agriculture led to higher productivity, income tax was lowered, unemployment was low and National Service was ended in 1960.

How much this prosperity was due to government policies is a matter of debate. Some historians argue that it was primarily caused by the growth in world trade and that the government's policies actually prevented Britain's economy from developing as rapidly as it should have done. Economic policy in the period came to be called '**stop-go**'. The Conservatives inherited a balance of payments deficit and inflation in 1951. They tackled the situation by credit restrictions and import controls. When the balance of payments moved into surplus, the government cut interest rates and taxes, which led to a period of boom. This in turn caused rising wages, prices and increasing imports and thus the balance of payments moved into deficit again. The boom had to be curbed by credit restrictions and tax increases.

> The link between the political and economic cycles was no accident.

The timing of the 'go' phases helped the Conservatives to win the elections of 1955 and 1959, but by the early 1960s it was becoming clear that the underlying growth of the economy was lagging behind Britain's European competitors. Ominously, unemployment was rising towards the million mark by 1963. One reason for this was that 'stop-go' discouraged long-term investment in industry. Some would argue that the Conservatives' failure to join the European Economic Community (EEC) when it was set up in 1957 was a crucial mistake.

> **KEY POINT**
>
> Economic policy in the period 1951–64 produced the 'affluent society', but no solution to Britain's long-term economic problems. This is why it has been described as 'thirteen wasted years'.

The election of 1964

AQA   U3   Edexcel U2
OCR   U1

As well as the economic problems, the Conservatives were losing popularity in the early 1960s for other reasons.

- An application to join the EEC was vetoed by France in 1963.
- The government was damaged by the Profumo scandal.
- Some Conservatives opposed Macmillan's policy of granting independence to African colonies.
- Home, who succeeded Macmillan as Prime Minister in 1963, was an electoral liability because of his aristocratic background and lack of experience in the Commons and the way he was chosen was seen as undemocratic.

Meanwhile, Labour's fortunes were reviving. In the 1950s Labour was torn by divisions, firstly about health service charges and then, more seriously, about nuclear disarmament. Under the leadership of Harold Wilson, elected in 1963 on the death of Hugh Gaitskell, Labour presented a more dynamic image, offering modernisation and planning of the economy and encouragement for technological change. In the 1964 election Labour won a small overall majority and Wilson became Prime Minister.

You should be able to explain the significance of each of these dates.

KEY DATES

1951	Conservative election victory; Churchill Prime Minister
1955	Eden Prime Minister; Conservative election victory
1956	Suez campaign
1957	Macmillan Prime Minister
1959	Conservative election victory
1963	Retirement of Macmillan; Home Prime Minister
1964	Labour victory in general election; Wilson Prime Minister

9.3 Conservative and Labour governments, 1964–79

LEARNING SUMMARY

After studying this section you should be able to understand:

- the political instability of the period
- the record of Wilson as Prime Minister, 1964–70
- the record of Heath as Prime Minister, 1970–4
- the Labour governments of 1974–9 and in 1979 the reasons for the Conservative election victory

A period of political flux

AQA **U3** Edexcel **U2**
OCR **U1**

Between 1964 and 1979 there were six general elections, four of which led to a change of government. In February 1974 no party gained an overall majority, while in two others (1964 and October 1974) Labour had majorities of four and three. These figures explain why there was an election only 18 months after the 1964 election, why there were two elections in 1974 and why the Labour government, which won the second election of 1974, lost its majority through by-elections in 1978 and had to rely on Liberal support in a Lib-Lab pact. The most important reason for this political uncertainty was the inability of governments of either party to deal effectively with the country's economic and industrial relations problems.

Wilson and Labour 1964–70

AQA **U3** Edexcel **U2**
OCR **U1** WJEC **U4**

Harold Wilson came to power in 1964 with a very small majority. His decision to call another election in 1966 was fully justified by the large majority he won.

The economy

As with all the governments of this period, the dominant problem was the economy. Wilson fulfilled his electoral promises by creating two new ministries.
- The Department of Economic Affairs, headed by George Brown, to plan the economy.
- The Ministry of Technology to encourage industrial modernisation.

The results were disappointing because the government had to concentrate on the more immediate problem of the adverse balance of payments which it inherited from the Conservatives. Wilson tried to remedy this by deflation – raising taxes and cutting government expenditure – in the attempt to avoid **devaluation**, but was nevertheless forced into it in 1967.

> Devaluation had been forced on a previous Labour government in 1949 and was seen as a sign of economic weakness.

A government reshuffle followed. Callaghan was replaced by **Roy Jenkins** as Chancellor of the Exchequer. Jenkins introduced more stringent deflationary measures and the balance of payments slowly improved. By 1968, however, inflation was rising and a prices and incomes policy was introduced. But this attempt to control wages led to a series of damaging strikes, many of which ended in submission to trade union demands.

> **KEY POINT**
>
> Devaluation actually helped the balance of payments as it made exports cheaper and imports dearer.

Trade unions

The strikes led Wilson to the conclusion that the trade unions were causing wage inflation. He called on Barbara Castle to draw up a plan for changes in the law governing trade unions – **'In Place of Strife'**. Opposition from the Trades Union Congress (TUC), and from union-backed MPs in the Labour Party itself, forced the government to abandon it.

> **KEY POINT**
>
> The trade unions miscalculated. When the law was finally changed in the 1980s by a Conservative government, the restrictions on union activity were much more severe.

Domestic policies

- Education: the government put pressure on local authorities to reorganise secondary education along comprehensive lines. The Open University was founded.
- Social reforms: capital punishment was abolished and the laws on homosexual acts, abortion and divorce were liberalised. Many of these reforms were initiated by backbench MPs, and passed on a free vote, but they were encouraged by the Home Secretary Roy Jenkins.
- The Race Relations Board was set up.
- Immigration: the Commonwealth Immigration Act (1968) restricted the right of entry to Britain in response to the arrival of thousands of Kenyan Asians with British passports. Immigration became a big political issue through a speech by the Conservative MP Enoch Powell, in which he warned that it would eventually lead to racial violence.

> Powell predicted that racial disturbances would end in 'rivers of blood'.

- Northern Ireland: see pages 135–6.

Foreign and colonial issues

- Europe: in 1967 another application to join the European Economic Community (EEC) was again vetoed by General de Gaulle.
- Rhodesia (modern Zimbabwe): originally a British colony, Southern Rhodesia was governed by the white minority who refused to allow any progress towards

majority rule. In 1965 the right-wing Prime Minister, Ian Smith, proclaimed UDI – a Unilateral Declaration of Independence. This was illegal, but Wilson was unwilling to use force to overthrow Smith and sanctions had little effect. It remained an unsolved problem until 1979.

The 1970 election

> Wilson need not have called an election until 1971, but in the early part of 1970 the opinion polls turned in his favour.

Despite the many unsolved problems listed above, most observers expected Wilson to win. The economy seemed at last to be in fairly good shape. The Conservative leader, Edward Heath, was thought to be uninspiring. But the result was a Conservative majority of 30.

Three issues account for Wilson's defeat.

- The immigration issue was given great prominence in the press and probably worked to the Conservatives' advantage despite the fact that Heath had dismissed Powell after his 'rivers of blood' speech.
- The failure of the attempt to curb trade union power made Wilson look weak.
- The crucial issue was the economy: just before the election, bad balance of payments and inflation figures were published.

Heath's Conservative government, 1970–4

AQA	U3	Edexcel U2
OCR	U1	

Edward Heath, a grammar school boy, became leader of the Conservative Party as a result of a change in the rules for choosing the leader after the 1964 election. He changed the image of the party by bringing into the party leadership more MPs who were, like Heath himself, from less privileged backgrounds. Heath's greatest achievement was the **entry of the United Kingdom into the EEC** in 1973.

The economy

> According to Conservative free market ideas they should have been allowed to collapse.

Heath was faced by a combination of rising unemployment and inflation which forced him to abandon the free market policies on which he had fought the election.

- When Rolls Royce faced bankruptcy, Heath nationalised it. He subsidised the re-structuring of Upper Clyde Shipbuilders when it too collapsed.
- In an attempt to reduce unemployment, the Chancellor, Anthony Barber, cut taxes and made a 'dash for growth' (the Barber Boom). The effect was inflationary – and matters were made worse by the oil price rise of 1973, which added fuel to the fire of inflation. Another twist was added to the inflationary spiral when the USA ended the post-war international exchange rate system under the Bretton Woods Agreement of 1944.
- An **incomes policy** was introduced in an attempt to control wage inflation. But in the end this depended on the co-operation of the trade unions.

> **KEY POINT**
>
> The oil price rise and the end of Bretton Woods were key changes in the global economy. Britain was ill-equipped to deal with them.

Trade unions

Victory by the Mineworkers' Union in a strike in 1972 brought the government face-to-face with the problem of **trade union militancy**. Heath introduced the

Industrial Relations Act. Trade union hostility quickly made this virtually a dead letter. This victory encouraged further trade union militancy in opposition to Heath's incomes policy. In 1974 the Mineworkers' Union called another strike which led to a three-day week in industry and then to the decision to call a general election on the issue 'Who governs the country?'

The General Election, February 1974

The miners' strike and the three-day week undermined confidence in Heath, but the election result, a hung Parliament, showed that the electors also had little confidence in Labour's ability to deal with the country's economic problems. Heath tried to do a deal with the Liberals, but failed. Wilson became Prime Minister of a minority government.

> **KEY POINT**
>
> Heath had lost two elections out of the three since he became leader of the Conservative Party in 1965. In 1975 he was overthrown by Margaret Thatcher.

The Wilson and Callaghan governments, 1974–9

AQA **U3**   Edexcel **U2**
OCR **U1**

The government

With a hung Parliament it was clear that another election would take place soon. Wilson called it in October in 1974, but the result was much the same, giving Labour an overall majority of just three. However, with the support of the Liberals, Labour was able to govern for over four years, even when it lost its overall majority in by-elections. In 1976 Wilson resigned. The Labour Party elected Jim Callaghan to succeed him as leader and Prime Minister.

The European Economic Community

This was Wilson's way of healing the divisions in the party. Labour ministers were allowed to campaign on both sides.

After talks with other European leaders to renegotiate the terms on which Britain had entered the EEC in 1973, Wilson called a referendum. The Labour party was divided on the issue, as it had been when Heath took Britain into Europe. The referendum produced an overwhelming majority in favour of membership, which settled the issue for the time being.

The economy and industrial relations

The economic and industrial relations problems which had destroyed Heath's ministry continued to dominate politics. Wilson began by settling with the miners. He then pursued a voluntary incomes policy (the Social Contract). There were fewer strikes, but higher wage settlements which added to inflation.

Inflation was the immediate problem. The government's deflationary measures in 1975 were not enough to avert a run on the pound in 1976. The Chancellor of the Exchequer, Denis Healey, was forced to seek a loan from the International Monetary Fund (IMF). In return stringent cuts had to be made in public spending. This was regarded as a great humiliation, but in combination with a strict incomes policy, it did succeed in reducing inflation.

Among the more unpleasant results there was uncollected rubbish in the streets.

The trade unions expected a return to normal collective bargaining in 1978. But the government's decision to impose a 5% limit on wage settlements in an attempt to cure inflation led to a confrontation with the unions. The result was the **Winter of Discontent** – strikes by public sector workers.

> **KEY POINT**
>
> The Winter of Discontent in 1978–9 convinced public opinion of the need to curb the power of the trade unions and prepared the ground for Thatcher's trade union reforms.

Devolution

Labour promised elected assemblies for Scotland and Wales in its October 1974 election manifesto. In 1978 bills to this effect were passed, but subject to referenda. In Wales, the majority voted against devolution. In Scotland, there was a majority in favour, but it did not meet the criterion of 40% of the total electorate. Devolution had to wait another two decades. But the anger of the 11 Scottish Nationalist MPs brought the government down.

The Conservative opposition

There were two important developments in the Conservative Party in the second half of the 1970s. Firstly, Heath was overthrown and replaced by **Margaret Thatcher** and secondly Sir Keith Joseph converted Thatcher to a monetarist approach to running the economy.

The 1979 election

Callaghan missed the opportunity to call a general election in the autumn of 1978 when the economy seemed to be in better shape and he would probably have won. By the spring of 1979, after the Winter of Discontent the government was deeply unpopular. In March, the government was defeated by one vote on a motion of no confidence. The Scottish Nationalists and the Liberals voted with the Conservatives. Callaghan was forced to call a general election. It was no surprise that the Conservatives under Thatcher won with a sound majority.

> **KEY POINT**
>
> The Winter of Discontent was the key reason for Callaghan's defeat.

You should be able to explain the significance of each of these dates.

KEY DATES

1964–70	Wilson government (Labour)
1967	Devaluation; Application to join EEC vetoed by de Gaulle
1970	General election; victory for Heath (Conservative)
1973	United Kingdom joins the EEC
1974	February – general election; Hung Parliament: Labour minority government
	October – general election; Small Labour majority
1976	IMF loan
1978–9	Winter of Discontent
1979	General election; Victory for Thatcher

9.4 Mrs Thatcher, 1979–90

LEARNING SUMMARY	**After studying this section you should be able to understand:** ● why Margaret Thatcher won three successive elections ● Thatcher's record in domestic policy ● why Thatcher was overthrown in 1990 ● why Thatcher's policies were so controversial

Three election victories

AQA **U3**   Edexcel **U2**
OCR **U1**

1979 marked a turning point in British political history, inaugurating a period of 18 years of Conservative government. The main reason for the Conservative victory in 1979 was disillusion with the Labour government after the Winter of Discontent. Many working class voters swung to the Conservatives and *The Sun* newspaper may have played a part in this. By 1982, however, the government was very unpopular because of the growth of unemployment and cuts in government expenditure.

In 1982, the political landscape was transformed by the **Falklands War**, which gave Thatcher a huge boost in the opinion polls. In 1983 she called an election. Facing a Labour Party which had swung to the left under Michael Foot, and had been weakened by the defection of some prominent Labour figures to form the Social Democratic Party (SDP) in 1981, she won a convincing victory.

With the economy apparently improving the Conservatives again won a substantial majority in the 1987 election. Voters were still wary of Labour despite the expulsion of the far left (the Militant Tendency) in 1986 by its leader, Neil Kinnock. The alliance between the newly formed SDP and the Liberals was weakened by strained relations between their leaders.

> **KEY POINT**
>
> Thatcher's political dominance was greatly assisted by the Labour Party which had become unelectable in the eyes of the majority of the electors.

Domestic policies

AQA **U3**   Edexcel **U2**
OCR **U1**

The economy: Thatcherism

The key features were monetarism, i.e. reducing the money supply to curb inflation, a belief in free markets and the reduction of the size of the state.

Geoffrey Howe, Chancellor of the Exchequer 1979–83, put these principles into effect.
● Public expenditure was cut.
● Income tax was reduced and VAT increased to compensate for the loss of revenue.
● Interest rates were raised.
● Exchange rate controls were abolished.

The result was a deep recession, leading to a steep rise in unemployment and many company failures. But Thatcher stuck to this policy. She refused to consider state intervention to prop up failing companies. In practice this meant a shift from manufacturing industry to the service sector – a shift in the balance of the economy which hit the old manufacturing areas particularly hard.

Nevertheless, by the mid 1980s inflation had been brought down, the balance of payments was under control and the economy was booming. By 1989 inflation was taking off again. Nigel Lawson, Chancellor of the Exchequer since 1983, advocated joining the Exchange Rate Mechanism (ERM) and this was one of the issues which eventually brought Thatcher down.

> The ERM linked together the exchange rates of all the major European currencies.

KEY POINT

Thatcherism brought about a significant re-balancing of the British economy.

Trade unions

Thatcher saw the trade unions as a major problem. She believed they had too much power, and were undemocratic in the way they were run and in the way they exercised their industrial muscle and were a barrier to economic modernisation. Her battle to curb their powers came to a head in the **miners' strike** of 1984–5. Thatcher won the battle, which paved the way for changes in trade union law. The 1984 Trade Union Act required trade unions to ballot their members before calling a strike and further restrictions followed. By 1991 trade union membership had fallen by a third.

> Thatcher's victory was aided by the stubbornness of the miners' leader, Arthur Scargill.

KEY POINTS

- The defeat of the miners' strike was a turning point in British industrial relations.
- Thatcher's handling of the strike showed steely determination.

Other key features of domestic policy

- **Privatisation** of state-owned assets: Thatcher believed that private enterprise was always more efficient than public control because it involved the discipline of the free market. Important examples were BT, the water authorities, British Gas and the electricity companies. Privatisation served two purposes: it shrank the size of the state and it provided income for the Treasury. But, because some of the privatised enterprises were virtual monopolies, nationalisation had to be replaced by regulation.
- **Deregulation** of financial markets, especially the London Stock Exchange.
- Housing: council house tenants were given the right to buy their houses at a discount (Housing Act 1980). This proved to be very popular – over a million houses had been sold by 1990.
- Health: growing financial pressures on the National Health Service led to the introduction of the internal market in 1990.
- Education: under the Education Reform Act (1988) a national curriculum was introduced and schools were encouraged to opt out of local authority control and receive their funding direct from the government (which also meant government control).

Thatcher's downfall

AQA **U3**   Edexcel **U2**
OCR **U1**

Despite her success in leading the Conservatives to three successive election victories, by the late 1980s Thatcher was losing support in her party.

- She had made many enemies. Her conviction that her policies were the right ones had, from the first, led her to remove opponents from her cabinet.
- The Westland affair led to the resignation of Michael Heseltine in 1986.
- Her increasingly sceptical views on Europe divided the party. In the Bruges speech (1989) she voiced her fear that it was developing into a centralised federal Europe.
- She opposed the ERM as contrary to her free market principles, but pressure from leading members of her cabinet, especially the Chancellor, Nigel Lawson, forced her to agree to it.
- The Community Charge (**poll tax**) was a key factor in Thatcher's fall. It was introduced in Scotland in 1989 and then in England in 1990. It proved to be very unpopular. A mass demonstration in London ended in rioting.
- A strong attack on her by Geoffrey Howe led to a leadership contest and her resignation, to be replaced by John Major.

> It was seen as deeply unfair because rich and poor paid the same amount.

KEY POINT

Towards the end of her prime ministership, Thatcher was so convinced that she was right that she failed to realise the strength of the feeling against her.

Assessment

AQA **U3**   Edexcel **U2**
OCR **U1**

Thatcher was (and is) a very controversial figure. Her admirers point to:
- the increased efficiency of the British economy
- the taming of the trade unions
- more efficient management in privatised companies
- the growth of a property-owning democracy through the sale of council houses.

They also claim that she raised Britain's international prestige (Falklands War, close relationship with President Reagan). For Conservatives she is also the leader who won three general election victories. Her critics point to the price paid for these achievements.
- The destruction of Britain's manufacturing base.
- Greater inequality between rich and poor.
- High unemployment (especially in the old industrial areas).

Critics see her as a divisive figure, most obviously in the way she handled the miners' strike. They claim that her legacy is excessive individualism (she famously claimed that there is no such thing as society). Her scepticism about Europe led to divisions within the Conservative Party which nearly tore it apart in the 1990s.

KEY POINT

Thatcher has been described as a 'conviction politician'. This explains why she succeeded in making fundamental changes in the political landscape and the economy, but it is also why she was eventually overthrown by leading members of her own party, who found her too domineering.

9.5 Major and Blair, 1990–2007

LEARNING SUMMARY	After studying this section you should be able to understand: • the main features of the Major governments • the rise and achievements of 'New Labour'

Major, 1990–7

AQA   U3

John Major was elected by the Conservative Party to replace Thatcher. One of the first things he did was to replace the poll tax with the Council Tax. Although he won the election of 1992 – somewhat against the odds – his authority was constantly under challenge from within his own party. The main cause of dissension was Britain's relationship with Europe. A significant section of the Conservative Party was 'eurosceptic'. Many thought Britain had ceded too many powers to Europe and some advocated complete withdrawal from the European Community.

The Conservatives' claim to economic competence was severely dented in 1992. There was a sharp recession and a deficit in the balance of payments. The conventional remedy for this would have been devaluation, but Major and the Chancellor, Lamont, were determined to defend Britain's membership of the ERM. On **Black Wednesday**, a run on sterling forced them to withdraw. It was a great humiliation, from which the government never really recovered, even though the new Chancellor, Kenneth Clarke, was successful in restoring public finances by 1997.

> **KEY POINT**
>
> The Conservative Party after the overthrow of Thatcher was disintegrating and there was little Major could do to retain the confidence of the electorate.

'New Labour'

AQA   U3

The rise of 'New Labour'

After the 1979 election, Labour moved to the left. When Callaghan resigned as leader in 1980, the Parliamentary Labour Party elected Michael Foot. This victory for the left led to a split, with Roy Jenkins, David Owen and Shirley Williams forming the Social Democratic Party (SDP), which then made an alliance with the Liberals (eventually this produced the Liberal Democrats). Under Foot, Labour was comprehensively beaten in the 1983 election on a left-wing, anti-nuclear, anti-Europe manifesto.

Famously described as 'the longest suicide note in history'.

Foot was succeeded by Neil Kinnock. He made a crucial move towards the revival of Labour in 1986 when he forced through the expulsion of the hard left Militant Tendency from the party. Although Labour was again defeated in the 1987 election, its performance improved. By 1992, Labour had moved sufficiently towards the centre to offer a real challenge to the Conservatives. In the end, however, the electorate did not trust Kinnock, who had originally been a left-winger, though he had now moved towards the centre. Labour suffered from accusations that it would increase taxation.

Kinnock was succeeded by John Smith, who died in 1994. Tony Blair then became leader and pushed ahead with modernising the party. He forced through the abandonment of Clause 4, which committed Labour to nationalisation, and promoted the image of 'New Labour'. His reward came in the landslide victory of 1997.

> **KEY POINT**
>
> The electorate regarded Labour as unelectable until it had modernised and moved to the centre ground of politics.

Blair: 'New Labour' in government

The 1997 election gave '**New Labour**' a landslide victory.
- 'New Labour' appealed to the centre ground in politics.
- The Conservatives were discredited by Black Wednesday and by accusations of sleaze. They were at war with each other over Europe and they were seen as out of touch with the country.

Blair went on to win two further elections in 2001 and 2005, though with declining majorities. Gordon Brown, the Chancellor of the Exchequer, was determined to prove Labour's economic competence. He inherited improving public finances and stuck to existing spending targets for two years. He handed control of interest rates to the Bank of England. By 2001, the public finances were in surplus and the economy was booming. He instituted a national minimum wage and tax credits for poor working families and families with children. Brown's success as Chancellor played a big part in the 2001 election victory. After 2001, the government embarked on a massive boost to spending on education, the health service and welfare benefits.

At the heart of the Blair governments, however, was a dysfunctional relationship between Blair and Brown. This was partly a difference over the way the Welfare State should be run, but also a personal rivalry reaching back to Blair's election to the leadership of the party. Brown believed there had been a deal for him to succeed Blair as Prime Minister.

The polarisation between Blair and Brown played a part in reducing Labour's majority in 2005, but there were two other important factors.
- **The Iraq War**: Blair, who believed in the importance of the 'special relationship' with the USA, joined President Bush in the invasion of Iraq in 2003. It was a divisive decision, based on faulty intelligence.
- The continuing weakness of the Conservative Party. After 1997 the Conservatives had a succession of leaders who failed to regain the trust of the country or restore the party's unity and sense of purpose: William Hague, Ian Duncan Smith and Michael Howard.

Two significant achievements attributable to Blair should be noted.
- The Good Friday Agreement concerning Northern Ireland.
- Devolution for Scotland and Wales was finally implemented.

Blair stepped down as Prime Minister in 2007 and was succeeded by Brown.

> **KEY POINT**
>
> The key flaw in the New Labour governments was the relationship between Blair and Brown.

You should be able to explain the significance of each of these dates.

KEY DATES

1979	General election victory for Thatcher
1982	Falklands War
1983	General election; Thatcher re-elected
1984–5	Miners' strike
1987	Thatcher's third election victory
1990	Thatcher overthrown; Major becomes Prime Minister
1992	General election; Fourth Conservative victory
1994	Blair becomes leader of the Labour Party
1997	Landslide victory for 'New Labour'

9.6 Northern Ireland, 1968–98

LEARNING SUMMARY

After studying this section you should be able to understand:

- the development of the troubles in Northern Ireland from the start of the civil rights movement to the Good Friday Agreement

The troubles in Northern Ireland

OCR   U1

The underlying problem of Northern Ireland dates back to the partition of Ireland in 1921. The boundaries of Northern Ireland – the six counties – left a substantial Catholic minority in a Protestant dominated province. They continued to hope for the eventual incorporation of Northern Ireland within the Republic of Ireland. This was also the declared policy of the Republic itself.

As well as this underlying aspiration, Northern Irish Catholics had three specific grievances.
- In politics, the constituency boundaries were rigged to maximise representation of Protestants.
- In housing there was blatant discrimination against Catholics.
- Employers discriminated against Catholics.

KEY POINT

The underlying problem was discrimination against Catholics.

A **civil rights** movement was founded in 1967 to protest against discrimination. In 1968 a march in Derry was met by police violence. Sectarian violence between Nationalists (Catholic) and Loyalists (Protestant) escalated. Harold Wilson sent in the British army. In Northern Ireland, the Provisional IRA came into existence determined to pursue the dream of a united Ireland by violence. Soon Unionist paramilitaries appeared to oppose them.

The troubles in Northern Ireland worsened in the 1970s. On **Bloody Sunday** 1972 thirteen unarmed men were killed in Derry by British soldiers during an illegal march (another man died later). Edward Heath suspended the Northern Ireland Assembly and introduced direct rule. He then tried to broker a power-sharing agreement (the **Sunningdale Agreement**), but this failed.

Throughout the 1970s and 1980s terrorists on both sides engaged in what became in effect a low-level civil war. The effects were felt in mainland Britain with a number of terrorist attacks. The most notable, perhaps, was the bombing of the Grand Hotel in Brighton during the Conservative Party conference in 1984, which almost succeeded in killing Prime Minister Margaret Thatcher and most of the cabinet.

> **KEY POINT**
>
> There was no chance of a solution while the Provisional IRA believed it could achieve a united Ireland by violence.

British governments were unable to do much more than use the army to preserve some sort of order. The army became a target, accused by the Nationalists of favouring the Protestants. An attempt to achieve a political solution was made in 1985 with the **Anglo-Irish Agreement**, but this failed. It was not until the 1990s, when the leaders of Sinn Fein, the political wing of the IRA, began to think that the terrorist campaign was not succeeding, that progress was made towards a political solution. The key steps were:

- The **Downing Street Declaration** (1993). The British and Irish governments committed themselves to working towards a solution. John Major declared that if both parts of Ireland voted for unification, the British government would not stand in the way. This unlocked the door for negotiations and was probably John Major's finest achievement.
- In 1994 the IRA announced a ceasefire, later matched by a Loyalist ceasefire.
- The **Good Friday Agreement** (1998), provided for an elected assembly and a power-sharing executive. The agreement gave the people of Northern Ireland the right to decide their future by majority vote. The Republic removed its claim to Northern Ireland from its constitution, but was given a share in a council to oversee cross-border cooperation. The details would take years to work out, but nevertheless this was a major achievement for Blair.

> **KEY POINT**
>
> A settlement had eluded British governments for twenty years – but probably that length of time was needed for attitudes to change.

KEY DATES

1968	Foundation of civil rights movement
1972	Bloody Sunday
1973	Sunningdale Agreement
1984	Brighton bombing
1985	Abortive Anglo-Irish Agreement
1993	Downing Street Declaration
1998	Good Friday Agreement

You should be able to explain the significance of each of these dates.

Exam practice questions

1 How successful were the Labour governments of 1945–51 in tackling Britain's post-war economic problems?   **[50]**

2 How far were divisions in the Labour Party responsible for Mrs Thatcher's victories in the elections of 1983 and 1987?   **[50]**

3 How successful were the Wilson governments of 1964–70?   **[50]**

10 The development of democracy in Britain, 1868–1997

The following topics are covered in this chapter:

- The electoral system
- Politics and parties, 1868–1918
- Politics and parties, 1918–45
- Political parties and government, 1945–97
- Government, Parliament and people
- The influence of trade unions and the media

10.1 The electoral system

LEARNING SUMMARY

After studying this section you should be able to understand:

- the development of the electoral system since 1867
- the relationship between the electoral system and the two-party system
- the importance of the women's suffrage movement in the development of democracy

The franchise and elections

OCR **U4** WJEC **U4**
Edexcel **U2**

In the mid nineteenth century Britain had a parliamentary system of government, but it was not democratic. The franchise was restricted in the counties to £10 copyholders and £50 leaseholders and in the boroughs to £10 householders. Although the worst anomalies of rotten and pocket boroughs had been eliminated in 1832, there were still a number of small boroughs returning two members to Parliament, while some larger towns were not represented.

- **The Second Reform Act (1867)** added £12 ratepayers (£14 in Scotland) to the county franchise, but the major change was in the boroughs, where the vote was given to all male householders and £10 lodgers. As a result one in three males had the vote but no women. The new voters were predominantly from the urban working class. There was also a redistribution of seats – 52 borough seats were abolished; 25 were re-allocated to counties; 19 to existing or newly created boroughs and seven to Scotland. An important feature was that Birmingham, Leeds, Liverpool and Manchester became three-member boroughs.

> This was important for allowing the new electors to exercise their votes independently.

- **The Secret Ballot Act (1872)** ended the system of voting in public and reduced bribery and intimidation in elections.
- **The Corrupt Practices Act (1883)** laid down limits for election expenses and prescribed penalties for bribery and corruption in elections.

The 1884 Reform Act extended the vote to working class men in the counties.

- **The Reform and Redistribution Acts (1884–5)** introduced a uniform franchise for counties and boroughs – male householders and £10 lodgers. The electorate was increased to 5.7 million, but about 40% of men were still excluded by this definition. There was a major redistribution of seats. Previously most constituencies had returned two MPs to Parliament. Except in a few big cities they were split into single-member constituencies.
- **The Parliament Act (1911)** limited the powers of the House of Lords and reduced the maximum interval between general elections from seven years to five. In the same year payment for MPs was introduced.

This meant a mass electorate, including women, for the first time.

- **The Representation of the People Act (1918)** gave the vote to all men over 21 and women over 30. The electorate was now over 21 million. There was a redistribution of seats to achieve equality of size between constituencies.
- **The Equal Franchise Act (1928)** gave the vote to women over 21. This meant that Britain finally had universal suffrage, with men and women having the vote on equal terms.

> **KEY POINT**
>
> Between 1868 and 1928 the electorate had been expanded from a minority of men to include all adults of both sexes and so government by the middle and upper classes had given way to democracy.

- **The Representation of the People Act (1948)** abolished plural voting (the right of people with property in two constituencies to vote in both). Postal voting was introduced. Seats were redistributed in accordance with the recommendations of the Boundary Commission set up in 1944. Boundary changes have been made at intervals since then.
- **The Representation of the People Act (1969)** lowered the voting age to 18.

Elections and the two-party system

OCR **U4**

For most of the period 1868–1997 British elections have been dominated by two parties. Before the First World War elections were essentially a contest between the Liberal and Conservative parties, with the added complication of the Irish Home Rule Party and, from 1906, the nascent Labour Party. After the war the southern Irish members disappeared as a result of the partition of Ireland.

The rise of Labour and the decline of the Liberals resulted in a three-way election in 1923 and a hung Parliament in 1929. Although the 1931 election, held in the shadow of the Great Depression, almost wiped out Labour, the 1930s was still an era of two-party politics – a National Government which was essentially Conservative facing a Labour opposition. From 1945 to the 1970s there was never more than a handful of MPs who were not either Labour or Conservative (the Ulster Unionists voted with the Conservatives). From the mid-1970s, however, support for other parties – Liberals and Nationalists – grew, but this was not reflected in election results. In 1983 Labour won 209 seats with 27.6% of the votes while the Liberal/SDP Alliance won only 23 seats with 25.4% of the votes. This was the consequence of the 'first past the post' electoral system, but while this continued to suit the two dominant parties calls for proportional representation fell on deaf ears.

> **KEY POINT**
>
> The 'first past the post' system results in a squeeze on third parties and thus produces a two-party system.

Two other developments in the 1970s should be noted.

- In 1973 the Conservatives took the United Kingdom into the EEC. In 1975 the Labour government which came into office in 1974 held a referendum on continued membership. This resulted in a 'yes' vote. This was the first (and so far the only) national referendum, though there have been local ones in Scotland, Wales and Northern Ireland.
- The 1970s saw a rise in support for Scottish and Welsh nationalism. In October 1974 the Scottish won eleven seats. As a result devolution schemes were proposed for Scotland and Wales, but referendums failed to produce the level of support required by the legislation.

The women's suffrage movement

OCR **U4**   Edexcel **U2**

The extension of votes to working class men in 1867 and 1884 raised the question of allowing women to vote. John Stuart Mill proposed this in the debates on the 1867 Reform Act. The late nineteenth century saw some movement towards improving the position of women. Girls' schools and women's colleges at Oxford and Cambridge were founded. In 1882 the Married Women's Property Act gave married women the right to hold property in their own name. Suffrage societies were formed in many areas in the 1870s and 1880s. The National Union of Women's Suffrage Societies (founded 1897) and the Women's Social and Political Union (WSPU, founded 1903) formed powerful pressure groups.

Most Liberals favoured votes for women, but some feared that women were more likely to vote Conservative.

It also made it difficult for the government to agree without seeming weak.

The election of the Liberals in 1906 gave hope to both groups and the WSPU drew a great deal of attention to the issue by its increasingly militant tactics. There were, however, powerful forces working against the women. Ideas about the role of women in the family and the community, which today would be regarded as prejudice, were deep-rooted and sincerely held. The issue was tied up with the question of granting the vote to the 40% of men who still could not vote. The militancy of the WSPU convinced some men that women were not fit to have the vote. Asquith, the Liberal Prime Minister, stalled as long as he could and the issue had still not been resolved in 1914.

> **KEY POINT**
>
> The pre-war suffrage movements failed to achieve their objective, but in 1918, in recognition of the contribution they had made to the war effort, women over the age of 30 were given the vote. But at the same time it was given to men over 21.

The first woman MP was elected in 1918, but progress towards equality in other areas of life, such as employment and pay, was slow. It was not until 1970 that the Equal Pay Act was passed, followed in 1975 by the Sex Discrimination Act.

10.2 Politics and parties, 1868–1918

LEARNING SUMMARY	After studying this section you should be able to understand:
	• how the expansion of the electorate affected the political parties in this period

The political parties

OCR **U4**   WJEC **U1**

> From 1867 Birmingham had three MPs, but electors had only two votes, so they had to be carefully organised to use them to maximum effect.

The changes in the electoral system led to the development of party organisation. In Birmingham, **Joseph Chamberlain** set up a network of ward organisations, partly to make the most effective use of Liberal votes. From this developed the National Liberal Federation, which provided help for constituency parties in fighting elections.

The Conservatives set up the National Union of Conservative Associations in 1867, following this in 1870 with the appointment of a National Agent (J.E.Gorst) and the establishment of Conservative Central Office.

Electoral changes also forced both parties to seek support from all classes. The Liberals gained support across the social range from Whig aristocrats to working class radicals. A few trade unionists were elected as Lib-Labs. The importance the Conservatives attached to winning working class support is shown by the setting up of Conservative working men's associations and clubs. In the 1880s Lord Randolph Churchill founded the Primrose League, which had two million members by 1910. Some historians would claim that Disraeli created the modern Conservative Party by associating it with '**Tory democracy**', a phrase actually coined after his death by Lord Randolph Churchill. The growth of working

> Especially in Lancashire.

class Conservatism was an important feature of late Victorian politics.

The growth in the size of the electorate made it necessary for political leaders to devote much more effort to gaining support in the country through election campaigns. Gladstone's victory in 1868 was achieved partly by a vigorous campaign in which he spoke all over the country and his Midlothian Campaign was equally important in the 1880 election.

> **KEY POINT**
>
> In response to the widening of the franchise, the political parties had to develop national and local organisations and draw up programmes to win the support of the electors.

From 1868 to 1886 politics was dominated by Gladstone and Disraeli. An important change in party politics occurred in 1886, when Gladstone's Home Rule Bill for Ireland split the Liberal Party with 93 Liberals voting against the bill. In 1895, most of them, led by Joseph Chamberlain, joined the Conservative Party, which then became the Conservative and Unionist Party. This party in its turn was split in 1903 by Chamberlain's tariff reform campaign. Meanwhile, after the retirement of Gladstone the Liberal Party began to develop in a new direction with the emergence of '**New Liberalism**'. The New Liberals advocated social reform and state intervention in the interests of national efficiency and social justice. Gladstonian Liberalism believed in a cheap, but efficient state, with much more emphasis on self-help. These two different interpretations of liberalism contained the seeds of later Liberal decline, but the campaign against tariff reform brought them together to win a convincing victory in the 1906 election.

The foundation of the Labour Party

The granting of the vote to working class men suggested the possibility of a separate party to represent the interests of labour. The leaders of the New Unions which developed from the 1880s advocated political action to improve social conditions by legislation and government action. The formation of the Independent Labour Party (ILP) by **Keir Hardie** in 1893 was an important step, but the key development came in 1900 when the Labour Representation Committee was set up, with representatives from the trade unions, the ILP the Fabian Society and the Social Democratic Federation (SDF). This became the Labour Party in 1906.

> The first Secretary of the Labour Party was Keir Hardie.

The development of a more democratic electoral system also led to the formation of extra parliamentary pressure groups. The Fabian Society and the SDF were two such groups, but there were also temperance societies (particularly influential among nonconformist Liberals), peace societies and women's suffrage societies. Joseph Chamberlain's tariff reform campaign, which he started in 1903, may also be regarded as a pressure group.

> You should be able to explain the significance of each of these dates.

KEY DATES	
1868–74	Gladstone's first ministry
1874–80	Disraeli's second ministry
1880–5	Gladstone's second ministry
1886	Liberal Party split over Home Rule
1900	Formation of Labour Representation Committee
1906	Liberal election victory
1911	Parliament Act

10.3 Politics and parties, 1918–45

LEARNING SUMMARY

After studying this section you should be able to understand:
- the decline of the Liberals and the rise of the Labour Party
- the development of the Conservative Party in the 1920s and its role in the National Government in the 1930s

The decline of the Liberals and the rise of Labour

OCR **U4** WJEC **U2**

The First World War led to a re-shaping of the party system. In 1915 Asquith formed a coalition, but he was widely regarded as the wrong man to lead the country in a war. In 1916, he was overthrown and replaced by Lloyd George. The bitterness this caused ensured that the Liberal Party would never again hold office, though many historians would argue that this was only one, and perhaps not the most fundamental, reason for the decline of the Liberals. At the end of the war, Lloyd George was re-elected as Prime Minister with the support of the Conservatives and the Coalition Liberals. By 1922 the Conservatives felt they had no more use for him and he was overthrown. There was then a short period of three-party politics, but by 1924 it was becoming apparent that Labour was replacing the Liberals as the alternative to the Conservatives.

The divisions among the Liberals facilitated the rise of **Labour**, but perhaps it would have happened anyway as a result of the enfranchisement of the working classes. At the end of the war the Representation of the People Act produced a genuine mass electorate. In 1922 Labour became the official opposition and in 1924, after an election which gave no party a majority, Ramsay MacDonald formed the first Labour government. It depended on Liberal support and lasted for less than a year, but it demonstrated that Labour was now the alternative to the Conservatives. The formation of a second Labour ministry in 1929 – again a minority government, but this time with the largest number of seats in a hung Parliament – underlined this.

> In the 1929 election Labour won 288 seats, the Conservatives 260 and the Liberals 59, so no party had an overall majority.

KEY POINT

It can be argued that with universal franchise and a large working class, the rise of Labour was inevitable and therefore the decline of the Liberals was equally inevitable.

The Conservatives and the National Government

OCR **U4**   WJEC **U2**

These developments in the Liberal and Labour parties obviously benefited the Conservatives. They were the dominant partners in Lloyd George's coalition government (1918–22) and then held office themselves until 1929, except for the brief interlude of the first Labour ministry. But this might not have happened if the Conservatives themselves had not adjusted to the new era of the mass electorate. They had a solid basis of upper and middle class support and by the 1920s had become clearly the party of business. Their leaders, Bonar Law and Baldwin, were both industrialists rather than landowners. They also attracted substantial support from the working classes, building on the foundations laid by the Conservative working men's associations and the Primrose League. Baldwin took pains to present himself as an 'ordinary' man. Under his leadership the Conservatives rejected the notion of class war and accepted the need for government to engage in social reform and management of the economy.

> He also made good use of the new medium of radio.

The National Government

The Great Depression cut across the development of the party system. The collapse of the Labour ministry in 1931 led to the formation of the National government with MacDonald as Prime Minister and Baldwin as his deputy. The National government was overwhelmingly Conservative. In the 1931 election, Labour was reduced to 52 MPs, but it still had one-third of the vote and gradually rebuilt its strength. The Second World War brought a suspension of normal politics with the formation of the wartime coalition. The inclusion of a number of Labour ministers in this was important in preparing Labour for office.

> Most Labour MPs regarded MacDonald as a traitor, especially after this catastrophic election result.

> You should be able to explain the significance of each of these dates.

KEY DATES

1916	Lloyd George replaces Asquith – split in Liberal Party
1918–22	Lloyd George Coalition
1924	First Labour Ministry
1924–9	Baldwin's Conservative government
1929–31	Second Labour Ministry
1931–40	National government

10.4 Political parties and government, 1945–97

<table>
<tr>
<td>**LEARNING SUMMARY**</td>
<td>**After studying this section you should be able to understand:**

● the changing fortunes of each of the three main political parties between 1945 and 1997</td>
</tr>
</table>

Labour

OCR   U4

Attlee and Gaitskell

The 1945 election not only marked a reversion to normal party politics, but produced a sweeping victory for Labour under Attlee – the first time it had won an overall majority. The result demonstrated that electors blamed the Conservatives, who had dominated the National governments, for the social evils of the 1930s, especially unemployment, as well as for foreign policy failures. Labour offered a more wholehearted commitment to social reform – full employment, a housing drive and a National Health Service.

Labour's hope that, with a mass electorate, it was now the natural party of government were, however, to be dashed. It gained widespread credit for establishing the Welfare State, but its belief in government planning of the economy, of which nationalisation was part, was less popular. Nationalisation of key sectors of the economy was accepted, though the results did not arouse great enthusiasm among either workers in the nationalised industries or consumers. But, by 1951, electors were questioning both the need for further nationalisation and the competence of the government in managing the economy. Controls and austerity were increasingly unpopular.

Labour's defeat in 1951 opened a debate in the party which continued for the rest of the century. The left believed that Labour should commit itself to a wholeheartedly socialist programme of nationalisation, state control of the economy and redistributive taxation – essentially waging a class war. To this was added from the late 1950s nuclear disarmament. The more moderate wing of the party argued that electoral success would only come by making Labour attractive to middle class voters, as well as traditional Labour supporters. These divisions helped to keep Labour out of power from 1951 to 1964. Gaitskell, leader from 1955 to 1963, failed to persuade the party to water down its commitment to further nationalisation.

Wilson and after

He promised to do so through 'the white heat of technology'.

In 1964 Labour regained office under Harold Wilson, who promised to provide managerial efficiency in modernising the British economy. A key element in this was the reform of industrial relations, but opposition from the trade unions forced the government to abandon its plans. This, along with the devaluation of the pound in 1967, left electors feeling that Labour was no more able to solve Britain's economic problems than the Conservatives. Labour lost the election of 1970.

Edward Heath's Conservative government (1970–4) had equal difficulty in tackling the problems of the economy and industrial relations. Not surprisingly, the two elections of 1974 showed that the electorate had no real confidence in either party. Labour returned to office in February 1974 without a majority. It gained a small majority in a second general election in October, but lost it again in by-elections. It was overtaken by an economic crisis resulting from a combination of Britain's poor economic record and the 1973–4 oil crisis.

> **KEY POINT**
>
> Labour's claim that its links with the trade unions would enable it to handle them more successfully than the Conservatives was undermined by a series of strikes (the 'Winter of Discontent') in 1978–9.

Labour was decisively defeated in 1979. The left, which believed that Labour had been defeated because it had not been socialist enough, gained control of the party. Michael Foot, who was elected leader in 1980, led it to a disastrous defeat in the 1983 election. Some Labour moderates defected and formed the Social Democratic Party (SDP). Neil Kinnock, who replaced Foot in 1983, drove out the militant extremists and strove to return Labour to the centre ground. By 1992, it was able to offer a real challenge to the Conservatives.

This process continued with the election of Blair as leader in 1994. He forced through the abandonment of Clause 4, the commitment to nationalisation. In 1997 he won a landslide victory.

> **KEY POINT**
>
> Labour had regained public confidence sufficiently to win an overwhelming majority over a demoralised Conservative Party.

The Conservatives

OCR **U4**

After their unexpected defeat in 1945, the Conservatives rebuilt their organisation and developed the idea of 'One Nation' Conservatism, which accepted the Welfare State. They also accepted most of Labour's nationalisation measures and the commitment to full employment. The 1950s and 1960s were therefore a period of **consensus politics**. The Conservatives won three successive elections in 1951, 1955 and 1959 because they appeared to offer greater unity and competence than Labour, which was divided by the issue of nuclear disarmament. By 1964, however, Britain's sluggish economic performance cast doubt on the government's competence. At the same time as it was hit by the Profumo scandal and a squabble over the succession to Macmillan.

Consensus politics: the two parties agreed on the main social and economic policies.

Hence the charge that the period 1951–64 was 'thirteen wasted years'.

The Conservatives returned to power in 1970 under Edward Heath, who was elected leader by a process more in keeping with a democratic party than that which had produced Douglas-Home in 1963. Heath was troubled, and eventually brought down, by the problem of the trade unions – a problem which also played a major part in bringing down the Labour governments which preceded and followed.

Monetarism: an economic policy which aims to control inflation by controlling the money supply.

Following their defeat in 1974 the Conservatives looked for a new leader and new policies. With the election of Mrs Thatcher as leader in 1975 and as Prime Minister in 1979, they adopted monetarism as their economic policy. Government spending was cut, nationalised industries were privatised and trade union law was reformed. These policies, known as **Thatcherism**, combined with Thatcher's handling of the Falklands crisis, the popular sale of council houses and the turmoil in the Labour Party, enabled the Conservatives to win the 1983 and 1987 elections. Thatcher's increasingly authoritarian attitude towards her colleagues and her refusal to back down over the highly unpopular poll tax led to her overthrow in 1990.

She was succeeded by John Major, who, contrary to expectations, won the general election in 1992, but found himself saddled with a party divided over Europe. The authority of his government was severely dented by a sterling crisis on '**Black Wednesday**' in 1992. Despite an attempt by Major in 1995 to restore his authority by resigning as leader and seeking re-election, the Conservative Party was increasingly fractious. In the 1997 election it was overwhelmingly defeated.

> **KEY POINT**
>
> The 1979 election marked a turning point in post-war politics. Thatcherism represented the end of the consensus which had characterised the policies of the two parties in the previous thirty years.

The Liberals

OCR   U4

Liberal candidates often came second in individual constituencies.

The Liberals never recovered from the split between Asquith and Lloyd George. They came together sufficiently during the 1920s to gain 59 seats in 1929, but were again divided by the formation of the National government. Half of the Liberals elected in 1931 supported the National government. The independent Liberals were reduced to 33 MPs. In post-war elections the electoral system meant that they were squeezed between the two main parties and were reduced to six MPs by 1951. Lacking the support of either business or the trade unions, they were at a considerable financial disadvantage. The number of Liberal MPs did not reflect the number of votes they gained even when their fortunes were at their lowest ebb. Not surprisingly, one of their main demands was proportional representation. In 1974 the Liberals' share of the vote increased to 19%, but they still gained only fourteen seats.

In the 1980s the Liberals formed an alliance with the SDP, which had split away from Labour in 1981. The Liberal-SDP Alliance won 23 seats in 1983, 22 in 1987 and, as the Liberal Democrats, 20 in 1992.

You should be able to explain the significance of each of these dates.

> **KEY DATES**
>
> | | |
> |---|---|
> | 1945 | Election; Labour victory |
> | 1951–64 | Conservative ministries under Churchill, Eden and Macmillan |
> | 1964 | General election: Victory for Labour led by Wilson. |
> | 1970 | General election: Wilson defeated by Heath |
> | 1974–9 | Labour ministries under Wilson and Callaghan |
> | 1979 | General election: Thatcher becomes Prime Minister |
> | 1990 | Thatcher replaced by Major |
> | 1997 | General election: Labour victory |

10.5 Government, Parliament and people

LEARNING SUMMARY

After studying this section you should be able to understand:

- how the powers of the House of Lords were restricted, making it subordinate to the House of Commons
- the growth of the power of the executive

Parliament

OCR   U4

The House of Lords

Over the period since 1868 the House of Commons has become the dominant house. In the nineteenth century the House of Lords was equal in power to the House of Commons. Between 1886 and 1892, and again between 1895 and 1902, the Prime Minister was a peer, Lord Salisbury. The widening of the franchise in 1867 and 1884 meant that a House elected by 60% of the adult male population could be overruled by a hereditary House. This was particularly galling to Liberals since the House of Lords had a permanent Conservative majority. In 1893 the Lords rejected the Second Home Rule Bill and between 1906 and 1908 they rejected several Liberal bills, despite the huge majority won by the Liberals in 1906.

> The Conservatives encouraged them to do so, hence the nickname 'Mr. Balfour's poodle'.

The issue came to a head over Lloyd George's 1909 budget. After two general elections in 1910, the powers of the Lords were curtailed by the **Parliament Act** of 1911. They were not allowed to reject a money bill and could only delay other bills for two years. This meant that the will of the elected House would ultimately prevail. In 1949 the delaying power was reduced to one year. By the second half of the twentieth century it was unthinkable for the Prime Minister to be in the Lords. When the Earl of Home became Prime Minister in 1963 he renounced his peerage and returned to the Commons. The influence of the Lords, as distinct from its power, was enhanced by the **Life Peerages Act** of 1958, but demands for reform of a House still dominated by hereditary peers had not been met by 1997.

> **KEY POINT**
>
> The development of a more democratic House of Commons made the power of the hereditary House of Lords anomalous.

The Executive

OCR   U4

Over the period since 1868 the government has gained increasing control over the House of Commons and within the government the power of the Prime Minister has grown. As far back as 1882, in the face of obstruction by Irish Home Rule MPs, the government introduced the closure to limit the length of debates. By the second half of the twentieth century, party whips maintained strict discipline over their MPs, with the ultimate sanction of expulsion from the Parliamentary party. This could mean deselection as a candidate and the end of a political career at the next election. To counter the loss of power of ordinary MPs, select committees of backbench MPs were set up in 1980 to monitor the work of government departments.

The basis of the Prime Minister's authority throughout the period rested on two powers: **patronage** (the right to appoint or dismiss ministers) and the right to decide on the timing of a general election. The creation of a Cabinet Secretariat by Lloyd George in 1916 gave the Prime Minister's office more effective control over other departments of government than had been enjoyed by nineteenth century Prime Ministers. In the later twentieth century Prime Ministers have increasingly relied on their own advisers, reducing the collective influence of the cabinet. Wilson's advisers were known as his 'kitchen cabinet'. The importance of the Prime Minister's power of patronage was dramatically illustrated in 1962 when Macmillan sacked seven cabinet ministers in what came to be called '**the night of the long knives**'. It was Macmillan, too, who first used television to good political effect. The media focus on the Prime Minister since then is another factor in the growth of what some believe to be a more 'presidential' style of prime ministership.

The power of the state

Compared with 1868, the size and power of the state by 1992 had increased enormously. Three main factors lie behind this.

- Firstly, the two world wars required governments to take extraordinary powers such as conscription, direction of labour, control of industry and transport. Some of this increased power was retained when the wars were over.
- The second factor has been the Welfare State, with its origins in the 'social service state' created by the Liberal government of 1905–15.
- The third factor was the nationalisation programme of the 1945–51 Labour government, though this was substantially reversed by the Thatcher government.

Ponting had released information about the Falklands War which was covered by the Act. He claimed that what he had done was 'in the public interest' and the jury agreed.

Another aspect of the growth of government power (and of reduced accountability) is the **Official Secrets Act**, which prevents unauthorised disclosure of official information and is binding on all government employees. The purpose of the original act in 1911 was to combat spying, but its effect was to keep much of the work of the government secret. It was successfully challenged in 1986 by Clive Ponting, but a new Official Secrets Act in 1989 closed off the defence he used.

10.6 The influence of trade unions and the media

LEARNING SUMMARY	**After studying this section you should be able to understand:** • the changing role of the trade unions in political life • the effects of the growth of mass media on British democracy

The trade unions

OCR   **U4**

The political influence of the trade unions in the nineteenth century was limited. The **New Model unions,** founded in the middle of the century, were mainly concerned to improve their members' wages and conditions of work and to provide insurance against sickness and unemployment. Their main political interest was in combating legal threats to their activities. To co-ordinate their activities they founded the Trades Union Congress in 1868. Since many of their members gained the vote in 1867, both Gladstone and Disraeli enacted legislation in their interest. A few trade unionists were elected as Lib-Lab MPs from the 1870s onwards.

The leaders of the '**New Unions**' formed in the 1890s were more politically minded, arguing that political action was necessary to improve social conditions. As a result the trade unions played a key role in the formation of the Labour Party. The Taff Vale Case (1901) convinced many previously sceptical union leaders that it was in their interests to have a political party to represent labour. The success of the infant Labour Party in persuading the Liberals to pass the Trade Disputes Act (1906) and the Trade Union Act (1913) seemed to confirm this. The Trade Disputes Act reversed the Taff Vale judgment. The Trade Union Act arose out of the Osborne judgment which ruled that unions could not use their funds to support a political party. This was a threat to the very existence of the Labour Party. The Trade Union Act allowed them to do so, on the condition that individual members of the union could opt out of paying that part of the subscription. The link between Labour and the unions was strengthened by the decision of the mineworkers in 1909 to give their support to the party.

The formation of a political party to represent labour and trade union interests did not prevent serious industrial trouble breaking out. There was a series of strikes in 1910–2 and further industrial trouble in 1920–1. Both sets of disputes led to violence and confrontation with the government. Some trade unionists were attracted by **syndicalism** and argued that workers should use the strike weapon for political ends.

> *Syndicats* is French for Trade Unions; syndicalism meant taking direct action, i.e. strikes, and even violence, to seize power.

In 1914 the miners, the transport workers and the railwaymen made an informal agreement to support each other (the Triple Alliance). This created a danger that they could bring the country to a standstill, but in 1921, when there was widespread industrial unrest, the Triple Alliance broke down. In 1926, however, when the miners were faced with further wage cuts and longer hours, the other unions supported them in the **General Strike**. Baldwin's Conservative government saw this as a threat to the democratically elected government and organised counter-measures. The TUC itself belatedly realised that the General Strike could lead to revolution and backed down. Many of its leaders had never wanted a general strike in the first place.

The failure of the General Strike weakened the trade union movement. In any case in an era of high unemployment trade union activity was difficult to sustain. Moreover, although the support of trade unionists enabled Labour to emerge as the largest party in the 1929 election, the collapse of the second Labour ministry in 1931 left both the party and the trade unions weakened throughout the 1930s.

With the election of Labour in 1945 the trade union movement at last had a government sympathetic to its aims and ideas. For much of the next thirty years the unions were at the height of their power. Under the constitution of the Labour Party they played the key role in formulating party policy. MPs, sponsored by trade unions, ensured that their views were heard in the Commons. Whichever party was in power, gaining their co-operation seemed to be essential for successful management of the economy. At the same time their activities seemed increasingly, especially to Conservatives, to be one of the causes of Britain's economic decline. Thus the Conservative victory in 1979 can be ascribed partly to the series of strikes known as the '**Winter of Discontent**' in 1978–9.

> At party conferences the big unions had 'block votes' based on their membership.

Thatcher's defeat of the miners' strike in 1984–5 opened the way for a major reform of trade union law. Even before the strike collapsed, the 1984 Trade Union Act imposed a number of restrictions on unions, including a requirement to ballot members before a strike.

> **KEY POINT**
>
> Thatcher abandoned the practice of consulting the unions over economic policy and curbed their activities by enacting new trade union laws.

The media

OCR   U4

In the mid-nineteenth century newspaper readership was confined to the educated middle class. There was no national press, but most provincial towns had their own newspapers. The London papers were naturally the ones which had most influence, but they concentrated mainly on factual reporting, e.g. detailed accounts of parliamentary proceedings.

The extension of the franchise, the expansion of elementary education and the growth of a **popular press** went hand-in-hand. The 1867 Reform Act was followed by the 1870 Education Act, which made elementary education available to all. Consequently most children attained a basic standard of literacy. This development lay behind the foundation of the *Daily Mail* by Alfred Harmsworth, later Lord Northcliffe, in 1896. This was the first mass circulation newspaper and soon reached a readership of over a million – mainly lower middle class rather than working class. It was written in a style to appeal to people with limited education and it aimed to capture attention by turning the news into stories or even making news by looking for 'scoops'. It also encouraged popular prejudices which it believed would help to sell the paper, e.g. fostering hostility to the French and the Boers in the 1890s and to the Germans in the years before 1914. It was soon followed by other newspapers, notably the *Daily Express* (1900), the *Daily Mirror* (1904) and the *Daily Herald* (1912). The popular press became the main means by which the voters enfranchised in 1867 and 1884 gained their political knowledge and often their political opinions.

> Some provincial newspapers, especially the *Manchester Guardian*, were important for their influence on middle-class voters.

The role of the popular press as opinion formers became perhaps even more important with the creation of a mass electorate in 1918 and has remained important ever since, as shown by the claim of *The Sun* to have won the 1992 election for the Conservatives. Two important points should be noted. First, the majority of the mass circulation newspapers throughout the twentieth century supported the Conservatives. Second, their circulation gave their proprietors the potential to exercise great political influence and some, e.g. Beaverbrook, exercised it to the full.

> Proprietor of the *Daily Express*.

The extension of the vote to a mass electorate in 1918 almost coincided with the rise of a new medium of mass communication, **radio**. In 1922 the British Broadcasting Company (BBC) was formed and in 1927 it became a public corporation, the BBC. By 1939, 90% of households had a 'wireless'. The BBC became an important source of news and politicians soon realised that radio provided a direct means of communication with voters in their own homes. Baldwin proved particularly adept at using it, while Lloyd George and Ramsay MacDonald, who were accustomed to addressing large meetings, were less able to adapt their style. Churchill's use of radio to boost national morale during the Second World War was masterly.

In the 1950s the rapid spread of **television** produced an even more powerful vehicle of mass communication. The first election in which television played a significant part was in 1959 and the first major politician to make effective use of it was Macmillan. From the 1960s, the ability to perform effectively on television was a vital attribute for the successful politician. By the end of the period, questions were being raised about whether parliament was being devalued by the attention politicians gave to television.

> **KEY POINT**
>
> The rise of the mass media was essential for the development of democracy, but also gave the media great power.

Exam practice questions

1 Examine the reasons for the changing fortunes of the Liberal and Labour parties in the period 1868–1997. **[60]**

2 Examine the reasons for the changing influence of trade unions in British politics during the period 1868–1997. **[60]**

3 How far has the influence of the media in British politics changed during the period 1868–1997? **[60]**

11 France, 1814–71

The following topics are covered in this chapter:

- The restored Bourbons and the Orleans Monarchy
- Napoleon III
- The Third Republic

11.1 The restored Bourbons and the Orleans Monarchy

LEARNING SUMMARY

After studying this section you should be able to understand:

- how far the restoration of the monarchy under Louis XVIII was a success
- the reign of Charles X and the reasons for his overthrow in 1830
- the rule of Louis Philippe

Louis XVIII

AQA	U3	CCEA	AS2
OCR	U1		

Louis XVIII was restored in 1814 by the victorious allies after the abdication of Napoleon I. He was, therefore, to many Frenchmen the symbol of defeat in the Napoleonic Wars. The enthusiastic reception given to Napoleon when he returned to France from Elba underlined this. Louis had to flee and was then restored again by the allies after Waterloo. To make matters worse for the restored monarchy, the allies then imposed on France a harsher treaty, including an indemnity and an army of occupation.

Political divisions in France

The revolutionary period left France politically divided between republicans, Bonapartists and royalists. Republicans saw the monarchy as a symbol of a hated social and political system. They believed that only a republic would guarantee political liberty. They were also largely anti-clerical. Bonapartism was relatively weak after Waterloo, but it became a powerful element in French politics later in the century, when many Frenchmen began to look back to the Napoleonic era as a period when France had dominated Europe and had a strong, centralised, progressive government. Royalists saw the return of the monarchy as offering stability against the possibility of revolution and as the best way to restore normal relations with the rest of Europe.

> Make sure you understand these divisions. They are fundamental for the understanding of nineteenth century French politics.

The Charter

Louis XVIII had the good sense to realise that the monarchy must win the loyalty of the French nation. He began by issuing the **Charter** in 1814. He promised to rule as a constitutional monarch in co-operation with an assembly elected on a narrow middle class franchise. He guaranteed freedom of speech and of the press, religious toleration and equality before the law. Thus, he made it clear that there was to be no return to the *ancien régime*. He also won the support of the middle classes by a prudent financial policy and kept the Napoleonic legal and administrative systems.

Louis and the 'Ultras'

Nevertheless Louis was subject to much pressure to restore at least some features of pre-Revolutionary France. The restored monarchy brought with it a host of émigré nobles who wanted to recover their land and their social and political power. In 1815 the **'Ultras'**, who favoured these policies, won a majority in the Assembly and proceeded to carry out a purge of the Bonapartists (the 'White Terror'). Louis realised that this was a mistake and checked it by appointing new ministers, first Richelieu and then Decazes, both of whom pursued moderate policies. In 1820, however, after the murder of the Duc de Berry, Decazes was attacked by the Ultras and resigned. The Ultras then persuaded the king to reduce some of the freedoms granted in the Charter, especially freedom of the press. In 1821 he appointed **Villèle**, a leading Ultra, as Prime Minister.

Foreign affairs

At the Congress of Aix-la-Chapelle (1818) the army of occupation was withdrawn and France was admitted to the **Quintuple Alliance**. Credit for this goes to Richelieu.

In 1823, following the Congress of Verona, the French army suppressed a revolt in Spain, with the approval of Russia and Austria, but against the opposition of Britain.

Charles X

AQA	U3	CCEA	AS2
OCR	U1		

Compare the attitudes and personalities of Charles X and Louis XVIII. Remember that Louis died in his bed, while Charles was overthrown in a revolution.

The triumph of the Ultras came when **Charles X** succeeded Louis in 1824. With Villèle as his chief minister, he pursued reactionary and clerical policies. The Law of Indemnity provided for compensation to be paid to émigré nobles who had lost their estates during the Revolution. Press censorship, which had briefly been relaxed in 1824, was tightened. The religious ceremonies he insisted on at his coronation alarmed anti-clericals, who were further upset when the church was given control over education. Even more extreme was the Law of Sacrilege, which prescribed savage penalties for irreligious behaviour. These measures were so unpopular that after the election of 1827 Charles had to dismiss Villèle.

In 1829, however, Charles appointed one of the most extreme of the Ultras, **Polignac**, as his chief minister. The result was a clash with the Chamber of Deputies. A general election produced an even more hostile Chamber. Polignac then issued the **Ordinances of St Cloud**, dissolving the new chamber before it met and reducing the already tiny electorate by three-quarters. This virtually destroyed the Charter of 1814. Economic hardship gave the liberals who protested against Polignac's measures the support of the working classes in Paris. In July 1830 revolution erupted and Charles was overthrown.

> **KEY POINT**
>
> Louis XVIII ruled as a constitutional monarch and tried to heal the divisions in post-Napoleonic France. Charles X pursued right-wing policies which appeared to be an attempt to restore the pre-revolutionary monarchy.

The July Monarchy

AQA **U3**   CCEA **AS2**
OCR **U1**

The restored Bourbons had ruled by divine right, so this was an important change.

The revolution of 1830 had been a spontaneous uprising against Charles X. The rebels had no plans for replacing him. In this confused situation a liberal journalist, Adolphe Thiers, took the lead and the outcome was that the crown was offered to Louis Philippe, head of the House of Orleans, a junior branch of the Bourbon family. The offer was made by the Chamber of Deputies, so in effect Louis Philippe was elected king.

Louis Philippe, the 'Citizen King'

Consider why Louis Philippe was called the 'Citizen King'.

Despite his aristocratic origins, Louis was a typical bourgeois in his habits. He seemed the ideal choice. As a member of the royal family he was acceptable to royalists, yet moderate republicans also approved of him because he was willing to accept the role of a constitutional monarch and because his father, Philippe Egalité, had been a supporter of the revolution of 1789. The constitution was based on the Charter of 1814. The widening of the franchise to include those who paid 200 francs a year in taxes placed electoral power in the hands of the middle classes. Press censorship was abolished and the power of the church was again restricted.

In domestic affairs the Orleans monarchy had some reforms to its credit: a Factory Act, elected district councils and an Education Act which planned state-aided primary schools in every commune. There was rapid industrial development in some areas. Nevertheless, the benefits of economic prosperity were not felt by the working classes. The government was unwilling to interfere in the economy by introducing legislation which would have protected the working classes. The combination of social unrest and the French revolutionary tradition caused sporadic outbreaks of violence. The worst of these were risings in Paris and Lyon in 1834, which were brutally suppressed. Following this, press freedom was restricted in 1835.

Foreign affairs

Louis Philippe avoided an adventurous foreign policy because of the expense of war and because he was uncertain whether his regime enjoyed sufficient support in France to take the risk. His critics accused him and Guizot, his Foreign Minister from 1840 to 1847, of subservience to Britain.

- He co-operated with Palmerston over Belgium, withdrawing his original idea of establishing a French king there and accepting Leopold of Saxe-Coburg instead.
- In the Middle East he hoped to gain influence, by backing Mehmet Ali against the Turks, but was outwitted by Palmerston, who had gained the support of Russia and Austria. Thiers, Prime Minister in 1840, threatened war, but was dismissed by the king. Mehmet had to surrender his conquests.
- **Guizot**, Foreign Minister 1840–7, scored a diplomatic victory over Palmerston in the affair of the Spanish marriages in 1846. Unfortunately, this deprived him of British sympathy when he most needed it in 1848.
- The Tahiti affair (1843–4) also caused friction with Britain. In the eventual settlement a French protectorate was established over Tahiti.

Causes of the 1848 Revolution

In the 1840s Louis Philippe faced increasing opposition.

- The economic hardship of the 'hungry forties' aroused working class discontent.
- A new revolutionary movement grew up: the early socialists, led by **Louis Blanc**. Blanc preached the 'right to work' and advocated state-aided 'social workshops' in which workers would be fairly treated. Since this was a period of industrial growth in some areas of France, particularly Paris, an urban proletariat developed which provided Blanc with considerable support.
- The failure of Louis Philippe's government to tackle social problems added to working class discontent.
- The King's advisers, such as Guizot, were anti-liberal and the regime became corrupt and inefficient.
- Bonapartism experienced a revival. Napoleon I's nephew, Louis Napoleon, exploited the mood of disillusion with Louis Philippe's foreign policy (it was claimed that 'France was bored' with it) to build up support.

> Louis Napoleon had written two books in which he built up the Napoleonic Legend and portrayed Napoleon I as the champion of progress.

> You should be able to explain the significance of each of these dates.

KEY DATES	
1814	Restoration of Louis XVIII; Charter issued
1815	Return of Napoleon; The Hundred Days; Louis XVIII restored again
1824	Accession of Charles X
1830	Ordinances of St Cloud; Revolution: Abdication of Charles X.
1830–48	Louis Philippe
1848	Revolution; Abdication of Louis Philippe

11.2 Napoleon III

LEARNING SUMMARY

After studying this section you should be able to understand:

- the course and outcome of the 1848 Revolution in France
- the establishment of the Second Republic
- the constitution of the Second Empire
- the social and economic development of France in the Second Empire
- the foreign policy of Napoleon III
- why the Second Empire was overthrown in 1870

The 1848 Revolution in France

AQA	U3	CCEA	AS2
OCR	U1	WJEC	U4

By 1848 Louis Philippe faced opposition from republicans, socialists (with growing working class support) and Bonapartists. Discontent focused on the demand for extension of the franchise. In February, revolution broke out when Guizot banned a 'reform banquet' in Paris. On 24 February Louis Philippe was forced to abdicate.

> You need to be aware of the division between republican Paris and conservative rural France – a key feature of French politics.

The rebels then set up a provisional government which included liberals, radicals and the socialist Louis Blanc. At his suggestion 'National Workshops' for the unemployed were set up in Paris. Arrangements were made for elections to a National Constituent Assembly on the basis of universal male suffrage in April.

Most of the members of the Assembly were royalists, liberals or moderate republicans. The radicals and socialists, who were powerful in Paris, were heavily outnumbered.

In May, the provisional government was replaced by a new government, from which the radicals and socialists were excluded. An attempt by the socialists and the Paris mob to overthrow this government (which had an overwhelming majority in an assembly elected by the largest electorate in French history) was frustrated by the National Guard. Louis Blanc fled and other socialist leaders were arrested.

A final desperate attempt by the Paris mob to overthrow the government was provoked by the decision to close the National Workshops. Without leaders or organisation, the working classes of Paris seized control of the city. The army under General Cavaignac turned the guns on the rebels and hundreds were massacred. Afterwards, 11 000 prisoners were punished by imprisonment or exile. These '**June Days**' turned the mass of Frenchmen outside Paris, especially the middle classes, against socialism and even liberalism.

The National Constituent Assembly finished drawing up the constitution by November. In December elections were held for a President. Five and a half million out of seven and a half million votes went to Louis Napoleon.

KEY POINT

Napoleon triumphed because:
- the name of Napoleon was known to all as a symbol of France's past glories
- he offered stability against the 'red peril' which had arisen in the June Days
- his schemes for social reform won working class support.

The Second Republic

AQA	**U3**	CCEA	**AS2**
OCR	**U1**	WJEC	**U4**

> The Electoral Law of 1850 did restrict the electorate despite his opposition.

Under the constitution Napoleon was President for four years only and not allowed to seek re-election. He was not prepared to accept this, so he set out to consolidate the support which had led to his triumph in the presidential election of 1848.
- He opposed demands by the Assembly to reduce the electorate.
- He won support from the Catholics by sending troops to Rome in 1849 to overthrow the Roman Republic set up by Mazzini and restore the Pope.
- The **Loi Falloux** (1850) was also intended to win support from the Catholics. The influence of the church over education was greatly extended by providing state funds for church schools.

> Plebiscite: vote by the people on an issue, i.e. a referendum.

By December 1851 Napoleon felt confident enough to take the first step towards making his power permanent. In a well-organised **coup d'état**, many of his leading opponents were arrested during the night. The next day, the anniversary of the coronation of Napoleon I as Emperor, he declared himself President for ten years. A year later he abolished the Second Republic and made himself the Emperor Napoleon III. Both these steps were approved by plebiscites. There is no doubt that he had widespread support among the French people.

The Constitution of the Second Empire

AQA	U3	CCEA	AS2
OCR	U1	WJEC	U4

Napoleon was in effect a dictator – but with popular approval.

The constitution of the Second Empire gave Napoleon III autocratic powers. His power was based on popular approval through plebiscites. He appointed ministers, was commander-in-chief of the armed forces and had the right to declare war, make treaties and institute legislation. The Legislative Assembly, elected by universal male suffrage, met for only three months a year and had very little power. In any case the elections were managed. There was strict press censorship. Many political opponents were exiled to Algeria. Political associations were suppressed. Provincial administration was in the hands of prefects appointed by the Minister of the Interior.

In 1859 Napoleon granted an amnesty to political opponents exiled in 1851. From 1860 he began to liberalise the system of government. The Legislative Assembly was given the right to debate its reply to the address from the throne and the press was allowed to report parliamentary debates. During the 1860s there were further concessions. Press censorship was relaxed and opposition journals and newspapers sprang up. Trade unions were legalised and it became increasingly accepted for ministers to be questioned in Parliament. A liberal and republican opposition developed, which won 32 seats in the elections of 1863 and 71 in 1869.

In 1869–70 a new constitution, known as the '**Liberal Empire**', gave the Legislative Assembly the power to propose laws and vote on the budget. A ministry representing the majority in the Assembly was formed in January 1870, led by Olivier. These reforms received overwhelming support in a plebiscite. But the Emperor still retained considerable powers, including the power to change the constitution, subject to a plebiscite.

KEY ISSUE

Historians debate whether these changes sprang from a genuine desire to liberalise the constitution or were concessions forced on Napoleon by a succession of failures in foreign policy.

Social and economic developments

AQA	U3	CCEA	AS2
OCR	U1	WJEC	U4

The Second Empire saw considerable economic growth. New banks were founded to raise capital for commercial and industrial development. Low interest rates encouraged investment. The railway network was vastly increased and mining and heavy industry were expanded. The Cobden-Chevalier Treaty (1860) marked a move to free trade. A great deal of slum clearance was undertaken in Paris and new boulevards and squares were created under the guidance of Baron Haussmann. Many of those involved with economic policy in this period were **Saint Simonians**, who believed in industrialisation as the means to social advance.

In his early days Napoleon had written a pamphlet on *The Ending of Poverty* and as Emperor he made a genuine attempt to improve social conditions. 'Conciliation Boards' were set up which negotiated improvements in wages and working conditions. Public works helped to create full employment.

KEY POINT

This goes a long way to explaining why many Frenchmen approved of the Second Empire.

Foreign policy

AQA **U3** CCEA **AS2**
OCR **U1** WJEC **U4**

Napoleon wanted – and was expected – to restore France to the glory it had had in his uncle's day. He therefore pursued a more active foreign policy than Louis Philippe. At first he had some success. France and its allies were victorious in the Crimean War of 1854–6, though the French army did not earn the glory Napoleon had hoped. The fact that the peace conference was held in Paris gave the Second Empire prestige.

Italy

Then, in 1859, Napoleon went to war against Austria in alliance with Piedmont, winning victories at Magenta and Solferino. The French did, however, suffer heavy losses and the intervention in Italy aroused opposition from both Catholics and liberals. The Catholics feared that the unification of Italy would endanger the papacy, while the liberals felt that Napoleon had let the Italians down by making the Truce of Villafranca. But he did acquire Savoy and Nice as his reward.

> Napoleon managed to offend Frenchmen at opposite ends of the political spectrum.

The 1860s

In the 1860s Napoleon's foreign policy was largely a catalogue of failures.

- He lost prestige by the ill-considered **Mexican adventure** of 1861–7. He sent French troops to overthrow the anti-religious republic in Mexico and set up a Catholic empire under Maximilian, brother of the Austrian emperor. He hoped to win the approval of Catholic opinion, as well as glory for his regime. Under pressure from the USA he had to withdraw his troops, leaving Maximilian to be executed.

> Napoleon miscalculated. He expected a long war, not a quick Prussian victory.

- In 1866 Napoleon was persuaded by Bismarck to remain neutral while Prussia defeated Austria. Prussia's victory left France facing a much more powerful Prussia. It was a long-standing principle of French foreign policy to prevent the emergence of a powerful state in Germany.
- Napoleon's unsuccessful attempt to restore the balance of power by trying to annex Luxemburg as compensation discredited him further. By revealing that Napoleon aimed to do this, Bismarck humiliated France.

The overthrow of the Second Empire

In view of these failures it is doubtful how much longer the Second Empire would have survived after 1870, but what destroyed it was the catastrophic failure of its armies at the beginning of the **Franco-Prussian War**. Napoleon tried to use the issue of the Hohenzollern candidature for the Spanish throne to score a diplomatic victory over Prussia and thus restore his prestige. He demanded that William I of Prussia should guarantee that the candidature would not be renewed. This provided Bismarck with the opportunity to provoke a war by editing and publishing the **Ems Telegram**. Napoleon gave way to French public opinion and declared war.

The French armies were unprepared for war. One army was driven into **Metz**, where it was besieged and eventually surrendered in October 1870. The other suffered a disastrous defeat at **Sedan** in September and Napoleon himself was taken prisoner. The Legislative Assembly proclaimed the overthrow of the Second Empire and the establishment of a republic and a provisional government.

You should be able to explain the significance of each of these dates.

KEY DATES

1848	Abdication of Louis Philippe; Second Republic proclaimed; Louis Napoleon elected President
1851	Louis Napoleon's coup d'état
1852	Establishment of the Second Empire
1854–6	Crimean War
1859	War against Austria in Italy
1861–7	The Mexican Adventure
1866	Austro-Prussian War
1870	Franco-Prussian War; fall of Second Empire

11.3 The Third Republic

LEARNING SUMMARY

After studying this section you should be able to understand:

- the outcome for France of the Franco-Prussian War
- the Paris Commune
- the establishment of the Third Republic in 1875

The Establishment of the Republic

AQA   U3

The End of the Franco-Prussian War

The first task facing the provisional government was to rally resistance against the Prussians. Paris was besieged in September 1870. Despite heroic efforts, especially by Gambetta, to raise resistance in the provinces, it fell in January 1871 after a four month siege. By the Treaty of Frankfurt, negotiated between Thiers and Bismarck, France was forced to surrender Alsace and Lorraine, to accept an army of occupation and to pay an indemnity. Thiers played a leading role in raising the money to pay this and in 1873 the army of occupation was withdrawn.

The Paris Commune

The Republic faced a grave threat from the left almost immediately after the end of the siege of Paris in the rising of the Paris Commune (March–May 1871). The Commune had many causes.

- The humiliation of defeat, rubbed in by a Prussian victory march through Paris.
- Social distress caused by the siege. The Assembly's decision at the end of the siege that payment of rents must be resumed made matters worse and sparked off the rising. Many of the Paris working class simply could not pay.
- Opposition by republican Paris to the newly elected National Assembly, which had a royalist majority. The decision of the Assembly to meet at Versailles rather than Paris was greatly resented.
- The influence of revolutionaries, including socialists, though the Commune was not primarily a socialist movement.

On the orders of Thiers, the head of the provisional government, the army suppressed the Commune. There was great brutality on both sides and the episode left deep divisions in French society.

> **KEY POINT**
>
> The Commune was an expression of the deep division between republican Paris and conservative rural France.

The Constitution of 1875

After the suppression of the Commune, the way was clear for the National Assembly to draw up a new constitution. The republic was now threatened from the right, as royalists had a majority in the Assembly. However, they were divided between the supporters of the Comte de Chambord (Bourbon) and the Comte de Paris (Orleanist). Since they were unable to agree who should be king, in the end the Assembly in 1875 accepted a republican constitution, with a President as head of state, a Chamber of Deputies elected by universal male suffrage and an indirectly elected Senate. The inclusion of the word republic in the constitution was adopted by a majority of one vote (the Wallon Amendment).

> **KEY POINT**
>
> A republic had been set up, but France remained deeply divided.

Exam practice questions

1 Why was Charles X overthrown in 1830? **[50]**

2 How far does his conduct of foreign policy explain the growing unpopularity of Louis Philippe? **[50]**

3 'A catalogue of failures.'

How far do you agree with this view of the foreign policy of Louis Napoleon (Napoleon III) as President and Emperor, 1848–70? **[50]**

4 Why, and to what extent, did Napoleon III liberalise the Second Empire between 1859 and 1870? **[50]**

12 Russia, 1855–1917

The following topics are covered in this chapter:

- Tsarist Russia, 1855–94
- Nicholas II, 1894–1917
- The 1917 revolutions

12.1 Tsarist Russia, 1855–94

LEARNING SUMMARY

After studying this section you should be able to understand:

- the significance of the reforms of Alexander II, 1855–81
- the importance of the reign of Alexander III, 1881–94

Alexander II, 1855–81

AQA U1 OCR U4

Russia in the middle of the nineteenth century was perhaps the most reactionary state in Europe. The system of government by a Tsar with absolute authority is generally termed **autocracy**. Russia's social structure was distinguished by the survival of **serfdom**, which had disappeared everywhere else in Europe. The majority of Russians were serfs, owned either by the crown or by the landed aristocracy. The middle class was tiny, reflecting the lack of industry and the relative unimportance of trade in Russia's backward economy. The **Orthodox Church** had a central role in the state and acted as a brake on change.

Reforms

The backwardness and inefficiency of Russia were highlighted by defeat in the Crimean War (1854–6). Tsar Nicholas I (1825–55) died in the middle of the war, leaving Russia in need of reform. Alexander II recognised this and the first half of his reign was in marked contrast to that of Nicholas I. The most important reform was the **emancipation of the serfs** in 1861. The peasants were freed from all their obligations to the landlords, whether money payments or labour services. The government compensated the landlords and reclaimed the money from the peasants by redemption payments over a period of 49 years. The land was not transferred to individuals, but to the 'mir' or village commune, which was responsible for the redemption payments.

> This section sets out the case for regarding Alexander as the 'Tsar Liberator'.

KEY POINT

The emancipation of the serfs was a fundamental change in Russian society and the economy. It involved over 40 million people and it was inevitable that other reforms would follow.

In 1864 '**zemstva**' were set up. These were elected district councils which were made responsible for roads, hospitals, schools, sanitation and poor relief. They were particularly active in setting up elementary schools. They were elected on a system which favoured the nobility and gentry, but they were nevertheless a step towards democracy. In 1870 town councils were also set up. Alexander introduced important legal reforms, including trials in public, trial by jury and salaries for judges (to reduce bribery). The army was reformed – the general staff was reorganised and all classes became liable for conscription which played an important part in reducing illiteracy, since conscripts were taught to read and write.

There was also some economic development. Some 20 000 km of railways were built. A State Bank was set up and there was some industrial development.

How effective were these reforms?

Although the emancipation of the serfs was a huge step, the way it was carried out had serious weaknesses. Generally, the peasants got the poorer land and their farms were small. Because the mir was collectively responsible for the redemption payments, it was very difficult for peasants to leave the village. Since the land was communally owned and regularly redistributed, there was no incentive to improve it. Russian agriculture therefore remained backward and inefficient. As the population grew, famines became more frequent. Since the peasants were tied to the mir, there was little migration either to the towns or to the underpopulated territories of Siberia. Industrial progress was therefore slow.

Although serfdom had been abolished, the other key features of nineteenth century Russia, the autocracy and the Orthodox Church, remained untouched. Both were hostile to reform.

This section and the next set out the case against regarding Alexander as the 'Tsar liberator'.

A drift to the towns began in the 1870s with the rise of factories.

Repression again

After the Polish Revolt (1863) Alexander's rule became more repressive. The powers of the zemstva were reduced. Press censorship was strict, the secret police were active and political cases were tried without a jury. Over 150 000 people were sent to penal servitude in Siberia.

Nevertheless, in the last years of his reign it was still uncertain whether the Tsardom would remain repressive or move gradually towards a constitutional system of government. A wave of revolutionary violence in 1879–81 resulted in many executions, but at the same time, under the influence of Loris-Melikov, Alexander was on the point of calling a partly-elected national assembly. His assassination in March 1881 ended the proposal.

Populists and anarchists

One reason why Alexander adopted more repressive policies was the rise of revolutionary movements among the intellectuals. As a class the intellectuals were small in number, but they produced a remarkable cultural outburst at this time – Tchaikovsky, Tolstoy and Dostoievsky were all active in this period. Many intellectuals were desperately aware of Russia's backwardness. Their disappointment at Alexander II's reforms led to the formation of reformist movements. Repression turned some of them into revolutionary movements. The two most important were the '**Narodniki**' (populists), who wanted to educate the peasants to demand reforms, and the **anarchists**, led by Bakunin, who called for armed rebellion. Anarchists made several unsuccessful attempts on the life of Alexander II. They succeeded in 1881.

This was the beginning of the revolutionary tradition which culminated in the revolutions of 1917. Can Alexander be accused of stimulating it?

Alexander's reforms gave hope of modernising Russia, but they failed to make the Tsarist system popular.

Alexander III, 1881–94

AQA	**U1**
Edexcel	**U1**
OCR	**U4**
WJEC	**U4**

The keynote of the reign of Alexander III was repression. His chief minister, Pobedonostsev, firmly believed in autocracy. The **Okhrana** (secret police) were actively hunting down revolutionaries, many of whom were executed or exiled to Siberia. There was strict press censorship and education was controlled. The zemstva were put under the supervision of Land Captains – gentry appointed by the Tsar. Anti-Semitism was encouraged by the government and by the Orthodox Church, which was also controlled by **Pobedonostsev** as Procurator of the Holy Synod. Pogroms (armed attacks on Jews) were common. The non-Russian minorities in the empire were also persecuted.

> The combination of economic advance and political repression was likely to lead to trouble in the end.

There were important developments in the economy. Industrialisation increased and Alexander authorised the beginning of work on the Trans-Siberian Railway. In 1892 he appointed Witte as Minister of Finance. There was also an important change in foreign relations in 1893 when Russia allied with France.

> You should be able to explain the significance of each of these dates.

KEY DATES

1854–6	Crimean War
1855–81	Reign of Alexander II
1861	Emancipation of the serfs
1863	Polish Revolt
1881	Assassination of Alexander II
1881–94	Reign of Alexander III

12.2 Nicholas II, 1894–1917

LEARNING SUMMARY

After studying this section you should be able to understand:

- the main political and economic developments, 1894–1905
- the outbreak of the Revolution of 1905 and its failure
- political and economic developments in Russia, 1905–14
- the strengths and weaknesses of Tsarist Russia in 1914
- the consequences for Russia of involvement in the First World War

Economic advance and political repression, 1894–1905

AQA	**U1**
OCR	**U1, 4**
Edexcel	**U1**
WJEC	**U4**

Nicholas II has been described as weak-willed, negative and of limited intelligence. He was easily influenced, especially by his wife, Alexandra. She was a deeply religious woman who was a strong believer in autocracy and constantly urged him to be a strong ruler. The combination of Nicholas and Alexandra was ultimately fatal for the Tsarist autocracy.

Nicholas continued the policies of Alexander III. Repression continued unabated. Nevertheless, reformist and revolutionary movements continued to develop.

- In 1898 the **Social Democratic Party** was founded by Plekhanov. Its ideas were Marxist and it sought support from Russia's newly emerging industrial working class. At its 1903 Congress, held in exile in Brussels and London, it divided into two wings. The **Bolsheviks**, led by Lenin, wanted membership restricted to a small number of dedicated activists who would bring about a socialist revolution and the dictatorship of the proletariat. The **Mensheviks** wanted a mass party of the working class which would aim to overthrow the Tsar, set up a democratic republic and then introduce an eight-hour working day and other social reforms. The two groups continued to work together until 1912.
- In 1901 the **Social Revolutionary Party** was formed. This aimed to unite the intellectuals, workers and peasants and to bring about revolution by propaganda and terror.
- In 1904 at a meeting of zemstva leaders the **Liberals** set up the Union of Liberation which demanded political reform.

The economy

Economic development gained momentum. The state played a key role. **Witte**, Minister of Finance from 1892 to 1903, achieved rapid industrial growth by increasing tariffs, encouraging foreign investment, especially from France, and stabilising the currency. The rail network more than doubled between 1890 and 1914, the outstanding achievement being the Trans-Siberian Railway. The rate of growth of industrial production was the highest in the world, particularly in coal, iron, oil and cotton. The urban population grew with corresponding speed, especially in Moscow and St. Petersburg, where housing and working conditions were appalling. The growth of an industrial proletariat played a major part in the development of a more western type of socialist movement.

The 1905 revolution

AQA	U1	WJEC	U4
OCR	U1, 4	CCEA	AS2
Edexcel	U1		

The Russo-Japanese War

At the beginning of the twentieth century Russia was seething with unrest. The peasants and the urban working class were equally discontented, as shown by the frequency of peasant uprisings and strikes. Political repression was as fierce as ever. Discontent boiled over into revolution as a result of the Russo-Japanese War (1904–5). The cause of this was the conflicting ambitions of Russia and Japan in Manchuria and Korea. The Russian government expected 'a short victorious war that would stem the tide of revolution'. In fact the Japanese won handsomely – in Manchuria they won the great battle of Mukden, while the Russian fleet, after sailing half-way round the world, was virtually wiped out in the battle of Tsushima.

The revolution

News of defeat in the Far East brought discontent to a head on 22 January, 1905, when government troops opened fire on a procession of peaceful, unarmed demonstrators carrying a petition to present to the Tsar at the Winter Palace in St. Petersburg. Several hundred were killed and the incident, known as **Bloody Sunday,** marked a turning point. This atrocity provoked a wave of strikes and peasant uprisings. In June there was a mutiny on the battleship *Potemkin* and in

The first appearance of a soviet.

September a general strike. In St. Petersburg a **Soviet** (committee of workers' representatives) was set up with Trotsky as co-chairman.

The Tsar was forced to make concessions.

- In August he promised to set up a **Duma** (assembly), though with a narrow franchise which would exclude industrial workers.
- On the advice of Witte, he issued the **October Manifesto** promising a wider franchise and legislative powers for the Duma. This satisfied the Liberals and divided them from the workers in the Soviet.

The government was then able to suppress the revolution. The leaders of the Soviet were arrested and a rising in Moscow was brutally suppressed. By April 1906 the Tsarist government was back in control and some 15 000 people had been killed.

> **KEY POINT**
>
> Tsarist Russia was shaken by the 1905 Revolution, but recovered. However, it never fully regained the loyalty it lost on Bloody Sunday.

Why the revolution failed

- The revolutionaries were not united, so eventually the Tsar was able to split the liberals from the socialists.
- There was no central leadership – the strikes and peasant uprisings were spontaneous and not organised.
- Lenin and other revolutionary leaders were in exile abroad and arrived too late to influence events.
- At the critical moment the Tsar made concessions in the October Manifesto (though only under pressure from Witte).
- The army and navy for the most part remained loyal (mutinies such as that on the *Potemkin* were the exception). This enabled the Tsar to revert to repression once he had regained the upper hand.

This was crucial.

From revolution to war, 1905–14

AQA	**U1**	WJEC	**U4**
OCR	**U1, 4**	CCEA	**AS2**
Edexcel	**U1**		

The Dumas

Nicholas II believed in autocracy and saw political concessions as weakness. He had no intention of observing the spirit of the October Manifesto. In January 1906 he issued the Fundamental Law of the Empire, asserting his 'supreme autocratic power'. In May Witte, whom he blamed for having pressed him to issue the Manifesto, was forced to resign. Stolypin replaced him.

The First Duma met in May 1906. The electoral system was rigged to favour the landowners and middle classes over the peasants and workers. The biggest political grouping in the Duma was the Cadets (Liberals). The Duma demanded sweeping reforms, including a democratic electoral system. Nicholas dissolved it after ten weeks.

Perhaps, given time, Russia might have developed a form of constitutional monarchy. The main obstacle was Nicholas himself.

The Second Duma (1907) was also soon dissolved because its demands were unacceptable to Nicholas. The Third Duma (1907–12) and the Fourth Duma (1912–17) were elected on a revised franchise, which increased still further the power of the gentry and middle classes. They were dominated by Octobrists (moderate liberals) and achieved some modest reforms, e.g. factory legislation. They had little power and the regime remained fundamentally autocratic.

Stolypin

Stolypin introduced important agrarian reforms which were intended to win the support of the peasants.

- Redemption payments were ended.
- Peasants were given complete freedom to leave the mir and they were allowed to turn their holdings into their own individual properties.
- Government assistance enabled three and a half million people to emigrate to Siberia.

Stolypin hoped that this would create a class of prosperous peasant farmers and would make agriculture more efficient. His reforms offered a solution to Russia's agrarian problems, but they needed many years to succeed.

> **KEY POINT**
>
> - The Dumas could have been the foundation for the gradual development of democracy in Russia, but the attitude of Nicholas II and the onset of the war prevented this.
> - Stolypin's reforms might have transformed Russian agriculture eventually, but only over a lengthy period.

Tsarist Russia in 1914

AQA	U1	WJEC	U4
OCR	U1, 4	CCEA	AS2
Edexcel	U1		

At the outbreak of the First World War there were indications that Tsarist Russia might survive.

- The Third and Fourth Dumas co-operated with the government.
- A class of prosperous peasants was slowly beginning to emerge.
- There were some signs of improvement in the conditions of industrial workers.
- Industrial output was growing, especially in coal and iron. Other industries were slower to grow.

But Russia's problems were enormous.

- The regime was still autocratic and repressive. The power of the Dumas was limited – they had no control over ministers and they were only allowed to make reforms of which the Tsar approved.
- The reputation of the monarchy never fully recovered from Bloody Sunday.
- Industry was still small in scale and inefficient by Western European standards.
- Agricultural productivity was still poor despite Stolypin's reforms, which in any case needed many years to have a real effect.
- Nicholas II lacked the intelligence to deal with his problems. His outlook was reactionary. He only gave the Dumas grudging approval. He also failed to acknowledge the need for change and did not realise how much prestige the monarchy had lost in 1905.
- The growing influence of Rasputin further discredited the court.
- The advisers of Nicholas II were mediocre. Only two had real ability – Witte, who was forced to resign in 1906 and Stolypin who was assassinated in 1911.

Don't exaggerate the importance of Rasputin as a factor in the downfall of the Tsar.

Russia and the First World War

AQA	**U1**	WJEC	**U4**
OCR	**U1, 4**	CCEA	**AS2**
Edexcel	**U1**		

- The war exposed the inefficiency of Tsarist Russia. Millions of men were drafted into the armed forces, but were not provided with adequate clothing, training or equipment.
- Against the highly efficient German army defeat was inevitable. In 1914 the Germans inflicted crushing defeats at the battles of **Tannenberg** and the **Masurian Lakes**. In 1915 the Russians were driven out of Poland. In 1916 an offensive against Austria met with some success, but then equipment began to run short.
- Since the Tsar unwisely decided to take personal command of the army in September 1915, military defeats were blamed on him.
- The civilian population suffered great hardship. Germany and Turkey closed Russia's Baltic and Black Sea ports and thus virtually cut Russia off from its allies. The internal transport system was in chaos. Food and fuel became increasingly difficult to obtain in the towns and prices rose dramatically.
- The government became increasingly unstable. Between 1914 and 1917 there were four prime ministers. In the absence of the Tsar at army headquarters continuity was provided only by the Tsarina Alexandra and her favourite Rasputin, whose corrupt influence and debauched private life discredited the monarchy even further.

KEY POINT

The war exposed the weakness of Tsarist Russia and brought about its downfall.

> You should be able to explain the significance of each of these dates.

KEY DATES

1894	Accession of Nicholas II
1898	Foundation of the Social Democratic Party
1903	Social Democratic Party split between Bolsheviks and Mensheviks
1904–5	Russo-Japanese War
1905	Bloody Sunday; Revolution of 1905
1906	First Duma; Witte resigned and replaced by Stolypin
1907	Second Duma
1907–12	Third Duma
1911	Assassination of Stolypin
1912–7	Fourth Duma
1914	Outbreak of First World War
1917	February Revolution; Abdication of Nicholas II

12.3 The 1917 revolutions

LEARNING SUMMARY	After studying this section you should be able to understand:
	• the establishment of the Provisional Government in February 1917 and its overthrow in October 1917
	• the roles of Kerensky and Lenin in these events

The February revolution, 1917

AQA	**U1**	WJEC	**U1, 4**
OCR	**U1, 4**	CCEA	**AS2**
Edexcel	**U1**		

At this stage it seemed possible that Russia would develop into a democratic republic.

On 23 February, 1917 (Russian calendar) a great wave of strikes and food riots broke out, particularly in Petrograd (formerly St. Petersburg). Troops sent to quell the rioters joined them. The authority of the government had collapsed. Six days later the Fourth Duma established a **Provisional Government** under Prince Lvov. Most of its members were Liberals, but there was one socialist, **Kerensky**. The next day the Tsar abdicated.

The Provisional Government

This proved to be a crucial mistake – but was any other decision possible?

The Provisional Government never enjoyed widespread support. In July Prince Lvov was replaced as Prime Minster by **Kerensky**. The Provisional Government decided to continue the war, which led to further military disasters and continuing food shortages. When rumours began to spread that land was to be redistributed, the peasants in the army deserted and went home to claim their land with the consequence that the Russian armies disintegrated. A disastrous offensive in Galicia in July provoked a rising in Petrograd, which the Bolsheviks tried unsuccessfully to turn into a coup (the July Days – see below). By the autumn the Provisional Government was discredited.

Lenin

In April Lenin returned to Russia. On his arrival in Petrograd, he issued the **April Theses**, in which he argued for an end to co-operation with the Provisional Government. Instead, power must be transferred to the soviets. Capitalism must be overthrown and the land and banks nationalised. These ideas were the practical application of Lenin's view that Russia could move straight from Tsarism to the dictatorship of the proletariat.

Soviets had been set up all over the country. The most important was the Petrograd Soviet of Workers' and Soldiers' Deputies, set up three days before the Provisional Government. The soviets claimed that, as their members were elected by the workers, they represented the will of the people more faithfully than the Provisional Government. They certainly enjoyed more popular support. When Lenin returned to Russia, the soviets were dominated by Social Revolutionaries and Mensheviks. The Bolsheviks, despite being a minority, had one advantage – they were a highly disciplined body of determined revolutionaries.

In July an attempt was made to overthrow the Provisional Government in Petrograd. This rising, known as the **July Days**, was poorly organised and soon collapsed. It gave the government the opportunity to arrest a number of Bolshevik leaders. Lenin himself fled to Finland to escape arrest.

The October revolution, 1917

AQA	U1	WJEC	U1, 4
OCR	U1, 4	CCEA	AS2
Edexcel	U1		

The crucial factor in the revival of the Bolsheviks after this setback was the **Kornilov affair** – an attempted right-wing coup by General Kornilov. They played the leading role in organising resistance by the soviets and as a result soon afterwards gained control of the Petrograd and Moscow Soviets. The membership of the Party rose to 200 000.

With the growth of Bolshevik support in the autumn of 1917 Lenin saw the opportunity for the Bolsheviks to seize power. The Central Committee of the Party decided to organise an armed coup. Lenin was supported by Trotsky, Stalin and seven others. Only **Zinoviev** and **Kamenev** voted against.

The revolution took place on the night of 6–7 November (24–25 October by Russian dating), the day before a meeting of the All-Russian Congress of Soviets. The Congress immediately confirmed the Bolsheviks in power.

> **KEY POINT**
>
> In the October Revolution a determined minority seized power from a weak Provisional Government, which had failed to address the problems which led to the downfall of the Tsar.

Why the October revolution succeeded

Trotsky argued in 1918 that the support of the Russian workers would have brought the Bolsheviks to power, but counter-revolutionary forces headed by Kerensky and Kornilov tried to prevent this. Thus the October Revolution simply ensured that the will of the workers was fulfilled. A later Soviet version stressed the logic of the class struggle and argued that the role of the Bolsheviks and Lenin, in particular, was to mould events to bring about the inevitable triumph of the proletarian revolution.

Western historians tend to stress the role of Lenin, stamping his personality on events, and to portray the October revolution as a coup rather than a popular revolution with mass support. Others emphasise the importance of the war, which they claim halted Russia's progress towards liberal institutions and gave extremists the opportunity to seize power.

> You should be able to explain the significance of each of these dates.

> **KEY DATES**
>
> **1917**
>
> | March | Abdication of Nicholas II; Provisional Government; Soviet set up in Petrograd (the February revolution) |
> |---|---|
> | April | Return of Lenin to Russia; April Theses |
> | July | Kerensky Prime Minister; July Days |
> | August | Kornilov's attempted coup |
> | November | Bolshevik revolution (the October revolution) |

Sample question and model answer

How successful were the domestic policies of Alexander III and Nicholas II before 1905? **[50]**

The key issue is 'success'.

Alexander III came to the throne as a result of the assassination of Alexander II. The late Tsar had adopted a more repressive policy in the late 1860s as opposition movements sprang up. The assassination confirmed Alexander III, who was a firm believer in autocracy, in pursuing a policy of political repression. He refused to make any concession to liberalism. The policies he initiated were continued by Nicholas II. Pobedonostsev, the chief advisor to Alexander III and still an influential figure under Nicholas II, was an equally firm believer in autocracy. How successful were the repressive policies of the two Tsars?

- From the start of his reign Alexander III clamped down on opposition. The Okhrana (secret police) sought out revolutionaries. Many were executed or exiled to Siberia. There was strict press censorship and education was strictly controlled.
- Alexander III limited the power of the zemstvos - the only representative institutions in Russia - by the appointment of Land Captains.
- Minority nationalities were subjected to Russification.

You should amplify these points from your own knowledge.

- Anti-Semitism was encouraged, and there were widespread pogroms.

Despite these measures, opposition was never totally suppressed. In the early twentieth century illegal parties were formed: the SDs, SRs, Liberals.

Turning to other aspects of domestic policy.

- There was little progress in tackling social problems.
- Peasants remained tied to the commune (mir), with a low standard of living.
- Little attempt was made to combat the problems of urbanisation resulting from industrial growth.
- There was little advance in education: universities were restricted and there was a low level of literacy among the masses.
- Economic policies were more successful. Witte achieved rapid expansion of railways and industry. This was financed by foreign investment and tariffs (which also protected industry).

But ...

Success and failure are balanced here.

- A failure to tackle the problem of the communes meant that the peasants were heavily taxed and yet unable to increase production sufficiently to provide the exports needed to finance industrialisation and the grain to feed the growing urban proletariat.
- The failure to tackle social problems, especially those resulting from urbanisation and peasant poverty, meant that despite repression there was increasing disaffection. In 1905 opposition broke out into revolution - the surest sign of the failure of the policies of Alexander and Nicholas.

13 The unification of Italy

The following topics are covered in this chapter:

- Nationalism and the 1848–9 revolutions
- The forging of the Italian nation

13.1 Nationalism and the 1848–9 revolutions

<table>
<tr><td rowspan="2">LEARNING SUMMARY</td><td>After studying this section you should be able to understand:</td></tr>
<tr><td>

- the development of Italian nationalism in the first half of the nineteenth century and the obstacles which it faced
- the failure of the revolutions of 1848

</td></tr>
</table>

The growth of the Italian nationalist movement

OCR	U2	CCEA	AS1
Edexcel	U1	WJEC	U1
CCEA	A2.1		

- ▉ Kingdom of Sardinia, 1859
- ▉ Added to Sardinia by conquest, 1859
- ▉ Added to Sardinia by plebiscite, March 1860
- ▢ Added to Sardinia by plebiscite, Oct–Dec 1860
- --- Territories claimed by Italy, but still under Austrian rule
- — Boundary of Kingdom of Italy, 1870

The Unification of Italy, 1859–70

In 1815 Italy was divided up into a number of states, as it had been before the Napoleonic wars. It was dominated by the influence of Austria and its Chancellor, Metternich. Lombardy and Venetia were part of the Austrian Empire. Parma, Modena and Tuscany were ruled by relatives of the Austrian Emperor. The Kingdom of the Two Sicilies (Naples and Sicily) and the Papal States looked to Austria as their protector. Only Piedmont-Sardinia was independent of Austrian influence. In all the Italian states the system of government was autocratic.

> These ideas were the legacy of the French Revolution, exported by Napoleon's armies.

The Napoleonic period stimulated liberal and nationalist ideas in Italy. Secret societies, the most famous of which was the Carbonari, spread these ideas. There were liberal revolts in Naples (1820), Piedmont (1821) and the Papal States, Parma and Modena (1830–1). All were suppressed with Austrian help.

Three possible national leaders emerged.

> The kingdom of Sardinia which comprised Sardinia and Piedmont, is generally referred to as Piedmont.

- **Mazzini** founded the Young Italy movement in 1831 with the aim of making Italy 'united, independent and free'. He believed the Italians could do this themselves in a popular uprising which would establish a democratic republic.
- **Charles Albert**, who became King of Sardinia in 1831, aimed to create a kingdom of north Italy rather than to unite the whole peninsula. To bring this about, he embarked on economic reforms to strengthen Piedmont. But he was not a liberal and his rule was repressive.
- **Pius IX**, who became Pope in 1846, had the reputation of being a liberal. He began his papacy by releasing political prisoners, an act which played a part in touching off the revolutions of 1848. For many Italians the papacy was the natural focus of leadership. Some, such as **Gioberti**, aimed not for unification, but for a confederation of Italian states under the papacy.

KEY POINTS

Obstacles to unification were:
- the domination of Italy by Austria
- differences among Italian nationalists as to what sort of united Italy they aimed for
- catholic fears that the Papacy might lose the Papal States.

The revolutions of 1848–9

AQA U2
OCR U2
Edexcel U1
CCEA AS1, A2.1
WJEC U1

Revolts in Sicily and Naples in January 1848 forced King Ferdinand to set up a constitutional government and touched off a series of uprisings. Charles Albert and Pius IX granted constitutions in Piedmont and Rome. Revolts in Milan and Venice expelled the Austrians. Charles Albert then declared war on Austria, but was defeated at the battles of Custozza (1848) and Novara (1849). In 1849 he abdicated in favour of Victor Emmanuel II. The Austrian general, Radetzky, regained control of Milan.

Meanwhile, in Rome Pius IX, whose reputation for liberalism had been greatly exaggerated, fled when faced by further demands. Mazzini set up the Roman Republic, but France then intervened. Louis Napoleon, President of the newly created Second Republic, sent troops to restore the Pope. His motive was to win support from French Catholics. In Naples King Ferdinand dismissed his liberal government and restored his autocracy by bombarding Sicily into submission. Finally, in August 1849, Austria regained control of Venice.

The 1848 revolutions in Italy failed for two main reasons.

- The Italians could not defeat Austrian military power unaided.
- The Italian revolutionaries were divided over their aims. Mazzini aimed for a republic, Charles Albert for a monarchy (of northern Italy only). Many Italians gave higher priority to setting up constitutional government in the separate states than to a unified Italy.

> **KEY POINT**
>
> 1848 marked an important step towards the unification of Italy.

Piedmont had emerged as the only Italian state capable of challenging Austria. It was clear that it would need allies to do so effectively – a lesson learnt by Cavour. Mazzini's Roman Republic, and especially the heroic resistance led by **Garibaldi** during the siege of Rome by the French, was an inspiration to Italian nationalists.

13.2 The forging of the Italian nation

LEARNING SUMMARY

After studying this section you should be able to understand:

- the role of Cavour in the unification of Italy by 1861
- the role of Garibaldi in the unification of Italy by 1861
- how Venice and Rome were incorporated into the Kingdom of Italy
- the main features of the constitution and economy of the unified Italy

Cavour and Piedmont

AQA	U2
OCR	U2
Edexcel	U1
CCEA	AS.1, A2.1
WJEC	U1

By 1849 only Piedmont, under its new king Victor Emmanuel II, still had a constitutional government. It was now the focus of nationalist hopes. **Cavour**, who was appointed Prime Minister in 1852, aimed to build up Piedmont's strength. His reforms expanded trade and strengthened finance. Roads, railways and canals were built. The army was reorganised. By 1859 Piedmont was a model to the rest of Italy for efficient government and thriving trade. The foundation of the National Society in 1857 added strength to Piedmont's leadership of the Italian cause. It organised propaganda in support of Piedmont and attracted the support of many leading nationalists, including Manin (leader of the revolution in Venice in 1848) and **Garibaldi**.

Cavour also realised that Piedmont would need a powerful ally against Austria. He sought the friendship of Napoleon III of France. Piedmont's participation in the Crimean War as an ally of France and Britain helped. The attempted assassination of Napoleon by Orsini in 1858 had the paradoxical effect of reviving his sympathy for the Italian national cause. Later that year, he made a secret agreement with Cavour, the **Pact of Plombières**, by which France promised to help to expel Austrian troops from Lombardy and Venetia. Cavour then organised military manoeuvres which provoked Austria to declare war in April 1859.

France was to receive Savoy and Nice in return.

The Franco–Piedmontese war against Austria was the first crucial stage in unification. The Franco–Piedmontese armies occupied Lombardy, defeating the Austrians at Magenta and Solferino. The heavy losses on both sides in these

Contrast this with the Austrian victories in 1848. The French alliance made all the difference.

battles shocked Napoleon and he made the **Truce of Villafranca**, leaving Venetia in Austrian hands. The terms of the truce, including the incorporation of Lombardy into Piedmont, were confirmed in the Treaty of Zurich.

The war inspired rebellions in other parts of northern Italy and this enabled Cavour to use plebiscites to join Parma, Modena, Tuscany and the Romagna (the north-eastern part of the Papal States) to Piedmont and Lombardy in a new Kingdom of North Italy in 1860.

> **KEY POINT**
>
> In 1859–60 Piedmont took over northern Italy, as Cavour had planned. The crucial factors in this were the modernisation of Piedmont by Cavour and the French alliance.

Garibaldi and Sicily

AQA	U2
OCR	U2
Edexcel	U1
CCEA	AS.1, A2.1
WJEC	U1

Public opinion made it impossible for him to stop Garibaldi, so he aimed to control him.

Inspired by Cavour's success, Garibaldi collected a force of a thousand volunteers and later in 1860 sailed from Genoa to Sicily. Landing in the west, he quickly gained control over the whole island. In August he crossed to the mainland and in September captured Naples. He then intended to march on Rome.

At this point Cavour became alarmed, for he realised that if Garibaldi attacked Rome, the Catholic powers of Europe might intervene. Rome was still protected by a French garrison and Napoleon III. He therefore sent troops into the Papal States from the north to forestall Garibaldi. The Italian army occupied the Marches and Umbria (the eastern part of the Papal States), but kept well clear of Rome itself. It then linked up with Garibaldi, who handed over his conquests to Victor Emmanuel. Thus, by the end of 1860, the whole of Italy, except Venetia and the area around Rome, had been annexed by Piedmont. In January 1861 the first all-Italian parliament met in Turin. Less than six months later Cavour died.

> **KEY POINT**
>
> Garibaldi's expedition forced Cavour to change his plans and accept the southern states as part of a unified Italy.

Venice and Rome

AQA	U2
OCR	U2
Edexcel	U1
CCEA	A5.1, A2.1
WJEC	U1

Italian nationalists could not rest content until Rome and Venetia had been 'liberated'. Venetia became part of Italy in 1866 as a by-product of the Seven Weeks' War, in which Italy fought against Austria as the ally of Prussia.

Rome presented more of a problem as, since 1848, the Pope had the protection of French troops. Napoleon III, in deference to French Catholic opinion, could not withdraw them and Italy could not contemplate a war against France. Consequently two attempts by Garibaldi in 1862 and 1867 to occupy Rome were unsuccessful and it was not until the Franco-Prussian War of 1870–1 that Rome was acquired. Because of the war, French troops were withdrawn from Rome, which was then occupied by Italian troops and became the capital. The Pope refused to recognise this and became a virtual prisoner in the Vatican until an agreement was made with Mussolini in 1929.

By 1871 the ambitions of Italian nationalists had been almost completely realised. Only South Tyrol, Trentino, Trieste and Istria remained 'unredeemed' – 'Italia Irredenta'.

The Kingdom of Italy

AQA **U2**
OCR **U2**
Edexcel **U1**
CCEA **AS.1, A2.1**
WJEC **U1**

The system of government of Italy after unification was based on that of Piedmont. The republican ideas of Mazzini and Garibaldi were rejected. Victor Emmanuel II of Piedmont, the first King of Italy, was the head of a constitutional monarchy, rather like that of Britain, which Cavour admired. The ministers were responsible to a Parliament elected on a rather narrow middle class franchise. This system survived for over half a century, but eventually it failed to give effective government and gave way to the dictatorship of Mussolini.

United Italy, unlike Germany, did not enjoy rapid economic development. This was partly because it lacked coal and iron, which were essential for industrial development in this period. Industry did develop in the north, but Italy remained comparatively poor and was, therefore, unable to play as effective a part in European affairs as many Italians had hoped. In the south, industrial development made no progress at all and the extreme poverty and ignorance of this region remained one of Italy's most serious social problems.

KEY POINT

The division between north and south worked against the development of national political parties.

You should be able to explain the significance of each of these dates.

KEY DATES

1831	Foundation of 'Young Italy' by Mazzini
1846	Pius IX elected Pope
1848	Revolutions throughout Italy; Roman Republic set up by Mazzini; Heroic, but unsuccessful, defence by Garibaldi
1852	Cavour Prime Minister of Piedmont
1859	War; Piedmont and France against Austria; Victories at Magenta and Solferino; Lombardy annexed by Piedmont
1860	Kingdom of North Italy set up after plebiscites in Parma, Modena, Tuscany and the Romagna; Garibaldi's invasion of Sicily; Sicily, Naples, the Marches and Umbria taken over
1861	Kingdom of Italy set up
1866	Venetia added to Kingdom of Italy
1870	Rome occupied by Italian troops and incorporated into Italy

Sample question and model answer

The words 'how important' indicate that the question is not just about Cavour, or even his modernisation of Piedmont.

How important was Cavour's modernisation of Piedmont after 1852 in bringing about a united Italy by 1861? **[50]**

The lesson of the failure of the 1848 revolutions was that Piedmont was no match for the military power of Austria. Cavour recognised this and set about modernising Piedmont. His aim was to make Piedmont strong enough to expand into a kingdom of Northern Italy. In doing so, he laid the foundation for the eventual unification of Italy, though this was not what he envisaged.

There were two main strands to modernisation.
- Economic: Cavour admired British economic achievements and aimed to imitate them through the expansion of trade by free trade treaties. Railways were built and financial institutions developed. Piedmont's trade trebled.
- Political: He also admired Britain's parliamentary system of government. The liberal constitution, granted in 1848, was retained and Piedmont's administration modernised. The privileged position of the Catholic Church was reduced. All this won for Piedmont admiration from European liberal opinion.

Thus Piedmont became a model to the rest of Italy for efficient government and thriving trade. This enabled Cavour to harness the forces of patriotism, which had been stimulated by Mazzini in 1848, to his aim of expanding Piedmont into northern Italy.

So far the answer has considered Cavour's modernisation of Piedmont. Now it moves on to other aspects of Cavour's role.

This was not all. Cavour also recognised the need for powerful allies. By sending Piedmontese troops to join with those of Britain and France in the Crimean War he gained European recognition for Piedmont and won the sympathy of Napoleon. In 1858 Napoleon made the Pact of Plombiéres with Piedmont, an agreement to attack Austria. Piedmont was to gain Lombardy and Venetia, while Savoy and Nice would be Napoleon's reward.

This part of the argument also draws attention to Napoleon's role.

The alliance with Napoleon III made victory possible over Austria, which was the principal obstacle to Cavour's ambitions for Piedmont. However, Napoleon, horrified by the bloodshed at Magenta and Solferino, backed out at the Truce of Villafranca. As a result Piedmont gained only Lombardy and not Venetia.

Disappointed by this outcome, Cavour resigned, but then returned to negotiate the union of the Central Italian duchies (Parma, Modena and Tuscany) with Piedmont. The resulting Kingdom of Northern Italy was probably as far as Cavour wanted to go.

Now the essay moves on to Garibaldi, leading to a conclusion which sets Cavour's modernisation in the context of French aid and Garibaldi's role.

Garibaldi's expedition to Sicily and Naples forced him to change his plans. He feared that Garibaldi would go on to attack Rome, which could endanger all that had been achieved. So, he sent troops into the Papal States, which linked up with Garibaldi. Naples and Sicily were handed over to Victor Emmanuel, who thus became King of a united Italy (except Venice and Rome). Although this was not what Cavour had intended when he went to war against Austria in 1859, he handled a potentially dangerous development with great skill, simultaneously restraining Garibaldi and bringing his conquests into a kingdom ruled by Victor Emmanuel.

Cavour's modernisation of Piedmont was crucial in making possible the defeat of Austria, but on its own it is not sufficient to account for the emergence of a united Kingdom of Italy by 1861. Piedmont could probably not have defeated Austria without French aid, so his diplomacy must be seen as just as important as his modernisation. The union of Naples and Sicily with northern Italy owes as much to Garibaldi as to Cavour, though here too Cavour's intervention was crucial.

14 The unification of Germany

The following topics are covered in this chapter:

- Germany, 1815–62
- Bismark and unification, 1862–71
- Bismark's Germany, 1871–90
- The Kaiserreich, 1890–1914

14.1 Germany, 1815–62

LEARNING SUMMARY

After studying this section you should be able to understand:

- the growth of German nationalism
- the failure of the Frankfurt Parliament to unite Germany
- the importance of the Zollverein

The growth of German nationalism

CCEA	AS.1, A2.1
OCR	U4
WJEC	U1, 4

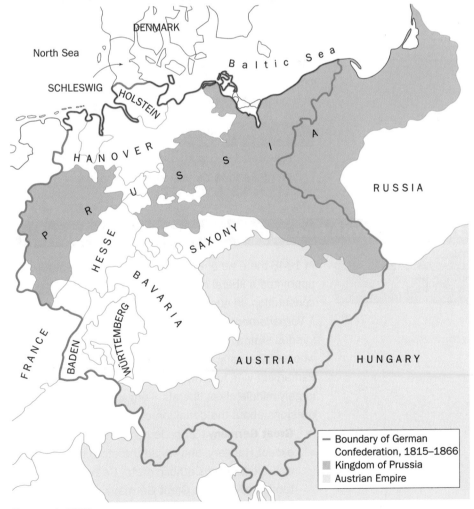

Germany in 1815

DENMARK

North Sea

Baltic Sea

SCHLESWIG

HOLSTEIN

HANOVER

P R U S S I A

RUSSIA

HESSE

SAXONY

BAVARIA

WÜRTTEMBERG

FRANCE

BADEN

AUSTRIA

HUNGARY

— Boundary of German Confederation, 1815–1866
Kingdom of Prussia
Austrian Empire

Prussia included part of modern Poland. Austria ruled modern Czechoslovakia, Hungary, Slovenia and parts of Italy, Romania and Poland.

The political map of pre-unification Germany was laid down in the Vienna settlement of 1815. Germany was divided into 39 states, of which Prussia and Austria were far and away the biggest. A new German Confederation was set up, with a Federal Assembly (Bundestag) consisting of delegates from the states meeting under Austria's presidency. Essentially Germany was a federation of princes. The two biggest states were Austria and Prussia, both of which also ruled territories outside the borders of the Confederation. It is important to note that Austria's non-German territories were much more extensive and more racially diverse than Prussia's.

The German nationalist movement

The Napoleonic period had witnessed the growth of liberal and nationalist ideas in Germany. The French armies which occupied much of Germany during the Napoleonic Wars brought with them **liberal** ideas of freedom and equality. By the end of the Napoleonic period, however, the French were resented as an occupying power rather than as the liberators they professed to be. This stimulated the growth of **nationalism**, which was closely linked with liberalism since freedom came to be seen in terms of freedom from foreign domination, as well as freedom from oppressive rulers. Logically this meant that the German states should be unified into a nation-state strong enough to stand alongside other nation-states such as France.

The universities were the main centres of liberal and nationalist ideas. The ideas of Hegel were particularly influential. He taught, in essence, that the development of the nation was the motive force in the unfolding logic of history.

Between 1815 and 1848, however, the German Confederation was dominated by **Metternich**, the Austrian Chancellor. Under his influence the princes pursued a policy of repression against liberals and nationalists, imposing strict censorship and putting the universities under close supervision.

> **KEY POINT**
>
> Between 1815 and 1848 neither liberals nor nationalists made much progress towards achieving their aims.

The 1848 revolution and the Frankfurt Parliament

Edexcel	**U1**
CCEA	**AS.1, A2.1**
OCR	**U4**
WJEC	**U1, 4**

In 1848 there were revolutions throughout Germany. In Prussia, Frederick William IV appointed a liberal ministry and summoned a National Assembly to draw up a constitution. In Austria, Metternich was overthrown after demonstrations in Vienna. A *Vorparlament* (pre-Parliament), with members drawn from the assemblies of the various states, met in March and arranged for the election of a Parliament for the whole of Germany, the Frankfurt Parliament of 1848–9. The purpose of the Frankfurt Parliament was to draw up a constitution for a united Germany. Its members – largely middle class liberals – engaged in endless debate, which revealed deep divisions about the definition of 'Germany'. There were two possibilities.

- **Great Germany** (Grossdeutschland), which would include the Austrian lands, except Hungary, and would therefore include many Slav peoples. Since Austria was the biggest Catholic state, Catholics in the other South German states tended to support Great Germany.

Think about the arguments for and against each point of view.

- **Little Germany** (Kleindeutschland), which would exclude the Austrian lands altogether, but would include the whole of Prussia. This view was more attractive to North German Protestants.

While the members of the Frankfurt Parliament were debating, the German princes were regaining control of their states. The Parliament offered the crown of a federal Germany in turn to the Austrian Emperor and the King of Prussia, but they both declined. Frederick William IV of Prussia said he would not accept 'the crown from the gutter' and ordered the Prussian delegates to resign from the Parliament. Soon afterwards it collapsed.

> **KEY POINT**
>
> 1848 left many Germans disillusioned with liberalism: the attempt to set up a united Germany by constitutional means had failed. Nationalist feeling had been roused and then disappointed.

Results of the failure of the 1848 revolutions

Despite the failure of 1848, nationalist sentiment remained strong in Germany. The legacy of 1848 was that many Germans regarded parliamentary democracy as ineffective. If liberalism had failed to create a German nation state, other means must be found.

The failure of the Frankfurt Parliament allowed Austria to revive the Confederation. An attempt by Prussia to set up a new federation, which excluded Austria, (the Erfurt Union) failed and in 1850, in the **Submission of Olmütz**, Frederick William IV of Prussia rejoined the revived Confederation.

The revival of the Confederation suited Austrian interests. Austria, however, had a number of weaknesses.
- The multi-national nature of the empire created great problems, particularly the relationship between Austria and Hungary.
- The army, widely thought to be one of the greatest in Europe, was actually less efficient than Prussia's, as was shown in 1866.
- In the 1850s it became increasingly isolated. It alienated Russia, which had been a key ally during the 1848 revolutions, by its attitude in the Crimean War. It fought – and lost – a war against France in northern Italy in 1859.

Prussia, with troops in the Rhineland, began to seem a better defence against the growing power of Napoleon III's France. Moreover it had some important sources of strength.
- It was by far the biggest state in northern Germany, with territories stretching from the Rhineland to East Prussia. Unlike Austria, it was largely German in population, with only one significant national minority (Poles in the east).
- Its economy was strong, with valuable natural resources, including the Ruhr coalfields, and good river communications (the Elbe, Oder and Rhine). From the 1850s it benefited from rapid development of the railway system and growing industrial strength.

Economic Nationalism: the Zollverein

Edexcel **U1**
CCEA **AS.1, A2.1**
OCR **U4**
WJEC **U1, 4**

Free trade was established within Prussia in 1818 and extended by negotiation to several other north German states in the 1820s. In 1834 negotiations with the Bavaria–Württemberg customs union led to the establishment of the Zollverein (customs union) of 17 states with a population of 25 million. Crucially, the Zollverein excluded Austria and thus gave Prussia economic leadership in Germany. Economic integration thus preceded political unification by several decades.

Until the middle of the century German economic development was comparatively slow. Agriculture still employed more than two-thirds of the population and the size of the middle class was small. The building of railways from the 1840s was the turning point: transport costs were reduced by 80% and trade was stimulated. By 1860 Germany was producing more coal than France and the output of iron and steel was growing rapidly. Much of this expansion took place in Prussia, which not only had great natural resources, but also the capital to exploit them and to finance the building of railways and investment in industry.

> **KEY POINT**
>
> The economic and military power of Prussia provided the foundation for the unification of Germany under its leadership.

14.2 Bismarck and unification, 1862–71

LEARNING SUMMARY	After studying this section you should be able to understand:
	• how the budget crisis of 1862 brought Bismarck to power in Prussia
	• the importance of the Danish and Austrian wars
	• how the Franco–Prussian war brought about the unification of Germany
	• why Bismarck was successful in bringing about unification

Bismarck and the budget crisis of 1862

Edexcel **U1**
CCEA **AS.1, A2.1**
OCR **U4**
WJEC **U1, 4**

William I (Regent in 1858 and King of Prussia from 1861) appointed **Roon** as Minister of War to build up Prussia's military strength. Roon was assisted by **Moltke** (Chief of the General Staff from 1857), the first general to recognise the strategic importance of railways. Roon proposed to expand the infantry, reduce the size of the militia and re-equip the army with breech-loading rifles. The Liberals, who had a majority in the Prussian Parliament, opposed the cost of these reforms. At this point William turned to **Bismarck**, appointing him Minister President of Prussia in 1862.

Bismarck came from a family of Junkers (Prussian landowning gentry). His main aim, many historians would argue, was to preserve the social and political power of the Junkers. But he also aimed to expand Prussia's power within Germany and end Austria's predominance. From 1851 Bismarck was the leader of the Prussian delegation to the Diet of the German Confederation, where he took every opportunity to challenge Austria's predominance. He had a reputation for strong anti-liberal views, which was why William called on him in his battle with the Liberals in the Prussian Parliament.

Bismarck used a dubious constitutional technicality to enforce the taxes needed to enlarge the army, even though the Parliament refused to approve them. The expansion of the army was crucial in the three wars between 1864 and 1871, which brought about the unification of Germany.

The Danish and Austrian Wars, 1864–6

Edexcel	**U1**
CCEA	**AS.1, A2.1**
OCR	**U4**
WJEC	**U1, 4**

Note that Bismarck did not plan a war against Denmark – he simply took advantage of a situation that arose.

Schleswig–Holstein and the Danish war

The King of Denmark was also Duke of Schleswig-Holstein. Christian IX, who succeeded to the throne in 1863, wanted to make Schleswig part of Denmark. The majority of the people of Schleswig were German and there was an outcry in Germany. Bismarck took the opportunity to present himself as the champion of German interests. In co-operation with Austria, which would not let Prussia act alone, he made war on Denmark, which was quickly defeated. By the Convention of Gastein (1865), Prussia took Schleswig and Austria Holstein. This gave Bismarck the chance to pick a quarrel with Austria whenever he liked.

The Seven Weeks' War, 1866

Edexcel	**U1**
CCEA	**AS.1, A2.1**
OCR	**U4**
WJEC	**U1, 4**

The German Empire, 1871

Compare this with the Danish war. This time Bismarck created the situation himself.

Bismarck's second war was against Austria. He had made his mark as a diplomat by challenging Austria's predominance in the German Confederation in the 1850s. This war was one he seems to have planned.

- Firstly, he gained the support of the Tsar by supporting Russia in the suppression of the Polish Revolt of 1863.
- He made an alliance with Italy, which wanted Venetia.
- At a meeting with Napoleon III at Biarritz he made vague promises of future compensation for France.

Venetia and Holstein were the only territories Austria lost. Bismarck did not want territory, but to deprive Austria of its predominant position in Germany.

In 1866 Bismarck provoked war by proposing that the German Confederation should be dissolved and a new confederation set up excluding Austria. The war, which only lasted seven weeks, proved the efficiency of the Prussian army with its new breech-loading rifle. The main Austrian army was overwhelmingly defeated at Sadowa in Bohemia. By the Treaty of Prague the German Confederation was abolished and a new **North German Confederation** was set up. The South German states were to be independent. Schleswig–Holstein was handed over to Prussia and soon afterwards Prussia annexed Hanover and several other north German states. Venetia was duly handed to Italy, even though Austria had defeated the Italian army.

The Seven Weeks' War had several important consequences.

- Austria was pushed out of Germany by the abolition of the German Confederation and turned its attention to the Balkans.
- The Prussian-dominated North German Confederation was set up.
- The Prussian Liberals abandoned their battle with Bismarck over the army and passed the 'iron budget' in 1866.
- French opinion was alarmed by the sudden emergence of a powerful new state to its east.

Many historians think that the establishment of the North German Confederation was all Bismarck wanted. They see it as a Prussian takeover of northern Germany to serve Prussian ends rather than the aims of the German nationalists. They argue Bismarck's aim was to protect the Junker domination of Prussia against liberals and nationalists. Unification achieved by a liberal revolution would threaten the Junkers. If this is true, the war with France and the creation of the Second Reich were not part of his plans.

The Franco–Prussian War, 1870–1

Edexcel	**U1**
CCEA	**AS.1, A2.1**
WJEC	**U1, 4**
OCR	**U4**

Historians debate whether a war against France was part of Bismarck's long-term plans, but after 1866 it became increasingly difficult to avoid one. Public opinion in France regarded the defeat of Austria by Prussia and the establishment of the North German Confederation as, in effect, a defeat for France. It had long been an aim of French foreign policy to prevent the emergence of a strong power in western Germany. Prussia's gains in the war were greatly resented and between 1866 and 1870 relations between France and Prussia were tense. Bismarck's disclosure that Napoleon had asked for compensation in the Rhineland or Belgium inflamed relations further.

This was really a pretext for war – the problem could easily have been solved without it.

The issue which sparked off the Franco–Prussian War in 1870 was the succession to the Spanish throne. One of the candidates, Prince Leopold, was a member of the Hohenzollern family, of which William I was the head. Napoleon III, fearing the encirclement of France if a Hohenzollern should become King of Spain, demanded that Leopold should withdraw. This was agreed, but Napoleon then demanded guarantees that the candidature would not be renewed. It was clear that he was seeking a diplomatic victory at Prussia's expense in order to boost his prestige. Bismarck altered the telegram in which William announced his rejection of the latest French demands (the **Ems Telegram**) so that the French government could only take it as a rebuff. Public opinion in Paris was outraged and demanded war.

Did Bismarck provoke the war? There is some evidence that he encouraged Leopold's candidature, perhaps with the aim of provoking a crisis. He certainly altered the Ems telegram with that aim. He appears to have thought war was inevitable in the end.

The war was a triumph for Prussia. One French army was surrounded at Metz and another which was sent to relieve it was itself surrounded and forced to surrender at Sedan. Napoleon was taken prisoner and a republic was set up in Paris. Paris was besieged between September 1870 and January 1871. The French were unable to find allies as Bismarck's diplomacy had kept Napoleon isolated. In January an armistice was signed and in May 1871 peace was made at Frankfurt. Alsace and Lorraine became part of Germany and France was to pay an indemnity and accept the occupation of its northern provinces.

The war enabled Bismarck to complete the unification of Germany. It aroused nationalist enthusiasm throughout Germany, and the southern states of Bavaria, Baden and Württemberg, which had remained outside the North German Confederation of 1867, were swept into a unified Germany. On 18 January 1871 William I was proclaimed **Emperor of Germany**. The new Empire excluded Austria.

Why Bismarck was successful in uniting Germany

Edexcel **U1**
CCEA **AS.1, A2.1**
WJEC **U1, 4**
OCR **U4**

Three factors were of great importance in this issue.

- The first was **Prussian military power**. Only military strength could overcome the hostility of Austria, in whose interest it was to keep Germany divided. Similarly it was likely that sooner or later France would try to prevent the emergence of a greater power to its east. Thus the roles of Roon, the Prussian Minister of War, and Moltke, the Chief of the General Staff, in building up the Prussian army, were crucial to Bismarck's success.

- The **economic development of Prussia** underlay its military power. Prussia was already the most industrialised state in Germany before Bismarck came to power and through the Zollverein it had gained economic supremacy over the other German states. It was the economic and military strength of Prussia which allowed Bismarck to achieve political unification.

- Bismarck's own contribution through his cynical and unscrupulous **diplomacy** was vital. He believed that 'reasons of state' justified any action. He could only have been thwarted if those powers threatened by the unification of Germany (or the growth of Prussian power) had worked together, but his diplomacy prevented this. The two powers which certainly should have worked together were France and Austria, but Bismarck's deception of Napoleon III at Biarritz kept Austria isolated in 1866, while his lenient treatment of Austria after the Seven Weeks' War ensured Austria's neutrality in the Franco–Prussian War. He ensured Britain's neutrality in 1870 by revealing that Napoleon III had his eye on Belgium in 1866 as 'compensation' for Prussia's gains in the Seven Weeks' War. He encouraged Russia to take advantage of France's involvement in war to repudiate the Black Sea clauses of the Treaty of Paris of 1856.

You can relate this to Bismarck's remark (made much later) that Prussia's aims would be achieved not by speeches but by 'blood and iron'.

This is known as Realpolitik.

You should be able to explain the significance of each of these dates.

KEY DATES

1815	Establishment of the German Confederation
1834	Zollverein set up
1848–9	Frankfurt Parliament
1850	Submission of Olmütz
1862	Bismarck Prime Minister of Prussia
1864	War against Denmark over Schleswig–Holstein
1866	Seven Weeks' War (Prussia vs. Austria)
1867	Establishment of the North German Confederation
1870–1	Franco–Prussian War
1871	German Empire set up

14.3 Bismarck's Germany, 1871–90

LEARNING SUMMARY

After studying this section you should be able to understand:

- the nature of the 'Bismarckian' political system
- how successful Bismarck was in dealing with the liberals, the socialists and the Roman Catholic Church

The German political structure

AQA	**U1**	Edexcel **U1**
OCR	**U4**	WJEC **U4**

The new German Empire (the Second Reich) was a federal state. William I of Prussia was the Emperor (Kaiser) and Bismarck the Chancellor. The Emperor was head of the executive and the army. He had the right to declare war or martial law in an emergency. The Chancellor was appointed by and responsible to the Emperor.

There were two houses of Parliament. The upper house (**Bundesrat**) consisted of representatives of the German states. Prussia, as the biggest state, had the most representatives in the Bundesrat. Prussia's government was controlled by the Junkers, who were thus able to block constitutional change through their representatives in the Bundesrat. While Bismarck was Chancellor he was able to control the Bundesrat through his position as Minister President of Prussia. The lower house (**Reichstag**) was elected by universal male suffrage and this made the constitution appear unusually democratic for its time.

Make sure you understand the arguments for describing the constitution as autocratic even though it was superficially democratic.

In reality, however, the constitution was autocratic, since the Reichstag had little power. German Chancellors, unlike British Prime Ministers, did not owe their position to their ability to command a majority in parliament (the Reichstag). The Reichstag did not have the power to remove the Chancellor, nor did the defeat of a government measure in the Reichstag force him to resign. It did, however, have the power to veto legislation and it controlled the non-military part of the imperial budget. This meant that it was desirable, but not essential, for the Chancellor to try to gain the support of enough parties or groups to approve his policies, but he could not be overthrown if he was unable to do so. Ultimately power lay with the Emperor. While William I was emperor Bismarck was allowed to carry on the government with relatively little interference, but things changed when William II came to the throne.

Domestic affairs

| AQA | U1 | Edexcel | U1 |
| OCR | U4 | WJEC | U4 |

The Liberals

At first Bismarck relied on the Liberals for a majority in the Reichstag, partly because he needed their support in his quarrel with the Catholics (see below). From 1874, however, his relationship with the Liberals cooled. The first dispute was over the size of the army, which accounted for 90% of the federal budget. In 1874, Bismarck forced through a proposal that its size should be fixed for seven years, thus greatly reducing what little power the Reichstag had. The second issue was protection. After a brief economic boom prompted by the euphoria of unification, a prolonged period of economic depression began in 1873. Bismarck decided to abandon free trade in favour of protection. This not only won him support from both industrialists and landowners, but had the further advantage of making the imperial government's finances less dependent on contributions from the states. Strong opposition from the liberals, who supported free trade, led to a decisive break with them in 1879 when **tariffs** were introduced. Henceforth, Bismarck relied on the Conservatives and the Catholic Centre Party in the Reichstag.

> Tariffs would be part of the federal budget. The contributions paid by the states were often a source of dispute.

The Kulturkampf

The North German Confederation was predominantly Protestant, but southern Germany was Roman Catholic. When the German Empire was set up in 1871, it therefore had a substantial minority of Catholics. Bismarck feared that their loyalty to Rome would conflict with their loyalty to the Empire. The growth of ultramontanism in the Roman Catholic Church, highlighted by the proclamation of the doctrine of Papal Infallibility in 1870, strengthened his suspicions. In the 1870s he conducted a struggle with the Catholics, known as the **Kulturkampf**. By the **May Laws** of 1873–5 education was brought under state control and state approval was required for the licensing of priests. The campaign backfired. Catholics rallied round and the Catholic Centre Party made gains in the Reichstag elections of 1874 and 1877. Since Bismarck needed their support against the Liberals over tariffs, he toned down the Kulturkampf and withdrew some of the May Laws.

> Ultramontanism placed great emphasis on the authority of the Pope over Catholics.

> **KEY POINT**
>
> Little was achieved by the Kulturkampf and it is generally thought that it was a mistake.

The Socialists

Another reason why Bismarck relaxed the Kulturkampf was the growth of socialism. There were socialist groups in Germany as early as the 1840s, but the establishment of the Empire with a Reichstag elected by universal suffrage provided the spur to bring them together. In 1875 the Social Democratic Party was founded on the basis of the Gotha Programme. In 1877 the party won half a million votes in the Reichstag election. Bismarck was alarmed and in 1878 introduced the **Anti-Socialist Laws** which banned socialist organisations, meetings and newspapers. The socialists were not, however, banned from membership of the Reichstag. Although it was handicapped, the Socialist Party continued to grow in strength. The Anti-Socialist Laws were renewed every three years until the fall of Bismarck, but were then allowed to lapse.

> **KEY POINT**
>
> 1878–9 was a turning point in Bismarck's relations with the political parties. He broke with the liberals, introduced the Anti-Socialist Laws, ended the Kulturkampf and began to rely on the Conservative and Catholic Centre parties.

State socialism

Bismarck also introduced 'state socialism'. In 1883–4 he instituted sickness and accident insurance and in 1889 old age pensions. The benefits were not generous, but were far in advance of what was provided in any other industrial country at the time. One reason for the introduction of these welfare measures was to undermine support for the socialists, but they were also a response to concerns about the growing gap between rich and poor as a result of the combination of industrialisation and the prolonged depression.

> You should be able to explain the significance of each of these dates.

> **KEY DATES**
>
> | | |
> |---|---|
> | 1871–90 | Bismarck Chancellor of the German Empire |
> | 1873–5 | May Laws |
> | 1878 | Anti-Socialist Laws |
> | 1879 | Introduction of tariffs; Break with the Liberals; Dual Alliance – Germany and Austria |
> | 1883–4 | State Socialism |
> | 1888 | Death of William I; Accession of William II |

14.4 The Kaiserreich, 1890–1914

LEARNING SUMMARY	After studying this section you should be able to understand:
	• the political structures and the role of the Kaiser in Wilhelmine Germany
	• the importance of economic developments in imperial Germany
	• the political influence of the agrarian and industrial elites and the army

The structure of politics

AQA	**U1**	OCR	**U4**
Edexcel	**U3**	WJEC	**U4**

The Kaiser

In 1888 William I died. After the brief reign of Frederick III, **William II** succeeded as Kaiser aged 29. He was a rather neurotic man whose behaviour was unpredictable. He was convinced of Germany's world-historic mission. Although he was the grandson of Queen Victoria, he was anti-British, although at the same time he admired Britain.

William was an autocrat at the head of an autocratic system. Under the 1871 constitution the Kaiser appointed the Chancellor and thus was in ultimate control. William II was determined to use his powers personally and exercised a much more direct control over government than his grandfather. As he was also head of the army his personal power was very considerable.

> It was because the system was autocratic that the Kaiser's character mattered so much.

The significance of this quickly became apparent. William disagreed with Bismarck about the anti-socialist policies, colonial expansion and relations with Russia. In 1890 Bismarck retired 'because of his health'.

The Reichstag and the political parties

The imperial constitution made it desirable – though not essential – for the Chancellor to gain the support of enough parties or groups to approve his policies. The divisions in German society, reflected in the Reichstag, made this difficult.

The most notable development in the Reichstag in the reign of William II was the steady rise of the **Socialist Party**. In the 1890 election – after the lapse of Bismarck's Anti-Socialist Laws – it gained 20% of the votes. By 1912 this had risen to 35%. In that year it gained 110 seats, even though the electoral system was weighted against urban voters. It was therefore the biggest party.

Other groups with a significant presence in the Reichstag were the Catholic Centre Party, the Liberals (divided into National Liberals and Progressives) and the Conservatives. Because of social changes in the 1890s support for the Conservatives declined. At the same time small right-wing, anti-Semitic fringe parties gained seats in the Reichstag. The Conservatives responded by adopting anti-Semitic policies themselves after 1900, along with strong support for protection of agriculture.

Chancellors

There were four Chancellors between 1890 and 1914.
- **Caprivi** (1890–4) shared William II's views on the Anti-Socialist Laws and the alliance with Russia, both of which were allowed to lapse. Social welfare laws were passed to regulate working conditions and child labour, in pursuit of William II's idea of winning over the working class by appearing as the 'social Kaiser'. But William became alarmed by the growth of the Socialist Party and abandoned this aim. After a series of intrigues, Caprivi was forced to resign.
- **Prince Hohenlohe** (1894–1900) was an elderly and rather weak Chancellor. The real power lay with the Kaiser, whose direct interventions in government were increasingly frequent. From 1897 he often by-passed Hohenlohe and gave his confidence to Bülow (Foreign Secretary) and Tirpitz (Secretary for the Navy). It was during this ministry that Germany embarked on the policy of **Weltpolitik** and began the expansion of the navy with the **Naval Law** of 1898.

> Weltpolitik is explained on pages 236–7.

> This meant distracting the German people from social issues by using foreign policy to display Germany's power.

- **Bülow** (1900–9) pursued a policy of '**social imperialism**', appealing to nationalistic fervour and enthusiasm for the naval building programme. He hoped by this to win the electorate from support for the Socialist and Liberal Parties. In this he had some success but at the cost of growing budget deficits. His parliamentary support, the 'Bülow bloc', broke up over his tax proposals to meet this deficit in 1909. At the same time William II's *Daily Telegraph* interview led to an open rift between the Kaiser and the Chancellor, who resigned in 1909.

- **Bethmann–Hollweg** (1909–17) faced continued financial crisis, though he was able to secure the passing of the army bills in 1912–3. When the Socialists emerged as the largest party in the Reichstag in 1912, it became increasingly difficult to achieve stable parliamentary majorities. The Chancellor was therefore dependent on the Emperor and the army, with the Pan–German League in the background. This was the situation in the crisis of 1914.

> **KEY POINT**
>
> Chancellors had to manoeuvre between the Kaiser, the political parties in the Reichstag, the elites and the army. In 1914 the crucial decisions were made by the Kaiser and the army leaders.

The economy

| AQA | **U1** | OCR | **U4** |
| Edexcel | **U3** | WJEC | **U4** |

> Germany's economic growth was an important reason for fears that it was a threat to the balance of power, especially after 1890.

In the period after 1870 Germany's economy developed very rapidly, so that by 1914 its industrial strength rivalled and in some spheres overtook Britain's. By 1914 coal production, which had quadrupled since 1870, almost equalled that of Britain, while iron and steel production was higher. The rail network trebled between 1870 and 1910. Newer industries such as electrical engineering and chemicals expanded rapidly. By 1914 Germany's merchant navy was the second largest in the world after Britain's. Behind this growth was an equally impressive expansion of the financial sector.

Industrialisation was accompanied by urbanisation. Germany's population increased by 65% between 1870 and 1914, from 41 millions to 68 million. At the same time there was considerable internal migration from the countryside to the towns, many of which doubled or trebled in size. Migrants to the towns were attracted by the hope of employment and higher wages and undoubtedly wages did rise, reflecting the growth of the economy. Nevertheless, many of the new town-dwellers found themselves living in slums, working long hours in poor conditions and liable to periodic unemployment.

Economic change had political consequences. The rise of the Socialist Party, which had caused Bismarck so much concern, was closely linked to the growth of an urban proletariat. At the other end of the scale, the development of large-scale industrial concerns led to a rise of an industrial elite with considerable political influence, but with interests which sometimes conflicted with those of the older agrarian elite, e.g. over protection.

> **KEY POINTS**
>
> - Germany's industrial strength added to the unease about the European balance of power since the unification of Germany.
> - Industrialisation created unresolved social and political tensions in the German Empire.

Pressure groups and the political elites

| AQA | **U1** | OCR | **U4** |
| Edexcel | **U3** | WJEC | **U4** |

Because of the relative powerlessness of the Reichstag, much of the political activity of Wilhelmine Germany took place outside the parliamentary system. Pressure groups played an important part.

- The **Pan–German League** (founded 1891) built up support for William II's Weltpolitik.

- The **Navy League** (1891) helped to drum up enthusiasm for Tirpitz's naval expansion programme.
- The **Army League** (1912) put pressure on the Reichstag to pass the army bills of 1912–3.
- The **Agrarian League** (1893), founded in response to Caprivi's commercial policies, campaigned for protection for agriculture. Its success in mobilising peasant discontent played an important part in the radicalisation of the Conservative Party.

Much political influence was wielded by three powerful interest groups.

- **Agrarian interests**: The Prussian Junkers (landed gentry) had a disproportionate political influence. The Prussian Parliament was elected on a system which favoured them and allowed them to control the government of Prussia. Since Prussia was the largest state in the Empire, the Junkers controlled the Bundesrat (Federal Council), which consisted of representatives of the states. Although their economic importance had declined relative to the industrialists, their political power remained and was exerted to block political reform and to protect the interests of agriculture, e.g. by pressing for tariffs directed against Russian grain imports in 1902.

- **Industrialists**: Industrialisation led to the emergence of a powerful and wealthy group of big industrialists. They supported William II's Weltpolitik as a means of securing markets for Germany's manufactures and sources of raw materials and provided the finance for the Pan–German League and the Navy League. They supported Tirpitz's plans for expansion of the navy because it would underpin the Weltpolitik and also provide contracts for shipbuilders. German industry would benefit directly and at the same time the appeal to German nationalism would divert support from the socialists. Opposition to socialism united the industrialists and the landowners and this combination was one of the cornerstones of politics in the period. But there were also tensions between them – industrial and agrarian interests were difficult to reconcile over the issue of protection.

- **The army**: Members of the army swore loyalty and obedience exclusively to the Kaiser. William took his role as head of the army seriously. The court was full of generals. Many historians argue that the army leaders, and especially Moltke, the Chief of the General Staff, had more influence than the Chancellor in 1914.

> Krupp was an example.

> Socialism and protection were two of the main issues in Wilhelmine politics.

Germany's part in the build-up to the First World War is explained on pages 235–9.

KEY POINT

The political structures of the German Empire were not democratic. Power lay with the agrarian and industrial elites, the army and the bureaucracy.

> You should be able to explain the significance of each of these dates.

KEY DATES

1888	Accession of William II
1890	Retirement of Bismarck
1890–4	Caprivi Chancellor
1894–1900	Hohenlohe Chancellor
1900–9	Bülow Chancellor
1909–17	Bethmann–Hollweg Chancellor
1914	Assassination at Sarajevo; Outbreak of First World War

Exam practice questions

1 Why was Bismarck more successful than the revolutionaries of 1848–1849 in ending Austria's influence in Germany? **[50]**

2 **(a)** Why did Bismarck break with the Liberals in 1879? **[12]**

(b) How successful were Bismarck's policies towards the Catholics and the socialists? **[24]**

3 **(a)** Why was Bismarck forced to resign in 1890? **[12]**

(b) How important was the political influence of pressure groups and the army in Germany between 1890 and 1914? **[24]**

4 'The emergence of a unified and powerful German state was rooted in its economic development.' **[50]**

How far do you agree with this view of German history in the period 1815–1914?

5 Why did German liberalism achieve so little in the period 1815–1914? **[50]**

15 Italy, 1896–1945

The following topics are covered in this chapter:

- Italy 1896–1915: a troubled nation
- The rise of Fascism
- The Fascist dictatorship
- Mussolini's Italy
- Foreign affairs

15.1 Italy, 1896–1915: a troubled nation

> **LEARNING SUMMARY**
>
> After studying this section you should be able to understand:
>
> - why Italy can be described as a troubled nation in this period
> - the role of Italy in the First World War

Italy in the 1890s

OCR **U1**   Edexcel **U1**

The Kingdom of Italy was a relatively new state. Most of Italy had been unified in 1859–60; Venetia had been added in 1866 and Rome in 1871. It proved difficult to make it a strong nation state. The new state had many problems.

- Lack of unity. National feeling was weak and local loyalties remained strong. Most importantly there were big social and cultural differences between the backward south and the rest of the country.
- Political parties were weak and lacked discipline.
- There was a parliamentary system of government, but only about 10% of the population had the vote because of the property and literacy qualifications. Moreover, there was little experience of parliamentary government in the states which had existed before unification.
- Participation in the political process was limited by the papacy, which decreed that Catholics should not vote or stand for election.

These political problems were accompanied by social unrest. Agricultural depression and slum conditions in the growing towns led to widespread rioting in the late 1890s. Socialism and anarchism grew in strength. The government responded with repression, culminating in 1898 when troops fired on demonstrators in Milan, killing about one hundred. In 1900 an anarchist assassinated the king in revenge.

> **KEY POINT**
>
> Italy failed to develop an effective system of parliamentary government.

Giolitti and 'transformism'

The weaknesses of the system of government led to the development of the system known as '**transformism**'. Created by Depretis in the 1870s, it enabled **Giolitti** to dominate political life between 1901 and 1914. It involved using patronage, which Giolitti controlled as Minister of the Interior, and playing off factions against each other to control Parliament. In theory transformism was supposed to ensure government by the best qualified men, regardless of party

He was Prime Minister as well as Minister of the Interior for much of this period.

allegiance. In practice it was a corrupt system. In order to maintain control over Parliament, the support of deputies was obtained by promises of political appointments or money for local projects. It destroyed faith in the parliamentary system. Nevertheless Giolitti had a number of achievements.

- Trade and industry expanded rapidly.
- Government finances improved as a result.
- Social reforms such as public health regulations, pensions and health insurance were introduced.
- The vote was extended to all men over 30 and illiterates were allowed to vote.
- More money was provided for education – though illiteracy remained high, especially in the south.

In spite of this, unrest remained high and in June 1914 Italy seemed to be on the verge of revolution.

The quest for colonies

The late nineteenth century was a period of European imperial expansion and many Italians saw it as a matter of prestige to acquire colonies. As a new and relatively weak state, Italy had largely missed out in the European scramble for African colonies in the 1880s and 1890s and its attempt to secure control of Ethiopia had ended in humiliating defeat at Adowa (1896). The conquest of Tripolitania (modern Libya) in 1912 was therefore greeted with approval, though as it turned out the colony was of little real value economically.

The First World War

OCR **U1**   CCEA **AS2**
Edexcel **U1**

The Italians called these territories 'Italia Irredenta' – that part of Italy which had not been recovered.

Italy had been a member of the Triple Alliance with Germany and Austria–Hungary since 1882, but there were always tensions because of Italian claims to South Tyrol, Trentino and Trieste – all part of the Austrian Empire. For Italians these were Italian territories, which had not yet been brought into the new state. When war broke out in 1914 Italy remained neutral. In 1915, she entered the war on the Allied side against Germany and Austria in return for a promise that she would receive the disputed territories and also Istria at the end of the war.

The war highlighted the weaknesses of the Italian army. Defeat at **Caporetto** (1917) led to the occupation of much of Venetia by Austrian forces. In the dying days of the war in 1918, however, the Austrians were pushed back after an Italian victory at Vittorio Veneto. At the end of the war Italian forces had advanced into and beyond the disputed territories.

KEY POINT

The First World War revealed Italy's weakness.

15.2 The rise of Fascism

LEARNING SUMMARY

After studying this section you should be able to understand:
- the problems faced by Italy at the end of the First World War
- Mussolini's rise to power

Italy at the end of the First World War

AQA **U1, 2** CCEA **AS2**
OCR **U1** WJEC **U1**
Edexcel **U1**

Italy was in poor shape at the end of the First World War. Its military record had been mixed. After entering on the Allied side in 1915, its armies were heavily defeated at Caporetto (1917) by the Austrians and Germans, who then advanced almost as far as Venice. This disaster, however, produced a spirit of national resistance and in 1918 the Italians defeated the Austrians at **Vittorio Veneto**. Austria was forced to seek an armistice. In view of this, the Italians were bitterly disappointed by the peace settlement. They gained South Tyrol, Trentino, Trieste and part of Istria, but their claims to the remainder of Istria, part of Dalmatia and a protectorate over Albania were rejected. All of these had been promised by the Allies in the Treaty of London when Italy entered the war. Particularly galling was the failure to get Fiume, the population of which was largely Italian. Italy was also disappointed that it gained none of the former German colonies. It seemed small reward for the loss of nearly 700 000 men plus over half a million deaths.

The economy

The Italian economy was weak even before the war. Because of the lack of coal and minerals, industrial development was slow. Agriculture was backward and peasants' standards of living were low, especially in the south. The war made matters worse: the total cost was as much as Italian government expenditure in the previous fifty years. Italy had to borrow heavily from the USA. Inflation became a serious problem, affecting the middle classes particularly badly as their savings were virtually wiped out. The end of wartime production led to widespread unemployment, which was added to by the demobilisation of 2½ million soldiers. Many unemployed ex-servicemen joined the various para-military organisations which sprang up. Others resorted to banditry and lawlessness was rife.

> These were the sources of Mussolini's Fascist fighting groups.

The political system

Italy's parliamentary democracy was discredited and failed to cope with Italy's post-war problems. In the half-century from the unification of Italy in 1859–60 to the First World War, governments had managed parliament by a system of bribery and corruption. This was known as **transformism**. Regional differences, particularly between the north and the south, were strong and worked against the growth of truly national parties. Disagreements about whether Italy should enter the war added a further source of political division. There were many small parties in Parliament and the introduction of proportional representation in 1919 made matters worse. The two largest parties, the Socialists and the Catholic Popular Party, were unable to co-operate and it was therefore impossible to form stable ministries. Between 1918 and 1922 there were five different governments.

> Thus the results of unification had been profoundly disappointing.

> **KEY POINT**
>
> Many Italians thought that what Italy most needed was strong government rather than democracy.

Gabriele d'Annunzio

The weakness of the government was dramatically illustrated in 1919–20 when the poet Gabriele d'Annunzio with a band of nationalists and ex-soldiers in a uniform of black shirts captured Fiume and held it for 16 months. The government could not support this venture, as d'Annunzio was acting in defiance of the peace settlement; neither could it oppose him since public opinion regarded him as a national hero. Eventually, it had to send troops to remove d'Annunzio and his followers and Fiume became an international free city. The episode was a lesson to Mussolini in the use of force to achieve nationalistic ends.

Mussolini's rise to power

AQA	U1, 2	CCEA	AS2
OCR	U1	WJEC	U1
Edexcel	U1		

By these tactics the Fascists helped to create disorder and then claimed that fascism stood for the restoration of law and order by strong government.

The combination of weak government, anger at the peace settlement and social unrest made the period 1918–22 chaotic. Strikes, riots and lawlessness became widespread. The appearance of factory councils and leagues of farm workers aroused fears of a communist revolution. The anti-communists responded by forming armed bands, of which the most important were the *Fasci di combattimento* (fighting groups) formed in Milan in 1919 by **Mussolini**. Mussolini's message was that Italy needed strong government. Fascist groups were formed throughout Italy and began attacking socialists and communists. In 1921 Mussolini founded the National Fascist Party. He won the support of landowners and industrialists, who began to finance the party. In the general election of 1921 the Fascists won 35 seats.

A general strike in 1922 provided Mussolini with the chance to gain power. The Fascists helped to defeat the strike by taking control of public buildings and organising street battles with the socialists. Meanwhile, the government stood by, apparently helpless, and failed to take on the socialists. In October 1922 Mussolini organised a '**march on Rome**' (by train!) by 30 000 Fascists. The Prime Minister, Facta, wanted to use the army and police to disperse them, but King Victor Emmanuel III refused and instead invited Mussolini to form a government.

KEY POINT

Mussolini was invited to take office merely by threatening the use of force. At the time his party had only 35 MPs.

15.3 The Fascist dictatorship

LEARNING SUMMARY	After studying this section you should be able to understand:
	• how Mussolini established himself as a dictator
	• the reasons for Mussolini's success in doing so

The consolidation of Mussolini's power

AQA	U1, 2	CCEA	AS2
OCR	U1	WJEC	U1
Edexcel	U1		

When Mussolini became Prime Minister, he formed a coalition with only four Fascists in the government. But he also persuaded Parliament to grant him dictatorial powers for a year. This enabled him to place Fascists in key positions in local government and the police. In 1923 a new Electoral Law (the **Acerbo Law**) provided that the party that gained most votes in a general election should have two-thirds of the seats in the Chamber of Deputies. The other parties agreed to this because they wanted to end the political paralysis that had afflicted the parliamentary system since 1918. In the election of 1924, the Fascists and their allies easily achieved the necessary number of votes. The election was marked by

Another example of the Fascists promoting disorder while claiming to be the party that would restore law and order.

a good deal of violence, with the Fascist blackshirts destroying the printing presses of opposition newspapers and beating up socialists in the streets. Even so, 2.5 million votes were cast against the Fascists.

Shortly afterwards **Matteotti**, who had publicly blamed Mussolini for the violence in the election campaign, was murdered. Public opinion was outraged and there were demands for Mussolini's dismissal. When the King refused to dismiss him, opposition members left Parliament. This was known as the **Aventine Secession**. It was a mistake, as it left Mussolini in complete control of Parliament.

In 1925, he took advantage of the situation to establish himself as dictator. All other parties were banned, non-Fascists removed from the government and opposition newspapers taken over. In December 1925 Mussolini became responsible to the King, and not to Parliament, and at the same time the King's right to appoint or dismiss ministers was taken away. In January 1926 Mussolini gained the power to make laws by decree.

> **KEY POINT**
>
> These changes made Parliament a consultative body and Mussolini a dictator.

Why was Mussolini able to establish a dictatorship?

AQA	**U1, 2**	CCEA	**AS2**
OCR	**U1**	WJEC	**U1**
Edexcel	**U1**		

Probably the most important reason was the virtual breakdown of parliamentary government between 1918 and 1922. For this the leaders of the existing Parliamentary parties bear much of the responsibility. The Prime Ministers of the period 1918–22, unable to provide effective government, came to rely on the Fascist paramilitary bands as a counterweight to the left-wing paramilitaries who seemed to threaten Italy with revolution. **Giolitti**, the Liberal Prime Minister in 1921–2, actually encouraged the Fascists by including them in his list of government candidates in the 1921 election, with the result that 35 Fascists were elected.

The socialists, the biggest party after the 1919 election, refused to co-operate with other parties and this was a major reason why no stable government could be formed. Furthermore, the socialists split in 1921 when the communist party was formed. This made the parliamentary situation even more complicated and the street battles between the various paramilitary bands even more frequent.

Support for the Fascists

In these circumstances Mussolini won the backing of important groups who were afraid of a communist revolution.
- Landowners, who welcomed Fascist attacks on leagues of farm workers.
- Industrialists, who similarly welcomed their attacks on the trade unions.
- The middle classes, who had lost their savings in the wartime inflation and feared that a communist revolution would reduce them to the level of the working classes.
- The Catholic Church, which saw a communist revolution as a major threat. Mussolini, formerly an atheist, went out of his way in 1921–2 to court the support of the papacy.

- The royal family. Mussolini abandoned his earlier republican views. The ling, while not giving open approval to Mussolini, helped to bring him to power by refusing to allow the army to be used against him.

> Don't underestimate Mussolini. He created the Fascist Party and gained power in three years.

Mussolini himself played an important part. Not only did he found the Fascist Party and gain it a foothold in Parliament, but he also provided leadership. At this stage in his career he had presence and the ability to project himself both by his oratory and his journalistic skills.

15.4 Mussolini's Italy

LEARNING SUMMARY	After studying this section you should be able to understand:
	- the main features of the Fascist state in Italy and the effectiveness of its control of opinion
	- the economic policies adopted by Mussolini and their social effects

The Fascist state

AQA	**U1, 2**	CCEA	**AS2**
OCR	**U1**	WJEC	**U1**
Edexcel	**U1**		

Fascist ideas

Fascism had no coherent philosophy. Mussolini's changing political views (he was a socialist and a republican before the war) suggest that his main aim was simply to get power. Fascism did, however, have some basic ideas.

- It stood for strong, centralised government (the name Fascist was derived from an ancient Roman symbol of authority).
- It placed great emphasis on the cult of the leader: Fascist propaganda depicted Mussolini (Il Duce) as a hero.
- It taught the subordination of the interests of the individual to the state.
- It was anti-democratic (hence a one-party state) and anti-communist.
- It aimed for economic self-sufficiency (autarky).
- It emphasised national pride.

Il Duce

> Mussolini seems to have believed in his own propaganda about his unique abilities.

At the heart of the Fascist state was Mussolini – **Il Duce** (the leader). Much emphasis was placed on the cult of the Duce. Mass rallies were organised to glorify Mussolini and the media were harnessed to propaganda. With the power to make laws by decree, he was a dictator. He alone appointed ministers and he was personally in charge of a number of ministries. Since all other parties were abolished, the electoral system was changed in 1928 so that electors could only accept (or, in theory, reject) a list of four hundred candidates drawn up by the Fascist Grand Council.

Mussolini's dictatorship

The Grand Council itself was the centrepiece of Mussolini's **Corporate State**. It consisted of representatives from each of the corporations Mussolini set up to organise workers and employers. In 1938, the Chamber of Fasces and Corporations replaced the Chamber of Deputies (Parliament). It had little real power, however. It only met when Mussolini summoned it. He played off its members against one another and this ensured that it did what he wanted. Thus Mussolini ensured that his authority was not challenged by the Fascist Party. No party elite grew up.

The system was not, however, a dictatorship like that of Hitler or Stalin. Much of the existing machinery of government remained in operation. At local level the prefects continued to be in charge and the local party officials were subordinated to them. The monarchy, the army and the police all remained. In central government Mussolini's reforms simply made the administration more complicated and less efficient.

The control of opinion

Much effort was devoted to developing the cult of the Duce through the media, but with only partial success.

- Newspapers and books were strictly censored and the radio was state-controlled. The media churned out government propaganda.
- The government regarded the film industry as important and tried to regulate it to serve its propaganda purposes, but its control was limited.
- Similarly the Ministry of Popular Culture failed to impose its ideas of Fascist culture in the spheres of literature, music and art.

Education was closely supervised. University teachers had to take an oath of loyalty to Mussolini. Schoolteachers had to be party members. Textbooks were re-written to glorify the Fascist state. State interference in education intensified from 1936, when textbooks became a state monopoly. Even so, it was not wholly effective, especially in universities, where the historian Croce and others continued to criticise the regime.

The indoctrination of the young was also pursued through **Fascist youth groups** which encouraged hero-worship of Mussolini and glorified war. Members often became enthusiastic Fascists, but 40% of Italy's youth did not join them.

Anti-Semitism

Anti-Semitism was not a part of Fascist ideology at first, but in 1938 Mussolini reversed his previously tolerant attitude to the Jews. Decrees were issued prohibiting inter-marriage between Jews and non-Jews and removing Jews from important positions. This was probably because Mussolini wished to compete with Hitler by emphasising Italy's racial purity. The policy was unpopular and was condemned by the Pope.

Church and the state

One of Mussolini's successes was the **Lateran Treaty** (1929). The Papacy had refused to recognise the state of Italy since 1870. Mussolini realised the value of the support of the Catholic Church. By the Treaty he recognised the Vatican City as a sovereign state and paid for lands taken from the Papal States during the process of unification before 1871. Catholicism was recognised as the official state religion. Bishops and priests were to receive state salaries and religious education was made compulsory in schools.

The economy

AQA	U2	CCEA	AS2
OCR	U1	WJEC	U1
Edexcel	U1		

The Corporate State

The central feature of Mussolini's economic policy was the creation of the Corporate State. Corporations were set up for each industry or occupation. They replaced trade unions, which were abolished, and consisted of representatives of employers and workers. In 1926 thirteen corporations were set up under a Minister of Corporations. In 1934 they were reorganised into 22 corporations and in 1938 the whole system was tied into the political structure when the Chamber of Deputies was replaced by a Chamber of Fasces and Corporations. The aim of the Corporate State was to replace the capitalist system, in which employers and labour were often in conflict, with a system of co-operation. Strikes were therefore forbidden and the corporations were empowered to draw up labour contracts and settle labour disputes. It was, however, an inefficient system. It favoured the employers, with whom the government was closely allied. The labour contracts were, therefore, often weighted against the workers.

Note the emphasis on state intervention in the economy.

The economic 'battles'

The other main features of Mussolini's economic policies were as follows.

- Public works schemes were introduced to reduce unemployment. Motorways, blocks of flats, sports stadiums and schools were built. Railways were electrified. But many projects were not completed and a lot of money disappeared through corruption.
- Government subsidies were provided to develop industry. In 1933 the Institute for Industrial Reconstruction (IRI) was set up. Industrial production increased: iron and steel production was doubled, as was production of hydroelectric power. But Italy still remained industrially weaker than the other European great powers, with low productivity and high costs.
- A programme of land reclamation was started, the most famous result being the draining of the Pontine Marshes near Rome.
- In the 'Battle for Grain', farmers were subsidised to produce more wheat. The aim was self-sufficiency. Wheat production doubled between 1922 and 1939, but to achieve this, land which would have been better suited to dairy or fruit farming was given over to wheat. Agriculture remained backward and consequently the south remained poverty-stricken.
- Mussolini regarded maintaining the value of the lira as a matter of national prestige. Unfortunately it was revalued at too high a level in 1926 and this led to a loss of exports. Even before the Great Depression many workers suffered wage cuts as a result. The Depression made matters worse: unemployment rose and Mussolini tried to defend the lira by wage cuts. Standards of living fell and discontent grew. In 1936 he finally accepted devaluation.
- Mussolini believed that a strong Italy needed a bigger population. Large families were encouraged by payment of child benefits and bachelors faced extra taxation. In spite of this the birth rate fell.

> **KEY POINT**
>
> The Italian economy remained comparatively weak in the 1930s. It was slow to recover from the Great Depression.

The social effects of Fascist policies

AQA	**U2**	CCEA	**AS2**
OCR	**U1**	WJEC	**U1**
Edexcel	**U1**		

Industrialists, big landowners and some of the middle classes benefited from Fascist policies. The Corporate State favoured industrialists, as did government subsidies to industry in the 1930s. The landed gentry were helped by policies which made it difficult for agricultural workers to leave the land and therefore kept agricultural wages down. Many of the middle classes benefited from the expansion of the civil service. Those working in private enterprises, however, did not do so well in the Depression years.

The working classes were worse off. Real wages declined, food prices rose and there was high unemployment, especially in the 1930s. Agricultural workers fared even worse than urban workers, with a fall in real wages of up to 40% in the 1930s. The working classes did, however, benefit from improvements in welfare provision. Pensions and unemployment benefits were increased, more schools were built and medical care was improved. They were also provided with leisure facilities by the OND (*dopolavoro*). Its sports facilities were particularly popular.

> In this respect Fascist Italy compared well with other industrialised countries.

Finally, the status of women was significantly lowered. Because of Mussolini's obsession with raising the birth rate, the state discouraged women from seeking employment.

15.5 Foreign affairs

> **LEARNING SUMMARY**
>
> After studying this section you should be able to understand:
> - the development of Mussolini's foreign policy between 1922 and 1939
> - his relationship with Hitler
> - his overthrow in 1943 and subsequent execution

Building the New Roman Empire 1922–39

AQA	**U2**	CCEA	**AS2**
OCR	**U1**	WJEC	**U1**
Edexcel	**U1**		

Fascism was nationalistic and aimed to make Italy great. It was to be expected that Mussolini would pursue an aggressive foreign policy:
- He had an early success in the **Corfu Incident** (1923), when he gained compensation from Greece for the murder of an Italian general on an international commission surveying the border between Greece and Albania. He did this by bombarding Corfu and refusing to recognise the competence of the League of Nations in the matter.
- In 1924 he gained further prestige when he annexed **Fiume** (Treaty of Rome with Yugoslavia).

His foreign policy over the next ten years was mainly directed towards counteracting French influence in Eastern Europe and especially Yugoslavia. In the process he made Albania virtually an Italian protectorate. He also had some success in establishing Italy's international prestige. Italy was one of the four permanent members of the Council of the League of Nations. In 1925 it was one of the guarantors of the Locarno Treaty (along with Britain). In 1928 it was a signatory to the Kellogg-Briand Pact.

Compare this with Mussolini's reaction to Hitler's seizure of Austria in 1938.

The rise of Hitler presented Mussolini with a problem. He regarded it as vital to preserve an independent Austria as a buffer between Italy and Germany. When the Nazis tried to seize control in Austria in 1934 and murdered the Chancellor, Dollfuss, he moved troops to the Austrian frontier. Hitler abandoned his plans to unite Austria with Germany, at least for the time being. This success boosted Mussolini's prestige. In the following year he joined Britain and France in the **Stresa Front** to condemn German rearmament.

The invasion of Abyssinia (Ethiopia)

The turning point in Mussolini's foreign policy came in 1935 when he invaded Ethiopia (commonly known as Abyssinia in the 1930s). Italians had felt, since the late nineteenth century, that they had not got their fair share of colonies in the 'scramble for Africa'. They had tried unsuccessfully to take over Ethiopia in 1896. Mussolini had already tried to establish economic domination there. He now saw the conquest of Ethiopia as the answer to Italy's economic problems and as a way of boosting his regime at a time when unrest was growing because of the effects of the Great Depression. The diplomatic situation seemed favourable. Britain and France were anxious to keep on good terms with Italy because of their concern about the growing strength of Germany. Mussolini thought they would therefore accept the Italian conquest of Ethiopia without much protest.

Mussolini aimed to divert social unrest by a prestigious victory.

The Italian armies had little trouble in taking over Ethiopia, though in the process they used poison gas. The real importance of the episode lay in its effects on Italy's relations with Britain, France and Germany and on the **League of Nations**. The League declared Italy an aggressor and imposed sanctions, but coal, steel and – most importantly – oil were excluded. The sanctions therefore had little effect on Italy's war effort. The failure to impose effective sanctions was largely because Britain and France were not prepared for war and, as Mussolini had calculated, were anxious to maintain good relations with Italy. For the same reasons they allowed Italy free passage through the Suez Canal, which they controlled. They even proposed, in the **Hoare-Laval Pact**, to allow Mussolini to keep two-thirds of Ethiopia, but public outrage in Britain and France forced the withdrawal of this plan. Nothing was done to stop Italy completing the conquest of Ethiopia.

The Hoare-Laval Pact demonstrated how keen Britain and France were to keep on good terms with Mussolini.

> **KEY POINTS**
>
> - The League had been shown to be ineffective.
> - Even the mild sanctions which had been applied angered Mussolini. He withdrew from the League and drew closer to Germany, which had not applied the sanctions.

Mussolini and Hitler, 1936–9

AQA	U2	CCEA	AS2
OCR	U1	WJEC	U1
Edexcel	U1		

Between 1936 and 1939 Mussolini's relations with Hitler became closer:
- In October 1936 Mussolini reached an understanding with Hitler which came to be known as the **Rome-Berlin Axis**.
- When the Spanish Civil War broke out both Italy and Germany gave military assistance to Franco. Italy's contribution, however, was the greater and it was a serious drain on its military resources. Moreover, Italian involvement widened the breach with Britain and France and increased Mussolini's dependence on Germany.

Mussolini could not have stopped the Anschluss but many Italians thought he should have protested.

- In 1937 Italy joined Germany and Japan in the **Anti-Comintern Pact**.
- When Germany took over Austria in the Anschluss (March 1938), Mussolini accepted it without question – a complete reversal of the policy he had pursued in 1934 and one which damaged his prestige in Italy.
- His role at the Munich Conference in September 1938, when he seemed to have played a key part, revived his popularity a little.
- In April 1939, following Hitler's take-over of the rest of Czechoslovakia, Mussolini imitated his aggression by sending troops into Albania. This was unnecessary as Italy already had economic control over Albania. Its main effect was to demonstrate that Italy's armies were not prepared for a full-scale war.
- Although Mussolini made the '**Pact of Steel**' with Hitler in May 1939, he stayed out of the Second World War in September.

KEY POINT

It became increasingly obvious between 1936 and 1939 that Mussolini was the junior partner in the relationship with Hitler.

The fall of Mussolini

AQA **U2** CCEA **AS2**
OCR **U1** WJEC **U1**
Edexcel **U1**

Consider whether Mussolini's regime would have survived if he had stayed out of the war.

By the middle of 1940 Mussolini was convinced that Hitler would win the war and wanted to make sure that Italy would share the spoils. He entered the war in June 1940, just before the fall of France. The war was a disaster for Italy. In 1940 Italian troops invaded Greece and advanced from Libya into Egypt. On both fronts they were driven back and had to be rescued by the Germans. Most of the navy was destroyed by Allied bombing. British troops captured all of Italy's African colonies. The war was unpopular in Italy. Civilian morale quickly dropped as a result of military disasters, food shortages and the Allied bombing of Italian cities. In July 1943 Allied troops invaded Sicily from North Africa. In August they crossed to the mainland.

In July 1943 Mussolini was overthrown and imprisoned. The Fascist Grand Council turned against him and persuaded the King to dismiss him even before the Allied troops crossed from Sicily to the mainland, which they did in August.

The new government surrendered to the Allies in September 1943, but German troops still occupied much of Italy. The Germans captured Mussolini four days later and set him up as the head of a puppet government in northern Italy. It took until April 1945 for the Allies to push the Germans back over the Alps. Mussolini himself was captured by Italian partisans and executed on 28 April 1945.

Mussolini was directly responsible for Italy's defeat. He went to war in 1940 knowing that Italy could not sustain a prolonged war. The Italian armed forces were ill equipped and had not made good the losses suffered in the invasion of Ethiopia and the Spanish Civil War. Italy's industrial base was much inferior to that of Britain, let alone the USA.

KEY POINT

Mussolini brought about his own downfall by the foolish decision to enter a war for which Italy was ill prepared.

You should be able to explain the significance of each of these dates.

KEY DATES

1923	Corfu Incident
1935–6	Conquest of Ethiopia
1936	Rome-Berlin Axis
1936–8	Spanish Civil War
1937	Anti-Comintern Pact
1939	Invasion of Albania; Pact of Steel
1940	Declaration of War against Britain and France
1943	Allied invasion of Sicily; Mussolini overthrown, captured by Germans and set up as head of a puppet government
1945	Execution of Mussolini.

Exam practice questions

1 'The experience of the years 1918–22 demonstrated that parliamentary democracy was incapable of providing Italy with effective government.' **[50]**

How far do you agree or disagree with this statement?

2 Assess the success of Mussolini's economic policies between 1922 and 1940. **[50]**

3 Why was there so little opposition to the establishment of a Fascist dictatorship in Italy? **[50]**

4 **(a)** Explain why Mussolini invaded Abyssinia in 1936. **[12]**

(b) 'Mussolini's policies towards Hitler were not in Italy's best interests'. **[24]**

How far do you agree or disagree with this statement?

16 Germany, 1918–45

The following topics are covered in this chapter:

- The Weimar Republic
- The rise of Hitler, 1930–3
- Nazi Germany, 1933–9
- Nazi Germany at war

16.1 The Weimar Republic

LEARNING SUMMARY

After studying this section you should be able to understand:

- the establishment of the Weimar Republic, 1919–20
- the Weimar constitution
- the challenges which the Weimar Republic faced
- the currency crisis of 1923 and its significance
- why the period 1924–9 is called the 'Golden Era' of Weimar

The establishment of the Weimar Republic, 1919–20

AQA	U1	CCEA	AS1
OCR	U1, 4	WJEC	U4
Edexcel	U1, 3		

The impact of the war

Germany's industrial development and its reserves of coal and steel were sufficient to sustain a massive war effort. However, its geographical position made it vulnerable to the effects of the Allied blockade and imported raw materials such as cotton, rubber and lubricating oil became scarce. Total industrial production declined by 30% between 1914 and 1918. German merchant shipping virtually came to a halt. At the same time the demands of the army for men and horses led to a drop of about 50% in agricultural production. Not surprisingly, Germany was the first power to introduce rationing. There were severe food shortages in the 'turnip winter' of 1916–7. By the end of 1918 malnutrition was widespread and there were food riots in German cities in November 1918.

The November Revolution

Be sure you understand why German nationalists regarded the members of the provisional government as 'the November criminals'.

In November 1918 the German Empire collapsed in defeat. The generals in command of the army on the Western Front said they could no longer prevent the allied forces advancing into Germany. The navy in Kiel mutinied. The civilian population faced starvation. Germany asked for an armistice. In the November Revolution, the Kaiser abdicated and a provisional government was set up under a Social Democrat, Ebert. In January 1919 a National Assembly was elected which met at Weimar and drew up a new constitution.

KEY POINT

The German people were totally unprepared for defeat. When the armistice was signed, the German armies were still in France and the people did not realise how desperate the military situation was. The generals did not disillusion them.

The Weimar constitution

The main features of Germany's government under the Weimar constitution were:

- The President was elected by the people for a term of office of seven years. His most important function was to appoint the Chancellor, but he also had emergency powers to suspend the constitution and rule by decree. These powers became very important in the early 1930s.
- The Chancellor was normally the leader of the largest party in the Reichstag.
- The Reichstag, elected every four years by universal suffrage and proportional representation, controlled taxation and legislation.
- The Reichsrat consisted of representatives of the provinces and had only limited delaying powers.

> **KEY POINT**
>
> The Weimar constitution was highly democratic. Its weakness lay in the system of proportional representation, which had the result that no single party ever gained a majority and therefore all governments were coalitions. As a result there were frequent changes of government.

The circumstances in which the Weimar Republic was set up were not favourable. Many Germans believed that the defeat was caused by a '**stab in the back**' by socialists. They argued that the November revolution had caused the surrender rather than the other way round. The Republic was further handicapped by being blamed for the Treaty of Versailles. The provisional government only accepted the treaty with great reluctance when it realised that there was no alternative. The treaty was bitterly resented by most Germans because of:

> Make sure you can elaborate these points if necessary – see pages 242–3.

- the way it was drawn up (the 'diktat')
- the extensive losses of territory (14% of Germany's land area and all its colonies)
- the heavy reparations (fixed in 1921 at £6600 million)
- the severe limits on the size of the armed forces
- most of all, the 'War Guilt' clause.

Challenges from right and left

AQA	**U1**	CCEA	**AS1**
OCR	**U1, 4**	WJEC	**U4**
Edexcel **U1, 3**			

At the end of the war, the communists hoped to seize power, as the Bolsheviks had done in Russia a year earlier. During the November Revolution, soviets sprang up all over Germany. An Independent Socialist republic was set up in Bavaria and in January 1919 the **Spartacists** (communists) attempted a revolution in Berlin. The provisional government had to use the army and the Freikorps (bands of anti-socialist ex-soldiers) to regain control. There was street fighting in Berlin and the Spartacist leaders, Karl Liebknecht and Rosa Luxemburg, were murdered. In Bavaria there was also civil war.

> Putsch: attempt to seize power by force.

In 1920 in the **Kapp putsch** members of the Freikorps attempted to seize power. The putsch was badly organised and soon brought to an end by a general strike in Berlin. Ominously, however, the army refused to come to the aid of the government and few of those responsible for the putsch were punished.

> **KEY POINT**
>
> - These challenges showed that some Germans were prepared to overthrow democracy by force.
> - The government had not been able to overcome its enemies by using its own armed forces.

The currency crisis of 1923

AQA	U1	CCEA	AS1
OCR	U1	WJEC	U4
Edexcel	U1, 3		

Post-war problems

At the end of the war Germany faced severe economic problems: food shortages, inflation, high unemployment and a large national debt. The Weimar government had to accept a peace treaty which deprived Germany of the rich mineral resources of Alsace–Lorraine and the Saar and required it to pay reparations. These were fixed in 1921 at £6600 million – a figure which many Germans claimed was beyond their power to pay.

The great inflation

The French government thought Germany was trying to wriggle out of paying what it owed.

The government decided it was impossible to raise the sums required from taxation, so it resorted to printing paper money, which led to further inflation. In 1923 Germany defaulted on its reparations payments, resulting in the occupation of the Ruhr by France. The economic consequences were catastrophic. Passive resistance in the Ruhr brought Germany's greatest industrial area to a standstill. The government met the situation by printing yet more paper money and by November 1923 hyper-inflation left the mark worthless.

The crisis was defused by **Stresemann**, who became Chancellor in August 1923. He called off the campaign of passive resistance and dealt effectively with communist attempts in Saxony and Thuringia to take advantage of the situation. In 1924 a new currency, the Rentenmark, was introduced and the **Dawes Plan** scaled down the annual payments of reparations. The French then withdrew from the Ruhr.

The Beer Hall Putsch

The crisis led to the **Beer Hall Putsch** in Munich. Hitler saw the abandonment of the struggle for the Ruhr as an opportunity to seize control of the Bavarian government and then march on Berlin. However, the army remained loyal to the government, even though General Ludendorff supported Hitler. The rising was suppressed and Hitler was imprisoned.

> **KEY POINT**
>
> The most important result of the currency crisis was that it wiped out the savings of the middle classes and thus undermined their loyalty to the Weimar Republic. The working classes were also badly affected, but landowners and industrialists profited.

The 'Golden Era' of Weimar, 1924–9

OCR	U1	Edexcel	U1, 3
WJEC	U4	CCEA	AS1

Economic recovery

After the troubles of the early 1920s, the period 1924–9 saw Germany emerge into an era of relative stability and prosperity. The economy recovered and with a stable currency, industry entered on a period of expansion. Unemployment decreased and living standards rose. The basis of this prosperity was, however, rather shallow, as it depended heavily on foreign loans, beginning with an American loan as part of the Dawes Plan of 1924. The Dawes Plan also reduced Germany's annual reparations payments and the **Young Plan** of 1929 reduced them and re-scheduled them over a period of fifty-nine years. Both these plans were negotiated for the Germans by Stresemann, who was Foreign Minister between 1923 and 1929.

Locarno

Stresemann also restored Germany's position among the great powers. By the **Treaties of Locarno** (1925) Germany accepted the 1919 frontiers with France and Belgium. They were also guaranteed by Britain and Italy, which gave France greater security. Moreover, unlike the Treaty of Versailles, the Locarno Treaties were negotiated by Germany, not dictated. Treaties were also signed between Germany, Poland and Czechoslovakia, but these did not include guarantees of Germany's eastern frontiers. The restoration of Germany to its position among the great powers was recognised in 1926 when it was admitted to the League of Nations and made a permanent member of the Council of the League. In 1928 it was a signatory of the Kellogg–Briand Pact to outlaw war as an instrument of policy.

> **KEY POINT**
>
> Locarno took some of the bitterness out of Franco–German relations and for this reason the late 1920s are often described as the period of the 'Locarno honeymoon'.

Politics

Politically, too, there was relative stability. Coalitions came and went, but they were all different combinations of moderate parties. In the elections of 1924 and 1928 the extremists gained relatively small numbers of seats. There were, however, some worrying features of the political scene. Despite their small numbers, extremists of right and left were an unsettling influence, engaging in regular street battles.

> The Nationalist Party, led by the press baron Hugenberg after 1928, was strongly anti-Weimar.

It proved to be unfortunate that the 1925 presidential election was won by **Hindenburg**. Though he was much respected, as the former German commander on the western front in the First World War, he was authoritarian in outlook and had little faith in democracy. He was not the man to defend the Weimar Republic in the crisis which Germany faced in the early 1930s. It was also unfortunate that in 1929, just before Germany was hit by the effects of the Great Depression, Stresemann died.

Weimar culture

The 1920s were also a golden era culturally. They were the era of the Bauhaus (founded by the architect Walter Gropius), of major writers, for example Thomas Mann, Franz Kafka, Bertolt Brecht, composers, such as Hindemith and Kurt Weill, and an array of outstanding figures in various academic disciplines. Berlin was regarded by many as the centre of the most exciting developments in the arts. Cinema, theatre and cabaret were second to none in Europe.

> You should be able to explain the significance of each of these dates.

KEY DATES	
1918	November Revolution: Armistice
1919	Spartacist Rising; Weimar Constitution; Treaty of Versailles
1920	Kapp Putsch
1923	Currency Crisis; Stresemann Chancellor, then Foreign Minister; Beer Hall Putsch; Hitler imprisoned
1924	Dawes Plan
1925	Locarno Treaties
1926	Germany admitted to the League of Nations
1928	Kellogg–Briand Pact
1929	Young Plan; Death of Stresemann

16.2 The rise of Hitler, 1930–3

The rise of the Nazi Party

OCR	U1	CCEA	AS1
Edexcel	U1, 3	WJEC	U2, 4
AQA	U1		

Hitler joined the German Workers' Party in 1919. By 1921 he was its leader and the party had been re-named the **National Socialist Party**. Hitler quickly became known because of his oratorical gifts, which he used to attack Jews and Communists and to promise the restoration of national pride. Some of the distinctive features of Nazism date from this period – the swastika badge, the use of songs and slogans, the brown shirt uniform of Hitler's private army, the *Sturmabteilung* (SA), led by Captain Röhm. Röhm was one of the early recruits to Nazism, as were Göring, Hess and Himmler.

In the early 1920s the National Socialist Party was one of a number of extremist groups opposed to the Weimar Republic. The currency crisis of 1923 brought a rapid increase in its membership, which prompted Hitler to embark on an attempt to seize power by force – the Beer Hall putsch. The putsch was a rather pathetic failure, but Hitler's subsequent trial gained him national publicity. While in prison he wrote **Mein Kampf**. After the failure of the putsch, he decided to seek power through elections.

Support for the Nazis declined after 1924. In the November 1924 elections they won only 14 seats and in 1928 only 12 seats. Nevertheless, there were important developments between 1924 and 1930. Hitler consolidated his hold over the party. Party organisation was greatly strengthened: in each district cells of party extremists were set up under the control of 'gauleiters' appointed by Hitler. The SA was gaining recruits and was conducting an increasingly bitter and violent campaign against communist gangs. A threat to Hitler's authority led by Strasser in north Germany was defeated at the Bamberg conference of 1926 and led to the development of the **Führerprinzip**, the cult of Hitler as the leader. Strong leadership, Hitler claimed, was needed to save Germany from a Jewish–socialist conspiracy. In 1930, with the Weimar system falling into crisis, his message appealed to many Germans and the Nazis gained 107 seats in the Reichstag.

> The Nazi Party also gained some respectability by its association with Hugenberg's Nationalist Party in campaigning against the Young Plan.

> **KEY POINT**
>
> Before 1930 the Nazi Party was no more than a small extremist fringe organisation.

Hitler's beliefs and policies

AQA	U1, 2	CCEA	AS1
OCR	U1, 2	WJEC	U2, 4
Edexcel	U1, 3		

Hitler's **racial theories** were based on Social Darwinism, which had been popularised in Germany by Houston Stewart Chamberlain. He believed that some races were inherently superior to others. In the highest category were the Aryan races, of which the Germans were the purest example. This was the basis for Hitler's anti-Semitism. He believed that the Jews were polluting other races (especially the Germans) by inter–marriage. He accused the Jews of causing the Russian Revolution and of stabbing the German army in the back in 1918. He seems to have believed stories of a Jewish conspiracy to dominate the world.

Hitler's racial theories provided the basis for his nationalist policies – the overthrow of the Treaty of Versailles and the union of all German peoples in a Greater Germany. They also provided a justification for his demand for '**lebensraum**' – living space for the Germans, which could only be acquired by conquests in Eastern Europe and Russia. Other important features of Hitler's political outlook were hostility to communism and to democracy. He saw the democracy of the Weimar Republic as a source of weakness and believed that for Germany to regain its greatness it needed a strong leader or **Führer**.

> **KEY POINT**
>
> Nazi ideas were racist, anti-Semitic, nationalist, anti-Communist and anti-democratic.

Another example of the 'big lie' was the idea that there was a Jewish conspiracy to dominate the world.

All these ideas appeared in *Mein Kampf*. So too, did Hitler's ideas about propaganda and especially the value of the 'big lie'. He made particularly effective use of the myth of 'the stab in the back', which he exploited by labelling the politicians who took over when the Kaiser abdicated 'the November criminals'. The Nazis' propaganda machine was run from 1929 by **Goebbels**.

The appeal of National socialism

OCR **U1, 2** WJEC **U2, 4**
AQA **U1** CCEA **AS1**
Edexcel **U1, 3**

None of Hitler's ideas were original, but the policies he advocated appealed to many sections of German society:

- Nazism drew its greatest support from the middle classes. The political weakness of the Weimar Republic led many of the middle classes to look for an alternative to the democratic parties, especially since they feared that weak government might lead to a communist revolution.
- Shopkeepers were attracted by Hitler's promise to help them compete with department stores.
- Peasant farmers were won over by pledges to reduce interest on agricultural debts. Darré won much support for the Nazis among the peasants.
- The working classes on the whole remained loyal to the Socialist Party, but the socialist element in the Nazi programme, which amounted to little more than vague promises of land reform and an attack on profiteering, did win some working class support.
- Nazism appealed to the nationalist and anti-Semitic strands in German society.
- It made a strong impact on the young and particularly young males.
- In the 1920s the Nazis gained more votes from men than women, but after 1930 it won more support from women due to its support for the institution of the family.
- Support for the Nazis was stronger among Protestants than Catholics.

It was the Great Depression which transformed the Nazi Party into the largest party in the Reichstag. Many of the middle classes, frightened by the growing support for the Communists in the early 1930s, turned to Hitler because of his extreme anti-Communist views. Industrialists also saw him as a bulwark against 'red revolution' and began to finance the Nazis. The SA gained recruits from among the unemployed because it offered food, accommodation and a small wage.

> **KEY POINT**
>
> One of the strengths of National Socialism was that it appealed to people from a variety of social backgrounds.

The crisis of Weimar, 1930–3

AQA	**U1**	CCEA	**AS1**
OCR	**U1, 2**	WJEC	**U2, 4**
Edexcel	**U1, 3**		

The **Wall Street Crash** affected Germany particularly badly. As share prices collapsed in the USA, American investors withdrew their loans from Germany, ruining many businesses. This had a knock-on effect on other businesses which did not depend directly on American investment. Unemployment, which was already rising in 1929, shot up to four million in 1931 and six million in 1932. For those in work wages fell, and for the unemployed benefits were cut. This was the situation which led to the collapse of the Weimar Republic and the rise of the Nazis.

In 1930 the coalition between the Social Democrats, the Centre Party and the People's Party led by Müller collapsed because of disagreements about measures to deal with the budget deficit. President Hindenburg appointed **Brüning**, leader of the Centre Party, as Chancellor. Unable to get a majority in the Reichstag, Brüning used the President's emergency powers to force through his proposed expenditure cuts. On the streets the Communists and Nazis were increasingly turning to political violence. In September 1930 a general election was called. Brüning hoped the violence of the extremists would increase support for the moderate parties, but instead the instability of the Weimar system led many to turn to the extremes. The Nazis gained 107 seats and the Communists 77 seats. With the moderate parties at odds with each other, and no party willing to co-operate with the Nazis or the Communists, it was impossible to construct a government with a majority. Brüning had to continue to rely on the President's emergency powers.

> In other words the Weimar constitution became unworkable, since the Chancellor was supposed to command a majority in the Reichstag.

> **KEY POINT**
>
> In 1930 the Weimar Republic ceased to be a functioning democracy.

As the economic crisis worsened in 1931 and 1932, violence continued and confidence in the government ebbed away. The sequence of events in 1932–3 was complicated:

- In April 1932, the growing strength of National Socialism was clearly demonstrated in the Presidential elections. Although Hindenburg was re-elected, Hitler gained 37% of the votes in the second ballot.
- In June, Hindenburg, on the advice of General Schleicher, dismissed Brüning and appointed **Papen** in his place.
- In July, the Nazis won 230 seats in the Reichstag elections, thus becoming the biggest party. The election showed that because of the economic crisis a large part of the electorate had turned to the extremist parties, for the Communists also did well, winning 89 seats.
- Papen invited Hitler to join his cabinet, but Hitler was not willing to accept any position other than that of Chancellor and Hindenburg would not agree to this.

> The extremist parties, both of which opposed the Weimar system, had more than half the seats in the Reichstag between them.

- Papen therefore called a second general election in November. This time the Nazis lost two million votes and 34 seats, while the Communists made substantial gains. Papen was still unable to gain a majority and resigned.
- Hindenburg then appointed **Schleicher** as Chancellor. He too failed to put together a coalition with a majority in the Reichstag.
- Papen, resenting the way Schleicher had replaced him, did a deal with Hitler. He would become Chancellor of a coalition government with only three Nazis and Papen as Vice Chancellor. Hindenburg believed that Papen would be able to keep Hitler under control and agreed.
- On 30 January, 1933 Hitler was appointed Chancellor.

> **KEY POINT**
>
> Hitler came to power by manipulation of the Parliamentary system, which he then proceeded to destroy.

Why did the Weimar Republic fail?

| OCR | **U1** | Edexcel | **U1, 3** |
| WJEC | **U4** | CCEA | **AS1** |

- The Weimar Republic was handicapped from the start because it was born of defeat in war and had to accept humiliating terms at Versailles. Nationalist opinion could not forgive the politicians who had set up the republic in these circumstances.
- Proportional representation led to unstable coalitions. In the end it was impossible to form a government which commanded a majority in the Reichstag. This instability discredited democracy.
- The political leaders had no experience of democracy because under the constitution of the Empire Chancellors had been responsible to the Emperor and not the Reichstag.
- The government had to rely on former servants of the Empire as civil servants, judges, teachers and, most importantly, army officers.
- Anti-democratic parties (Communists, Nationalists and National Socialists) had much support. They were responsible for much violence, which the government failed to control.
- The mainstream political parties failed the republic. The Socialists were more concerned with fighting their battle with the Communists than with saving democracy. The Centre Party under Brüning was happy to connive at the undermining of democracy by the use of the President's emergency powers. The Liberals lost the middle class support on which they depended.
- The Weimar Republic faced two severe economic crises. It survived the currency crisis of 1923 and there was then a period of relative prosperity. But the second crisis – the **Great Depression** – stretched the loyalty of the middle classes to breaking point.
- Hindenburg's political outlook was authoritarian and anti-parliamentary. He was happy to allow democracy to wither through the use of his emergency powers. In the crisis of 1932 he turned to men of an equally anti-democratic outlook, Papen and Schleicher.
- The manoeuvrings of the politicians in 1932 created the opportunity for Hitler to gain power by legal means. Papen, especially, was foolish to believe that he could control Hitler.

16.3 Nazi Germany, 1933–9

After studying this section you should be able to understand:

- how Hitler established his dictatorship
- the National Socialist state and its policies on education, youth, the churches, control of the army and race
- the persecution of the Jews
- Nazi economic policies
- the response of the German people to Nazism

The consolidation of Hitler's power

AQA   **U1, 2**   CCEA **AS1**
OCR   **U1, 2**   WJEC **U2, 4**
Edexcel **U1, 3**

Hitler's first aim as Chancellor was to secure his hold on power. He began by calling another general election in March 1933. Nazi propaganda used the Reichstag fire to whip up anti-Communist feeling. Hitler made effective use of the radio to project his image. The *Sturmabteilung* (SA) made violent attacks on their opponents during the campaign. Even so, the Nazis only gained 44% of the votes. With the support of the Nationalist Party, Hitler had a bare majority. He needed a two-thirds majority to change the constitution. He secured this by arresting the Communist deputies under an emergency law issued after the Reichstag fire and by doing a deal with the Catholic Centre Party. In return for their support he would allow them to continue to control their schools.

> This cannot be regarded as a genuinely free election, yet the Nazis still did not win an overall majority.

On 23 March 1933 the **Enabling Law** was passed. This gave Hitler dictatorial powers and he then dissolved all other political parties and took over control of all branches of national activity.

> So Hitler had used the Weimar constitution to set himself up as a dictator.

The Night of the Long Knives

The only remaining sources of potential opposition were the army and the radical wing of the Nazi Party itself. Röhm, the leader of the SA, wanted Hitler to introduce a more socialist programme. He also wanted to absorb the army into the SA. Hitler could not afford to alienate the army; the alternative was to eliminate Röhm and destroy the influence of the SA. On 30 June 1934 (the Night of the Long Knives) Röhm was murdered and some 400 others – old enemies or potential dissidents – were removed. The SA survived, but with little influence. The Schutzstaffel (SS), which had played the leading part in the **Night of the Long Knives**, became ever more powerful.

> The result was hardly surprising since the there was no secret ballot and voters were watched by the Gestapo.

In August 1934 Hindenburg died. Hitler proclaimed himself President, Chancellor and Führer. This was completely unconstitutional, but Hitler gave it some spurious legitimacy by holding a plebiscite which gave it 90% approval.

The National Socialist State

AQA   **U1, 2**   Edexcel **U1, 3**
OCR   **U1, 2**   CCEA   **AS1**
              WJEC   **U2, 4**

Totalitarianism

Nazi Germany was a totalitarian state. Its ethos was summed up in the phrase 'Ein Volk, ein Reich, ein Führer' (one people, one empire, one leader). Everything was subordinated to the good of the state. Nazi propaganda rammed home the message that the Germans would achieve their destiny as the 'master race' by

The title of Führer (leader) expressed Nazi ideology about leadership. For members of the army it meant that they had to take an oath of personal loyalty to Hitler rather than to the state.

their loyalty to their great Führer. This was the **Führerprinzip**, or 'leader principle', which, according to Nazi theory was the unifying principle of the Nazi state. A highly developed personality cult depicted Hitler as the supremely wise leader, the focus of his people's aspirations. Mass rallies at Nuremberg, using all the techniques of flags, banners, music, etc., allowed Hitler to use his rabble-rousing oratorical gifts to the full.

All organisations which might rival the Nazi party were either abolished or absorbed into the party. The German state and the Nazi Party became synonymous. No other political parties were allowed. Trade unions were abolished and replaced by the German Labour Front. The state governments were put under the control of Nazi Reich Governors. All social organisations, down to the level of village clubs, were subjected to **Gleichschaltung** (co-ordination), which in fact meant nazification.

In practice the Nazi state was not as highly organised and tightly controlled as these measures would suggest. Much of the existing machinery of government survived alongside the Nazi organisations. The civil service continued to function efficiently. The powers of government and party authorities often overlapped. Thus the work of the Party Chancellery under Martin Bormann overlapped with that of the Ministry of the Interior, as did that of the Nazi Bureau for Foreign Affairs with the Foreign Office. Alongside the provincial governments were the Nazi Gauleiters, though sometimes the same person was both Gauleiter and provincial minister-president or governor. Another complicating feature was Hitler's tendency to create special commissions for specific tasks: Todt, for instance, was given the job of building the autobahns. Himmler as head of the SS was made directly answerable to Hitler, which led to conflict with both the Ministry of the Interior and the Party Chancellery.

This has led some historians to describe Hitler as a 'weak dictator'. He was lazy, frequently getting up late and doing little work. He was bored by administrative detail, seeing himself as the visionary leader who made the big decisions and left their implementation to subordinates. The Cabinet rarely met. The Führerprinzip, however, meant that if Hitler was not involved decisions were not made.

> **KEY ISSUE**
>
> Some historians argue that competition between subordinates strengthened Hitler's authority: it was a process of divide and rule. Others claim that he was remote and indecisive and therefore the overlapping functions of the state and the Party led to inefficiency.

Some leading Nazis

The effect of this system was to give some of Hitler's associates considerable power:

- **Goering** was appointed President of the Reichstag in 1932 and Minister President of Prussia and Air Minister in 1933. He was responsible for building up the Luftwaffe and took charge of the Four-Year Plan which was introduced in 1936.
- **Goebbels** was put in charge of Nazi party propaganda in 1929. His appointment as Minister for Information and Propaganda followed naturally when the Nazis came to power in 1933. He was also gauleiter of Berlin.

- **Himmler** was appointed head of the SS in 1929. The role of the SS in the Night of the Long Knives in 1934 left him in a powerful position. In 1936 he became chief of the unified German police forces. His power was enormous: he controlled the police, the SS, the SD (the party's spy service headed by Heydrich), the Gestapo and the Death's Head Unit, which ran the concentration camps.

A police state

Nazi Germany was a police state. The **Gestapo** (secret police), set up in Prussia in 1933 by Göring, kept a close watch on possible opponents (communists, socialists, trade unionists) and people the Nazis disapproved of, such as Jews, gypsies and homosexuals.

In 1934, the Gestapo came under the control of Himmler, the head of the SS, and in 1936 he became the police chief for the whole of Germany. The SS (Schutz Staffel) was formed in 1925 as an elite paramilitary body within the Nazi Party. It played the leading role in the Night of the Long Knives in 1934 and from then grew in power and influence. It had its own security service (the SD) under **Heydrich**, who was also, under Himmler, the head of the Gestapo.

The SS ran **concentration camps**, the first of which was opened at Dachau in 1933. The regime in the concentration camps was brutal. but they were not extermination camps in the 1930s and the number of inmates was relatively small, though it increased to 25 000 in 1939. The influence of the SS was more limited than it became during the Second World War and Himmler's power was challenged by other powerful figures outside the SS such as Göring and **Bormann**.

Through the Waffen SS, set up in 1938, it had a leading role in the army. In the Second World War it administered occupied territories and ran the extermination camps.

With the 'legal revolution' the law courts were also an instrument of Nazi coercion. Judges were appointed for their loyalty to Nazi ideas and had to undergo training in Nazi ideology.

> **KEY POINT**
>
> The combination of the SS, Gestapo and SD provided the Nazi state with the means to suppress any opposition by terror.

Propaganda

Goebbels was a convinced advocate of the 'Big Lie'.

Goebbels was put in charge of a new Ministry of Propaganda in 1933. He established strict censorship of the press, books, films and the arts. News agencies were amalgamated into one central source of 'correct' information. 'Un-German' books were burnt. The works of Jewish composers were banned. The government-controlled radio was used to good effect to spread Nazi ideas.

Education and youth

Education was particularly important. In the schools Nazi racial views were taught and textbooks in subjects such as history and biology were re-written. Teachers were required to join the Nazi Teachers' Association and were watched to ensure that they followed the party line. Universities were placed under the control of government-appointed rectors and academics who were not willing to toe the Nazi line were forced out.

All youth movements were absorbed into the **Hitler Youth**, which boys joined at the age of 14. From 1936 membership was compulsory. Boys were indoctrinated with nationalist and racist ideas. They took an oath to Hitler as 'saviour of our country' and were taught to look forward to their future role in military service to the Nazi state. The parallel girls' organisation, the **League of German Maidens**, prepared girls to serve the state as wives and mothers.

The churches

Historians continue to debate how far the churches compromised their principles in their dealings with Hitler.

For the Nazis, with their belief in the total subordination of the individual to the state, the churches were bound to be a problem. This was particularly true of relations with the **Catholic Church**, which owed loyalty to the Pope in Rome. Hitler quickly tackled this problem: in 1933 a Concordat with Rome ensured that the Catholic Church withdrew from politics in return for keeping some control over its schools. The Catholic Centre Party dissolved itself voluntarily. But the Nazis then dissolved the Catholic Youth League and tried to set up a Nazi organisation within the Church. Relations deteriorated and in 1937 Pope Pius XI issued an encyclical criticising the Nazi regime. Some Catholic bishops and priests continued to speak out against the Nazis and many were imprisoned.

Many **Protestants** initially welcomed the Nazis in preference to what they regarded as the ungodly Weimar Republic. This encouraged Hitler to attempt to bring the Protestant Churches under Nazi control by amalgamating the 28 provincial Churches into a Reich Church under a Reich Bishop, Müller. The nazification of the Reich Church, which attempted to combine Christianity with anti-Semitism and Führer-worship, resulted in a split and the emergence of the Confessional Church, led by Pastor Niemöller. This was banned in 1937 and some hundreds of pastors, including Niemöller and Bonhoeffer, were sent to concentration camps.

By the late 1930s the Nazi regime was becoming openly anti-Christian, recognising that Nazi ideology was not compatible with Christianity. Some Nazi leaders began to revive pagan ceremonies.

> **KEY POINT**
>
> Persecution of priests and pastors ensured that the Churches did not become centres of opposition. On the whole, however, the loyalty of Church members to their faith seems to have survived Nazi hostility and the Churches continued to be a source of mute protest.

The success of Hitler in gaining control of the army

Until 1938 the army was the most powerful institution which was not fully under Hitler's control. One of the main reasons for the Night of the Long Knives was his fear that the activities of Röhm and the SA would provoke an army coup. By removing Röhm and other SA leaders, Hitler earned the goodwill of the army. A few weeks later, in August 1934, when Hindenburg died and Hitler took the title of Führer, all members of the army were required to take an oath of personal allegiance to him. Military ideas of personal honour made it difficult for army officers to oppose Hitler after this.

As younger officers were promoted, the army became increasingly nazified.

Between 1934 and 1938 the army was gradually brought under Nazi control. The swastika was adopted as a badge on army uniforms. Officers were given instruction in Nazi ideology. The adoption of a policy of large-scale rearmament naturally won army support. But the general staff became increasingly worried by the trend of Hitler's foreign policy. They regarded the remilitarisation of the Rhineland as risky. In November 1937, as recorded in the **Hossbach memorandum**, Hitler announced to his chief military advisers his plans for the expansion of Germany, which would involve attacking Austria and Czechoslovakia. Horrified by the risk that this would lead to war with Britain and France, the generals protested. Hitler's response was to reorganise the command structure of the army. The War Minister, Blomberg, and the Commander-in-Chief of the Army, Fritsch, were both dismissed in 1938 on charges of personal misconduct. Hitler put the army under his direct command through the OKW (Army High Command).

Another attempt was made in 1944 – see page 222.

It was, however, from the army that an attempt was made to remove Hitler. In 1938 General Beck tried to persuade the General Staff to remove him, but he received no support and resigned.

> **KEY POINT**
>
> By 1938 the army, the last institution with a degree of independence, was under Hitler's direct control.

Nazi racial policies

Hitler's belief in the superiority of the Aryan races, of which the Germans were the purest example, was given practical effect from the very beginning of Nazi rule. The Jews (see section below) were not the only victims.

- In 1933 compulsory sterilisation of people with hereditary diseases or mental illness was introduced.
- In 1939 the Nazis began a programme of euthanasia for the mentally ill or retarded, code-named Action T4. About 72 000 people were murdered before it was stopped in response to public protests in 1941. But it continued unofficially up to the end of Nazi rule.

The public outcry was sparked off by a sermon condemning it by a Catholic Cardinal.

- Gypsies were sent to concentration camps. Over 80% of gypsies in Germany died during the Nazi era (and about half a million gypsies in the territories occupied by Germany during the war).
- Tramps, beggars and other 'undesirables' were treated similarly.

The persecution of the Jews

AQA U1, 2 CCEA AS1
OCR U1, 2 WJEC U2, 4
Edexcel U1, 3

The Jews were singled out for special persecution as the scapegoats for all Germany's ills. They were blamed especially for the '**stab in the back**', a myth which Goebbels' propaganda machine made great play with.

- In 1933 there was a boycott of Jewish shops and businesses. Jews were dismissed from the civil service and excluded from universities and in due course from most of the professions.

The German people seem to have approved this. How far they approved of more brutal methods, culminating in the Holocaust, is a matter of historical debate.

- In 1935 the **Nuremberg Laws** deprived Jews of German citizenship and forbade them to marry 'Aryans'.
- Persecution intensified in 1938. Jews were banned from commerce. In November, attacks on synagogues and Jewish houses and businesses took place all over Germany (**Kristallnacht** – the Night of Broken Glass). This was allegedly a spontaneous outburst in retaliation for the assassination of a German embassy official in Paris by a Jew, but was largely the work of the SA. Jews were encouraged to emigrate – and many did.

- In 1939 30 000 Jews who had not emigrated were rounded up and sent to concentration camps. There were still over 200 000 Jews in Germany.

See pages 221–2.

The '**final solution**' began in 1941 with mass deportations of Jews to concentration camps. Between 1942 and 1945 some 3 to 4 million Jews died in the gas chambers. A further 2 million died in other ways, for example disease, mass shootings, etc.

> **KEY POINTS**
>
> Up to 1939 there was no suggestion of an intention to exterminate the Jews altogether.
> - Some historians claim that Hitler intended to exterminate the Jews from the outset.
> - Others argue that it was only decided upon as the result of the war in the east, which closed off the possibility of mass deportation.
> - It has been argued that Hitler himself was not responsible for the Holocaust, but the overwhelming majority of historians reject this view.

The economy

AQA	**U2**	CCEA	**AS1**
OCR	**U1, 2**	WJEC	**U2, 4**
Edexcel	**U1, 3**		

Nazi economic policies had two main aims: to reduce unemployment and to revive Germany's military and industrial might. To achieve these ends economic activity was state-controlled. Wages, food prices, rents, investment and foreign exchange were all controlled. Trade unions were abolished and strikes made illegal. Farm prices were fixed so that farmers made a reasonable profit. Public works were started, financed by the state; the most famous example is the building of autobahns. Under **Dr. Schacht** an elaborate system of exchange controls was developed, which exploited the dependence of much of Eastern Europe upon Germany as a market for food exports. Bilateral trade agreements were made with Eastern European and South American countries to boost German exports and secure essential raw materials. As a result, by 1935 exports exceeded imports.

It does not follow that he intended to go to war in 1940.

In 1936 a **Four-Year Plan** was introduced with the explicit aim, stated in a memorandum from Hitler, of making Germany ready for war within four years. The basic purpose was to achieve self-sufficiency (autarky) by boosting domestic production and developing synthetic substitutes for oil and other imports. At the same time, a programme of large-scale rearmament was undertaken. Under state direction industrialists produced what the Nazis thought Germany needed and, where necessary, labour was directed where it was needed.

Assessment of Nazi economic policies

The reduction of unemployment was one of the reasons why the German people supported Hitler. When you have studied this paragraph, you should be able to assess how much credit he deserved for it.

The Nazis were successful in reducing unemployment to three million by 1935 and to virtually nil in 1939. Unemployment had already begun to fall before Hitler came to power and the upturn in world trade from 1934 helped to reduce it further. The public works schemes and rearmament provided the sort of stimulus advocated by Keynesian economics. Rearmament also took half a million men out of the labour market by conscription into the army. But the reduction in unemployment also owed something to more questionable aspects of the Nazi regime. The expansion of the civil service and the party organisation created jobs, but both were over-staffed. The removal of political opponents and 'undesirables' to concentration camps reduced unemployment, because they were not counted.

Neither were Jews who had been forced out of their jobs, since they were no longer citizens after 1935.

In other respects, too, the success of Nazi economic policy may be doubted. Despite massive investment, synthetic substitutes for oil and rubber only produced a small proportion of Germany's needs. Agriculture failed to meet its targets and Germany continued to depend on food imports. Although there was some economic growth, it was not fast enough to pay for the massive cost of rearmament. By 1939 Schacht, as President of the Reichsbank, was warning of the danger of runaway inflation.

> **KEY ISSUE**
>
> Some historians argue that by 1939 war was the only answer to Germany's economic problems. A short, successful war would win lebensraum – land in Eastern Europe, which would supply Germany's food needs and thus free foreign exchange to buy the raw materials required by its industry.

The response of the German people to Nazism

OCR	**U1, 2**	Edexcel	**U1, 3**
AQA	**U1, 2**	CCEA	**AS1**
WJEC	**U4**		

- Industrialists saw Hitler as a bulwark against communism. They welcomed the abolition of trade unions. Big business grew at the expense of smaller businesses. It profited from rearmament and from the war effort. In return it provided much of the money to finance the Nazi party.
- The middle classes, who had lost so much under the Weimar Republic, were impressed by Hitler's success in restoring prosperity, in warding off the threat of communist revolution and in rebuilding national pride.
- The working class were pleased by the drop in unemployment, by rent controls and by the benefits offered by the **Strength through Joy** organisation, such as subsidised holidays. On the other hand wages only increased slowly and in many industries there was a drop in real wages. Hours of work were now generally longer.
- Farmers were won over by fixed prices for their products and by a law which made farms hereditary estates. This was the work of Darré, Hitler's Minister of Food and Agriculture. On the other hand, this meant that many peasant farms remained small; agriculture was inefficient and peasant incomes low. The standard of living of agricultural workers was even worse and increasing numbers of them migrated to the towns in search of better paid work.

> Nevertheless the Nazis enjoyed much support among women because they stressed the importance of the family.

- The status of women suffered. The Nazis taught that their function was to serve the state by producing children. Women were eased out of professional positions and the civil service. In the later 1930s, however, labour shortages created a demand for women workers in agriculture and industry.

Successive plebiscites gave over 90% approval for Hitler's policies and, although intimidation may have exaggerated support for the Nazis, there is little evidence of serious discontent and much evidence of general approval. There was some passive opposition (non-co-operation) or refusal to join the party. Those who expressed open opposition, for example communists, were likely to end up in a concentration camp.

You should be able to explain the significance of each of these dates.

KEY DATES

1933	January: Hitler appointed Chancellor
	February: Reichstag Fire
	March: Enabling Law
1934	Night of the Long Knives; Death of Hindenburg; Hitler Führer, President and Chancellor
1935	Nuremberg Laws
1935	Kristallnacht (Night of the Broken Glass)
1939	Outbreak of Second World War

16.4 Nazi Germany at war

LEARNING SUMMARY

After studying this section you should be able to understand:

- the impact of the war on life in Germany and the occupied territories in the Second World War

Germany and the occupied territories during the war

AQA	**U2**	OCR	**U1, 2**
Edexcel	**U1, 3**	WJEC	**U4**
CCEA	**AS1**		

In the early years of the war life was fairly normal for most Germans. Hitler believed that loss of morale on the home front had caused Germany's collapse in 1918 and was anxious to prevent this happening again. Rationing was introduced in 1939, but shortages were few. Germany's food needs were met by exploiting the occupied territories in Eastern Europe. The occupied territories also provided labour to tackle manpower shortages: some eight million foreign workers (mostly 'Slav sub-humans') were employed altogether, though most were either reluctant conscripts or slave labour. With his belief that the place of women was in the home, Hitler resisted bringing women into the workforce.

The final solution

The invasion of Poland in 1939 brought three million more Jews under Nazi rule in areas which the Nazis intended to Germanise as part of the policy of acquiring *lebensraum*. The Jews were rounded up and confined to ghettoes. In the most notorious, the Warsaw ghetto, over 100 000 Jews died of starvation or disease. Large numbers of Jews were murdered by the SS murder squads, the *Einsatzgruppen*.

Hitler was careful not to be at Wannsee himself, but almost certainly knew what was decided.

In 1942 leading Nazis at the **Wannsee Conference** decided on a 'final solution', i.e. to exterminate the Jewish race. At **Auschwitz** and other death camps Jews from all over occupied Europe ended in the gas chambers. Nearly six million Jews died in the Holocaust.

The occupied territories

Remember that in 1939 the eastern half of Poland was invaded by the Russians and treated with equal brutality. It was conquered by the Nazis in 1941.

By 1942 the Nazis occupied much of Eastern Europe as well as Denmark, Norway, the Netherlands, Belgium and northern France. All these were effectively under Nazi military rule and Nazi policies were enforced, particularly anti-Semitic policies. Western Poland was incorporated into the Reich, as were Bohemia and Moravia. Most of the rest of Poland formed the General Government, with an entirely German administration headed by Hans Frank. It was in effect a German colony. The Nazis aimed to make it purely German within 15–20 years. They began by murdering the greater part of the Polish elite immediately after the invasion in 1939. The aim was to deprive Poland of leaders. A million Poles had their land confiscated and taken over by Germans by 1941. The Baltic states and part of northern Poland were similarly formed into Ostland. When the USSR was invaded in 1941, the Ukrainian nationalists at first welcomed the Nazis as liberators from Soviet rule, but then found that the Nazis treated Ukraine as a colony and its people as 'Slav sub-humans'. The occupied territories, especially those in Eastern Europe, were regarded as a source of labour for German factories.

Total War

Things changed after Stalingrad. In February 1943 a speech by Goebbels signalled a switch to **Total War**. Rations had to be increasingly cut. Women were brought into the labour force, though still not to the extent that they were in Britain. The Armaments Minister, Todt, and his successor, Speer, tackled administrative problems with measures to co-ordinate production, notably the Central Planning Board set up in 1942. Speer achieved considerable success, despite the activities of the SS under Himmler and of Bormann's Gauleiters which often cut across his planning.

The Hitler myth faded and terror, organised by the increasingly powerful Himmler, took its place. There were more signs of resistance, but the various groups were hopelessly divided: some were anti-democratic nationalists with quite different aims from the Kreisau Circle of Christian conservatives. A group of aristocratic officers led by **Stauffenberg** came closest to removing Hitler in the **July Bomb Plot** in 1944. The effect, paradoxically, was to revive German support for Hitler.

From 1943 onwards, however, the economy was under increasing stress. Allied bombing raids on German cities caused terrible damage to industrial plants and to housing, though it is doubtful how far they had the intended effect of destroying German morale. In the last months of the war conscription was extended to all males between the ages of 15 and 60. The final invasion of Germany in 1944–5 and Hitler's refusal to contemplate surrender led to enormous physical destruction.

Exam practice questions

1. To what extent, by 1929, had the Weimar Republic overcome the problems which it faced after 1919? **[50]**

2. How successful were the Nazis between 1933 and 1939 in solving Germany's economic problems? **[50]**

3. How successfully did the Nazis gain and retain the loyalty of the German people between 1933 and 1939? **[50]**

4. To what extent was the Nazi regime popular between 1933 and 1939? **[50]**

5. Study sources A, B and C and use your own knowledge.

'Hitler deliberately created confusion in government in Nazi Germany in order to increase his own authority.'

To what extent do you agree with this opinion? Explain your answer, using the evidence of sources A, B and C and your own knowledge of the issues related to this controversy. **[40]**

Source A: From *Twelve Years with Hitler*, by O. Dietrich, Hitler's Press Officer, published 1955.

In the twelve years of his rule in Germany, Hitler produced the biggest confusion in government that has ever existed in a civilised state. It was not laziness or an excessive degree of tolerance which led the otherwise so energetic and forceful Hitler to tolerate this real witch's cauldron of struggles for position and conflicts over competence. It was intentional. With this technique he systematically disorganised the upper echelons of the Reich leaders in order to develop and further the authority of his own will until it became a despotic tyranny.

Source B: From *Hitler, A Study in Tyranny*, by A. Bullock, published 1952.

Hitler bore the final responsibility for whatever was done by the regime, but he hated the routine work of government, and, once he had stabilized his power, he showed comparatively little interest in what was done by his departmental Ministers except to lay down general lines of policy. In the Third Reich each of the Party bosses, Göring, Goebbels, Himmler and Ley, created a private empire for himself. Hitler deliberately allowed this to happen; the rivalries which resulted only increased his power as the supreme arbiter. Nobody ever had any doubt where the final authority lay – the examples of Röhm and Gregor Strasser were there, if anyone needed reminding.

Source C: From *Hitler and Nazi Germany*, by F. McDonough, published 1999.

Hitler frequently by-passed formal government departments to set up rival institutions and specialist agencies. It has been estimated that there were 42 separate agencies with executive power to implement policy within the central government machine of Nazi Germany. Hitler was quite aware of this confusion, but he consistently blocked initiatives designed to make the governmental structure more efficient and co-ordinated. In essence, the political system in Nazi Germany was a complex maze of personal rivalries and overlapping party and state institutions, which resulted in chaos and confusion.

17 Soviet Russia, 1917–41

The following topics are covered in this chapter:

- Lenin 1917–24
- Stalin's dictatorship, 1924–41

17.1 Lenin 1917–24

LEARNING SUMMARY

After studying this section you should be able to understand:

- how Lenin established the Communist state in Russia
- the defeat of the Whites in the Civil War
- why War Communism was replaced by the New Economic Policy
- Lenin's achievements

The consolidation of Bolshevik power

OCR	**U1,4**	CCEA	**AS2**
Edexcel	**U1**	WJEC	**U1, 4**

For Lenin the survival of the Bolshevik regime was the top priority, whatever the cost.

Be prepared to explain why Lenin was wiling to accept such a harsh treaty.

Lenin later claimed that War Communism was an emergency measure to deal with the crisis, but it is more likely that it was an attempt to introduce doctrinaire communist ideas. By 1921 he realised that it did not work.

OGPU = secret police, a forerunner of the KGB.

Lenin took several crucial decisions in the early days of Bolshevik rule in order to fulfil the promises of 'land, peace and bread' and 'all power to the soviets':

- Land was confiscated from the crown, the Church and the landowners and redistributed to the peasants.
- The Constituent Assembly, which met in January 1918, was immediately dissolved by Red Guards because the elections had left the Bolsheviks in a minority. The All-Russian Congress of Soviets then considered Lenin's proposals for the constitution.
- The **Peace of Brest-Litovsk** was made with Germany and Austria (March 1918). The terms imposed by Germany were extremely harsh. Russia surrendered Poland and the Baltic States to Germany, recognised Finland and the Ukraine as independent and agreed to pay huge reparations. Despite the severity of the terms, Lenin insisted that there was no alternative to accepting it.
- **War Communism** was instituted. This was the name for the economic policies Lenin introduced in 1918. Industry and the banks were nationalised. Private trade was forbidden. Peasants were made to sell all surplus grain to the state at fixed prices.

The Red Terror

Lenin was ruthless in dealing with opponents. In December 1917 he set up the Cheka (secret police) which instituted the '**Red Terror**'. The first victims were the leaders of the other political parties. Over 140 000 people had been executed by February 1922 when the Cheka was replaced by the OGPU. By then Lenin was satisfied that all opposition had been suppressed.

The Soviet constitution

In July 1918 the new Soviet constitution was introduced. Russia became the Russian Soviet Federated Socialist Republic. Russia was declared to be a classless society with no private ownership of property. Supreme power was nominally given to the All-Russian Congress of Soviets, consisting of representatives of city and village soviets elected by universal suffrage, but this only met for about one week each year. The Congress elected an Executive Committee, which in turn elected the ten members of the Council of People's Commissars (ministers). Lenin was the Chairman of this Council and thus the head of the government. There was only one political party, the Communist Party. All other parties were held to be counter-revolutionary. Real political power, therefore, lay with the Communist Party and especially its **Politburo**. Since there was only one party, membership was essential for political advancement.

At the end of the Civil War there was a further constitutional change. Pre-revolutionary Russia was a multi-national state. The danger that some of the nationalities would break away in the Civil War was overcome by the Red victory. To incorporate them into the new soviet system, the **Union of Soviet Socialist Republics** (USSR) was set up in 1922. This was a federation of republics, of which Russia was the most important.

> **KEY POINT**
>
> The soviet system of government was described by Lenin as 'democratic centralism'. This really meant that the state was subordinated to the Communist Party in both the USSR and the constituent republics.

The Civil War, 1918–20

OCR	U1, 4	CCEA	AS2
Edexcel	U1	WJEC	U1, 4

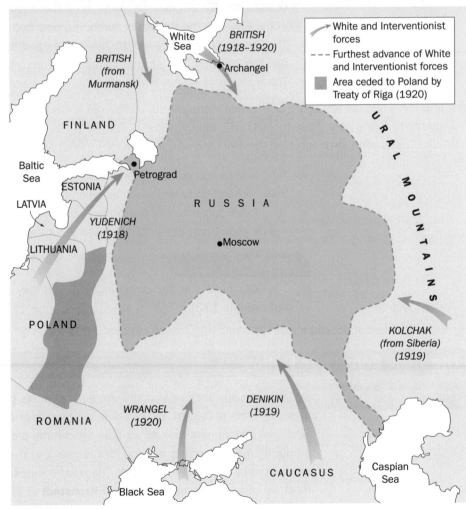

The Russian Civil War, 1918–20

Lenin had seized power by force and it was not surprising that this provoked counter-revolution and civil war. Nor was it surprising that there was foreign intervention in the Civil War. Foreign powers feared that the example of the Russian Revolution would be followed by the workers elsewhere. The founding of the Third Communist International by the Bolsheviks in 1919, with the purpose of promoting world revolution, gave substance to this fear. Britain and France were angry at Russia's desertion of the Allied cause and worried that the armaments they had supplied to Russia might fall into German hands. France, which had substantial investments in Russia, was also angered by Lenin's repudiation of all foreign debts.

The Civil War raged between 1918 and 1920. The Whites (counter-revolutionaries) attacked from three main directions. From the south they were led by Denikin and then by Wrangel. Kolchak attacked from the east and Yudenich from the Baltic towards Petrograd. Foreign forces landed at Archangel and Murmansk in the north and in the Crimea and the Caucasus in the south. A Japanese force went into Siberia from Vladivostok. For a time much of Siberia and southern Russia was under White control, but by 1920 the Bolsheviks had overcome most of the White forces. Then Russia was attacked by Poland, which, with French aid, succeeded in taking over a substantial part of White Russia and the Ukraine, leaving three million Russians in Poland (Treaty of Riga, 1921). The remaining White forces in central Asia and the Far East were mopped up in 1921–2.

Why did the Communists (Reds) win the Civil War?

- The Red Army was united under a single command, that of **Trotsky**, who created an efficient fighting machine by sheer personal dynamism. By the end of the Civil War the Red Army numbered over five million men.
- The Communists controlled the main cities and the railways. They therefore had the advantage of internal communications.
- The Russian peasants feared that the Whites would return the land to the landlords.
- Foreign intervention enabled the Communists to pose as Russian patriots.
- The Whites were not united in their aims. Some were Tsarists, others wanted a republic.
- They also lacked co-ordination. This was partly a matter of geography – transport and communication between the White forces was difficult.
- The foreign supporters of the Whites were half-hearted. They had other priorities – ending the Great War in 1918, working out the peace settlement in 1919.

> **KEY POINT**
>
> The Communists seized power in 1917, but they were not fully in control of Russia until 1921.

The New Economic Policy

| OCR | U1, 4 | CCEA | AS2 |
| Edexcel | U1 | WJEC | U1, 4 |

By 1921 the economy was on the verge of collapse, partly because of the strain of seven years of foreign and civil war, but also because of War Communism. Since the government took all surplus agricultural produce, the peasants stopped producing more than they needed for themselves. The result was famine, aggravated by droughts in 1920–1. There were widespread disturbances. The most serious was the naval mutiny at **Kronstadt** in 1921, which convinced Lenin that a change was needed. The **New Economic Policy** allowed the peasants to

A class of prosperous peasants emerged as a result – only to be destroyed by Stalin's collectivisation policies.

sell their surplus produce on payment of a tax of a percentage of the crop. It also restored private trading through 'Nepmen'. All major industrial installations, however, remained under state control, as did banking, transport and foreign trade. Economic recovery was delayed by continuing famine and financial crisis, but by Lenin's death things were improving.

KEY POINTS

- The New Economic Policy was a retreat from pure communism and a compromise with capitalism.
- By the time of Lenin's death in 1924 the Russian economy was beginning to recover as a result.

Lenin's achievements

OCR	**U1, 4**	CCEA	**AS2**
Edexcel	**U1**	WJEC	**U1, 4**

- Lenin played a crucial role in 1917 in the overthrow of the Provisional Government, persuading his colleagues to seize power and planning how to achieve it.
- His immediate decisions about the land and the peace with Germany were crucial in enabling the Bolsheviks to hold on to power.
- With the help of Trotsky and the Red Army he held the new communist state together through the Civil War.
- His decision to replace War Communism by the New Economic Policy was realistic, even though it involved compromising the basic economic principles of Marxism.
- He made a start on social reform with decrees providing free education and a national insurance scheme.
- He achieved some foreign recognition for the Communist government in Russia, including the resumption of full diplomatic relations with Germany by the Treaty of Rapallo (1922).

But...

- Lenin was completely ruthless: millions of Russians died in the civil war and the great famine of 1920–1 and thousands more were victims of the secret police in the Red Terror.
- The new Russian state which he created was a totalitarian police state. It had a vast bureaucracy, meshed with the communist party.
- Unfortunately he had made no arrangements for choosing his successor and this allowed Stalin to take over eventually.

KEY ISSUE

Did Lenin lay the foundations for Stalinism? Some historians argue that Stalinism was a direct consequence of the totalitarian system created by Lenin. Others claim that Lenin used terror in response to a crisis and would later have modified it if he had lived.

You should be able to explain the significance of each of these dates.

KEY DATES

1917	October Revolution; Bolshevik government
1918	Peace of Brest-Litovsk; War Communism
1918–20	Civil War
1921	Kronstadt Mutiny; New Economic Policy
1924	Death of Lenin

17.2 Stalin's dictatorship, 1924–41

LEARNING SUMMARY	**After studying this section you should be able to understand:**
	• Stalin's rise to power
	• Stalin's policies of industrialisation and the collectivisation of agriculture
	• the purges of the 1930s
	• the political, social, educational and cultural aspects of life in Stalin's Soviet Union in the 1930s
	• Soviet foreign policy in the 1930s

Stalin's rise to power

AQA	**U1, 2**	CCEA	**AS2**
OCR	**U1, 4**	WJEC	**U1, 4**
Edexcel	**U1**		

> This was crucial because it enabled him to manipulate the Politburo against his enemies.

Stalin, whose father had been a serf, became Commissar for Nationalities in 1917 and General Secretary of the Communist Party in 1922. The latter position enabled him to build up a power base. Membership of the Party at local level was carefully controlled by the Secretariat, i.e. Stalin. The local parties elected the Party Congress, from which the Central Committee and the Politburo were drawn. Thus, Stalin controlled promotion within the Party.

Shortly before he died Lenin advised the Communist Party to remove Stalin from the post of General Secretary, but the Central Committee ignored this. Kamenev and Zinoviev, who were jealous and mistrustful of Trotsky, joined Stalin in the Triumvirate. This isolated Trotsky, who was forced to resign as Commissar for War in 1925.

There was a complicated power struggle in 1926–7. Stalin allied himself to Bukharin and the 'rightists', who advocated continuing with the New Economic Policy, while the 'leftists' led by Trotsky, Kamenev and Zinoviev opposed further concessions to the peasants. At the Party Congress in 1927 Stalin triumphed. Trotsky, Kamenev and Zinoviev were removed from the Politburo. In 1929 Trotsky was sent into exile.

In the same year Stalin changed his views about the New Economic Policy. The procurement crisis of 1927–8, when the peasants refused to produce enough grain at the prices offered by the state, convinced him that it was failing. When Bukharin and his 'rightist' colleagues protested, they too were expelled from the Politburo. Stalin was left as undisputed dictator.

Underlying the struggle was a debate about the future path of the Communist regime – 'permanent revolution' or 'socialism in one country'.

> **KEY POINT**
>
> The struggle for power between Stalin and Trotsky was both a clash of personalities between a Georgian peasant and a middle class intellectual and a conflict of principles. Trotsky stood for 'permanent revolution' and Stalin for 'socialism in one country'.

Why Stalin won the battle to succeed Lenin

- He displayed great political skill in out-manoeuvring his rivals.
- As General Secretary he had built up solid support in the Party Congress.

'Permanent revolution' meant rapid industrialisation, the abolition of private farming and promoting revolution elsewhere in Europe so as to ensure the survival of Communism in Russia.

- **'Socialism in one country'** had more appeal than 'permanent revolution' to Russians, who simply wanted peace and prosperity after the hardships of the First World War and the Civil War. It also appealed to Russia's national pride and self-reliance.
- The case for 'permanent revolution' had been seriously weakened by the failure of attempts at Communist revolution in the west, especially the Spartacist Rising in Germany in 1919.
- Trotsky, who was in many ways the obvious successor to Lenin, was mistrusted. He was regarded as too clever, too western in his ways of thought and too inclined to think he was right and the Party wrong. He was suspected because he had been a Menshevik until 1917. He had great intellectual and organisational abilities, but lacked political skill.

Economic policy ('Socialism in one country')

AQA	**U1, 2**
OCR	**U1, 4**
Edexcel	**U1**
CCEA	**AS2, A2.1**
WJEC	**U1, 4**

The Five-Year Plans

'Socialism in one country' implied building up Russia's strength and this meant industrialisation. Stalin embarked on a series of **Five-Year Plans**, which were to be carried out under the supervision of the State Commission for Economic Planning (Gosplan). Targets were set for all major industries, to be achieved by a mixture of rewards and punishments.

The first Five-Year Plan (1928–32) concentrated on heavy industry. The second (1933–7) allowed for some limited production of consumer goods, but the third (1938–42) returned to the emphasis on heavy industry (and also, in view of the approach of war, armaments). The result of these plans was a remarkable rate of growth, which transformed Russia into a major industrial power, though it is questionable how efficient the new industries were. Between 1928 and 1941 coal and steel production quadrupled. Great new industrial areas were developed in the Urals and Siberia.

> **KEY ISSUE**
>
> Some historians claim that this industrialisation enabled Russia to defeat Germany in the Second World War and to emerge as a superpower afterwards. Another view is that the foundation for Russian industrial strength was laid by the Tsars and that Stalin merely built on it. On this view faster progress would have been made by different methods.

Direction of labour meant that the government sent workers to factories where they were needed.

Success was achieved by using the power of the state to put great pressure on the workforce. Conditions for the workers were very poor with low wages, poor housing in the new industrial towns, direction of labour and ruthless discipline in the factories. But there were also incentives: pay differentials and medals for outstanding workers (Stakhanovites). The emphasis on heavy industry meant that the Russians saw little benefit in terms of availability of consumer goods. Low wages meant that living standards fell, though by the mid 1930s workers began to see some benefits in education, health care and holidays with pay. Government propaganda stressed that the sacrifices were in a patriotic cause.

Since foreign loans were not available to Communist Russia, the capital needed for industrialisation had to be raised by Russia itself. This is why wages were held down. Government control of the economy allowed it to cut labour costs to the minimum and plough back all surpluses. But it was also vital to earn foreign exchange to pay for imports of foreign machinery. The success of the Five-Year Plans therefore depended on agriculture, since Russia's principal export was grain. Grain was also required to feed the growing industrial towns at the lowest possible cost.

The collectivisation of agriculture

For Stalin agriculture presented two problems. Firstly, there were 24 million separate peasant farms, many of them too small to use modern agricultural machinery. Secondly the richer peasants (kulaks), who had profited from the New Economic Policy, wanted high prices for their produce. In any case, the rise of a class of prosperous peasants, who owned their own land, was an affront to communist ideology.

> Be prepared to discuss the advantages and disadvantages of collectivisation as a solution to the problems of Russian agriculture.

Stalin's solution was **collectivisation**. In 1929 he decreed that all farms should be collectivised within three years. The kulaks resisted by burning their crops and slaughtering their cattle. Between 1929 and 1932 there was virtual civil war in the countryside, resulting in famine in 1932–3. A minimum of ten million kulaks were killed, died in the famine or were deported to Siberia. Ultimately Stalin triumphed: by 1939, 97% of all land had been collectivised. Along with the provision of agricultural machinery by motor tractor stations, this enabled Russian agriculture to produce record grain harvests in the late 1930s. Even so, it remained relatively inefficient. The number of livestock did not recover until the 1950s.

> **KEY POINT**
>
> The human cost of Stalin's industrialisation and collectivisation policies was enormous.

The purges

AQA **U1, 2** CCEA **AS2**
OCR **U1, 4** WJEC **U1, 4**
Edexcel **U1**

In the mid-1930s Stalin set about destroying all possible opposition to his rule. The murder of the Communist Party boss in Leningrad, Kirov, by a young Communist dissident in December 1934 sparked off the purges. In 1935 Zinoviev and Kamenev were arrested and imprisoned and in 1936 after a show trial they were executed on the evidence of their own confessions. Another show trial in 1938 removed Bukharin and Yagoda, the head of the NKVD (secret police). All the possible rivals to Stalin were liquidated: all the living members of Lenin's politburo, except Stalin himself and Trotsky (in exile), the Chief of the General Staff, Marshal Tukhachevsky, and about two thirds of the senior officers in the army were executed. About 300 000 lesser people were shot and seven million sent to labour camps in Arctic Russia and Siberia (the gulags). Many were condemned on the basis of confessions which were clearly untrue.

> Purges are a common feature of single-party dictatorships. What was extraordinary about Stalin's purges was their scale.

There have been many explanations for the purges. Some historians lay the emphasis on Stalin's paranoid personality. Others think that he saw the elimination of the entire generation of Bolsheviks of Lenin's time as the only way to ensure that there would be no threat to his position in the future. Another theory is that he wanted to make sure there would be no internal rivals in a position to profit from any external disaster such as defeat in war. Whatever the explanation, most of the victims presented only an imaginary threat.

The purges left Stalin in total control of a terrorised population, but they also deprived Russia of many of its best brains, slowed down its industrial growth and weakened the army, which lost more officers in the purges than in the Second World War.

Stalin's Russia

AQA	**U1, 2**	CCEA	**AS2**
OCR	**U1, 4**	WJEC	**U1, 4**
Edexcel	**U1**		

The 1936 Constitution

Nominally the USSR was a democracy. The **Constitution** of 1936 provided for all citizens over 18 to elect by secret ballot the Supreme Soviet. This apparently democratic constitution had some propaganda value for Stalin – it was applauded by left-wing sympathisers of the Soviet Union in the west. However, there was only one party to vote for. Real power lay with the Communist Party and within the Party with its Secretary, Stalin. Stalin's control over the Party was further strengthened by the purges. High office demanded unquestioning loyalty.

A police state

The Soviet Union was a **police state**. Guarantees of individual liberty in the constitution were meaningless, as the purges demonstrated. There was strict censorship of the press. There was no freedom of speech and little freedom of movement. Lenin's secret police, the Cheka, had been abolished in 1922, but its place had been taken by the OGPU, which Stalin used to enforce collectivisation. In 1934 the OGPU was merged with the NKVD (People's Commissariat for Internal Affairs), which became notorious as the instrument by which Stalin carried out the purges.

The USSR was also a **totalitarian state**. The influence of the state was felt in all areas of Russian life. All forms of opposition or disagreement were suppressed. Although there were over a hundred national groups within the USSR and 12 nominally separate republics, the national minorities were suppressed. Jews were regarded with particular disfavour and often persecuted. The government tried to diminish the influence of the Orthodox Church by persecuting the priests and closing churches.

Stalin's rule was a ruthless dictatorship, more repressive than the Tsarist autocracy.

Education

Education was closely supervised to ensure that Marxist doctrines of the class struggle and the dictatorship of the proletariat were inculcated. In both schools and universities teachers were required to accept unquestioningly Stalinist ideology, a combination of nationalist and Marxist ideas which portrayed the Soviet Union under its great leader as the epitome of 'all patriotic and progressive forces'. It was strongly anti-religious. The educational system did, however, succeed in its foremost aim: illiteracy was almost eradicated. It also made it possible for working class children to enter higher education, though in

This was a considerable achievement and should be set against the fact that education was used for indoctrination.

the 1930s Stalin moved away from favouring working class applicants to selecting those with the best qualifications.

Soviet culture

It also meant producing works which were readily accessible to ordinary Russians and which portrayed Russia as happy, successful and progressive.

Cultural life was state controlled. Writers, artists and musicians were required to produce works of '**socialist realism**'. Stalin defined this as 'National in form, Socialist in content'. Practitioners of the arts, scholars and intellectuals all had to be careful to produce what was acceptable to the state for fear of their lives. This meant glorifying the Soviet state and above all Stalin.

Stalin became the object of an extraordinary personality cult. Propaganda portrayed him as the great leader who cared for his people on whom everything depended. Everywhere there were statues or portraits of him.

The family

Policy towards the family changed in the 1930s. Under Lenin divorce and abortion became easy. By the 1930s family breakdown was becoming a serious problem. Stalin therefore made divorce more difficult and abortion illegal. Emphasis was placed on strict sexual morality.

Conclusion

The nature of the Soviet state makes it difficult to know how much suppressed discontent there was.

In spite of everything Stalin seems to have enjoyed much support among the Russian people. They accepted the sacrifices as the means to make Russia great and prosperous. Stalin appealed both to their desire for better conditions and to their sense of Russian nationalism and in the second half of the 1930s his policies did seem to be slowly paying dividends. Literacy was increasing, standards of living were at last beginning to rise and social services were improving. Opposition was largely suppressed.

> **KEY POINT**
>
> Propaganda portrayed Stalin as the great leader who was concerned for his people and on whom almost everything depended. In spite of his brutal methods, he enjoyed much support.

Foreign policy in the 1930s

Edexcel **U1**   WJEC   **U1**
CCEA   **A2.1**

For much of the inter-war period the USSR was isolated from international diplomacy. In the mid-1930s Stalin began to take more interest in European affairs, joining the League of Nations (1934) and sending forces to fight in the Spanish Civil War. At first he was not alarmed by the rise of Hitler, thinking his regime would not last. When he realised his error he tried to improve relations with the west. In the end, however, he came to the conclusion that the western powers would not help Russia in the event of a German attack. The policy of appeasement, which reached its climax at Munich, reinforced this view. He therefore decided to seek an agreement with Germany.

Stalin was not even consulted about the fate of Czechoslovakia.

The **Nazi–Soviet Pact** (1939) bought him time and enabled him to regain the territory lost to Poland at the Treaty of Riga in 1921. Stalin went on to attack Finland. Despite unexpectedly stiff resistance by the Finns, Russia gained territory in Karelia. It also annexed the Baltic States. Relations with Germany deteriorated, but Stalin was convinced that Hitler would not attack Russia while still at war in the west. Stalin expected a German attack, but not until 1942. He was taken by surprise when Hitler launched **Operation Barbarossa** in June 1941.

You should be able to explain the significance of each of these dates.

KEY DATES

1922	Stalin Secretary General of the Communist Party
1924	Death of Lenin
1925	Fall of Trotsky
1927	Kamenev and Zinoviev expelled from the Politburo
1928	First Five-Year Plan
1929	Collectivisation decree
1933	Second Five-Year Plan
1935	Purges begin with arrest of Kamenev and Zinoviev
1938	Third Five-Year Plan
1939	Nazi-Soviet Pact
1941	German invasion of Russia

Sample question and model answer

How far is terror an adequate explanation for Stalin's pre-eminence in Russia between 1929 and 1941?

[50]

Terror extended throughout the USSR under Stalin and was a major explanation of his pre-eminence, but not the only one.

- The use of terror was a long-standing feature of Russian government. Lenin established a one-party state, in which opponents were dealt with by terror (the Cheka). Before that the Tsars had used terror. Stalin inherited this tradition, but used terror on a different scale and for different purposes.
- From 1929 collectivisation was enforced by terror. Kulak class was destroyed. Famine resulted, but was ignored by Stalin who gave higher priority to transforming Soviet society and economy.
- For the same reason, industrialisation was pushed forward by force, as well as incentives. People were conscripted to work in factories. Failure to meet production targets was regarded as sabotage. Production did increase, but at the cost of great hardship and even so, industry remained fundamentally inefficient.
- Terror was used against political rivals. Trotsky was driven into exile and eventually murdered by Stalin's agents in Mexico.

- Terror reached its height in the purges. Stalin began with show trials of politicians who had links with the 1917 Revolution and Lenin. These `Old Bolsheviks' were seen as potential rivals. Kamenev and Zinoviev were executed. Stalin then turned on army generals and senior officers. Then the purges spread throughout the party and the army - thousands were executed or sent to gulags. The purges removed all elements which Stalin believed were not absolutely reliable, leaving Stalin in unchallengeable control.

However, terror was not the only explanation for Stalin's pre-eminence. Stalin's rise to power was based on his control of the party organisation as General Secretary of the Communist Party. This enabled him to remove Trotsky and other rivals in the 1920s and remained the basis of his power. Propaganda, films and the arts were used to build up an extraordinary personality cult of Stalin as the father of his people. He was indirectly compared to the heroes of Russian history such as Ivan the Terrible and Peter the Great. Artists and film-makers were required to produce works of `socialist realism', which meant glorifying the state and praising Stalin for its achievements. He seems not to have been held responsible for the hardship of the Russian people but looked up to.

Terror was a key feature of Stalin's Russia. It put Stalin in an unassailable position of power, where even his closest associates were afraid to step out of line. To a large extent, however, it was unnecessary. Stalin's position as party boss and the extraordinary personality cult which grew up were sufficient in themselves to ensure his dominance - certainly after 1929 when his remaining rivals were removed.

18 International relations, 1879–1941

The following topics are covered in this chapter:

- Causes of the First World War
- The First World War
- The Versailles settlement
- The League of Nations and international diplomacy in the 1920s
- The Versailles settlement challenged, 1931–7
- The outbreak of the Second World War, 1937–41

18.1 Causes of the First World War

LEARNING SUMMARY

After studying this section you should be able to understand:

- the making and importance of the alliance system
- the importance of the arms race
- the series of crises which led up to war
- the causes of the war

The Alliance system

| OCR | **U1** | WJEC | **U1** |
| Edexcel | **U3** | AQA | **U1** |

The first step in the formation of the alliances was taken by Bismarck in 1879. Fearful of a war of revenge for defeat in the **Franco-Prussian War** of 1870–1, he sought to isolate France. In 1879 he formed the Dual Alliance with Austria – a secret defensive alliance which was the cornerstone of German diplomacy until 1918. Three years later Italy joined Germany and Austria in the **Triple Alliance**.

Bismarck maintained good relations with Russia, as well as the alliance with Austria and Italy and thus kept France isolated. But after his dismissal in 1890, William II made little effort to keep on good terms with Russia. This provided an opening for French diplomacy and in 1893 France and Russia made a military alliance, each promising to help the other if attacked by Germany.

> **KEY POINT**
>
> By 1893 the Triple Alliance of Germany, Austria and Italy faced the Dual Alliance of France and Russia. Of the major powers, only Britain remained uncommitted.

The making of the Triple Entente

By 1900 Britain's policy of 'splendid isolation' was being questioned. Colonial disputes with France over Egypt and Sudan made it likely that she would favour an alliance with Germany. But William II's clumsy diplomacy, especially the Kruger

This is also known as the Entente Cordiale.

Telegram and his support for the Boers in the Second Boer War, turned British opinion against an alliance with Germany. Britain therefore sought an alternative route out of isolation. The result was the **Anglo-French Entente** (1904), by which France recognised British control in Egypt and Britain recognised French influence in Morocco.

Three years later a similar entente was signed with Russia, France's ally. Like the Anglo-French Entente this was an understanding, not an alliance. Britain was not committed to war in support of France or Russia, but the signing of the Ententes began a period of increasing co-operation between Britain and France, especially in naval matters. Consequently by 1914 Britain was morally committed to support France.

All the other powers were now involved in defensive military alliances. Neither alliance was intended as a preparation for war. Their intention was to provide security for their members against attack and thus prevent war. But their effect was that, if a war did start, it might drag in all the other members, as happened in 1914.

> **KEY POINT**
>
> By 1907 the Great Powers of Europe were divided between the Triple Alliance and the Triple Entente.

The arms race

OCR	**U1**	WJEC	**U1**
Edexcel	**U3**	AQA	**U1**

The result of the formation of the alliance system was an arms race. Each alliance thought it essential not to let the other gain sufficient military strength to risk an attack. All the continental powers built up their armies. By 1914 Germany was able to call on nearly four million men (including reservists). Russia and France both responded by increasing the period of compulsory military service.

> **KEY POINT**
>
> By 1914 Europe was divided into two 'armed camps'.

Alongside the arms race there was a **naval race** between Britain and Germany. Germany began to build up its navy in 1898, after Tirpitz was appointed head of the Admiralty in 1897. He argued that Germany needed an expanded navy to make it a world power and to compete with Britain. Britain relied on the navy as its first line of defence and began a programme of naval construction to maintain its naval supremacy. The race accelerated after 1906 when the *Dreadnought* was launched and continued unabated up to the outbreak of war. Attempts to negotiate with Germany cuts in naval building failed and Britain therefore made the 1912 **Anglo–French Naval Agreement**. Britain was to concentrate its naval strength in the North Sea and France in the Mediterranean.

This brought Britain and France close to being allies who would be obliged to help each other in a war.

Pre-war crises, 1905–1914

OCR	**U1**	WJEC	**U1**
Edexcel	**U3**	AQA	**U1**

Much of the tension between the powers before the First World War can be attributed to William II, whose foreign policy is summed up as '**weltpolitik**' (world policy). A mixture of nationalism and militarism, it meant that Germany demanded a place 'in the sun' and that nothing should be settled 'without the intervention of Germany'. In practice this meant colonial expansion, building up the navy and the extension of German influence in the Balkans (symbolised by William's proposed Berlin–Baghdad Railway).

A series of crises occurred between 1905 and 1914.

- The **first Moroccan crisis** (1905) arose when William visited Tangier and demanded a conference on the future of Morocco, in an attempt to undermine the Anglo-French Entente. When the conference met at Algeciras in 1906, only Austria supported Germany. Morocco was left under French influence. Germany's clumsy diplomacy had strengthened the Anglo-French Entente.

- The **Bosnian Crisis** (1908) arose when Austria annexed Bosnia, which was technically still part of the Ottoman Empire, though Austria had ruled it since 1878. This outraged Serbia, since there was a substantial Serbian population in Bosnia, and it looked to Russia for help. Russia, however, was unable to do anything since William made it clear that Germany would back Austria in the event of war. Russia was snubbed and Serbia became a bitter enemy of Austria.

- The **second Moroccan crisis**, which arose when the German gunboat *Panther* was sent to Agadir, provoked Lloyd George to threaten war. Germany backed down, though with some 'compensation' in the Congo. The crisis strengthened the Anglo-French Entente and led to the Anglo-French Naval Agreement of 1912.

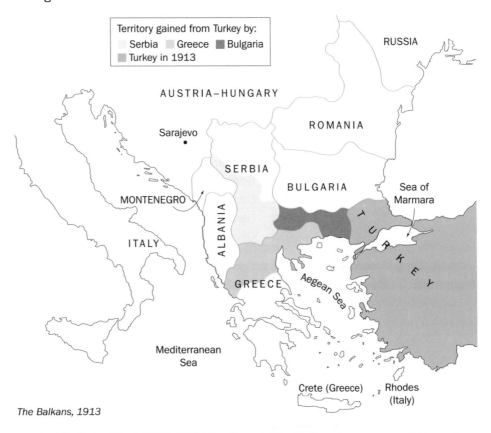

The Balkans, 1913

- In 1912 the **First Balkan War** broke out. The Balkan League, consisting of Serbia, Greece, Montenegro and Bulgaria, captured most of Turkey's remaining territory in Europe. Austria was alarmed that Serbia would become too powerful and especially that it would gain an outlet to the sea in Albania. There was a real danger that Austria and Russia would be drawn into the conflict and that a general war would result. The great powers called a peace conference in London, in which Germany, supported by Britain, insisted that

Albania should be independent. The remaining territory conquered from Turkey was carved up between the victors. Disappointed in its hopes for Albania, Serbia occupied part of Macedonia, which was claimed by Bulgaria. This resulted in the Second Balkan War in 1913, in which Bulgaria went to war with its former allies, but was defeated. By the Treaty of Bucharest, Greece kept southern Macedonia and Serbia kept northern Macedonia.

> **KEY POINT**
>
> The outcome of the Balkan Wars was to strengthen Serbia. Austria feared an eventual attack on Bosnia by a militant Serbia. This might herald the break-up of the multinational Austrian Empire.

The July Crisis, 1914

After the Balkan wars, Austria was determined to weaken Serbia. War between Austria and Serbia was almost inevitable. What was not inevitable was that such a war should lead to a general European war. The assassination of Franz Ferdinand at **Sarajevo** provided Austria with the excuse to crush Serbia. Austria consulted Germany before issuing an ultimatum. It is unlikely that it would have taken such a strong line but for the fact that William gave the Austrian chancellor a 'blank cheque' – a promise of German help without conditions.

Think about this when considering Germany's responsibility for the war.

Events then unfolded rapidly.

23 July	Austrian ultimatum to Serbia. Its terms were such that rejection was inevitable.
25 July	Serbia replied, accepting most, but not all, of the terms.
28 July	Austria declared war on Serbia. It is important to note that Russia could not allow herself to be humiliated again by failing to back Serbia, as she had in 1908.
30 July	Russian mobilisation was ordered.
31 July	Germany issued an ultimatum to Russia to stop mobilisation.
1 August	Germany declared war on Russia and activated the Schlieffen Plan.
2 August	German issued an ultimatum to Belgium.
3 August	Germany declared war on France.
4 August	German troops invaded Belgium; Britain declared war on Germany.

It was very difficult for Russia to do this in a short period of time.

Causes of the war

OCR	U1	WJEC	U1
Edexcel	U3	CCEA	A2.1
AQA	U1		

Explaining the outbreak of the First World War involves balancing a number of factors, each of which played an important part. The immediate cause was clearly the instability of the Balkans. Austria's fear of the rise of Serbia and its long-standing rivalry with Russia made the region a powder keg. What needs to be explained is why this problem led to a world war. Each of the following factors needs to be considered.

- The growth of German power: The nineteenth century balance of European power had been profoundly disturbed by the creation of the German Empire by Bismarck and was further upset when William II adopted the policy of weltpolitik.
- Economic rivalry: The threat posed by Germany's political power was increased by its growing economic strength.
- Colonial rivalry: This too played a part in creating an atmosphere of suspicion, especially between Germany and Britain. But note that all of the colonial disputes involving the great powers in the preceding twenty years had been resolved without a European war.

- The alliance system – Triple Alliance v. Triple Entente: But it is doubtful whether the existence of rival alliances was enough itself to cause a war. Indeed, it can be argued that before 1914 it created a balance of power.
- The arms race.
- Anglo-German naval rivalry: This was perhaps the most serious cause of friction between Britain and Germany before 1914.
- The mobilisation plans of the great powers: It was difficult to stop mobilisation once it had begun, which meant that the politicians lost control of events to the generals in 1914. The logic of the Schlieffen Plan made it impossible for a war involving Russia to be confined to Eastern Europe and led directly to the involvement of Britain.
- The role of public opinion in the growth of a nationalistic, warlike mood, fanned by the popular press in the main European states.

Army leaders had great influence in pre-1914 Germany – see page 191.

Germany must bear a considerable share of the responsibility. By 1914 the army leaders had more control over German policy than the Chancellor, Bethmann-Hollweg. The Kaiser, the ministers and the army leaders all held strongly nationalistic and militaristic opinions. There was a widespread feeling that a war was inevitable and many thought it was desirable as a way of winning popular support away from socialism and liberalism. At a war council in 1912 Moltke wanted an immediate war over the Balkans, but Tirpitz said the navy would not be ready for 18 months. Some historians argue from this that Germany was planning a war from then on.

You should be able to explain the significance of each of these dates.

KEY DATES	
1879	Dual Alliance of Germany and Austria-Hungary
1882	Triple Alliance: Germany, Austria-Hungary and Italy
1893	Dual Alliance: France and Russia
1904	Anglo-French Entente
1905	First Morocco Crisis
1907	Triple Entente: Britain, France and Russia
1908	Bosnian Crisis
1911	Second Morocco Crisis
1912	Anglo-French Naval Agreement
1912–3	Balkan Wars
1914	Outbreak of war

18.2 The First World War

LEARNING SUMMARY

After studying this section you should be able to understand:

- the development of the war on the Western Front
- the main features of the war on other fronts
- how the war ended with the defeat of Germany

The Western Front

OCR   U1

As soon as war was declared, the Germans put into operation the **Schlieffen Plan** which had been prepared before the war to deal with the threat posed by a war on two fronts against France and Russia. The plan was to deal a knock-out blow against France by striking through Belgium and northern France and sweeping west of Paris. The French capital would be cut off and forced to surrender. The German armies would then be transferred to the east to confront the Russians who, it was assumed, would be slower to mobilise.

The plan went wrong. The invasion of Belgium brought Britain into the war and the British Expeditionary Force (BEF) was sent to Belgium to assist the Belgian army. The German advance was slowed down. Meanwhile, the Russians invaded Germany from the east much sooner than the Schlieffen Plan had allowed for. Troops had to be transferred to the east. Moltke modified the plan and headed straight for Paris. At the **battle of the Marne**, the French and the BEF halted the German army. The Germans then fell back. The 'race to the sea' which followed was an attempt by both sides to turn the other's flank. At the **First Battle of Ypres** (November 1914) neither side could break through. Both sides then dug trenches which eventually stretched from the Swiss border to the North Sea.

> **KEY POINT**
>
> The failure of the Schlieffen Plan led to the stalemate of trench warfare.

The Third Battle of Ypres is often called Passchendaele.

Stalemate followed. For nearly four years tremendous efforts were made to break through the enemy lines, most notably at the Battles of **Verdun** and the **Somme** (1916) and the **Third Battle of Ypres** (1917). Despite enormous casualties it rarely proved possible to push back the enemy more than a few hundred yards. This was because:

- the weapons (machine guns and landmines) were better for defence than attack
- attackers had to overcome mud and barbed wire to get across No-Man's Land
- preliminary bombardments of the trenches took away the element of surprise
- the generals were unable to devise any other way of attacking than by sending large numbers of men on foot to attack the enemy trenches.

Attempts were made to devise new weapons to break the stalemate. The most notable were gas and tanks. Neither proved decisive, though towards the end of the war tanks became less prone to break down and did break through enemy lines at the battles of **Cambrai** (1917) and **Amiens** (1918).

> **KEY POINT**
>
> The basic problem on the Western Front was that defence was much stronger than attack.

The other fronts

OCR   **U1**

The Russians had huge resources of manpower, but could not provide them with proper equipment.

On the **Eastern Front** the Russians mobilised more quickly than expected, but they were defeated at the battles of **Tannenberg** and the **Masurian Lakes** in 1914. A major Russian offensive against Austria in Galicia in 1916 was at first successful, but then ground to a halt through shortage of equipment. The 1917 revolutions in Russia led to its withdrawal from the war by the Treaty of Brest-Litovsk in 1918.

In 1915 an attempt was made by Britain, supported by forces from Australia and New Zealand, to open up a new front in Turkey, which had entered the war alongside Germany and Austria. The **Gallipoli** expedition, however, proved to be a disaster.

The only major sea battle of the war took place in 1916 when the German Fleet ventured out of port into the North Sea and was confronted by the British Grand Fleet at **Jutland**. Although the British suffered heavier losses than the Germans, the German fleet withdrew to its base and did not venture out again. Thus the British fleet retained control of the seas, which enabled it to maintain a blockade of Germany throughout the war.

The German response to the blockade was a **U-boat** (submarine) campaign which aimed to cut off Britain's supplies. By 1917 this was proving very damaging to the British war effort, but British losses were then dramatically reduced by the adoption of the convoy system. The most important result of the U-boat campaign was the entry of the USA into the war in 1917. This was because the Germans had adopted a policy of attacking any ships approaching Britain and had sunk some American ships.

> **KEY POINT**
>
> The Germans calculated that unrestricted submarine warfare would bring Britain to its knees before the Americans could have a significant impact. They were wrong.

This was the first war in which aircraft played a part. At first they were very basic and used only for reconnaissance. As the war progressed, fighter planes equipped with machine guns were developed. By the end of the war, planes were also being used to drop bombs. But even then aircraft were still too basic to have a major impact.

The end of the war

OCR   U1

The **Treaty of Brest–Litovsk** released German forces from the east for a major offensive in the west. They made considerable gains, partly because of new tactics, but mainly because the Allies, united for the first time under a single commander, Marshal Foch, fell back and allowed the Germans to exhaust themselves. Foch then launched a counter-attack. With more and more American troops arriving, the Germans were pushed back. With increasing shortages, due to the success of the Allied blockade, Germany was on the point of exhaustion. There were strikes, riots and mutinies. Germany's allies were collapsing and Germany was forced to ask for an armistice.

> **KEY POINT**
>
> The blockade and the entry of the Americans into the war were probably the decisive factors.

18.3 The Versailles settlement

LEARNING SUMMARY

After studying this section you should be able to understand:
- the main features of the Paris Peace Conference, 1919
- the peace terms imposed on Germany
- the other main features of the settlement
- the weaknesses of the settlement

The Paris Conference, 1919

OCR **U1** WJEC **U1, 4**
Edexcel **U3**

The peace treaties were drawn up by a conference at Paris in 1919. There were 32 states represented, but not Germany and her allies, to whom the decisions of the conference were eventually communicated for acceptance. The main decisions were taken by three men: Woodrow Wilson of the USA, Lloyd George of Britain and Georges Clemenceau of France.

The dominant ideas which were eventually incorporated in the peace treaties can be traced back to Woodrow Wilson's **'Fourteen Points'**, issued in January 1918. Most of them concerned the territorial changes needed for a stable peace in Europe and embodied the principle of **national self-determination**, i.e. that boundaries should be determined by nationality. The last point was that 'a general association of nations' should be formed: this was the origin of the League of Nations.

In seeking a stable peace, Wilson thought that an excessively harsh peace with Germany would make her want revenge. Clemenceau, however, was determined to punish Germany and ensure that she should be so weakened that she could never again present a threat to France. Lloyd George's position was somewhere between the two.

As a result of the conference, five treaties were signed in 1919–20 with Germany (Treaty of Versailles), Austria (St. Germain), Hungary (Trianon), Bulgaria (Neuilly) and Turkey (Sèvres).

Germany: the Treaty of Verseilles

OCR **U1, 4** WJEC **U1, 4**
Edexcel **U3**

Germany's losses, 1919

Germany suffered a number of territorial losses. Alsace and Lorraine were restored to France. The Saarland was to be administered by the League of Nations for 15 years, during which the coalmines would be in French possession; at the end of that period its future would be determined by a plebiscite. In the east Germany lost West Prussia and Posen to the new state of Poland to form the Polish Corridor to the Baltic. Danzig became a free city under the League and Memel was also administered by the League until 1923, when it was taken over by Lithuania.

The area of Germany west of the Rhine and also a zone 50 kilometres to its east was demilitarised. Germany's army was reduced to 100 000 men and conscription was forbidden. She was also forbidden to make tanks, military aircraft or heavy artillery. The navy was limited in size and was not permitted any submarines. Germany's colonies became 'mandates' under the supervision of the League. This actually meant that they were transferred to other powers for their administration, though they did not become their colonies. Britain acquired the mandate over Tanganyika (Tanzania today), South Africa over South West Africa (Namibia), France over Togoland and the Cameroons, Belgium over Ruanda and Urundi, Australia over German New Guinea, New Zealand over German Samoa and Japan over Germany's North Pacific islands.

> But in practice they were treated as colonies.

The remaining provisions of the German treaty were extremely important. Article 231, the **'War Guilt Clause'**, asserted that the war and the losses caused by it were the result of the aggression of Germany and her allies. Article 232 required Germany to pay reparations to the Allies for their losses, at a figure fixed in 1921 at £6.6 million in gold.

> **KEY POINT**
>
> There was no negotiation with Germany. The German representatives were simply summoned in to sign a treaty drawn up by the Allies. This is why they regarded it as a dictated treaty and therefore unfair.

The treaties with Germany's allies

OCR **U1** WJEC **U1, 4**
Edexcel **U3**

Eastern Europe

The three great empires which had dominated Eastern Europe – Austria, Turkey and Russia – had collapsed and a new map was produced, based on the principle of national self-determination. Six new states were created: Estonia, Latvia and Lithuania (which had been handed over from Russia to Germany by the Treaty of Brest-Litovsk), Finland, Poland and Czechoslovakia. Serbia was transformed into Yugoslavia by the acquisition of Bosnia, Herzegovina, Dalmatia and Croatia from Austria-Hungary. Romania was doubled in size by acquisitions from Austria-Hungary and Russia. Italy gained Trentino and the South Tyrol from Austria. Thus Austria-Hungary (now two separate states) suffered considerable losses.

The Turkish Empire

By the Treaty of Sèvres the former Turkish provinces of the Arabian peninsula were given their independence. By 1926 most of the area had been united into one state, which was known as Saudi Arabia from 1932. Syria and Lebanon became French mandates and Iraq, Transjordan and Palestine British mandates.

The Treaty of Sèvres also gave Smyrna (Izmir today) to Greece. A revolution in Turkey brought to power Kemal Ataturk, who refused to accept the loss of Smyrna. A war between 1920 and 1922 resulted in a Turkish victory. The Treaty of Sèvres was superseded by the **Treaty of Lausanne** (1923): Smyrna remained Turkish and a million Greeks were expelled.

Weaknesses of the settlement

OCR **U1** WJEC **U1, 4**
Edexcel **U3**

The principle of national self-determination had to be tempered by economic or defensive considerations which left racial minorities in the new states. The three million Germans in the Sudetenland found themselves in Czechoslovakia, because the only defensible frontier was the Bohemian mountains. Altogether there were six million Germans outside Germany and Austria and there were substantial racial minorities in Poland, Czechoslovakia, Romania and Yugoslavia. In a Europe whose states were based on the principle of national self-determination, these minorities felt more insecure than they had under the old multiracial empires.

The new 'successor states' in Eastern Europe were smaller and weaker than the former empires and so they depended on western support in the 1930s when both Germany and Russia had recovered their strength. The absence of both Germany and Russia from the conference meant that the two most powerful states were not committed to maintaining the settlement.

In Germany the settlement aroused great bitterness. The Germans called it a **diktat**, which humiliated them by the War Guilt Clause, deprived Germany of territories they regarded as rightly hers, disarmed her and imposed a crippling burden in reparations.

J. M. Keynes condemned the amount demanded in reparations as far beyond Germany's ability to pay. Reparations were a major cause of the German currency crisis of 1923, which in turn played its part in the rise of Hitler.

18.4 The League of Nations and international diplomacy in the 1920s

LEARNING SUMMARY

After studying this section you should be able to understand:

- the origins and structure of the League of Nations
- its record in the 1920s
- the changes in relations between Germany and the international community in the 1920s
- the failure of the attempts to secure disarmament

The origins of the League of Nations

OCR **U1**   Edexcel **U3**

The League had its origins in Wilson's Fourteen Points. Under the Covenant of the League, which was written into each of the peace treaties, members undertook:
- to submit disputes with other members to the League for decision
- to preserve against aggression the territory and independence of other members
- to apply economic sanctions against aggressors and, if these failed, military sanctions
- to reduce armaments.

These obligations were intended to produce **collective security**.

> This meant that members of the League would act together (collectively), against an aggressor.

The structure of the League of Nations

OCR **U1**   Edexcel **U3**

The **Assembly**, which met annually, consisted of representatives of all members. For all major decisions, unanimity was required, which meant that a minor power could obstruct progress. The **Council** consisted of four permanent members (Britain, France, Italy and Japan) and four temporary members elected by the others. In 1926 Germany became a permanent member and the number of temporary members was raised to nine. It met at least four times a year. As in the Assembly, decisions had to be unanimous, which led to slow progress. Its power was limited, as it had no army at its disposal and therefore had to rely on the goodwill of members for action against an aggressor.

The League set up a number of special **Commissions**, including the Mandates Commission, the Minorities Commission, the Commission for Refugees and the World Health Organization. Much of the League's most valuable work was done by these bodies. The Disarmament Commission, however, had little success. Also associated with the League, but not technically part of it, were the International Labour Organisation and the Court of International Justice.

> Don't forget these Commissions when assessing the record of the League.

KEY POINT

The requirement for unanimity was intended to safeguard the rights of member states, but it weakened the League's ability to act.

The record of the League in the 1920s

OCR **U1** Edexcel **U3**
WJEC **U4**

The League suffered a significant blow at its very beginning: The US Senate refused to ratify the peace treaties and so the USA did not join the League.

The League succeeded in settling a number of minor international disputes in the 1920s.
- It settled the division of Upper Silesia between Poland and Germany (1921).
- It settled a dispute between Sweden and Finland over the Aaland Islands (1920–1).
- It halted the Greek invasion of Bulgaria in 1925 and forced Greece to pay compensation.

> The Conference of Ambassadors had representatives from Britain, France, Italy and Japan. It was not part of the League's structure but worked alongside it.

But an early indication of its weakness was the **Corfu Incident** (1923). Mussolini used the murder of an Italian general on an international commission surveying the border between Greece and Albania as an excuse to bombard Corfu. The Council of the League initially condemned Italy's action, but then handed the matter over to the Conference of Ambassadors, which ordered Greece to pay compensation to Italy. Thus the ambassadors, representing the Great Powers, had failed to back the Council of the League and the use of force had been shown to pay dividends.

KEY POINT

The League's record in the 1920s suggested that it was effective in disputes between lesser powers, but not when one of the great powers was involved.

Two other events suggest that there was limited confidence in the League as a guarantor of peace.
- The **Geneva Protocol**, 1924. The Covenant of the League left the definition of an 'aggressor' unclear. The Protocol stated that any country which refused to accept arbitration in a dispute was an aggressor. It was dropped when Britain refused to accept it after a change of government.

Signatories only made a pledge not to resort to war. There was nothing to enforce it.

- The **Kellogg–Briand Pact**, 1928, prohibited the use of war 'as an instrument of national policy except in self-defence'. Since this was already enshrined in the Covenant, it indicated a lack of faith in the League, and it had little effect. At the time, however, it was seen as another step towards a more peaceful world, and one in which, unlike the League, the USA took part.

The German question

OCR **U1**   Edexcel **U3**
WJEC **U4**

Relations with Germany were at the heart of much of the international diplomacy of the 1920s. At the Paris Conference in 1919 Clemenceau of France had been determined to punish Germany and ensure she could never fight another war – hence the demand for reparations. In 1922 Germany failed to make the required payments. France and Belgium responded by occupying the Ruhr.

The Little Entente was formed to resist Hungarian claims: France saw it as also a defence against Germany

French fears of the revival of German power were shared by the newly created states of Eastern Europe. In 1920 Czechoslovakia, Yugoslavia and Romania formed an agreement known as the **Little Entente** and France agreed to support its members with military aid. In 1921 France made a similar agreement with Poland.

See page 208 for further details of the occupation of the Ruhr and the Dawes Plan.

The diplomatic climate changed in 1924–5. The German currency crisis of 1923 prompted a review of reparations and the **Dawes Plan** (1924) reduced the annual instalments and linked them to Germany's ability to pay. This was facilitated by the new German Foreign Minister, Stresemann, who understood that Germany must allay French fears if it was to regain its place in European affairs. He cultivated good relations with Briand of France and Austen Chamberlain, the British Foreign Minister.

Locarno

The result was the **Locarno Treaties of 1925**.

- Germany, France and Belgium accepted as final the boundaries laid down at Versailles. Britain and Italy guaranteed these boundaries.
- Germany agreed that its frontiers with Poland and Czechoslovakia could only be altered by arbitration.
- France renewed its treaties of mutual assistance with Poland and Czechoslovakia.

Hitler exploited this in 1938.

Note that no guarantees were given for Germany's eastern frontiers, thus suggesting that they were open to change. Even so, these treaties were regarded as a triumph at the time and they were followed by a period of much greater harmony known as the 'Locarno honeymoon'. Germany was admitted to the League of Nations in 1926 and to the Kellogg–Briand Pact in 1928. In 1929 a further modification of reparations was agreed in the **Young Plan**. Relations between France and Germany were much more harmonious.

> **KEY POINT**
>
> Locarno and the Kellogg-Briand Pact were intended to strengthen the peace, but they indicated doubts about the Versailles settlement and the League.

Disarmament

OCR **U1**   Edexcel **U3**
WJEC **U4**

Many people believed that one of the main causes of the First World War had been the arms race. One way of ensuring that such a war could never happen again, therefore, was to reduce armaments, as proposed in the Fourteen Points and enshrined in the Covenant. A step towards this was the **Washington Naval Treaty** (1922), one of several treaties which resulted from a conference called by the USA because of its fears about Japanese ambitions in the Far East and Pacific. The aim of the Naval Treaty was to prevent a naval race. The USA, Britain and Japan agreed to limit their navies in a ratio of 5:5:3. In the end this was more beneficial to Japan than to Britain or the USA, since their commitments were worldwide, whereas Japan's ambitions were limited to the Pacific region.

In 1926 the League set up a Commission to prepare for a World Disarmament Conference, but progress was slow. The conference finally met at Geneva in 1932. In 1933, with Hitler in power, Germany withdrew, claiming that it was unfair that Germany had been disarmed by the Treaty of Versailles while other powers did not disarm. In 1934 the Conference broke up.

> **KEY POINT**
>
> The basic problem was that none of the great powers was willing to disarm while it suspected possible threats to its security.

You should be able to explain the significance of each of these dates.

> **KEY DATES**
>
> | | |
> |---|---|
> | 1919 | Versailles settlement |
> | 1922 | Washington Naval Treaty |
> | 1923 | Corfu Incident |
> | 1924 | Dawes Plan |
> | 1925 | Locarno Treaties |
> | 1928 | Kellogg-Briand Pact |

18.5 The Versailles settlement challenged, 1931–7

LEARNING SUMMARY

After studying this section you should be able to understand:

- the significance of the Japanese invasion of Manchuria, 1931
- Hitler's moves to rearm Germany
- the failure of the League of Nations to prevent Mussolini's conquest of Abyssinia
- the importance of the remilitarisation of the Rhineland

The Japanese invasion of Manchuria, 1931

OCR **U1** Edexcel **U3**
WJEC **U4**

Japan was hard hit by the Great Depression. Its government came increasingly under military control. In September 1931 Japan attacked China after a minor bomb explosion on the South Manchurian Railway, which was owned by Japan. Japanese troops quickly occupied Manchuria which, in March 1932, they renamed Manchukuo. A Japanese puppet government was set up. Both China and Japan were members of the League and China appealed to the League. A commission of inquiry (the Lytton Commission), sent to Manchuria by the League, condemned Japan's aggression, but no action was taken. The USA, to which China appealed under the Kellogg-Briand Pact, also refused to intervene. In 1933 Japan withdrew from the League and went on to invade more of northern China. The failure of the League to act against Japan was perhaps the turning-point in its history, for it showed that it was ineffectual in checking aggression.

> **KEY POINT**
>
> The episode seemed to show that the League's authority could be ignored – a lesson not lost on Mussolini and Hitler.

German rearmament

OCR **U1** Edexcel **U3**
WJEC **U2, 4**

Hitler's first moves were cautious. He continued for a while to participate in the Geneva **Disarmament Conference**, but in October 1933 withdrew on the grounds that Germany was not being given equal treatment. At the same time he withdrew from the League of Nations. He balanced these moves with a ten-year Non-Aggression Pact with Poland in 1934. The purpose of this was to break up the French system of alliances in Eastern Europe.

By March 1935 he felt confident enough to issue a direct challenge to the Versailles settlement by announcing that Germany now had an air force and by reintroducing conscription. This prompted Britain, France and Italy to make an agreement (the **Stresa Front**, April 1935) to resist by force any future attempt to change the settlement. This soon broke down as a result of the Anglo-German Naval Agreement (June 1935) and Mussolini's invasion of Abyssinia.

> This implied that the Versailles settlement could be renegotiated.

Mussolini's conquest of Abyssinia, 1935–6

OCR **U1** Edexcel **U3**
WJEC **U4**

Italians had felt since the late nineteenth century that they had not got their fair share of colonies in the 'scramble for Africa'. They had tried unsuccessfully to take over Abyssinia (modern Ethiopia) in 1896. Mussolini had already tried to establish economic domination there. Mussolini now saw the conquest of Abyssinia as the answer to Italy's economic problems and as a way of boosting his regime at a time when unrest was growing because of the effects of the Great Depression. The diplomatic situation seemed favourable. Britain and France were anxious to keep on good terms with Italy because of their concern about the growing strength of Germany. Mussolini thought they would therefore accept the Italian conquest of Abyssinia without much protest.

The Italian armies had little trouble in taking over Abyssinia, though in the process they used poison gas. The real importance of the episode lay in its effects on Italy's relations with Britain, France and Germany and on the League of Nations. The League declared Italy an aggressor and imposed sanctions, but coal, steel and – most importantly – oil were excluded. The sanctions therefore had little effect on Italy's war effort. The failure to impose effective sanctions was largely because Britain and France were not prepared for war and, as Mussolini had calculated, were anxious to maintain good relations with Italy. For the same reasons they allowed Italy free passage through the Suez Canal, which they controlled. They even proposed, in the **Hoare-Laval Pact**, to allow Mussolini to keep two-thirds of Abyssinia, but public outrage in Britain and France forced the withdrawal of this plan. Mussolini went on to take control of Abyssinia unopposed.

> **KEY POINT**
>
> This confirmed the ineffectiveness of the League of Nations.

Why the League of Nations failed

- Membership: There were never more than five of the great powers in membership. The USA never joined. Germany was only a member between 1926 and 1933, the USSR between 1934 and 1939. Japan withdrew in 1933, Italy in 1937. Only Britain and France were members throughout the existence of the League, making it too much of an Anglo-French alliance.
- Reluctance or inability to enforce its decisions: The League had no army. Aggressor states were willing to use war to further their aims, but members of the League were not willing to risk war to stop them.
- Sanctions: The only action taken against a powerful aggressor (the imposition of sanctions on Italy) was ineffective, partly because it was difficult to enforce when some of Italy's trading partners such as the USA were not members of the League. More importantly, however, it was because the sanctions did not include materials such as oil which were vital for Italy's industry and army.

Hitler and the Rhineland

OCR **U1** Edexcel **U3**
WJEC **U2, 4**

This was a gamble on Hitler's part, but its success encouraged him to make further aggressive moves.

This encouraged Hitler to gamble on the next major breach of Versailles, the **remilitarisation of the Rhineland** in March 1936. This was a crucial step. It allowed Hitler to fortify Germany's western frontier, thus protecting it against France and making it easier to concentrate on expansion to the east. France was unwilling to oppose Hitler without British assistance and Britain was unwilling to intervene. British opinion regarded Hitler's action as redressing a legitimate grievance.

KEY POINT

The remilitarisation of the Rhineland completed the destruction of the Versailles settlement so far as it applied to Germany itself and opened the way for the expansion of Germany to unite all Germans in a Greater Germany.

18.6 The outbreak of the Second World War, 1937–41

LEARNING SUMMARY

After studying this section you should be able to understand:
- the steps by which Hitler's aggressions led to war in September 1939
- how Japanese aggression brought about war in the Pacific

The road to war, 1936–9

OCR **U1** Edexcel **U3**
WJEC **U2, 4**

Lebensraum meant living space for the German people – in other words expanding German territory into Eastern Europe.

Hitler consolidated his position in 1936–7. Rearmament proceeded apace and the Four-Year Plan was put into effect with the aim of making Germany ready for war, if necessary, in that time. At the end of 1937, according to the **Hossbach memorandum,** he informed his military commanders of his intention to acquire *lebensraum*, beginning with the takeover of Austria and Czechoslovakia. This would have to be completed by 1943–5 at the latest, because by then Germany would have lost its military superiority. This appeared to suggest that Hitler had a timetable for his expansionist policies, though A. J. P. Taylor thought he was 'simply daydreaming' – speculating about the future rather than planning.

In 1938 the creation of an enlarged Reich got under way.

- The **Anschluss** with Austria (March 1938). The Austrian Nazis, led by Seyss-Inquart, caused growing disorder. Schuschnigg, the Chancellor, tried to defuse the situation by holding a referendum on the question of union with Germany. This provided an excuse for Hitler to intervene and take over Austria. It was another triumph for Hitler in the eyes of German nationalists.
- The **Sudetenland** (September 1938). Hitler used the excuse of discontent, stirred up by the Sudeten German Nazis, to demand that the Sudetenland be handed over from Czechoslovakia to Germany. At the Munich Conference Britain and France gave way to this demand. The USSR was not consulted.
- In March 1939 German troops occupied the rest of Czechoslovakia. Bohemia and Moravia became German protectorates; Slovakia was nominally independent. For the first time Hitler had taken over a country which was not German-speaking – a development which played a crucial role in changing British policy towards Germany.
- Memel was handed over by Lithuania (March 1939).
- In April 1939 Hitler demanded Danzig and a road and railway across the Polish Corridor. The Poles, fearing that this was a prelude to a German invasion, refused.
- The **Nazi–Soviet Pact** (August). Hitler believed that with Russia neutral the British government would revert to its policy of appeasement.
- Germany invaded Poland on 1 September 1939. On 3 September 1939 Britain declared war.

> **KEY POINT**
>
> Hitler calculated that Britain and France would either back down or offer only token support to Poland. He was wrong.

The Far East and the Second World War

OCR **U1**   Edexcel **U3**

The Japanese occupation of Manchuria in 1931 was followed by a period of intermittent localised warfare between China and Japan. Power struggles within China between the government of Chiang Kai Shek and the Communists under

Mao Zedong enabled the Japanese to extend their control within north-east China. The militaristic Japanese government aimed to conquer the whole of China and then the whole of East Asia. In 1937 the Marco Polo Bridge incident provided an excuse for full-scale war. Within months the Japanese conquered Shanghai and Nanking and gained control over most of the Chinese coastline. Chiang Kai Shek retreated to a new capital in Chungking. Mao and the communists, who controlled most of the north, led the resistance – often by guerrilla warfare – to the Japanese.

Pearl Harbour

The outbreak of war in Europe provided the opportunity for the next Japanese advance. Japan was already linked with Germany and Italy in the Anti-Comintern Pact of 1936 and in 1940 it formed a tripartite Axis with them. With the defeat of France by Hitler, Japan was able to occupy French Indo-China as part of its plan to set up a Greater East Asia Co-Prosperity Sphere. This was really another name for subordination of the economies of East Asia to the Japanese economy – a Japanese informal empire.

The USA was already alarmed by the growth of Japanese power in the western Pacific and the threat to American trade with China. President Roosevelt demanded that Japan should evacuate Indo-China and China. He reinforced this by stopping the sale of oil to Japan, a move which threatened to cripple Japan's army and industry. While negotiations took place in Washington, the Japanese prepared an unprovoked attack on the US navy at **Pearl Harbour** (December 1941). They also attacked British bases in Malaya and Hong Kong. The USA and Britain immediately declared war on Japan. At the same time Hitler declared war on the USA. Thus, Pearl Harbour linked the existing wars in Europe and China into a global war.

You should be able to explain the significance of each of these dates.

KEY DATES	
1931	Japanese invasion of Manchuria
1933	Hitler comes to power in Germany
1935	Stresa Front
1935	Italian invasion of Abyssinia; German rearmament
1936	Remilitarisation of the Rhineland
1938	Anschluss; Sudetenland crisis; Munich agreement
1939	Hitler takes over the rest of Czechoslovakia; Nazi-Soviet Pact; invasion of Poland; Britain and France declare war
1941	German invasion of Russia; Pearl Harbour

Exam practice questions

1. To what extent was German foreign policy between 1895 and 1914 'dangerously aggressive'? **[50]**

2. 'Germany's policies in North Africa and the Balkans between 1905 and 1913 were unwise and provocative.'

   How far do you agree with this statement? **[50]**

3. Why was there no serious threat to European peace in the 1920s? **[50]**

4. 'Hitler's foreign policy successes between 1933 and 1941 rested on his remarkable tactical skills and ability to exploit his opponents' weaknesses.'

   How far do you agree with this statement? **[50]**

19 Germany 1945–90: from defeat to unification

The following topics are covered in this chapter:

- From occupation to division, 1945–9
- The Federal Republic of Germany, 1949–63
- The German Democratic Republic, 1949–71
- The two Germanies, 1961–89
- Reunification, 1989–91

19.1 From occupation to division, 1945–9

LEARNING SUMMARY	After studying this section you should be able to understand:
	• the surrender and occupation of Germany in 1945
	• the division of Germany by 1949

The surrender and occupation of Germany

AQA	U3	OCR	U2
OCR	U1	Edexcel	U1
WJEC	U4		

In April 1945 Allied and Russian troops advancing through Germany from west and east linked up on the River Elbe. On 30 April Hitler committed suicide and on 7 May the new German head of state Admiral Doenitz surrendered unconditionally. Germany was devastated. There were food and fuel shortages. The transport system had broken down. The economy collapsed. Government at all levels had ceased to function. Refugees were streaming in from the east.

The Yalta Conference, 1945

In February 1945 the Allied leaders, Roosevelt (USA), Churchill (Britain) and Stalin (USSR) met at Yalta to make plans for post-war Germany and Europe. They decided:

- Germany would be divided into four zones of occupation (the fourth zone was for France), with Berlin correspondingly divided into four sectors
- Germany would be demilitarised and denazified
- war criminals would be punished.

The Potsdam Conference, 1945

At Potsdam in July–August 1945 the Allied leaders further decided that the border between Germany and Poland should be the Oder-Neisse line and that Germans living in Poland, Hungary and Czechoslovakia should be relocated into Germany (thus adding enormously to the refugee problem). Each occupying power was to determine what it would exact in reparations.

> **KEY POINT**
>
> The new German-Polish border involved massive population movements.

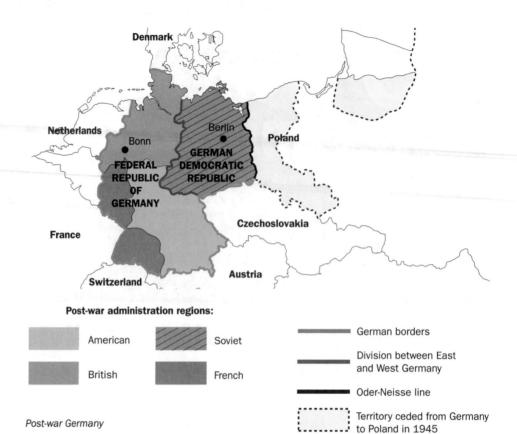

Post-war administration regions:

▢ American	▨ Soviet	━━━	German borders
▢ British	▢ French	━━━	Division between East and West Germany
		━━━	Oder-Neisse line
		┅┅	Territory ceded from Germany to Poland in 1945

Post-war Germany

The Nuremberg Trials, 1945–6

> Those sentenced to death included Bormann and Ribbentrop. Hess was sentenced to life imprisonment.

The International Military Tribunal tried 22 leading Nazis on charges of war crimes and crimes against humanity. There were four judges, one from each of the Allies. Twelve were sentenced to death, though Goering committed suicide the day before he was due to be hanged, seven were imprisoned and three were acquitted.

> **KEY ISSUE**
>
> The Nuremberg Trials were controversial. The evidence against most of the defendants was overwhelming, but the way the trials were conducted could be seen as imposing 'victors' justice'.

Denazification

At the same time the process of **denazification** affected a much wider section of German society. The aim was to remove from public office and positions of responsibility all committed Nazis. Implementation varied between the four zones. It was most thorough in the Soviet zone, where it was also a means of seizing assets of factory or estate owners – class enemies in communist theory. In the end many former Nazis were 'rehabilitated'.

The Allied Occupation

An **Allied Control Council** was set up to coordinate the administration of Germany. The immediate task facing the occupying powers was to restore basic services and prevent starvation and disease. This was carried out by the military governments of the occupying powers. They were also responsible for resettling the millions of refugees and for demilitarisation, which meant dismantling factories capable of making war equipment.

The division of Germany by 1949

AQA	**U3**
OCR	**U1, 2**
WJEC	**U4**
Edexcel	**U1**

Soon economic and political developments began to pull the western and soviet zones apart.

Economic developments

Soviet expansionism in Eastern Europe prompted Britain and the USA to change their policies towards Germany. They began to see western Germany as a potential buffer against Soviet aggression. The dismantling of German factories ceased and instead they began to build up the economy in their zones. In 1947 the British and the USA zones were joined for economic purposes into Bizonia. The French, anxious about the possible revival of German power, kept their zone separate until 1948. When the Organisation for European Economic Cooperation was set up in 1948 to administer the Marshall Plan, Bizonia was an associate member – a development which the Russians saw as an act of aggression.

> The Russians aimed to create a Soviet-style communist economy in their zone.

The Russians treated their zone quite differently. They exacted massive reparations by removing factories and industrial equipment to the USSR. Land reform and nationalisation of banks and industry set their zone on a different path which made the prospect of a unified Germany more remote.

Political developments

Creating a stable Germany in the western zones meant rebuilding German political and civic institutions. In 1946 local elections were held and in 1947 elections for provincial (Land) governments. The western allies encouraged the creation of democratic political parties. **The Social Democratic Party** was re-established under Kurt Schumacher. The conservative Catholic and Protestant parties which had existed in the Weimar Republic were brought together to form the **Christian Democratic Union** by Konrad Adenauer, who had been Mayor of Cologne from 1917–33. A third party, the **Free Democrats**, equivalent to the British Liberals, was formed in 1948.

In the Soviet zone the Communist Party was re-established in June 1945. In 1946 the Social Democratic Party amalgamated with it to form the Socialist Unity Party (SED). This was supposedly a voluntary merger, but in reality it was a takeover of the Social Democrats by the Communists.

The Berlin Blockade

To further the economic recovery the western powers introduced a currency reform on 20 June 1948. The new Deutschmark was also introduced into West Berlin. The Russians saw this as an attempt to undermine their efforts to build a socialist society in their zone. On 24 June they closed all land routes to West Berlin. The western powers overcame this by the Berlin airlift. The Russians lifted the blockade on 12 May 1949.

> **KEY POINT**
>
> The Berlin Blockade was a key development in the division of Germany – an attempt by the Russians to drive the western powers out of Berlin, met by a massive operation to supply Berlin by air.

The two Germanies

Negotiations between the four occupying powers over a peace treaty with Germany had reached stalemate by the end of 1947. In 1948 the three western powers started the process of drawing up a constitution for a German state formed from their zones. The **Federal Republic of Germany** (FRG) was set up in May 1949.

In the Soviet zone a People's Congress was elected in May 1949, but the only candidates were those appointed by the Socialist Unity Party. This Congress approved a constitution for the **German Democratic Republic** (GDR) which came into existence in October 1949. The division of Germany was complete.

19.2 The Federal Republic of Germany, 1949–63

LEARNING SUMMARY

After studying this section you should be able to understand:
- the constitution of the Federal Republic
- the reasons for the 'economic miracle'
- the success of Adenauer's foreign policy
- why Adenauer resigned in 1963

The constitution of the Federal Republic

AQA **U3**
OCR **U1, 2**
WJEC **U4**
Edexcel **U1**

The Basic Law set up a federal structure in West Germany. It aimed to create a democratic system of government while avoiding the weaknesses of the Weimar constitution and is the basis of the present constitution of Germany.
- The lower house of Parliament (the Bundestag) is elected by a mixture of direct and proportional representation. A party has to secure 5% of the votes to gain representation. Elections are normally held every four years.
- The upper house (the Bundesrat) consists of representatives of the Land (provincial) Parliaments.
- The Chancellor is elected by the Bundestag and can only be dismissed by the Bundestag electing a successor in a vote of no confidence.
- The President, who is the head of state, has largely ceremonial functions and cannot dismiss the Chancellor or dissolve Parliament (unlike in the Weimar Republic).
- The Federal Constitutional Court was set up to safeguard the constitution.

Adenauer and 'chancellor democracy'

The constitution places the Chancellor at the heart of the government, hence the term 'chancellor democracy' that arose to describe it. The centrality of the Chancellor was reinforced by Adenauer, who held this position from 1949–63. In the first elections under this constitution the Christian Democrats (CDU/CSU) emerged as the strongest party, but needed the support of the Free Democrats to form a government. Adenauer became Chancellor. Adenauer's success in foreign policy, combined with West Germany's economic growth, enabled the CDU/CSU to win the elections of 1953 and 1957 (in 1957 with an absolute majority over all other parties). After the 1961 election, however, Adenauer once again required the support of the Free Democrats in a coalition.

The CSU is the equivalent of the CDU in Bavaria.

The 'economic miracle'

AQA	U3	WJEC	U4
OCR	U1, 2	Edexcel	U1

The Marshall Plan provided American aid to European countries to rebuild their economies after the destruction of the war.

With the establishment of the Federal Republic in 1949 economic recovery gathered pace. In the 1950s the growth rate of the West German economy was 8% per annum. By 1952 it had a positive balance of trade and by 1960 its economy was the strongest in Europe. Apart from the kick-start given by the Marshall Plan there were other factors assisting this 'economic miracle'.

- West German factories were re-equipped with modern machinery after the destruction at the end of the war. This enabled West Germany to develop strong exports of industrial goods.
- The Federal Republic spent nothing on armaments for several years because it had been demilitarised.
- The Korean War provided a stimulus for the steelworks of the Ruhr.
- Labour relations were good and there was comparatively little disruption from strike action.
- The division of Germany freed West Germany from the demands of Prussian agricultural interests, which had been a continual problem from the time of Bismarck onwards. Post-war German economic policies therefore promoted industry, and the agricultural sector declined in size.

The 'economic miracle' was commonly attributed to Erhard's policies, making him very popular.

- The Economics Minister, **Erhard**, followed free market economic policies and kept interest rates low to encourage investment. He avoided state intervention in the economy except for investment in education and the infrastructure.
- The Bundesbank, established in 1957, was independent of the government and pursued policies which made the Deutschmark one of the world's leading currencies.
- The European Coal and Steel Community (founded 1951) created a much bigger 'domestic' market for these basic industrial products. This process was expanded by the creation of the **European Economic Community** in 1957. This development also ensured that the revival of Germany's economic strength would not be seen as a threat by its neighbours, since Germany's economy was integrated into the wider European economy. Indeed Germany was a motor for growth and prosperity in the EEC as a whole.

Economic growth slowed in the 1960s and unemployment rose. Nevertheless, West Germany remained the economic powerhouse of Europe.

> **KEY POINT**
>
> The 'economic miracle' produced a marked contrast in standards of living between West and East Germany.

Adenauer's foreign policy

AQA	U3
OCR	U1, 2
WJEC	U4
Edexcel	U1

Adenauer's main aim was to rehabilitate Germany as a sovereign state in Europe. The steps by which he achieved are detailed below.

- The **Petersberg Agreement** (1949). The Federal Republic joined the International Authority for the Ruhr.
- The **European Coal and Steel Community** (ECSC, 1951). West Germany was one of its six members. The ECSC was conceived by Robert Schuman, the French Foreign Minister as a means to European economic cooperation and also to reduce the possibility of future conflict between France and Germany.

- The proposed European Defence Community (EDC), within which West Germany could rearm. German rearmament was encouraged by the USA in the light of the escalating Cold War and Adenauer supported the plan. The plan failed because of French fears of a revival of German military power.
- A treaty with Israel (1952) to pay reparations as a recognition of guilt for the Holocaust enhanced West Germany's standing with public opinion in the west.
- The **Western European Union** (1954) was set up following the collapse of the EDC. This joined West Germany with the members of the Brussels Treaty Organisation, a defensive alliance set up in 1948 by Britain, France and the Benelux countries.
- This opened the way for West Germany to join **North Atlantic Treaty Organization (NATO)** in 1955 and to form an army. At the same time it gained full sovereignty.
- In 1957 West Germany joined France, Italy and the Benelux countries in setting up the European Economic Community by the Treaty of Rome.

> After the experience of militarism in Nazi Germany, many people both in Germany and neighbouring countries were hesitant about the formation of a German army.

> **KEY POINT**
>
> By 1957 West Germany was fully integrated diplomatically and militarily with the western powers and into the developing European movement.

Relations with the USSR and Eastern Europe

These developments inevitably had repercussions for relations with the USSR and Eastern Europe and for the prospect of reunification. The USSR refused to recognise the Federal Republic when it was set up, but by 1955, with Stalin dead, the USSR under Khrushchev was following a policy of co-existence. Adenauer was able to open diplomatic relations with Russia. At the same time the remaining German prisoners of war in Russian hands were repatriated – which gained Adenauer much acclaim in Germany. However, he was not prepared to recognise the regime in East Germany. By the **Hallstein Doctrine** the FRG announced that it would break off diplomatic relations with any country, except the USSR, which did recognise East Germany.

Opposition to Adenauer's foreign policy focused above all on its implications for reunification. In 1952 Stalin proposed reunification on condition that a unified Germany remained neutral. Adenauer suspected his motives and insisted on free elections throughout Germany as a precondition. Stalin rejected this and the proposal was abandoned. The opposition attacked him for this, but the electorate supported him in the 1953 election.

The resignation of Adenauer

AQA	**U3**	Edexcel	**U1**
OCR	**U1, 2**	WJEC	**U4**

Adenauer's power and popularity, at their height after the 1957 election, began to decline in the late 1950s.

- He was criticised by Erhard over the terms of entry to the EEC. Relations with Erhard were strained after this.
- The building of the **Berlin Wall** in 1961 ruined remaining hopes of reunification and seemed to show that his policies towards the USSR had achieved nothing.
- The CDU/CSU lost its majority in the 1961 election. Adenauer had to form a coalition with the Free Democrats (FDP), which insisted on a promise that he would resign before the next election. Adenauer was aged 85 in 1961.

- The Spiegel affair (the arrest of a magazine editor for publishing classified information about NATO) led to cabinet resignations and then to Adenauer's resignation in 1963.

But he had one last achievement: the **Elysée Treaty**, known as the **French-German Friendship Treaty**, 1963 – the result of Adenauer's warm relationship with de Gaulle.

> You should be able to explain the significance of each of these dates.

KEY DATES

1945	Yalta and Potsdam Conferences
1948–9	Berlin Blockade
1949	Establishment of Federal Republic and German Democratic Republic
1951	European Coal and Steel Community set up
1955	West Germany joined NATO; GDR joined Warsaw Pact
1957	European Economic Community set up
1961	Berlin Wall built
1963	Resignation of Adenauer

19.3 The German Democratic Republic, 1949–71

LEARNING SUMMARY

After studying this section you should be able to understand:

- the development of the German Democratic Republic under Ulbricht, 1949–71

The German Democratic Republic under Ulbricht, 1949–71

AQA	**U3**	Edexcel	**U1**
OCR	**U1, 2**	WJEC	**U4**

From 1949–71 the East German leadership was headed by Ulbricht, a communist who had spent the war years in Moscow and returned to Germany with the Russians in 1945. He played a key part in the formation of the Socialist Unity Party. The German Democratic Republic (GDR) was a one-party state on the Soviet model and Ulbricht's power came from his position as General Secretary of the Party. The People's Congress (Parliament) was a talking shop. Real power lay with the party, which controlled all aspects of society. The **Stasi** (State Security Service) had almost complete power over the population. There were state-controlled organisations for youth, trade unions and women. Membership of the party was essential for career advancement.

KEY POINT

The Stasi was one of the most efficient secret police services ever known. It had agents everywhere – nearly 100 000 full-time agents and twice as many informers.

The rising of June 1953

In June 1953 there were mass demonstrations in protest against increased production quotas, which effectively meant a pay cut. There was already unrest because of shortages of food and consumer goods. Ulbricht had to call on Soviet troops to suppress the protesters. There were over 1300 arrests afterwards.

The economy

Ulbricht's economic policies followed the Stalinist soviet model. The key policies were nationalisation of industry, collectivization of agriculture and central planning, with the emphasis on industrial products rather than consumer goods. Production quotas were set in the Five-Year Plans of 1951 and 1956. The economy did grow – in fact East Germany was the most successful industrial economy in Eastern Europe – but standards of living lagged behind those in the west. This remained true despite some loosening of central controls in the 1960s (the New Economic Policy).

The Berlin Wall

In the late 1950s thousands of East Germans were leaving the comparative poverty of East Germany to enjoy the fruits of West Germany's economic miracle. They were able to do this by using public transport from East to West Berlin. Efforts by Khrushchev to secure western recognition of the independence of the GDR and the evacuation of West Berlin in the late 1950s failed. By 1960 the number of East Germans leaving via West Berlin reached a thousand a week. To stop this, in August 1961 the Berlin Wall was built. The flow of refugees was halted. This and the New Economic Policy brought an improvement in the economy.

> To make matters worse, those leaving were largely young and skilled.

> **KEY POINT**
>
> The Berlin Wall lasted for 28 years. Between 100 and 200 people died trying to cross it. It became the symbol of the division of Germany.

Relations with the west

The geographical position of the GDR made it the USSR's front line in the Cold War. When the USSR set up the **Warsaw Pact** in 1955, the GDR was a member and in the following year it created the National People's Army. Throughout the 1950s and 1960s the two Germanies confronted each other. The atmosphere changed in the late 1960s, when the superpowers, the USA and the USSR, began to pursue détente. Moscow saw Ulbricht, who favoured confrontation with the west, as an obstacle to détente. In 1971 he was dismissed at Moscow's behest.

19.4 The two Germanies, 1961–89

LEARNING SUMMARY	After studying this section you should be able to understand:
	• developments in the FRG, 1963–89
	• developments in the GDR, 1971–89
	• the effect of Ostpolitik on relations between the FRG and the GDR

Developments in the FRG, 1963–1989

AQA **U3** Edexcel **U1**
WJEC **U4**

There were five Chancellors between the resignation of Adenauer and Reunification.
- **Erhard** (1963–6) led a coalition between the CDU/CSU and the FDP. He was less successful as Chancellor than he had been as Economics Minister. A recession and budget crisis in 1966 led to the break-up of the coalition and Erhard resigned.
- **Kiesinger** (1966–9) led a Grand Coalition with Brandt (SPD) as Vice-Chancellor. A coalition between the two main parties was seen as an essentially temporary measure to deal with the economic problems.

- **Brandt** (1969–74). The 1969 election enabled Brandt to form a coalition with the FDP. He resigned in 1974 following the revelation that one of his personal assistants was a spy for the GDR. Brandt's main achievement was Ostpolitik (see below).
- **Schmidt** (1974–82), who had been Minister of Finance, took over the leadership of the SDP–FDP coalition, but there were increasing strains between the partners by the 1980s. The coalition broke up when the FDP Minister of Economics proposed cuts in social services which were unacceptable to the SDP. Schmidt resigned after a constructive vote of no confidence in 1982.
- **Kohl** (1982–98) headed a CDU/CSU–FDP coalition, which gained a majority in the 1983 election.

> **KEY POINT**
>
> The Federal Republic was in many ways a model democracy.

The main internal problems in these years are detailed below.

- The student movement, inspired by similar movements in the USA and France in 1968, staged sit-ins and demonstrations, but gained little support in the population. But it did give rise to …
- The **Red Army Faction**, better known as the Baader-Meinhof Gang. This extreme left-wing student group carried out a number of acts of urban terrorism. Its leaders were arrested in 1972, and Baader committed suicide in prison in 1977, after which it was greatly weakened.

But it remained active into the 1990s.

- The oil crisis of 1973 led to a growing recognition of the limitations of economic growth. The economic optimism of the 1950s and 1960s declined amid growing economic problems. There was also a growing awareness of environmental issues, which resulted in the formation of the Greens in 1980. They won 27 seats in the 1983 election.

Developments in the GDR, 1971–89

AQA **U3** Edexcel **U1**
WJEC **U4**

West German television could be received in many parts of East Germany.

Honecker, who replaced Ulbricht as First Secretary of the SED Central Committee, had been responsible for security and had been in charge of the building of the Berlin Wall in 1961. His time as the GDR's leader was a period of economic and political stagnation in the GDR. Living standards were much lower than in West Germany and television made people aware of this – but they did improve and were the highest in the Eastern Bloc. There were always shortages. The lack of personal freedom was resented. Elections were meaningless.

But there was no open opposition. This is partly because of the way revolts in other East European states had been suppressed, partly because the Stasi was everywhere. This came to be known as the '**niche society**' – one where people got on with their lives, taking care to keep out of trouble and to do what was required by the state.

Relations between the two states: Ostpolitik

AQA **U3** Edexcel **U1**
WJEC **U4**

Détente is examined more fully on pages 281–2.

The pursuit of **détente** by the superpowers opened the way for a new phase in the relations between East and West Germany. In 1969 Brandt, newly elected Chancellor of West Germany, embarked on his **Ostpolitik**. The first result of this was the 1970 treaty between West Germany and the USSR and this led on to a Four Power Agreement on the status of Berlin. In 1972, by the Basic Treaty, West and East Germany recognised each other. In 1973 both states were accepted into the United Nations. Both states took part in the Conference on Security and Cooperation in Europe and signed the Helsinki Final Act in 1975. Trade and border agreements were made between the two states.

> **KEY POINT**
>
> Ostpolitik made relations between East and West Germany more normal, but also suggested that the division was to be permanent. With only limited exceptions, East Germans were still not allowed to travel to the West.

19.5 Reunification, 1989–91

LEARNING SUMMARY	**After studying this section you should be able to understand:** • why the GDR collapsed • how Kohl brought about reunification in 1990

The collapse of the GDR

AQA **U3** Edexcel **U1**
WJEC **U4**

The East German regime collapsed in 1989. The underlying causes were economic failure and lack of political freedom. But why did these longstanding weaknesses suddenly lead to collapse in 1989?

For further explanation see pages 285–6.

The policies of **perestroika** (restructuring) and **glasnost** (openness) introduced by Gorbachev in Russia from 1985 encouraged movements for reform throughout Eastern Europe. In Hungary, Kadar resigned in 1988 and, in Poland, **Solidarity** won free elections in June 1989. In East Germany, awareness of these events led to the emergence of political parties and protests in which the churches became a focus for unrest. The rigging of elections in May 1989 was met with demonstrations in Leipzig and other cities. The opening of the Hungarian frontier with Austria provided an escape route which thousands of East Germans took. Others took refuge in West German embassies in Prague, Budapest and Warsaw. Regular Monday demonstrations in Leipzig began in September. On 23 October 300 000 took part and the security forces took no action to disperse the crowd.

The opening of the Berlin wall

The SED leadership were out of touch. As late as 7 October, 1989, at the celebration of the 40th anniversary of the founding of the GDR, Honecker claimed that socialism would not be halted. But the politburo finally realised that the situation was serious and on 18 October forced him to resign in favour of Krenz. Gorbachev had already made it clear that the USSR would not intervene to crush the demonstrations. On 4 November, 1989 over a million people turned out for a demonstration in East Berlin. On 9 November the border to West Berlin was opened: the wall had fallen.

> **KEY POINT**
>
> The symbolism of the opening of the Wall was immense.

The SED leadership still hoped to reform the system and thus preserve the GDR. A new Minister President, Modrow, was appointed. In December, the entire politburo resigned and the SED's leadership role in the constitution was ended.

In February 1990 the SED changed its name to the Party for Democratic Socialism. It was all to no avail. When free elections were held in March, there was a clear majority for the Alliance for Germany, led by the CDU and with a programme of a market economy and reunification.

Kohl and reunification

AQA **U3** Edexcel **U1**
WJEC **U4**

In West Germany Chancellor Kohl's reaction to the opening of the Berlin Wall was the **Ten Point Plan** for step-by-step reunification. In February he met Gorbachev. Following the elections in East Germany, Kohl pressed for a speedy resolution of all the issues involved. In May, the two German governments signed a treaty for monetary, economic and social union, as a result of which in July the Deutschmark became the currency of East Germany.

The next step was to secure the agreement of the four wartime allies. When Kohl met Gorbachev in February, he got his agreement in principle to reunification. In May the **Two Plus Four Talks** between the German governments and the USSR, USA, Britain and France opened. With the support of the USA and in spite of some hesitation by Britain and France, a treaty was signed in September: the frontier between Germany and Poland was accepted and Germany was to be a member of NATO. In September the two Parliaments approved the Unification Treaty and in October unification took place. In December a new Bundestag for the whole of Germany was elected.

Unification came at a price for both East and West Germany. For the West, it meant bearing the financial burden of supporting the run-down East. For the East Germans, it meant high unemployment because their industries were uncompetitive and the loss of the social services to which they had become accustomed.

> **KEY POINT**
>
> The key to the collapse of the GDR and reunification was to be found in events in Russia.

You should be able to explain the significance of each of these dates.

> **KEY DATES**
>
> | | |
> |---|---|
> | 1969 | Brandt, Chancellor of the Federal Republic, begins Ostpolitik |
> | 1971 | Ulbricht replaced by Honecker as leader of the GDR |
> | 1972 | Basic Treaty between West and East Germany |
> | 1985 | Gorbachev comes to power in the USSR |
> | 1989 | Opening of the Berlin Wall |
> | 1990 | Reunification |

Sample question and model answer

The key issue is the loss of power by the Christian Democrats (CDU) to the Social Democrats (SDP). You are offered one explanation, which you should consider first and then consider others.

Note that the answer considers the state of the CDU before Adenauer's retirement as well as after.

The question is not only about the CDU, but also the SDP.

To what extent does the retirement of Adenauer explain the loss of power by the Christian Democrats to the Social Democrats in West Germany during the 1960s?

[50]

The retirement of Adenauer was an important milestone in the history of the CDU. It brought to power as his successor Erhard, who was seen as 'the father of the economic miracle'. Erhard was less successful as Chancellor than as Economic Minister. He lost the support of the Free Democrats in 1966 and had to resign. He was succeeded by Kiesinger, who put together a 'grand coalition' with the Social Democrats. This was regarded as essentially a temporary measure to deal with the economic problems, but it clearly marks a stage in the rise of the Social Democrats. Thus the retirement of Adenauer can be seen to have been followed by declining success for the CDU.

This is not, however, the same as saying that his retirement caused the decline. In fact his retirement came about because the CDU's dominant position in West German politics was already under threat in Adenauer's last years in power. In the 1961 election the CDU still emerged as the largest party, but with fewer seats in the Bundestag. This was perhaps above all because of the Berlin crisis (1961 was the year the wall was put up). Adenauer was only able to form a government by promising his coalition allies, the FDP, that he would retire before the next election. Relations with the FDP were fractious from the beginning. Adenauer's actual retirement was precipitated by the Spiegel affair, which prompted several resignations from his cabinet. So the CDU's position was already weakened in 1963. The succession of Erhard actually improved its popularity for a time - he was re-elected Chancellor after the 1965 election.

Erhard found it difficult, as Adenauer had done, to maintain good relations with his Free Democrat partners in the coalitions. Matters came to a head in 1966 when West Germany faced unaccustomed economic problems. A recession caused high unemployment and a relatively high budget deficit. As we have seen, this led the Free Democrats to withdraw from the coalition. Perhaps more important in explaining the decline of support for the CDU was the fact that its high standing in the 1950s was based on its economic record; now it was blamed for the loss of economic confidence.

The SDP would probably have made gains because of the decline of support for the CDU. But the SPD also had growing appeal in its own right. The reason for this was above all the leadership of Willi Brandt. Brandt had personal charisma and his record as Mayor of West Berlin made him a popular figure. The grand coalition gave him experience of office. Perhaps most important was his Ostpolitik, which offered the prospect of better relations with the East. After the building of the Berlin Wall hopes of reunification faded. Ostpolitik offered a realistic alternative. A further factor in the swing of opinion towards the Social Democrats was that, in 1959, they formally abandoned their commitment to Marxism and accepted the market economics which had made the economic miracle possible.

So in conclusion, the retirement of Adenauer was an important step towards the rise to power of the SDP, but probably more important was the economic downturn in the mid-1960s and the appeal of Brandt and Ostpolitik.

20 The USSR, 1941–90

The following topics are covered in this chapter:

- **Stalin, 1941–53: the Second World War and after**
- **Khrushchev and destalinisation**
- **The Brezhnev era, 1964–82**
- **The end of the Soviet Union, 1982–1991**

20.1 Stalin, 1941–53: the Second World War and after

LEARNING SUMMARY

After studying this section you should be able to understand:

- the victory of Russia in the war against Germany, 1941–5
- the record of the Soviet Union in the last years of Stalin's dictatorship, 1945–53

The Great Patriotic War

AQA	U3	Edexcel U1
OCR	U4	

In Russia the Second World War is known as the **Great Patriotic War** because of the heroic efforts and enormous sacrifices made to achieve victory.

> The German offensive was code-named Operation Barbarossa.

The military history of the war fell into two phases. In the first phase (1941–2) the Germans advanced deep into Russia. There were three main lines of attack: against Leningrad in the north, towards Moscow in the centre and through the Ukraine in the south. By the end of the year Leningrad was besieged and the Germans had almost reached Moscow, which the Russians successfully defended. In the south Kiev, Odessa and the Crimea had been captured, except for Sebastopol, which was under siege. Forced to retreat, the Russians employed a scorched earth policy. Even so, it was only the Russian winter that halted the German advance. But Hitler had failed to take full advantage of the situation by not deciding which was his main objective.

> Total German losses in and around Stalingrad were about half a million.

In 1942 the main German offensive was in the south. In September they attacked **Stalingrad**, the key to Russia's links with the Caucasus and its oil reserves. This was the limit of their advance. Hitler's refusal to allow a retreat from Stalingrad was a crucial mistake. In February 1943, the combination of the Russian winter and over-extended supply lines, forced the German army of about 100 000 men at Stalingrad to surrender.

> **KEY POINT**
>
> This was the turning point of the war on the eastern front.

> Zhukov's role in the battle may have been exaggerated.

In the second phase (1943–5) the Russian armies pushed the Germans back. In July 1943 Marshal Zhukov won the massive tank battle at Kursk. In November

Kiev was liberated and early in 1944 Leningrad. In the second half of 1944, the Red Army advanced into Eastern Europe, occupying Romania, Bulgaria and Poland. In January 1945, Russian troops entered eastern Germany, reaching Berlin in April.

Stalin's wartime leadership

But unlike Hitler, he did not interfere in the details of military strategy.

Stalin played a key part in achieving ultimate victory.
- The personality cult which had developed in the 1930s helped to focus Russians on his leadership role.
- He enlisted mass patriotism by identifying himself and the Russian nation with the spirit of Old Russia. Churches were reopened and the clergy were encouraged to preach resistance. Tsars such as Peter the Great were portrayed as heroes.
- He used the radio to encourage patriotic resistance.
- He set up the State Defence Committee in 1941 to organise and co-ordinate the war effort.
- He reorganised the army and promoted able officers.

By the end of the war Stalin's authority in Russia was unassailable.

> **KEY POINT**
>
> Stalin was regarded by most Russians as the heroic leader who had achieved victory.

The wartime economy

Russia's industrial strength, together with massive aid from the USA and Britain, enabled it to equip its vast army. Industrialisation in the 1930s underlay this. Industrial plants east of the Urals, e.g. Magnetogorsk, produced large numbers of aircraft and tanks. The State Defence Committee also organised a massive transfer of industrial plant from the war zone to Siberia and Central Asia. In the latter years of the war the USSR was producing more military equipment than Germany and of better quality.

Opposition in the USSR

Hitler's armies were initially welcomed by separatists in the Ukraine, as well as Cossacks and White Russians. Hitler threw away the chance to turn them against Stalin's dictatorship. German brutality, based on Nazi racial theories, alienated them. But note that the fact that they had initially welcomed the Nazis as liberators from Russian oppression made Stalin suspect them. On his orders thousands were slaughtered.

> **KEY POINT**
>
> The cost of the war to Russia was enormous. Overall the USSR had 23 million dead, including three million who died as prisoners of war in German hands, and some 5 million people were homeless. A quarter of all Soviet property had been destroyed.

Stalin's dictatorship, 1945–53

AQA	**U3**	Edexcel	**U1**
OCR	**U4**	WJEC	**U4**

The economy

The major task facing Russia in 1945 was reconstruction.

- The fourth and fifth Five-Year Plans rebuilt Russian industry. By 1950, the USSR was the world's second biggest industrial power. The emphasis was on capital goods rather than consumer goods. New industries, such as plastics, were not developed. Industrial equipment seized from East Germany as reparations helped reconstruction. Much of the new industry was east of the Urals, so as to keep it as far away as possible from any threat from the west.
- Particular attention was given to the development of a nuclear industry. By 1949 the USSR had an atomic bomb.
- Agricultural productivity, however, remained low and food prices were high. This was partly a result of destruction in the war, but mainly because of low investment and the inefficiency of the collective farms.
- The standard of living remained low, partly because of the emphasis on capital goods in the Five-Year Plans, but also because of the high level of military expenditure. There was a shortage of consumer goods and housing.

The Cold War

The Second World War temporarily transformed Russia's relations with the west. When the USA entered the war in 1941, the Grand Alliance of the USA, Britain and the USSR was formed. The leaders of the three countries met at three major conferences: **Teheran** (1943), **Yalta** (February 1945) and **Potsdam** (July–August 1945). It was, however, a somewhat uneasy alliance between the capitalist western powers and communist Russia. Stalin was always suspicious that the Western powers would ultimately try to overthrow communism in Russia. He therefore wanted a communist-controlled Eastern Europe as a buffer against the perceived threat from the west.

> Stalin remembered western hostility to Communist Russia in the Civil War of 1918–20 and through the 1920s and 1930s.

At the end of the war the presence of Russian troops enabled Stalin to set up Peoples' Democracies in Poland, Romania, Bulgaria and Hungary. At first these included both Communists and non-Communists, but the Communists soon took control and established one-party states. A Communist coup in Czechoslovakia in 1948 completed Soviet control of Eastern Europe.

When the western powers began to rebuild Western Germany, Stalin tightened his control over the Eastern European satellite states. In 1949, he set up **Comecon** to co-ordinate their economies and direct their trade towards Russia. The Soviet military presence in Eastern Europe was built up to a total of 5½ million Soviet troops by the early 1950s.

During Stalin's last years, the Cold War flared up twice: in 1948 when he instituted the Berlin blockade and in 1950–3 with the Korean War.

> **KEY POINT**
>
> Stalin suspected the western powers of wanting to overthrow the Communist regime in Russia. The western powers suspected Russia of wanting to set up Communist governments throughout Europe and then the rest of the world.

Government and society

Politically Stalin's last years were marked by a renewal of the repression of the 1930s: censorship, an omnipresent secret police (under Beria), persecution of the church, anti-Semitic tendencies, and state pressure on the arts and universities. His dictatorial powers were further increased: the Party Congress, the Central Committee and the Politburo rarely met.

In the Great Purge in the 1930s over 300 000 people had been executed and millions sent to the **gulags** (labour camps) in Siberia.

The Cold War intensified Stalin's obsessive fears of a hostile world seeking the first opportunity to destroy the USSR. He responded by cutting Russia off from the outside world. Because he feared they had brought back western ideas, returning prisoners of war were appallingly treated. He became obsessed by real and imaginary threats to himself; he believed in the Doctors' Plot – an alleged conspiracy by Jewish doctors to poison him. He was planning new purges when he died in 1953.

> **KEY POINT**
>
> After 1945 Stalin returned to the policies of the 1930s. The USSR was ruled by a savagely repressive dictatorship and its people were isolated from the rest of the world. But it was also one of the two superpowers.

You should be able to explain the significance of each of these dates.

> **KEY DATES**
>
> | | |
> |---|---|
> | 1941 | Operation Barbarossa begins |
> | 1943 | Stalingrad |
> | 1945 | Russian armies capture Berlin; surrender of Germany; Yalta Conference. |
> | 1948 | Communist coup in Czechoslovakia |
> | 1948–9 | Berlin Blockade |
> | 1953 | Death of Stalin |

20.2 Khrushchev and destalinisation

LEARNING SUMMARY

After studying this section you should be able to understand:

- the rise of Khrushchev to the leadership of the USSR
- how far destalinisation was successful
- the fall of Khrushchev, 1964

The rise of Khrushchev

AQA **U3**   WJEC **U4**
OCR **U4**

The NKVD was the ministry which controlled the police, the secret police and the gulags.

By 1955 Krushchev was the dominant figure in the collective leadership.

There was no obvious successor when Stalin died in 1953. The most powerful figure was Beria, the head of the NKVD. Because of his record as the ruthless enforcer of Stalin's terror, he was feared by the other leading members of the politburo, who joined forces against him. He was arrested three months after Stalin's death and later shot after a show trial. A 'collective leadership' of Malenkov (Prime Minister), Bulganin (Defence Minister) and **Khrushchev** (First Secretary of the Communist Party) emerged. A power struggle took place in 1957 over the policy of **destalinisation** (see below) between Khrushchev and the 'Anti-Party Group', which included Molotov and Malenkov. Khrushchev emerged victorious and his rivals were expelled from the **Presidium** (the new name for the Politburo). In 1958, Khrushchev became Prime Minister as well as First Secretary of the Party. He now had supreme power.

Destalinisation

| AQA | U3 | WJEC | U4 |
| OCR | U4 | | |

This speech caused a great stir because Stalin had previously been regarded as the saviour of the nation.

Khrushchev followed a policy of destalinisation. He introduced this in an extraordinary speech to the Twentieth Party Congress in 1956. He accused Stalin of building up a personality cult and denounced the purges of the 1930s. He also advocated a policy of co-existence with the west, arguing that capitalism would decay from within and communism would triumph without war. The impact of this speech was an important factor in Khrushchev's victory in the power struggle. But it also led to unrest in Poland and then to an attempted revolution in Hungary in 1956, which was brutally suppressed by Soviet troops.

Destalinisation involved releasing many political prisoners (though others replaced them) and reducing the power of the secret police, who were disarmed and reorganised into the KGB in 1954. This was accompanied by a degree of liberalisation, known as the **Khrushchev Thaw**. Censorship was relaxed a little. Religious organisations, however, were persecuted.

Liberalisation was limited – liberal compared with the Stalin era.

> **KEY POINT**
>
> Khrushchev's speech to the Twentieth Party Congress marked a turning point in the government of Russia.

The economy

The Khrushchev Thaw saw a shift in economic policy towards producing consumer goods, which brought about a rise in living standards. Khrushchev also sought to make the economy more efficient and at the same time weaken the power of the central state bureaucracy by a policy of **decentralisation**. In 1957, he replaced the central ministries in Moscow by regional economic councils, which were supposed to be more responsive to local needs but actually led to inefficiency.

Khrushchev tried to increase agricultural output by the **Virgin Lands** policy. Volunteers were sent to Siberia and provided with tractors to bring new land into cultivation. This led to increased food production, but poor management and problems of soil erosion hampered the scheme. In 1963 Russia had to import American and Australian grain.

Foreign policy

The Khrushchev Thaw also affected foreign policy. Khrushchev attempted to improve relations with the west by pursuing a policy of **peaceful co-existence**. Since this was a reaction against the isolation of Russian under Stalin, it was linked to destalinisation. There was, however, a lack of consistency and results were limited.

- In 1955 Russia set up the **Warsaw Pact**, a Soviet-dominated military alliance between the countries of Eastern Europe in answer to the North Atlantic Treaty Organization (NATO).
- Khrushchev aimed to secure western recognition of East Germany and the evacuation of West Berlin by the western powers. But his approach, alternately threatening and negotiating, was unsuccessful and culminated in the building of the Berlin Wall in 1961.
- Khrushchev walked out of the 1960 Paris Summit Conference over the U2 spy plane incident.

This is explained on page 280.

Fuller accounts of all these evens can be found in Chapter 21 The Cold War.

- His handling of the **Cuban Missile Crisis** (1962) was seen as a humiliating climbdown.
- Relations with Communist China deteriorated. Mao Zedong challenged Russia's leadership of the communist world, claiming his version of communism was a purer one. By 1960, there was an open split between the two leading communist powers.

The fall of Khrushchev, 1964

AQA	U3	WJEC	U4
OCR	U4		

In 1964, while Khrushchev was on holiday, the Presidium dismissed him. Why was he overthrown?

- He was accused of creating a personality cult.
- He alienated the military by cutting the defence budget, relying on the USSR's nuclear weapons for security.
- A reorganisation of the provincial party apparatus in 1962 alienated many party officials.
- His handling of foreign affairs was seen as a failure.
- Despite a shift in the emphasis of industrial policy, consumer goods remained in short supply. The Seven-Year Economic Plan introduced in 1959 had to be abandoned in 1963.
- The Virgin Lands policy had not worked. In 1963 the harvest failed. Russia had to import grain and bread rationing was introduced.

KEY POINT

By 1964 Khrushchev had lost the confidence of other members of the Presidium, who regarded his behaviour as increasingly unpredictable.

20.3 The Brezhnev era, 1964–82

LEARNING SUMMARY

After studying this section you should be able to understand:
- how Brezhnev came to dominate the leadership of the USSR
- the political, economic and social policies of the Brezhnev era.

Brezhnev and the leadership of the USSR

AQA	U3	WJEC	U4

After the fall of Khrushchev, the government of the USSR returned to the pattern of collective leadership set up after the death of Stalin. At first there was a triumvirate of Brezhnev (General Secretary of the Communist Party), Kosygin (Prime Minister) and Podgorny (Chairman of the Presidium). Though collective leadership remained in place, Brezhnev was the most important of the three and by the early 1970s had emerged as the effective ruler. In 1977 Podgorny was dismissed and Brezhnev became President as well as Party Secretary. He retained these positions, despite increasing ill health, until his death in 1982.

Political, economic and social policies

AQA	U3	WJEC	U4

Brezhnev failed to address the weaknesses in the system of government. The conservatism of the era amounted to inertia. The USSR was governed by an inflexible bureaucracy, which became increasingly corrupt. Promotion was dependent on bribery and nepotism and officials were lining their own pockets and living in a style not available to the rest of the population. Rather than seeking to reform the system, Brezhnev retreated from reform. Decentralisation was abandoned. The regional economic councils set up by Khrushchev were abolished. It has been argued that he realised that reform might bring the whole system down – as eventually happened under Gorbachev.

> **KEY POINT**
>
> Brezhnev was a cautious bureaucrat.

Brezhnev also reversed the liberalisation of the Khrushchev era. Censorship was tightened, for example in 1966 the writers Daniel and Sinyavsky were put on trial. Solzhenitsyn was exiled in 1974. Dissidents were sent to labour camps or mental hospitals. The KGB under Andropov regained much of the power it had lost under Khrushchev. Jews were persecuted and forbidden to emigrate. Baltic nationalism was severely repressed.

The economy

The early years of the Brezhnev era did see some attempts at reform in economic policy, in which Kosygin played an important role. Industrial machinery and skills were imported from the west, for example Fiat was commissioned to reorganise the car industry. The Five-Year Plans of 1966 and 1971 emphasised the production of consumer goods and this did produce some improvement in industrial output and living standards. The rigidity of the centralised planning system, however, meant that overall results were disappointing. The Russian workforce was plagued by absenteeism and alcoholism, with obvious effects on productivity. The targets set by the Five-Year Plans were not met. The growth rate of the Russian economy lagged further and further behind the west. The failure of Russia to keep up with the west was particularly apparent by the 1980s in computer technology. The economy was also distorted by unaffordable spending on armaments, which starved other sectors of investment. The Brezhnev era is therefore often described as a period of stagnation for the Russian economy.

Compare this with the policies of Stalin and Khrushchev. None of them overcame the inefficiency of Russian agriculture.

In agriculture Brezhnev did attempt to improve efficiency. He revived the Ministry of Agriculture, which Khrushchev had abolished. He gave collective farms more freedom and raised farm workers' wages. Production did increase, but even so a bad harvest in 1975 forced Russia once more to import grain from the USA. Moreover, the food distribution system was so inefficient that there were often food shortages in the cities.

In social policies, a big housing programme provided 11 million new flats, but most of them were tiny. Housing costs were, however, subsidised, as was health care. In education, the aim of universal secondary education was largely achieved, though the quality of education was much criticised. Pre-school education expanded.

The last years of the Brezhnev era

From 1975 to his death in 1982 Brezhnev suffered from ill health but refused to resign. This was the period of stagnation. Industry and agriculture remained inefficient. Corruption in the bureaucracy increased. Brezhnev filled the Politburo with his friends, with the result that Russia was governed by a group of old men.

Détente is explained on pages 281–2.

In 1979 Brezhnev made Russia's problems worse by invading Afghanistan. This caused outrage in the USA and the west and undid the improvement in relations between the USSR and the west achieved by détente. It also added to the already excessive burden of the military budget.

> **KEY POINT**
>
> The Brezhnev era was a period of stagnation, but for Russians it provided peace and stability.

20.4 The end of the Soviet Union, 1982–91

LEARNING SUMMARY

After studying this section you should be able to understand:
- the changes in leadership of the USSR, 1982–85
- the significance of Gorbachev's reforms

Leadership changes, 1982–5

AQA U3 WJEC U4

On the death of Brezhnev, **Andropov** was elected General Secretary of the Communist Party. He had played a key role in the suppression of the Hungarian Rising in 1956 and the Czech Rising of 1968 (the Prague Spring). As head of the KGB from 1967 to 1982 he was fierce in the pursuit of dissidents. Andropov attempted to introduce reforms in industry and agriculture and to root out corrupt Party and provincial officials. But within months he became seriously ill and died in February 1984.

On his death opponents of his reforms in the Presidium elected **Chernenko**, ignoring Andropov's wish that he should be succeeded by Gorbachev. Chernenko was already seriously ill and died in March 1985.

Gorbachev's reforms

AQA U3 WJEC U4

Gorbachev became First Secretary of the Communist Party in 1985. He recognised that the USSR faced serious problems. His aim was to preserve the USSR by modernising it, but he unleashed forces which destroyed it. The twin pillars of his policy were:
- **Perestroika** – restructuring of the economy. Production quotas were abandoned. Private ownership of businesses was allowed and foreign investment encouraged.
- **Glasnost** – openness. There was to be more press freedom and more transparency in government. The aim was to combat inertia and corruption in the bureaucracy by exposing it.

The two principles were inseparable – glasnost was required for perestroika to work. To carry out these policies Gorbachev had to overcome conservative opponents in the Politburo, led by Ligachev. Gorbachev avoided confrontation with Ligachev by appointing him his deputy, but at the cost of weakening the implementation of his reforms.

Ligachev was initially a supporter of Gorbachev.

To counteract opposition he gave more power to the local soviets and in 1989 set up a new elected Parliament, the Congress of People's Deputies. The prohibition of other political parties was lifted, but Gorbachev was careful to uphold the primacy of the Communist Party. Gorbachev took a new position as President of the Union.

He recognised that the burden of military expenditure was a major obstacle to the success of his economic reforms. It was leading to cuts in budgets for education, social services and medical care and preventing any rise in living standards. In 1989, he withdrew Russian troops from Afghanistan.

> **KEY POINT**
>
> Gorbachev was correct in his diagnosis of Russia's problems, but his attempt to solve them left Russian with neither a command economy nor a market economy.

The satellite states

This is explained more fully on page 286.

Gorbachev's reforms in the USSR naturally led to demands for reform in the satellite states in Eastern Europe. In 1989, one by one, the communist regimes in Poland, Hungary, East Germany, Czechoslovakia, Bulgaria and Romania were overturned. Gorbachev made it clear that soviet military aid could no longer be provided to prop them up.

The nationalities

The principle of glasnost led directly to the revival of nationalist movements in the non-Russian territories of the USSR – movements which had hitherto been repressed. This led to a virtual war between Azerbaijan and Armenia in 1988–9, violence in Georgia in 1989 and military intervention in Latvia and Lithuania in 1991. In 1989–91, however, all the non-Russian republics claimed and eventually achieved sovereignty, with the Baltic states in the lead. By 1991 the Union had virtually collapsed.

A further effect was the re-emergence of Russian nationalism, as many Russian came to the conclusion that the soviet system had worked to the economic disadvantage of Russia itself. This seriously weakened Gorbachev's position since he was President of the Union, but not of the Russian Republic (this position was held by Yeltsin from 1991).

The fall of Gorbachev

By the end of 1989, although the satellite states in Eastern Europe had overthrown their Russian-backed communist regimes, the USSR remained intact. Gorbachev was given wide powers in a newly created post of President of the Union in 1990. But his position was increasingly insecure.

Yeltsin had won popularity by cleaning up the corrupt city administration in Moscow when Gorbachev appointed him head of the city committee of the Communist Party.

- Perestroika had made little progress in improving the economy and delivering better living standards. The problem was that perestroika had only gone part way to creating a market economy. Economic chaos resulted.
- Nationalist movements in the Baltic states were demanding independence and were being followed by the Caucasian and Asian republics of the USSR.
- He was challenged by Yeltsin, who was very popular in Moscow and in June was elected President of the Russian Republic by a newly elected parliament. Yeltsin took advantage of the revival of Russian nationalism to put himself at its head.

An attempted coup in August 1991 by conservatives seeking to reverse Gorbachev's reforms was foiled by Yeltsin. There is some evidence that by this time Gorbachev himself was considering putting the brakes on reform. The plotters appear to have hoped Gorbachev would assume dictatorial powers to carry out their policies. His credibility was undermined and Yeltsin's standing greatly enhanced. Yeltsin took advantage of the situation to dissolve the Communist Party within the Russian Republic.

Gorbachev was now identified by Russians with the preservation of the Union and the primacy of the Communist Party. Economic failure had discredited the Party, so he tried to save himself by dissolving the Communist Party of the Soviet Union. It was too late. The nationalist tide swept him away, as the Union collapsed. At the end of 1991 Yeltsin forced him to resign as Union President and the Union was dissolved. It was replaced by the **Commonwealth of Independent States**.

KEY POINT

Gorbachev's reforms, which were intended simply to modernise the USSR, brought about the collapse of the Soviet Union and the Soviet empire in Eastern Europe.

You should be able to explain the significance of each of these dates.

KEY DATES

1956	Khrushchev's speech to the Twentieth Party Congress
1962	Cuban Missile crisis
1964	Fall of Khrushchev
1979	Invasion of Afghanistan
1982	Death of Brezhnev, succeeded by Andropov
1984	Death of Andropov, succeeded by Chernenko
1985	Gorbachev appointed First Secretary of the Communist Party
1989	Collapse of communist governments in Eastern Europe
1991	Fall of Gorbachev

Sample question and model answer

The key words are 'why' and 'disappointing'.

Why was the rate of economic growth in the Soviet Union from the late 1960s disappointing? **[50]**

In the 1970s the growth rate of the Soviet economy, which had been about 5% per annum, fell to no more than 2% per annum. Both economic growth and living standards in the USSR were increasingly falling behind the west.

Factual knowledge, which should be expanded in a full answer, is used to underpin judgements.

The key to this, because of its central importance in the Soviet economy, was the disappointing performance of agriculture. Ambitious plans to increase production were not matched by investment in transport and storage facilities. Even in the 1960s, much of the wheat produced by Khrushchev's Virgin Lands policy had to be thrown away because of the lack of infrastructure. Similar large-scale projects, planned and directed by an army of bureaucrats, continued in the 1970s with poor results. Large collective farms were inefficient despite efforts to introduce incentives.

Moving on to industry, the answer starts with a positive point, before going on to explain the weaknesses.

The situation in industry was rather better, at least in the late 1960s and early 1970s. Industrial machinery and skills were imported from the west and production increased. The basic problem, however, was the planning system. The Five-Year Plans set unrealistic targets, so results were felt to be disappointing. More importantly, central planning through the State Planning Commission (Gosplan) failed to adjust effectively to changing economic needs. A command economy had been reasonably effective in earlier times in building up Russia's heavy industry, but the lack of a market system meant that when the emphasis shifted to consumer goods there was no proper means of measuring demand. The result was shortages and bottlenecks. One area in which the planning system failed markedly was the production of computers. Attempts to improve matters by encouraging more local management were disappointing, mainly because years of central planning meant that local officials lacked the necessary experience and were often corrupt.

Other points you could make are summarised here.

There were other reasons for the USSR's poor growth record:

- Alcoholism and absenteeism in the workforce. There was also overmanning - it was almost unknown to make workers redundant.
- Failure to invest in the railway system - crucial for the movement of goods in a country the size of Russia.
- Poorly directed investment in prestige projects.
- The Chernobyl disaster - the result of mismanagement - halted the development of the nuclear industry, which had previously been promising.
- Above all, unaffordable spending on armaments, which starved other sectors of investment.

The conclusion links the issue with the collapse of the Soviet system.

The underlying problem was political. A totalitarian system with a command economy had become enmeshed in an unresponsive, inefficient and often corrupt bureaucracy. Reform, as Gorbachev recognised, required not only restructuring of the economy (perestroika), but also more openness (glasnost) so that weaknesses were brought out and could be addressed. But this in turn brought the whole system crashing down.

21 The Cold War, 1945–90

The following topics are covered in this chapter:

- The outbreak of the Cold War, 1945–53
- Peaceful co-existence and détente, 1953–82
- Eastern Europe, 1953–85
- The end of the Cold War

21.1 The outbreak of the Cold War, 1945–53

LEARNING SUMMARY

After studying this section you should be able to understand:

- the origins of the Cold War
- the development of the soviet bloc in Eastern Europe
- how the division of Europe between West and East hardened after 1948
- the cause and outcome of the Korean War

The origins of the Cold War

AQA	U3	Edexcel	U3
OCR	U1	WJEC	U4
CCEA	A2.1		

The USSR, USA and Britain were allies in the Second World War, but only because they had a common enemy: Nazi Germany. Before the war the USSR was regarded with great suspicion in Western Europe and the USA, as it was feared that the USSR aimed to spread communism throughout the world. This suspicion was returned by the Soviet leaders, who felt isolated in a hostile world. When the war ended, mutual antagonism re-surfaced.

Yalta and Potsdam

Two conferences in 1945 laid down the basis for post-war Europe:

- **Yalta** (Roosevelt, Stalin and Churchill). Germany was to be divided into four zones. Countries conquered by or allied to Germany, were to be liberated and prepared for free and democratic elections. A conference at San Francisco was to set up the **United Nations Organisation** to replace the League of Nations.
- **Potsdam** (July–August). Truman replaced Roosevelt, who had died. Churchill was at Potsdam initially, but Attlee replaced him as a result of the 1945 British election. Only Stalin remained from the Yalta conference. The division of Germany and Berlin was confirmed. New boundaries were agreed between Poland and Germany (the **Oder-Neisse Line**) and between Poland and Russia. Germans living in Poland, Hungary and Czechoslovakia were to be relocated to Germany. Poland was to have a free and independent government, including members of the government-in-exile.

The Oder-Neisse Line was only agreed for the time being – until a final peace treaty was made, but it eventually became permanent.

The USSR and the Eastern bloc

AQA	**U3**	Edexcel	**U3**
OCR	**U1**	WJEC	**U4**
CCEA	**A2.1**		

Between 1945 and 1948 Eastern Europe was brought under the control of the USSR. At the end of the war Russian troops occupied Poland, Czechoslovakia, Hungary, Romania, Bulgaria and the eastern half of Germany and Austria. The Russians set up Popular Front governments of communists, socialists and leaders of peasants' parties in Hungary, Romania and Bulgaria. But in 1946–7 the non-communist members were removed. In Poland, Stalin ignored the Potsdam agreement, arrested the leaders of the government-in-exile when they returned to Poland and imposed a communist government. There were also communist governments in Yugoslavia and Albania, where communist partisans had overthrown the German occupation. Thus as Churchill noted in his Fulton speech in 1946, 'From Stettin in the Baltic to Trieste in the Adriatic an **iron curtain** has descended across the continent'.

The communist coup in Czechoslovakia, 1948

> The coup set alarm bells ringing in the USA and helps to explain why Congress approved the Marshall Plan.

Russian control of Eastern Europe was completed in 1948 when non-communist members of the Czech government were removed. Elections held in an atmosphere of violence with a single list of candidates produced an overwhelming victory for the communists.

Cominform and Comecon

In all these states, with the exception of Yugoslavia, the communist governments owed their power to Russian support. They can therefore properly be described as satellite states. The establishment of the Communist Information Bureau (**Cominform**) in 1947 and **Comecon** in 1948 showed that the USSR and its satellites formed a Soviet bloc. Stalin saw control of Eastern Europe as essential for Russian safety. He remembered western support for the Whites in the Russian Civil War (1918–20) and the hostility with which the USSR had been regarded in the 1920s and 1930s. He saw American policy towards Germany after the war as proof of its aggressive intentions.

Yugoslavia, however, was different. Tito, the communist head of government, had led the partisans who liberated Yugoslavia from the Nazis and refused to take orders from Russia. In 1948 Yugoslavia was expelled from the Cominform.

The response of the USA

AQA	**U3**	Edexcel	**U3**
OCR	**U1**	WJEC	**U4**
CCEA	**A2.1**		

Greece and the Truman Doctrine

The first flashpoint of the Cold War was Greece where after the end of the German occupation civil war broke out between the monarchist government and the communists. The communists had support from the communist regimes in Bulgaria and Yugoslavia, while the government had the support of British troops who remained there after the liberation of Greece. In 1947 Britain decided she could no longer afford this. Truman, fearing that Russia would gain control of Greece, promised US support for free peoples resisting aggression – the **Truman Doctrine**. In pursuit of this US troops were sent to Greece and the communist rebels were defeated.

> **KEY POINT**
>
> The significance of the Truman Doctrine was that the USA would not retreat into isolationism (unlike 1920).

The Marshall Plan

Truman feared that economic hardship in Western Europe resulting from the destruction of the war would play into the hands of the communists. The communist parties in France and Italy had substantial support. To counter this, in June 1947 the US Secretary of State, George Marshall, announced a programme of aid to help European recovery. In response sixteen western European countries formed the **Organisation for European Economic Cooperation** (OEEC), with the western zones of Germany as an associate member. The offer of aid was not limited to Western Europe but Stalin saw the Marshall Plan as an American attempt to dominate Europe and forbade the Russian satellite states to accept it. This is why he set up Comecon in 1949 as a rival organisation to the OEEC.

East vs. West, 1948–55

AQA	**U3**	Edexcel	**U3**
OCR	**U1**	WJEC	**U4**
CCEA	**A2.1**		

The Berlin Blockade

Matters came to a head over Germany. Russia and the three western occupying powers disagreed about the future of Germany. Russia exacted massive reparations from its zone, dismantling factories and removing the machinery to Russia. It aimed to keep Germany as weak as possible. The western powers, regarding reparations after the First World War as a mistake, set about economic reconstruction in their zones. In 1947 the USA and Britain united their zones for economic purposes (Bizonia), with the French zone joining later. In 1948, after fruitless talks with the USSR, they introduced a new currency, the Deutschmark, in their own zones. They then extended it into the western sectors of Berlin. The Russians retaliated by trying to drive the western powers out of West Berlin. In June 1948 they closed all land links to West Berlin (the Berlin Blockade) but the western powers overcame this by the Berlin airlift. The Russians lifted the blockade in May 1949.

> Since Berlin was in East Germany, Stalin feared this would destabilise the currency and economy of the Russian zone.

The Berlin blockade hardened the division of Germany. The western powers were convinced that there was no hope of Russia agreeing to reunify Germany. In 1949 they set up the Federal Republic in West Germany. The Russians replied by setting up the Germany Democratic Republic in the east.

> **KEY POINT**
>
> The Berlin blockade was a turning point in relations between west and east.

NATO and the Warsaw Pact

The blockade convinced the western powers of the dangers of Russian aggression. Three months before the start of the blockade, Britain France and the Benelux countries had set up the Brussels Treaty, creating an organisation for joint military action if attacked. In 1949 the **North Atlantic Treaty Organisation** (NATO) was set up: the USA and Canada joined in a defensive military alliance with Britain, France, Italy, the Benelux countries, Norway, Denmark, Iceland and Portugal. Turkey and Greece joined in 1952.

The Russians responded by making military agreements with their East European satellite states, culminating in the formation of the Warsaw Pact in 1955.

Western fears of Soviet aggression were intensified by two further events in 1949–50.

- In 1949 Russia successfully tested an atomic bomb.
- In 1950 North Korea attacked South Korea.

So in 1952 it was proposed that West Germany should rearm within the framework of a new **European Defence Community**. French fears of a revival of German military power prevented this, but in 1954 the **Western European Union** was set up with West Germany as a member. In 1955 West Germany joined NATO and a West German army was formed. The USSR regarded this as further evidence of western aggression and responded with the **Warsaw Pact** (1955).

> **KEY POINT**
>
> After 1945 the Russians and the Americans suspected each other of aggressive intentions and responded with defensive measures which were then interpreted by the other side as further evidence of aggression.

The cause and outcome of the Korean War, 1950–53

Edexcel **U3**

> Russia, which had a veto in the Security Council, could have prevented this but was boycotting its meetings, which proved to be a mistake.

After the Second World War, Korea was partitioned. North Korea was communist and Russian-backed. South Korea had an American-backed government under Syngman Rhee. Both wished to reunite Korea – but under their own type of government. In 1950 North Korea invaded the south. The UN Security Council condemned North Korea as an aggressor. The USA, on behalf of the UN, then sent troops under the command of General MacArthur to support South Korea.

Sixteen other nations, including Britain, sent troops to join the Americans in the UN force. MacArthur's forces eventually drove the invaders back into North Korea and almost to the Chinese border. China, where the Communists had gained control in 1949, then sent troops into North Korea and drove the UN force back again. MacArthur proposed using the atomic bomb against China, but President Truman vetoed this and dismissed MacArthur. The war then developed into a stalemate around the 38th parallel. An armistice was finally signed in 1953, leaving Korea divided to this day.

> **KEY POINT**
>
> The war demonstrated how easily a local conflict could lead to nuclear war. It also marked the beginning of the US policy of containment – trying to stop the spread of communism from China into South East Asia. This eventually led to the Vietnam War.

> You should be able to explain the significance of each of these dates.

> **KEY DATES**
>
> | | |
> |---|---|
> | 1945 | Yalta and Potsdam Conferences |
> | 1947 | Cominform; Truman Doctrine; Marshall Plan announced |
> | 1948 | Communist coup in Czechoslovakia |
> | 1948–9 | Berlin blockade |
> | 1949 | NATO formed; Federal Republic of Germany and German Democratic Republic set up; Russia has the atomic bomb |
> | 1950–3 | Korean War |
> | 1955 | Warsaw Pact set up; West Germany joins NATO |

21.2 Peaceful co-existence and détente, 1953–82

LEARNING SUMMARY

After studying this section you should be able to understand:

- how far tensions were eased by Khrushchev's policy of peaceful co-existence
- the importance of the nuclear arms race in the development of the Cold War
- the importance of the Cuban Missile Crisis
- the results of Brezhnev's policy of détente
- the importance of the Sino-Soviet split

Khrushchev and 'peaceful co-existence'

AQA	U3	Edexcel	U3
OCR	U1	WJEC	U4
CCEA	A2.1		

With the death of Stalin in 1953, the Cold War entered a new phase. Khrushchev pursued a policy of peaceful co-existence. He argued that confrontation was unnecessary as communism would triumph without war because of the weaknesses of capitalism. In 1955 he met President Eisenhower at the **Geneva Conference**. His attack on Stalin's policies at the USSR's Twentieth Party Congress in 1956 signalled a change in outlook. By 1959 relations had improved sufficiently for Khrushchev to make a successful visit to the USA.

> Khrushchev was unpredictable and inconsistent in pursuing co-existence.

A summit conference in Paris was arranged for 1960 between Khrushchev and President Eisenhower, but it coincided with the **U2 spy plane incident**. An American spy plane was shot down over Russia and the pilot was caught. Khrushchev could not resist the temptation to make a propaganda coup out of the incident and stormed out of the summit.

The Berlin Wall

> Those leaving were mainly young and highly skilled – people East Germany could not afford to lose.

A major continuing obstacle to peaceful co-existence was the German question. The Berlin blockade had solved nothing. West Berlin was still, in Russian eyes, an affront to East Germany's sovereignty. It was also the route by which thousands of East Germans escaped to the West to leave the comparative poverty of East Germany and enjoy the fruits of West Germany's economic miracle. Khrushchev's attempts to secure western recognition of the independence of East Germany and the evacuation of West Berlin were rebuffed. By 1960 the number of East Germans leaving via West Berlin reached a thousand a week. To stop this, in August 1961 the **Berlin Wall** was built. The flow of refugees was halted. Berlin remained divided for 28 years, during which time over one hundred people lost their lives trying to escape over the wall.

In 1963 President Kennedy visited West Berlin to show solidarity and made his famous 'Ich bin ein Berliner' speech.

The nuclear arms race

| AQA | U3 | Edexcel | U3 |
| WJEC | U4 | | |

At the end of the Second World War the only power with atomic weapons was the USA, but in 1949 the USSR successfully tested an atomic bomb. Both sides in the Cold War now had this deadly weapon. In 1952 the USA tested the even more destructive hydrogen bomb, but Russia was only months behind in developing its

Sputnik, the first artificial satellite to orbit the Earth, was part of the same programme.

own H-bomb. The USSR was also working on the development of missiles to deliver nuclear warheads and in 1957 launched the **R-7**, the first Intercontinental Ballistic Missile (ICBM). The USA followed with its own ICBM in 1959 and in 1960 produced the Polaris missile, a submarine-based missile which could be launched even if missile bases on land had been destroyed. Both sides were also working on Anti-Ballistic Missiles – missiles that would destroy incoming missiles. By the 1970s the USA and the USSR each had over 2000 missiles and had reached a position of **Mutually Assured Destruction** (MAD). This meant that if either launched a nuclear attack they also would be destroyed themselves.

> **KEY POINT**
>
> This balance of destructive power probably helped to prevent the Cold War becoming an outright military conflict.

The Cuban Missile Crisis, 1962

AQA　**U3**　Edexcel **U3**

The Cuban revolution of 1959 brought to power **Fidel Castro**. The regime of Batista, which Castro overthrew, was corrupt and repressive. The Cuban economy was dominated by American corporations, which profited from the island's resources, especially its sugar, while leaving most Cubans in poverty. Castro, who was a socialist and a nationalist, but claimed not to be a communist, proceeded to nationalise American companies. The USA responded by stopping trade with Cuba and eventually broke off diplomatic relations. In 1961 President Kennedy allowed the CIA to back an invasion of Cuba by Cuban exiles at the Bay of Pigs; it was a disastrous failure and further poisoned relations between the USA and Cuba.

US policy probably drove Castro into the arms of Russia.

Castro turned to Russia for support. Khrushchev started to install medium range ballistic missile sites in Cuba. These posed a threat to most major cities in the USA. When US spy planes revealed the missile bases, Kennedy demanded that all missiles in Cuba should be destroyed and imposed a naval blockade. This meant that Russian ships approaching Cuba would be stopped and searched. The world was close to nuclear war, but Khrushchev ordered Soviet ships approaching Cuba to turn round. After a few more tense days an agreement was reached that Russia would dismantle the missile bases if the USA lifted the blockade and promised not to attack Cuba. There was also a secret agreement to remove American missiles from Turkey at some time in the future.

As a result of the crisis both the USA and the USSR tried to reduce the danger of nuclear war. A hotline was set up between the White House and the Kremlin. In 1963 the **Partial Test Ban Treaty**, which limited underground nuclear tests, was signed.

> **KEY POINT**
>
> The crisis was probably the most dangerous moment in the entire Cold War.

Brezhnev and détente

AQA　**U3**　Edexcel **U3**
OCR　**U1**　WJEC　**U4**
CCEA　**A2.1**

Détente meant seeking a relaxation of tensions.

After the fall of Khrushchev in 1964 Brezhnev emerged as the dominant figure in a collective leadership in the USSR. Aware of the escalating cost of the nuclear arms race and its effect on Russia's economy, he pursued a policy of détente. The cost of the arms race was also a problem for the USA, which had the additional burden of the Vietnam War. The fact that the two superpowers had achieved MAD meant that they could afford to limit the arms race. In 1968 the **Nuclear Non-Proliferation Treaty** was signed and in 1969 the Strategic Arms Limitation Talks (SALT 1) began, culminating in 1972 in a treaty to reduce anti-ballistic missile systems.

Détente provided a favourable climate for a change in West German policy towards its eastern neighbours. Willy Brandt, the West German Chancellor from 1969, who had previously been the socialist mayor of West Berlin, developed the **Ostpolitik**. This was based on the view that recognition of the status quo in Eastern Europe was more advantageous to West Germany than confrontation.

- In 1971 a Four Power Agreement over the status of Berlin was reached.
- In 1971 West Germany signed treaties with Russia and Poland which accepted the 1945 boundaries of Poland. This meant that West Germany accepted the Oder-Neisse Line.
- In 1972 in the Basic Treaty, West and East Germany recognised each other.
- In 1973 West Germany signed a treaty with Czechoslovakia.

> This was strongly opposed by the Christian Democrats in West Germany as it meant giving up the aim of reunification.

The Helsinki Accords, 1975

Détente reached its peak in the **Helsinki Final Act** (1975). This was the outcome of the Conference on Security and Co-operation in Europe (CSCE), which had been meeting since 1972. The western powers agreed to guarantee Europe's existing frontiers. This meant accepting Soviet domination of Eastern Europe. There was also an agreement to respect human rights and freedoms. Dissidents in Eastern Europe began to claim more freedom. Even in Russia itself there were groups claiming their rights under Helsinki, but they were still largely denied them.

> **KEY POINT**
>
> The Soviet leaders were very satisfied with the Helsinki Accords because of the guarantee of their control in Eastern Europe. They did not anticipate the effect of the agreement on human rights.

The 'New Cold War'

Relations between east and west deteriorated in the late 1970s. The failure of the USSR to honour its commitments on human rights under the Helsinki Agreement was one reason. Even more important was the Soviet invasion of Afghanistan, which marked the beginning of the 'New Cold War'. Russia was continuing to build up its stock of nuclear weapons. American opinion turned increasingly anti-Russian and saw the invasion of Afghanistan as a serious threat to world peace. President Carter called on athletes to boycott the 1980 Moscow Olympics and refused to sign the SALT 2 treaty. Under Reagan, President from 1981, the USA embarked on a massive build-up of military power, culminating in the **Strategic Defence Initiative** (SDI). In this atmosphere it was difficult to pursue Ostpolitik any further.

> The SDI, otherwise known as Star Wars, was a highly sophisticated defence against incoming missiles.

The Sino-Soviet split

AQA **U3**   Edexcel **U3**

In 1949 the Chinese Communists established the Chinese People's Republic after defeating Chiang Kai Shek in the civil war. In 1950 Stalin signed a Treaty of Friendship and Alliance with China, which provided a large loan and a military alliance. China and the USSR co-operated in the Korean War, but after Stalin's death, relations began to cool. Mao Zedong regarded Khrushchev's policy of co-existence with the west as a betrayal of Marxist–Leninist principles.

- In 1960 at a meeting of Communist Parties in Moscow he accused Khrushchev of 'revisionism'. Khrushchev withdrew Soviet technical experts from China.
- In 1962 Mao criticised Khrushchev for backing down over Cuba. By this time China and the USSR were in open competition for the leadership of the communist world as the true heirs of Lenin.
- The rivalry was sharpened in 1964 when China acquired its own nuclear bomb.
- In 1969 there was small-scale warfare in the form of border clashes.

In 1971 Mao changed his attitude towards the USA. 'Ping pong' diplomacy began with the invitation of western table tennis teams into China. Nixon responded by ending the USA's veto on the admission of Communist China into the UN in place of Taiwan. In 1972 Nixon visited Beijing. The rapprochement with China strengthened America's hand in the process of détente with the USSR.

> Mao and Khrushchev had clashed earlier in 1960 at the Romanian Communist Party conference.

KEY POINT

The split was both about the nature of communism (ideology) and about the leadership of the communist world.

> You should be able to explain the significance of each of these dates.

KEY DATES

1957	Launch of R-7 and Sputnik
1960	U2 spy plane incident; Sino-Soviet split
1961	Berlin Wall
1962	Cuban Missile Crisis
1968	Nuclear Non-Proliferation Treaty
1972	SALT I Treaty; Basic Treaty between East and West Germany
1975	Helsinki Final Act
1979	Soviet invasion of Afghanistan

21.3 Eastern Europe, 1953–85

LEARNING SUMMARY

After studying this section you should be able to understand:

- the reasons for opposition to Soviet control in Eastern Europe
- the suppression of the Hungarian rising of 1956
- the failure of the Prague Spring in Czechoslovakia in 1968
- the significance of the Solidarity movement in Poland

Underlying problems

OCR **U1** Edexcel **U3**
CCEA **A2.1** WJEC **U4**

Eastern Europe appeared to be completely under Russian control after 1948, but beneath the surface there was opposition to Russian-backed communist regimes. This was based on:

- nationalism – anti-Russian feeling
- economic problems – poor living standards
- lack of political and religious freedom.

But whenever there was a serious threat to a communist regime, Russia intervened.

Hungary, 1956

OCR **U1** Edexcel **U3**
CCEA **A2.1** WJEC **U4**

Destalinisation after 1953 seemed to point to less rigid control of the satellite states by Moscow, allowing 'different roads to socialism'. The result was the crisis in Hungary in 1956. Poor living standards and opposition to a strongly pro-Russian government, which relied heavily on the secret police, led to demonstrations demanding the appointment of **Imre Nagy** as Prime Minister. Russian troops were briefly withdrawn from Budapest but when Nagy proposed to allow press freedom and the formation of non-communist parties and to withdraw Hungary from the Warsaw Pact, Khrushchev sent in the tanks. About 2,500 Hungarians were killed and thousands fled. Nagy was deposed and later executed in Russia despite being promised his freedom.

Opinion in the West was horrified, but powerless, partly because of Suez.

KEY POINT

Khrushchev would not allow Hungary to leave the Warsaw Pact, as it could lead to the collapse of the pact and the break-up of the Soviet bloc.

Czechoslovakia: the Prague Spring, 1968

OCR **U1** Edexcel **U3**
CCEA **A2.1** WJEC **U4**

In the 1960s there was growing discontent within the communist party. The economy was weak. Industrial productivity was low and costs were high. Collectivized agriculture was producing less than in the 1930s. Reformers within the party blamed the hardliners who had controlled the country since the 1948 coup. There was also a demand in Slovakia for more autonomy within a federal system.

These tensions led to a power struggle within the party leadership in 1967 and the appointment of **Dubcek** as First Secretary of the Party. He introduced a programme of industrial and agricultural reform, greater political freedom and equality for Slovakia within a federation – 'communism with a human face'. The result was the Prague Spring: the emergence of new political and cultural groups. The Two Thousand Words manifesto in June demanded real democracy.

This was not Dubcek's work, indeed he disowned it.

The USSR feared that this was the beginning of counter-revolution, though in reality Dubcek was a convinced communist who had no intention of breaking with Moscow or bringing non-communists into his government. On 20 August 1968 forces drawn from all the Warsaw Pact countries invaded Czechoslovakia. There was some resistance but not on the same scale as in Hungary – partly because the lesson of Hungary was that resistance was futile. Hardliners took control. In 1969 Dubcek was replaced as First Secretary by Husak. The only concession to reformers was that Czechoslovakia became a federation, with a little more autonomy for Slovakia.

The justification for the Russian action was put forward by Brezhnev in what became known as the **Brezhnev Doctrine**. By this the USSR claimed the right to intervene in any communist state where the regime was endangered by counter-revolution.

KEY POINT

As in Hungary in 1956 the Soviet leaders feared that other countries in Eastern Europe might follow the Czech example.

Solidarity in Poland

| OCR | U1 | Edexcel | U3 |
| CCEA | A2.1 | WJEC | U4 |

In Poland as in other Eastern European countries, central planning produced a stagnating economy. A massive price rise in 1970 caused demonstrations and the replacement of Gomulka by Gierek as First Secretary of the Communist Party. Gierek tried to stimulate the economy by a switch to producing more consumer goods but serious problems continued. There were food shortages and price rises. A wave of strikes in 1976 led to the formation of a Workers' Defence Committee.

An important factor in Poland was the influence of the Catholic Church. The election of Karol Wojtyla as Pope in 1978 was a great boost to national pride in this deeply Catholic nation and this was further enhanced by a visit to Poland by the new Pope in 1979.

In 1980 renewed food shortages and a new round of price rises led to a wave of strikes. The main one was in the Gdansk shipyards and was led by **Lech Walesa**. The strikers succeeded in getting the government to agree to the formation of independent trade unions, along with greater freedom of religious and political expression. As a result **Solidarity** – the Independent Self-Governing Trade Union – was set up with ten million members and Lech Walesa as chairman. Solidarity made further demands in 1981 – economic reform and free elections. In 1980 Gierek was forced to resign. A year later General Jaruzelski became Prime Minister and First Secretary of the Party. Under pressure from the USSR he introduced martial law in December 1981. Solidarity was declared illegal and Walesa was imprisoned (though he was released in 1982). But Solidarity survived as an underground movement and its prestige was enhanced in 1983 when Walesa was awarded the Nobel Peace Prize.

> **KEY POINT**
>
> Under Jaruzelski the government was losing its legitimacy.

21.4 The end of the Cold War

LEARNING SUMMARY

After studying this section you should be able to understand:

- Gorbachev's reforms in the Soviet Union
- the effects of these reforms in soviet-controlled eastern Europe
- the collapse of the Soviet Union and assess its consequences in Russia
- the break-up of Yugoslavia in the 1990s

Gorbachev's reforms: Perestroika and Glasnost

AQA	U3	Edexcel	U3
OCR	U1	CCEA	A2.1
WJEC	U4		

Gorbachev became First Secretary of the Communist Party of the USSR in 1985. He recognised that the country faced serious problems. Agriculture was inefficient and industry was falling further behind the west. His aim was to preserve the USSR by modernising it but he unleashed forces which destroyed it. The twin pillars of his policy were:

- **Perestroika** – restructuring of the economy. Production quotas were abandoned. Private ownership of businesses was allowed and foreign investment encouraged.
- **Glasnost** – openness. There was to be more press freedom and more transparency in government. The aim was to combat inertia and corruption in the bureaucracy by exposing it.

Gorbachev also recognised that the burden of military expenditure was unsustainable and was preventing any rise in the standard of living. He announced cuts in the armed forces. In 1986 he met President Reagan at the Reykjavik Summit, which led to a treaty for the elimination of Intermediate Range Nuclear Missiles in 1988. In 1989 he withdrew troops from Afghanistan.

To gain support from the people in his struggle with the more conservative elements in the Politburo, he set up an elected Congress of People's Deputies in 1989, though he was careful to preserve the primacy of the Communist Party.

The effects of the reforms in Eastern Europe

AQA	**U3**	Edexcel	**U3**
OCR	**U1**	CCEA	**A2.1**
WJEC	**U4**		

Inevitably these reforms led to demands for reform in the satellite states.

- **Poland**: Solidarity had been banned but had survived and grown in strength. In June 1989 Jaruzelski was forced to hold free elections which were won by Solidarity. Solidarity formed a government and Walesa became President.
- **Hungary**: In 1988 Kadar was brought down. In May 1989 the border with Austria was reopened. This provided a route for East Germans to escape, making the Berlin Wall redundant. Free elections in 1990 brought in a centre-right government.
- **East Germany**: Mass demonstrations, most famously in Leipzig, demanded more freedom. Gorbachev told the government it could not expect help from Russia and it drew back from using force. In November the Berlin Wall was brought down.
- **Czechoslovakia**: In November and December 1989 there were huge demonstrations. Dubcek reappeared to address the crowds. The dissident poet, Vaclav Havel, was elected President.
- **Bulgaria**: In December 1989 demonstrations led to the resignation of the communist government.
- **Romania**: In December 1989 mass demonstrations overthrew the Ceausescus.

In all these events the USSR made no attempt to intervene. By 1990 all the former satellite states had overthrown their communist governments and established democracies. In the course of 1990–1 Soviet troops were withdrawn from them.

In October 1990 Germany was reunified. Gorbachev initially opposed this, but then approved it despite opposition from other members of the Politburo. He did, however, refuse to agree to the admission of the united Germany to NATO. Gorbachev had also dropped his opposition to this in July 1990.

> **KEY POINT**
>
> The collapse of the communist regimes in Eastern Europe brought the Cold War to an end. The underlying reason was the failure of the command economies of the Soviet bloc to match the growth rates of the west and to raise living standards.

The collapse of the Soviet Union

AQA	**U3**	Edexcel	**U3**
OCR	**U1**	CCEA	**A2.1**
WJEC	**U4**		

The fall of Gorbachev

At the end of 1989, although the satellite states in East Europe had overthrown their Russian-backed communist regimes, the USSR remained intact. The position of Gorbachev was apparently strengthened when he was given wide executive powers in a newly created post of President in 1990. But in reality his position was increasingly insecure.

- Perestroika had made little progress in improving the economy and delivering better living standards.
- Nationalist movements in the Baltic states were demanding independence, and were being followed in this by the Caucasian and Asian republics in the USSR.
- He was challenged by Yeltsin, who was very popular in Moscow and in June 1991 was elected President of the Russian Republic by a newly elected Parliament.

An attempted coup in August 1991 by conservatives seeking to reverse perestroika and glasnost was foiled not by Gorbachev, but by Yeltsin. The plotters claimed their aim was to give Gorbachev dictatorial powers. Gorbachev asserted he knew nothing about it but his credibility was undermined – and Yeltsin's standing greatly enhanced. He tried to revive his authority by dissolving the communist party, but to no avail. At the end of 1991 he was forced to resign as Union President and the Union was dissolved.

> **KEY POINT**
>
> A key factor in Gorbachev's fall was the revival of Russian nationalism, which Yeltsin exploited. Russians came to believe that the Union had not been to the benefit of Russia itself.

Yeltsin's Russia, 1991–2000

When Gorbachev resigned, the Union had effectively collapsed. The Baltic states, Ukraine, Belarus and several Asian republics had all declared their independence. At the end of December 1991 the USSR was officially dissolved and Russia, Ukraine and Belarus set up the Commonwealth of Independent States. Most of the former Soviet republics except the Baltic states and Georgia eventually joined this very loose federation of sovereign states.

> The Baltic states looked to the west and eventually joined the European Community.

In June 1991 Yeltsin was elected President of Russia, a position which he held until 2000. He carried Russia through a period of rapid transformation without major upheaval, leaving it with a more liberalised economy and a more democratic constitution. But there was severe hardship for the Russian people. The introduction of a market economy led to inflation and a sharp drop in living standards. Crime and corruption became serious problems. By the end of the 1990s Russia was also involved in an ongoing bloody conflict in Chechnya.

The break-up of Yugoslavia

AQA **U3** OCR **U1**

The nationalist tide which swept through Eastern Europe and the USSR spread to Yugoslavia in 1991. Yugoslavia was a multi-ethnic federation which had been held together by **Tito**. After his death in 1980 ethnic tensions increased. In 1990, following the fall of communist governments throughout Eastern Europe, democratic elections were held in the Yugoslav republics, producing majorities for independence in Croatia, Slovenia and Macedonia. In Serbia, however, the elections were won by Milosevic's Communist Party, which supported Yugoslav unity. Yugoslavia then disintegrated amid civil war and ethnic cleansing.

- Slovenia and Macedonia became independent in 1991.
- Croatia declared independence in 1991. Armed resistance by the Serb minority, backed by Serbia, was finally crushed in 1995.

- Bosnia declared its independence in 1992. The largest ethnic group in Bosnia was Muslim, but there were large minorities of Serbs and Croats. As a result neither Serbia nor Croatia recognised Bosnian independence. A vicious civil war ensued, which included the notorious Srebrenica massacre. Following intervention by NATO in 1995, the war was brought to an end by the **Dayton Accords**, which set up Bosnia as an independent federal state.

> You should be able to explain the significance of each of these dates.

KEY DATES

1956	Hungarian Rising
1968	Prague Spring
1980	Solidarity formed in Poland
1985	Gorbachev First Secretary of Communist Party of the Soviet Union
1989	Communist regimes collapse throughout Eastern Europe; Berlin Wall opened
1990	German reunification
1991	Gorbachev forced to resign; USSR dissolved.
1992	Yeltsin elected President of Russia
1995	Dayton Accords end civil war in former Yugoslavia

Exam practice questions

1 Why were the USA and the USSR allies in 1945, but enemies by 1948? **[50]**

2 'Between 1945 and 1955 both the USA and the USSR perceived the other as the aggressor.'
Assess the validity of this verdict. **[50]**

3 Study sources A and B.

How far do you agree with the view that the Cold War came to an end because the war in Afghanistan fatally undermined the Soviet Union's capacity to maintain control over its satellite states?

Explain your answer, using the evidence of sources A and B and your own knowledge of the issues related to this controversy. **[40]**

Source A: From *Europe, A History*, by Norman Davies, published 1996

Gorbachev's analysis of the Soviet crisis can be deduced from his subsequent actions. It was a sorry catalogue. Further expansion of the Soviet arsenal did not promise greater security. Military spending had reached levels which precluded any improvement in civilian living standards. Indeed, the Soviet economy could no longer sustain established patterns of expenditure. Communist planning methods had failed, the technology gap with the West was widening every day. The Party was corrupt and dispirited; the young were turning their backs on communist ideology; the citizenry had lost patience with empty promises. Soviet security was beset by apathy. Soviet foreign policy was in disarray. The war in Afghanistan was a bottomless drain: Soviet hegemony in Eastern Europe paid no dividends. Gorbachev's strategy lay first in defusing the Cold War climate of fear and hatred on which the old system had thrived, and then, having cleared the air, to move on to the trickier problems of internal reform.

Source B: From *Postwar*, by Tony Judt, published 2005

Afghanistan was a catastrophe for the Soviet Union. Its traumatic impact upon a generation of conscripted soldiers would emerge only later. But long before then even the Soviet leaders themselves could see the scale of their mis-step. In addition to the cost in men and material, the decade-long war of attrition in the Afghan mountains constituted an extended international humiliation. It excluded for the foreseeable future any further deployment of the Red Army beyond its frontiers: after Afghanistan there could no longer be any question of applying force in Eastern Europe.

It says something about the underlying fragility of the Soviet Union that it was so vulnerable to the impact of one – albeit spectacularly unsuccessful – neo-colonial adventure. But the disaster in Afghanistan, like the cost of the accelerating arms race of the early '80s, would not of itself have induced the collapse of the system. Sustained by fear, inertia and the self-interest of the old men who ran it, Brezhnev's 'era of stagnation' might have lasted indefinitely. Certainly there was no countervailing authority, no dissident movement – whether in the Soviet Union or its client states – that could have brought it low. Only a Communist could do that. And it was a Communist who did.

Exam practice answers

3 Nineteenth century Britain: protest and reform

1. Economic distress was a major reason for the rise of Chartism.

- Peak years of Chartist activity coincided with periods of economic depression: first and second Chartist petitions, Newport Rising, Plug Plot during depression of 1837–43. Chartist activity subsided with prosperity after 1843 but revived with economic difficulties of 1847–8.
- At local level Chartist activity was linked with distress and declining industries, for example handloom weavers in Lancashire and Yorkshire.

But there were other factors.

- **Social** distress another major cause. Chartism was strongest in newly industrialised areas, where living and working conditions caused unrest, for example the Plug Plots in Lancashire and the Black Country.
- **Political** leaders were also important. At its core Chartism was a political movement making political demands which had a pedigree stretching back to the eighteenth century radicals. For many Chartists the demand for the Charter was a phase in a lifetime of radical activity – Lovett is an example. Thus disappointment with the Reform Act was a key factor.
- Chartism drew on other sources of unrest such as the failure of trade unionism (collapse of GNCTU, Tolpuddle Martyrs) and hostility to the new Poor Law. Chartism drew some of its support from taking over the Anti-Poor Law movement.

Thus economic distress was only one among many causes of support for Chartism, but it was the one which turned it into a mass movement.

2. (a) All agree that the purpose is to enfranchise the middle classes, but Sources B and C disagree with A about the underlying purpose. Source A: to preserve power of aristocracy and keep down the lower classes. Source C ('security against revolution') supports this but sees it as a good thing. Source B sees positive virtue in votes for middle classes ('moral improvement'). Sources B and C link right to vote with property – so agree with A about no democracy. Language and tone of B and C very different from A – link this with provenance.

(b) The key issue is whether 'high tension' (Source E) amounted to a revolutionary situation. Evans says MPs thought so and argues that they saw the Act as a compromise – the minimum necessary to defuse it. Source D shows how far radicals were prepared to go to keep Wellington out of office. Own knowledge could include Bristol and Nottingham riots. Explain why governing class feared revolution – memories of the French Revolution, Peterloo and more recently the 1830 revolution in France. Would revolution actually have occurred? Impossible to say – failure of Chartists a few years later suggests perhaps not – but it was a reasonable fear.

4 Foreign affairs, 1815–1914

1. (a) Congress of Troppau – Troppau Protocol – continental powers claimed right to intervene to stop revolutions in Spain and Portugal. The State Paper of 1820 opposed intervention in internal affairs of other countries. Castlereagh's motive was not support for liberal revolutions, but suspicion of Russia and France using Congress System to increase their power.

(b)
- Congress of Verona – Canning opposed intervention in Spain and thus helped to undermine the Congress System.
- In Portugal and South America Canning promoted British trade, prevented intervention by Spain and France (thus maintaining balance of power) and promoted constitutional governments.
- Greece though was a big problem. Victory for the rebels would upset the balance of power in Russia's favour, but British opinion supported the Greeks. So Canning intervened jointly with Russia so as to keep control over the situation. A successful strategy, but after his death Wellington reversed it.

2. **(a)** The main reason why Canning recognised their independence was trade with the former Spanish colonies, which had increased over ten times in the revolutionary period. Also suspicion of France, which had helped the Spanish king against the liberals. Canning feared France would help Spain to regain control over the colonies. NB: Canning's motive was not support for liberalism.

   (b) The main issues which show Palmerston's suspicion of France were:
   - Belgian Revolt (1830). Palmerston feared French influence and worked with Louis Philippe to ensure it was genuinely independent.
   - Succession disputes in Spain and Portugal. Quadruple Alliance stopped France gaining too much influence.
   - Near East: Palmerston risked war with France when Thiers backed Mehmet Ali against the Turkish Sultan. Working with Russia and Austria, he checked French ambitions in the Eastern Mediterranean.

   But suspicion of France was not the only influence on Palmerston:
   - Suspicion of Russia, particularly in the Near East crisis.
   - Protection of trade was also important in the Near East.
   - Support for liberal movements, but not if they clashed with British interests. Spanish and Portuguese succession disputes relevant.
   - Balance of power. Probably the underlying main influence which explains the suspicion of France and Russia.

3. Note the word **main** – balance economic and other reasons for British involvement in Africa.

   Economic: Africa offered markets for exports, outlet for investment and sources of raw materials. The Great Depression (1873–96) and awareness that Britain was losing ground to Germany and the USA made this attractive. Chamberlain saw imperial expansion as the way forward for the British economy. NB: also Rhodes (diamonds).

   Other factors include:
   - Mission to spread the 'benefits' of European civilisation (Kipling: 'the white man's burden') and to spread Christianity. In the context of the time, these were genuine motives for many people.
   - Strategic – to prevent other powers colonising Africa. Especially rivalry with France over Egypt (protection of route to India also important in this). The 'scramble for Africa' was a phase in which European rivalries were worked out in Africa. National prestige was at stake.

   Conclusion: motives were mixed. You could argue either way for economic or strategic considerations – examiners would look for the quality of your argument.

4. The key words are **why** and **deteriorate**. The dates 1898 to 1914 refer to the German Naval Law and the outbreak of war. Start with relations in the 1890s – Germany was Britain's most likely continental ally if she came out of isolation. Poor relations with France (colonial issues). The main issues which caused deterioration are the naval race, Germany's attitude to the Boer war, the failure of Chamberlain's attempts to make an alliance with Germany, the effects of the Ententes on Anglo-German relations and the two Morocco crises. Each of these soured relations. The navy was particularly important to Britain. The main responsibility for the deterioration lies with Germany, so the character of William II, German ambitions and the Weltpolitik should be considered. On the British side, Chamberlain tried to make an alliance but William overplayed his hand. Grey tried to maintain good relations but had to deal with German actions which were against British interests.

8 Appeasement and world war, 1919–45

1. **(a)** Keynes regarded the Versailles settlement as unwise above all else because of reparations. He saw the sum demanded as beyond Germany's ability to pay and that the economic recovery of Europe depended on Germany, so unreasonable demands would hold up recovery throughout Europe. He thought the treatment of Germany was harsh and would lead to calls for revenge.

   (b) Begin with problems left by the Versailles settlement: the German question, making the League of Nations effective and bringing about disarmament.
   - Regarding Germany, the Genoa Conference failed to settle reparations problem, but MacDonald played key role in mediating between France and Germany over the Ruhr and getting the Dawes Plan accepted. Austen Chamberlain played a key role in the Locarno Treaties.
   - Regarding the League of Nations, discuss the Geneva Protocol (failed) and Kellogg-Briand Pact, which appeared to reduce the risk of war, but cast doubts on the League's effectiveness.
   - Regarding disarmament, discuss the Washington Naval Treaty, but point out that the promised World Disarmament Conference did not meet in the 1920s.

   All these were attempts to strengthen the peace settlement. Other foreign policy issues (the revision of the treaty with Turkey at the Lausanne Conference and relations with Russia) were important, but not enough to invalidate the statement in the question. It might be argued that the underlying purpose of strengthening the peace settlement was to avoid any European commitments, such as had drawn Britain into war in 1914.

2. - At the time there was a case for appeasement: public opinion; guilt over the Versailles settlement; Britain's comparative military weakness; the fear of the USSR as an even greater threat than Germany.
   - Appeasement of Italy over Abyssinia was understandable – Italy was a potential ally against Hitler (Stresa Front). Doubtful whether sanctions on oil would have worked or whether public opinion would have allowed military action. But sent out wrong message to Hitler, so doubtful if it was sensible.
   - Rhineland (1936). Many in Britain thought Hitler's action reasonable. Baldwin thought risk of war was too great to intervene, but this was probably last point when Hitler's aggression could have been checked.
   - Anschluss: appeasement inevitable – little Britain could do.
   - Munich. The case for appeasement: public opinion approved; Britain was not prepared for war – appeasement gave time for rearmament; Sudetenland was Hitler's 'last territorial demand' and a reasonable one, since the people were German.
   - Case against Munich: encouraged Hitler's belief that Britain would back down under pressure; proved not to be his last demand (events of 1939); betrayed a potential ally with a strong army; alienated USSR.

   Conclusion: 1936 as a dividing line is not helpful – with hindsight the least sensible act of appeasement was Rhineland. But there was a case for appeasement in 1938.

9 Post-war Britain, 1945–2007

1. The main economic problems in the 1945–51 period were: war damage, pre-war decline of old industries, loss of overseas investments, indebtedness to the USA, the need to export in order to pay for food and raw materials and balance of payments.

   The American loan of 1946 helped with the immediate post-war difficulties. This was given on condition that the pound sterling was made convertible, but when this was put into effect in 1947 it led to a balance of payments crisis.

   Marshall Aid and the appointment of Cripps as Chancellor in 1947 aided recovery. Cripps directed economic activity towards exports and there was a wage freeze between 1948 and 1950, even though prices were rising. Cripps believed that austerity was the solution to Britain's economic problems. Import controls were imposed. By 1950 exports were 75% above the 1938 level.

   But the balance of payments continued to be a problem – the 1949 devaluation made imports dearer and exports cheaper, which helped the balance of payments. Overall by 1951 much economic progress had been made, but at the price of continuing austerity. The underlying problems of the economy remained.

2. Begin with the suggested reason – Labour divisions. Refer to the election of Foot, formation of the Social Democratic Party (SDP) and problems with Militant Tendency. Point out that divisions were not Labour's only problem: the cause of the divisions was a move to the left – note the 1983 manifesto.

   Move on to other explanations for Thatcher's victories. The Falklands War was a big factor in 1983, counteracting unpopularity caused by unemployment and cuts in government services. By 1987 the economy was booming and inflation was down. Privatisations and sale of council houses were popular. Handling of the miners' strike, though divisive, was widely approved. Thatcher's style of leadership won as much admiration as disapproval. Brighton bombing probably boosted her image.

   Conclusion: Labour's divisions were important. It was widely perceived as unelectable. But, because of the Falklands War, they probably could not have won in 1983 anyway and by 1987 the economy was so favourable to Thatcher that again they probably would have lost even if they had been less divided.

3. Success for the Wilson governments of 1964–70 was mixed. Key failures were over the economy and trade unions.
   - The economy (most important issue). Discuss the balance of payments problem: deflationary policies at first, then devaluation, then more deflation by Jenkins, incomes policy and downturn just before 1970 election. Tackling balance of payments undermined George Brown's work at Department of Economic Affairs to improve the economy by planning. Overall a failure.
   - Trade unions. Attempt to reform ('In Place of Strife') failed – rejected by union leaders. Wilson could not force it through because of Labour's dependence on the unions.
   - Social reforms, such as capital punishment, homosexual acts, divorce, and abortion left an important legacy – work of backbenchers, but with government support.
   - Education. Pressure on local authorities to move to comprehensive education. Still a long way to go by 1970, but probably the turning point. Open University founded – perhaps Wilson's most permanent legacy.

   Assess also the handling of race relations, immigration, Northern Ireland, Rhodesia, entry to Europe (vetoed by de Gaulle).

10 The development of democracy in Britain, 1868–1997

1. The key theme in the changing fortunes of the Liberal and Labour parties, 1868–1997, is the replacement of the Liberals by Labour. Your answer should focus on the reasons for the turning points set out below.
   - Gladstonian **Liberal** Party (a coalition of Whigs, Peelites and Radicals) in power 1868–74 and 1880–5, but split over Home Rule (1886). Liberal Unionists eventually joined Conservatives.
   - 1905 Liberal election victory. In power until 1915 and implemented Liberal reforms. But there were underlying differences between Gladstonian and 'New' Liberals.
   - 1916 Asquith–Lloyd George split. In the 1922 election the Liberals won fewer seats than Labour. Third party thereafter, reaching lowest point in 1950s.
   - Underlying reasons for decline: rise of working class electorate and trade unionism; divided leadership; lack of organisation and funds; impact of electoral system on third parties. Not identified with any interest group or class, unlike Labour.
   - **Labour** emerged from growth of trade unions and socialist societies. Labour Representation Committee (1900); 29 MPs in 1906 as result of Gladstone–MacDonald Electoral Pact. In 1922 they emerged as the main opposition party. In 1924 and 1929–31 Labour minority governments, but overtaken by the 1931 financial crisis.
   - The 1945 election saw the first Labour majority government elected. In 1964–70 and 1974–9 the Wilson and Callaghan governments were increasingly weakened by economic difficulties and association with trade unions. The 1979 election was followed by bitter internal disputes which kept Labour out of office. Splinter group formed SDP, which later joined with Liberals as Liberal Democrats.

2. Start the examination of the changing influence of trade unions in British politics with the situation in 1868: New Model unions with industrial rather than political aims. Then explain the main turning points, focusing on the main reasons for them:
   - 'New Unions' in the 1880s – more political in outlook.
   - Formation of Labour Representation Committee in 1900; importance of Taff Vale Case (1901).
   - Liberals, Labour and trade unions; Trade Disputes Act (1906) and Trade Union Act (1913).
   - Wave of strikes 1910–13; syndicalism.
   - Industrial disputes of 1920–21; collapse of the Triple Alliance.
   - General Strike (1926) – impact of failure on trade unions and the Labour movement.
   - Rise of Labour Party in 1920s; two Labour ministries; collapse in 1931; weakness of the trade unions and Labour in the 1930s.
   - Labour victory in 1945; trade unions at height of influence 1945–79 under both Labour and Conservative governments.
   - Growing unease at effect of trade union power on economy; 'winter of discontent' 1978–9.
   - Miners' strike and Thatcher reforms curbing TU power.

3. The influence of the media on politics in 1868 was limited: no popular press, London and provincial papers catered for middle class. The main changes between 1868 and 1997 were:
   - 1867 Reform Act: working class electorate in boroughs, followed by 1870 Education Act; beginning of (almost) universal elementary education.
   - 1896 *Daily Mail* (Northcliffe) – the first mass circulation newspaper. Designed to appeal to people with limited education. Followed by *Daily Express* (1900), *Daily Mirror* (1904) and *Daily Herald* (1912).
   - 1918 Representation of the People Act – mass electorate. Role of popular press as opinion formers even more important. Most mass circulation newspapers throughout twentieth century supported Conservatives.
   - Radio: In 1922 the formation of British Broadcasting Company (became BBC in 1927). By 1939 90% of households had a 'wireless'. BBC became an important source of news, but aimed to be politically neutral. But radio changed relationship between politicians and voters. Baldwin particularly adept at using it. Churchill's wartime broadcasts.
   - Spread of television in 1950s – an even more powerful vehicle of mass communication. First major politician to make effective use of it was Macmillan. From 1960s ability to perform effectively on television was a vital attribute for the successful politician. Role of television interviewers in holding politicians to account – what was the effect on parliament?

   NB The answer should focus on the **reasons** for the significance of these developments. It should not simply be a long narrative.

11 France, 1814–71

1. Charles X was overthrown in 1830 because:
   - He tried to restore the *ancien régime*. The divisions in post-revolution France (republicans, Bonapartists, moderate royalists, Ultras) made this dangerous.
   - He made a series of early mistakes: compensation for émigré nobles; the ancient religious form of coronation; increased privileges for the Church; tighter press censorship.
   - The appointment of the extreme Ultra Polignac as chief minister in 1829 provoked a clash with the Chamber of Deputies, but a general election produced an even more hostile Chamber.
   - Instead of backing down, Charles X issued the Ordinances of St Cloud.
   - Economic hardship caused discontent among working classes in Paris.

2. Louis Philippe's foreign policy was unpopular for a number of reasons:
   - He avoided war because of the expense and because there was uncertainty of support for his regime.
   - Seen as subservient to Britain, for example in Belgium and the Mehmet Ali affair.
   - Scored diplomatic victory in Spanish marriages affair, but this was short-lived and deprived him of British sympathy in 1848.

   But unpopular foreign policy was not enough to cause his overthrow. Other reasons for his unpopularity were:
   - Louis Philippe had an uninspiring personality.
   - Lack of a political base: he was asked to become King in 1830 as a compromise which was acceptable to moderate royalists and republicans, but he never had the enthusiastic support of either.
   - In the 1840s under the influence of Guizot the regime became increasingly corrupt, inefficient and illiberal.
   - Perhaps most important, economic change led to widespread distress but the regime did little to tackle the consequent social problems.

3. Napoleon III's foreign policy was 'A catalogue of failures', but not entirely:
   - In 1848, as President of Second Republic, he sent troops to Rome to protect the Pope. A success.
   - Crimean War: France and the allies were victorious, but not an overwhelming, glorious victory. Peace conference in Paris brought prestige. A success.
   - Italy, 1859–60. France and Piedmont defeated Austria, but there were heavy losses in battle; Napoleon backed out (Truce of Villafranca). Offended liberal opinion in France by backing out and catholic opinion by intervening at all, because this endangered the papacy. So overall a failure.
   - Mexico. A clear failure.
   - Austro-Prussian War (1866). Failure: France had a clear interest in a struggle for power in Germany, but Napoleon stood aside.
   - Attempt to gain Luxemburg as compensation led to humiliation.
   - Final, fatal miscalculation over the Hohenzollern candidature for the Spanish throne – attempt to score a diplomatic victory over Bismarck led to Franco-Prussian War.

4. Between 1859 and 1870 Napoleon III attempted to liberalise the Second Empire:
   - 1859 amnesty to political opponents, followed in 1860 by the 'Liberal Empire'.
   - During the 1860s press censorship was relaxed and trade unions were legalised. In 1867 ministers were required to answer questions in Parliament. A Parliamentary opposition developed. Main reason was growing unpopularity because of foreign policy failures.
   - In 1869 a new constitution gave the Assembly power to propose laws and vote on the budget. A ministry representing the majority in the Assembly was formed in January 1870. A response to combined opposition of Liberals, Catholics and royalists.
   - But Napoleon still retained considerable powers, including the power to change the constitution, subject to a plebiscite. So only partial liberalisation.

14 The unification of Germany

1. Bismarck succeeded in ending Austria's influence in Germany whereas the revolutionaries of 1848–9 failed.
   - Main reason is that revolutionaries in 1848 were divided about their aims: some advocated Greater Germany, others supported Little Germany, excluding Austria; i.e. they were ambivalent about Austria; not all of them wanted to end Austria's influence. Religion was also a divisive factor – Greater Germany would be predominantly Catholic, Little Germany predominantly Protestant.
   - Bismarck, by contrast, was single-minded in his determination to assert Prussian predominance in Germany at the expense of Austria – unification was almost a by-product. Refer to his conduct in 1840s as Prussian ambassador to Diet of German Confederation.
   - Frankfurt Parliament lacked means to enforce the constitution of Little Germany against the princes – no army. Bismarck had well-equipped Prussian army.
   - 1849: Frederick William IV of Prussia refused to accept crown from Frankfurt Parliament. Bismarck had the confidence of William I.
   - Bismarck's diplomacy was crucial. Used Schleswig–Holstein dispute to win support of German nationalist opinion and provide excuse to pick a quarrel with Austria. Then isolated Austria – allied with Italy, kept Russia and France neutral. Aim achieved by victory in Seven Weeks' War.

2. **(a)** The immediate reason why Bismarck broke with the Liberals in 1879 was a dispute over protection – Liberals supported free trade. Underlying this was a shift in Bismarck's policies. The Liberals were never Bismarck's natural allies – he was at odds with them in 1874 over size of the army and the related issue of the power of the Reichstag. But he worked with them in 1870s because of struggle with Catholics (Kulturkampf). By 1879 he realised this was not succeeding and needed support of Catholic Centre party in battle over tariffs.

(b) Bismarck's policies towards the Catholics and the socialists were not very successful. The Kulturkampf was abandoned, partly in order to concentrate on attacking the Socialists. The Anti-Socialist Laws failed to prevent the continuing growth of the Socialist Party and lapsed after Bismarck's fall. He got his way in his quarrel with the Liberals over tariffs, but only by abandoning the Kulturkampf and allying with the Catholic Centre Party.

3. **(a)** Bismarck was forced to resign in 1890 by William II, who became Emperor after the death of William I and the brief reign of Frederick III. William disagreed with Bismarck about the anti-socialist policies, colonial expansion and relations with Russia. As Kaiser, William had the right to appoint and dismiss Chancellor – pressured Bismarck to resign.

(b) The importance of pressure groups and the army in Germany between 1890 and 1914. Outline the political system of the Empire, noting the relative powerlessness of the Reichstag and the power of the Emperor. Discuss William's character, especially his militarism. These factors meant that pressure groups and army leaders had considerable influence. Discuss the various pressure groups and interest groups: the Agrarian League and the influence of the junkers; industrialists (supported colonial expansion and military expenditure); the Pan-German League (supported Weltpolitik); the Navy League; the Army League. End with the influence of army leaders, especially Moltke, in the run-up to 1914.

4. 'The emergence of a unified and powerful German state was rooted in its economic development.' Items to discuss include:
   * Zollverein. Prussian-dominated customs union (from 1834) which corresponded closely with the eventual German Empire. Excluded Austria. Provided Prussia with internal market of 25 million people.
   * Development of the Prussian economy. Railways opened up German market and stimulated growth, especially in Prussia, which had good natural resources (e.g. coal in Ruhr). Prussia had capital to finance industrial development and railway building.
   * Industrial development and Zollverein underlay Prussian power and were basis for unification of Germany under Prussia. But this does not mean they were the **cause** of unification. Process of unification was political and military, the work of Bismarck.
   * Rapid industrial development after unification. Unification provided stimulus – common currency and uniform commercial law introduced – but Germany's natural resources and well-developed transport and banking systems were also important. Coal, iron and steel, electrical engineering and chemicals all highly developed. By 1914 Germany was the greatest industrial power in continental Europe.
   * This provided basis for, and made possible, William II's aggressive nationalism (weltpolitik), but was only part of the explanation for it. Political factors (character of William II, power of the emperor under the constitution, role of the army in imperial Germany) also important.
   * Industrial growth produced an elite of industrial magnates who encouraged nationalistic policies (for example the building of the navy as it provided industrial contracts).

5. German liberalism achieved so little in the period 1815–1914 because:
   * Liberalism in 1815 had limited appeal – mainly to intellectuals. Linked with nationalism. Seen as a threat by Metternich, who used Confederation against liberals – Carlsbad Decrees.
   * 1848 revolutions – Metternich overthrown, constitutions granted in many states. Frankfurt parliament aimed to create unified Germany, with a liberal constitution, but while it debated, counter-revolutionary forces regained control in Austria and Prussia. The Liberals had failed.
   * Liberals gained a majority in Prussian Parliament in 1858. Clash with William I over taxes for army – appointment of Bismarck (1862), who collected the taxes in defiance of Parliament.

- Bismarck's wars against Denmark and Austria, leading to North German Confederation, won over the Liberals. He succeeded where Liberals had failed: nationalism, previously associated with the Liberals, now linked with military strength rather than constitutionalism.
- The imperial constitution provided for a Reichstag elected by universal suffrage, which pleased Liberals; but it was not a liberal constitution – the Reichstag had little power.
- In the 1870s Bismarck allied with National Liberals against Catholics, but quarrelled with them over the size of the army (1874) and broke with them in 1879 over protection. Thereafter he relied on Conservatives and Catholic Centre.
- 1879–1914: Liberals divided into National Liberals and Radicals – lost ground to Conservatives and Socialists. The Liberals were a declining force.

15 Italy, 1896–1945

1. Outline the main features of Italian politics. Parliament was managed before the war by transformism, which meant bribery and patronage. Regional differences, especially between north and south, worked against formation of national parties. Further splits were caused by differences of opinion about Italy's entry into the war. After the war Socialists were unwilling to co-operate with any other party; also they split into Socialists and Communists. Result: five governments between 1918 and 1922. Thus governments were unable to cope with post-war problems: weakness of the economy, inflation, disappointment over the peace treaties, growth of para-militaries of both right and left. You could argue that this was due to a failure of political leadership rather than a failure of parliamentary democracy as such. The ablest politician, Mussolini, aimed to destroy democracy and the king did nothing to stop him.

2.
- The central feature of Mussolini's economic policies was the Corporate State which was supposed to produce co-operation between employers and labour. Strikes were forbidden.
- The government intervened actively in the economy. It funded public works (e.g. motorways, blocks of flats, electrified railways and, most famously, the draining of the Pontine Marshes). Industrial output was promoted by the Institute for Industrial Reconstruction and subsidies.
- The 'Battle for Grain' doubled wheat production. But dairy or fruit farming would have been more suited to some areas.
- But there were many weaknesses. The Corporate State was cumbersome and inefficient; in practice it favoured employers against workers. There was much corruption. Italy remained industrially weaker than the other great powers. Agriculture remained backward. The south remained poverty-stricken.
- The lira was over-valued, leading to a loss of exports.

3. The main reason why there was so little opposition to the establishment of a Fascist dictatorship in Italy was that Parliamentary government had virtually broken down between 1918 and 1922. There was widespread violence. Many important groups, including landowners, industrialists and the middle classes, began to see Mussolini as a bulwark against a communist revolution. The Catholic Church also saw communism as a threat. The reason why Parliament granted Mussolini dictatorial powers in 1922 was that MPs saw a strong leader as better than the growing anarchy of the preceding four years. In this they probably reflected public opinion. The King, in inviting him to be Prime Minister, was probably right in thinking this was what majority opinion wanted. The main groups which could have opposed Mussolini were the socialists, but they were divided between democratic socialists and communists. Between 1922 and 1925, when Mussolini finally established his dictatorship, a combination of violence by Fascist blackshirts and mistakes by opponents (the Aventine Secession) enabled him to overcome remaining opposition.

4. **(a)** Mussolini invaded Abyssinia in 1936 because he saw it as the answer to Italy's economic problems and as a way of boosting his regime. Italians felt they had not got their fair share of colonies in the 'scramble for Africa' (unsuccessful attempt to take over Ethiopia in 1896). Diplomatic situation seemed favourable. Britain and France were anxious to keep on good terms with Italy because of concerns about Hitler.

(b) Mussolini first saw Hitler as a threat, then allied with him. Which was in Italy's best interests? In 1934 moved troops to Austrian frontier to oppose German takeover of Austria and joined Stresa Front to oppose German rearmament. The turning point was the invasion of Abyssinia and this led to the break-up of Stresa Front. Mussolini turned to Hitler: 1936 Rome-Berlin Axis, 1937 Anti-Comintern Pact. Intervention in the Spanish Civil War widened the breach with Britain and France, increased dependence on Hitler. Dependence on Hitler meant he could not oppose Anschluss – reversal of 1934 policy. From 1939 he was trying to keep up with Hitler – the invasion of Albania to match Hitler's takeover of Czechoslovakia. Could have stayed neutral in Second World War, but entered it after German successes in 1939–40. Invasions of Greece and Egypt – Italian army failed and had to be rescued by Germans. Led to the eventual invasion of Italy by Allies and Mussolini's downfall. But note that from 1936 to 1940 Mussolini's relations with Hitler brought prestige to Italy (for example Mussolini's role at Munich).

16 Germany, 1918–45

1. By 1929, the Weimar Republic had overcome many of the problems which it faced after 1919.
   - **Political**: Much more stable. No extremist attempts to stage a coup since 1923. Extremist parties gained few seats in Reichstag. Mainstream parties worked together reasonably well in a series of coalitions.
   - **Economic**: The new currency and the Dawes Plan produced comparative prosperity.
   - **International position**: The end of the Ruhr crisis in 1924 produced better relations with France. Locarno guaranteed Franco-German border. Germany joined League of Nations and Kellogg-Briand Pact.

   So by 1929 it had apparently overcome most of its problems. But there were weaknesses which made it unable to meet the crisis of the depression and its political fallout. It had only shallow support from the people – it was associated with the defeat of 1918. Proportional representation meant that after 1929 it became impossible to form a government with a majority in the Reichstag. Many civil servants, judges and army officers had no commitment to democracy. Economy was dependent on American loans.

2. When evaluating how successful were the Nazis from 1933 to 1939 in solving Germany's economic problems consider:
   - Unemployment was virtually eliminated, partly by a revival of world trade and partly by Nazi policies – public works (e.g. autobahns), rearmament, expansion of the civil service and the party organisation. Jews who had been forced out of their jobs and political opponents in concentration camps were not counted as unemployed.
   - The state controlled wages, food prices, rents, investment and foreign exchange. Trade unions were abolished and strikes made illegal. Farm prices were fixed so that farmers made a reasonable profit.
   - Exports were boosted by Dr. Schacht's manipulation of exchange rates and trade agreements with Eastern European and South American countries.
   - In 1936 a Four-Year Plan was introduced. The aim was self-sufficiency (autarky) by boosting domestic production and developing synthetic substitutes for oil and other imports.

   But production of synthetics was disappointing and agriculture failed to meet its targets. Economic growth was not fast enough to pay for rearmament and by 1939 there was a danger of runaway inflation.

3. When evaluating the success of the Nazis in gaining and retaining the loyalty of the German people in the years 1933 to 1939, begin by explaining that they came to power because they seemed to offer economic stability, restoration of national pride, strong leadership and end of the Communist threat. Gaining loyalty depended on success in these.
   - Elimination of unemployment and the revival of the economy won much support. Policies appealed to many groups in German society. Core support came from lower-middle and skilled working classes, but also supported by peasants (benefited from import controls and fixed farm prices), industrialists (Nazis a bulwark against Communism), and even much of industrial working class (full employment). Weaknesses of economic policy, especially probability of inflation, not apparent by 1939.
   - Foreign policy restored national pride (give selected details).
   - Hitler projected an image of strong leadership – the Führer principle.
   - Propaganda reinforced loyalty. Skill of Goebbels.

   True extent of support hard to determine because of suppression of opposition. Some overt criticism from Churches. Probably many Germans ignored aspects they disliked because of (a) Nazis successes, (b) risks involved in open dissent. But overall Nazis seem to have had widespread support.

4. This question (To what extent was the Nazi regime popular from 1933 to 1939?) is very similar to the one above and the material is much the same. The focus is on popularity, which is not quite the same as loyalty, but there is the same problem of knowing what Germans really felt because it was unwise to express dissent. Overall the evidence seems to show that the Nazis were genuinely popular, mainly because of the improvement in the economy and the restoration of national pride. But there was also a good deal of low-level grumbling and it is hard to tell how much people resented the loss of freedom which was the price of the benefits. Can any conclusions be drawn from evidence such as the fact that membership of the Hitler Youth had to be made compulsory because too many young people were not joining?

5. Introduction: The key issue is whether Hitler **deliberately** created confusion. The question arises from the debate between 'intentionalists' who claim that Hitler's 'intentions' were at the heart of all Nazi policies and 'structuralists' who see him as a 'weak dictator', never in complete control of Nazi Germany and acting as an umpire in disputes between rival power blocks.

   Sources A and B support intentionalist view. Quote: Source A 'produced ... confusion', to create 'a despotic tyranny', 'was intentional'. Source B 'deliberately allowed', 'increased his power as the supreme arbiter'. Source C also implicitly supports intentionalist view ('was aware of confusion', blocked attempts to remedy it), but does not suggest it was deliberately to increase his power. Source A, Hitler's Press Officer, was well placed to observe confusion, not necessarily to know why. Sources B and C are historians taking one view in an ongoing debate.

   It remains debatable whether it was a deliberate policy of 'divide and rule'. Hitler was lazy, avoided routine work of government. Decisions often taken in response to last advice received. Specialist agencies created to cut through bureaucracy often created more rivalries. Himmler as head of SS overlapping with Ministry of Interior and Party Chancellery is one example of confusion. Hitler's 'intentions' were important in spheres which interested him, e.g. foreign affairs, but not organisation of government.

   Conclusion: created an organisational jungle, but doubtful if it was deliberate.

18 International relations, 1879–1941

1. Key words are 'dangerously' and 'aggressive'. Note that the question is not just about 1914. Begin with William II's weltpolitik. Discuss his unpredictable, vain, autocratic character and the influence of army leaders and nationalistic pressure groups in imperial Germany. Examine the successive crises in Morocco (1905), Bosnia (1908), Morocco (1911) and the Balkan wars (1912–3). Also examine German naval policy and ambitions in the Middle East (Berlin–Baghdad Railway). In each case assess whether Germany was aggressive and how dangerous it was. Generally, Germany had a case, though sometimes (e.g. First Moroccan Crisis) a flimsy one, but was exploiting its case aggressively. Germany could claim that it had a strong interest in the Balkans, and that as a great power it had the right to build up its navy and extend its trading interests in North Africa and the Middle East, along with Britain and France. End by discussing Germany's willingness to support Austria–Hungary in the Balkans as a major reason why Sarajevo led to war. Consider also the Schlieffen Plan as involving aggressive war, and its role in bringing Britain into the war.

2. Give details of the crises in North Africa and the Balkans between 1905 and 1913 and comment on each. Germany had a legitimate interest in Morocco, but in the Moroccan Crisis (1905–6), the Kaiser's real aim was to break up the Anglo-French Entente. This was a legitimate German aim but because it was clumsily carried out it backfired – Britain supported France. In Bosnia (1908) Germany backed Austria (as one would expect), but Serbia was embittered and, because Germany virtually threatened war, Russia was thwarted. From Russia's point of view this was provocative, but as German policy it was not unwise. In the Agadir Crisis (1911) Germany's interest was legitimate but sending a gunboat to Agadir was provocative to Britain. The result was to strengthen ties between Britain and France. In the Balkan Wars (1912–3) Germany supported Austria, insisting that Serbia should not gain Albania, but worked with Britain to achieve a negotiated peace (Treaty of London) and again co-operated with Britain to prevent the Second Balkan War escalating. Overall the view seems justified with regard to North Africa, but not the Balkans. (Note that this question does not include 1914.)

3. Serious threats to peace could only come from major powers – there were localised threats to peace, usually involving lesser powers. In the case of Greece and Bulgaria there was war. All these (except the Corfu incident) were settled by the League of Nations – one reason why there was peace in the 1920s. All major powers were exhausted by war and there was widespread anti-war feeling after the Great War. Austria–Hungary had disappeared. Germany had been disarmed; in the 1920s its leaders were mainly concerned to re-establish its position in Europe. Russia was feared, kept out of European affairs, but mainly concerned with its own internal problems. France was prickly because of security fears (hence Ruhr crisis). Britain was keen to strengthen the peace. Hence Locarno. But there was no progress on disarmament and there was resentment of Versailles in Germany. Kellogg-Briand Pact showed there was anxiety about keeping the peace.

4. Main examples of tactical skill and ability to exploit opponents' weaknesses:
   - Reoccupation of Rhineland – timed to exploit breakdown of Stresa Front as result of Mussolini's invasion of Abyssinia.
   - Rome-Berlin Axis – ditto.
   - Anschluss – exploited unfairness of Versailles to Germans. Since Austria was German, it was difficult to oppose.
   - Sudetenland – based on same tactics. Also successful tactics in pressuring Chamberlain and exploiting British reluctance to go to war.
   - Nazi-Soviet Pact exploited mutual mistrust between western powers and USSR. Purely tactical, as shown by invasion of Russia in 1941 – purpose was to enable Hitler to invade Poland.

   Overall Hitler exploited general fear of another war, British guilt feelings over harshness of Versailles and the slowness to rearm. His demands were often difficult to oppose because he had a case (Rhineland, Austria, Sudetenland, even Polish Corridor). But his successes were also the result of mistakes by Britain and France: Anglo-German Naval Agreement (suggested Versailles could be revised); failure to oppose reoccupation of Rhineland; Chamberlain's belief at Munich that Hitler could be trusted; failure to seek Russian support.

21 The Cold War, 1945–90

1. To explain why the USA and the USSR, allies in 1945, were enemies by 1948:
   - Begin with the Grand Alliance; they were held together by a common enemy. As soon as the Second World War ended suspicions re-surfaced. At Yalta, Truman suspected Stalin's intentions (more than Roosevelt, who had died).
   - Explain Soviet domination of Eastern Europe after the war; note specially events in Poland. 'Iron curtain' by 1946. Completed by Communist coup in Czechoslovakia in 1948.
   - America responded with the Truman Doctrine and Marshall Plan; seen by Stalin as American attempt to dominate Europe.
   - Explain different approaches to occupation zones of Germany; to avoid mistakes made after First World War, USA and Britain set about rebuilding German economy.
   - Crunch came with introduction of new currency. Discuss position of Berlin and effects of introduction of new currency to West Berlin. Berlin blockade and airlift, 1948.

   Underlying reasons: Stalin's fear, based on western attitudes to USSR 1917–1941, that USA's real aim was to overthrow communism was matched by a US fear that Stalin aimed to make Europe (and ultimately the world) communist. Both sides saw their actions as defensive, but the other side saw them as aggressive. At root, it was communism vs. capitalism.

2. The assertion that between 1945 and 1955 both the USA and the USSR perceived the other as the aggressor does seem valid. This is very similar to the question above, but covering a longer time span. The answer should begin with the main points in the previous answer.

   Between 1948 and 1955 there were developments on both sides which were seen by the other as aggressive. The USSR acquired an atomic bomb (1949), set up Comecon (1949), established the GDR in East Germany and set up the Warsaw Pact (1955). The establishment of the Chinese People's Republic was also regarded by the USA as part of a communist takeover of the world spearheaded by the USSR, as was the North Korean attack on South Korea. The west (which in soviet eyes meant the USA) set up NATO (1949), established the Federal German Republic, set up Western European Union which included a West German army and in 1955 admitted West Germany to NATO. In 1952–4 the USSR and the USA developed hydrogen bombs. With suspicions running high it was not surprising that each move by the other was seen as aggressive and met by a reaction which in turn seemed aggressive.

3. The question is about the reasons for the end of the Cold War. Was it because of the collapse of Soviet control over Eastern Europe? Or was that simply the result of deeper causes? How does the Afghanistan war fit in? There is no right answer.

   Source A suggests the Afghan war was one of a number of factors causing the 'Soviet crisis': unsustainable military expenditure, economic and technological failure, political corruption, disillusioned people. It does not make a direct connection between Afghanistan and Eastern Europe, simply arguing that control over Eastern Europe was no longer worth its cost.

   Source B makes a direct connection between them, thus supporting the view in the question. Like Source A it emphasises the role of Gorbachev as the catalyst. But it also suggests that the underlying problem was 'the fragility of the Soviet Union'. This theme can be developed from own knowledge, taking up the points in Source A.

Index

Abdication crisis (1936) 102, 104
Abyssinia 113, 202, 248–9
Act of Union 35, 84
Adenauer 255–9
Agrarian League 191
Alexander II 163–5
Alexander III 165
Anarchists 164
Andropov 271–2
Anglo-French Naval Agreement 64, 74, 236, 237
Anglo-German Naval Treaty 105, 113, 248
Anglo-Irish War (1919–21) 87
Anschluss 114, 203, 250
Anti-Corn Law League 26–7, 46
Anti-Semitism 165, 199, 211, 218–9, 221–2
Appeasement 104–5, 112–5
Asquith 67, 73, 76, 77, 80, 95, 140
Attlee 100, 102, 105, 107, 144
Austria 55, 59–60, 64, 174–6, 179–85, 194–5, 202–3, 236–8, 250

Baldwin 95, 96–8, 100, 102, 104, 113
Balfour 36, 69–70, 90
Balkan Crisis (1875–8) 38, 59–60
Balkan Wars (1912–3) 65, 237–8
Belgium 57, 65, 155
Berlin 255, 258, 260, 262, 278, 280, 286
Beveridge Report 118, 120
Bismarck 159, 182–9, 235
Blair 134, 136
Boer Wars 34, 38, 62, 66–7, 69
Bolsheviks 166, 170
Bosnian Crisis (1908) 64, 237
Brandt 260–2
Brezhnev 270–2, 281–2, 284
British army 33, 66, 81
British coal industry 50–1, 95, 97–8, 107

British economy 94–5, 98–101, 121–2, 124–8, 130–1, 133–4
British foreign policy 54–60, 63–6, 74–5, 110–5
British general elections 17, 20, 22, 25, 31, 33, 36, 37, 69–70, 72–3, 94–6, 99–100, 120, 122, 124–5, 127–30, 133–4, 139–40
British income tax 19, 26, 30, 72
British media 150–1

Callaghan 126, 128–9
Canning 20, 55–6
Castlereagh 20, 54–5
Catholic emancipation 20, 84–5, 89
Cavour 175–6
Chadwick 47–9
Chamberlain, Joseph 33, 36, 61, 69, 141
Chamberlain, Neville 96, 102, 105, 113–5
Charles X 154
Chartism 24–5, 43–6
Children's Charter 71
China 57, 113, 247–8, 250–1, 270, 279, 282–3
Churchill 71, 97, 102–7, 115–7, 120, 276–7
Cold War 267–8, 276–86
Collectivisation 230
Combination Acts 18, 20, 43
Comecon 267, 277
Congress of Berlin (1878) 38, 60
Congress System 55
Conservative Party and governments 25–7, 30, 37–9, 67, 69–70, 95–8, 120, 127–8, 129–34, 139, 141, 143, 145–6
Corfu Incident 201, 245
Corn Laws 19–20, 26–7
Corporate State 198, 200
Crimean War 59, 66–7
Cuban missile crisis 281

Czechoslovakia 114, 243–4, 246, 250, 267, 277, 284, 286

Dawes Plan 111, 208, 246
Destalinisation 269–70
Détente 261, 281
Disarmament 112, 246–7, 248
Disraeli 27, 30–1, 37–9, 59–61
Dubcek 284

East Germany (GDR) 256, 259–63, 278, 280, 282, 286
Easter Rising 87, 95
Eastern Question 58–60
Eden 123
Education Acts 32, 38, 69, 118, 121, 150
Education in Britain 23, 32, 51, 69, 81, 118, 126, 131
Egypt 34, 61
Emancipation of serfs 163–4
Erhard 257–8, 260
Ethiopia See Abyssinia
European Economic Community (EEC) 126–8, 140, 257

Factory Acts 23, 26, 39, 50–1
Fascism 194–203
Fenians 35, 85–6
First World War 65–6, 74, 80–1, 169, 194, 235–41
Five Year Plans (USSR) 229–30, 267, 271
France 153–61
Franco-Prussian War 159–60, 176, 184–5
Frankfurt Parliament 180–1
Free trade 20, 25–7, 30, 32, 69
French Second Empire 158–9
French Second Republic 157
French Third Republic 160–1

Gaitskell 122, 134, 144
Garibaldi 175–6
General Strike (1926) 97–8, 103, 149

Geneva Protocol 111, 245
German army 187, 191, 217–8, 239–41
German Confederation 179–81
German economy 190, 208, 212, 219–20, 255, 257
German Empire (1871–1918) 183, 185–91
German Liberals 187, 189
German socialists 187–90
German unification 179-85
Germany 179–91, 206–22, 253–63
Gestapo 216
Giolitti 193–4, 197
Gladstone 27, 29–30, 32–6, 59, 61, 90, 141
Goebbels 211, 215–6, 222
Goering 215–6, 254
Gorbachev 262, 272–4, 285–7
Grand Alliance 106–7, 116
Great Depression 98–9, 211–3
Great Patriotic War 265–6
Greek Revolt 56, 58
Grey 64–6, 74
Guizot 135–6

Heath 127–8, 135, 145
Helsinki Accords 282
Himmler 215–6
Hindenburg 209, 213
Hitler 112–5, 202–3, 208, 210–22, 248–51, 265–6
Hitler Youth 217
Hoare-Laval Pact 113, 202, 248
Holocaust 218, 221–2
Home Rule 35–6, 73, 86, 89, 90
House of Lords 72-3, 147
Hungary 284, 286

Imperialism 38–9, 60–2, 67
India 104
Ireland 26, 34–6, 73, 84–92, 95
Irish economy 90–2
Irish Land Act (1870, 1881) 35–6, 92
Irish nationalism 84–7
Irish potato famine 27, 91–2
Italian economy 195, 200
Italian unification 173–7
Italy 159, 173–7, 193–203

Japan 63, 113, 166, 247–8, 250–1
Jews 165, 199, 211, 218–9, 221–2
Junkers 182, 186, 191

Keir Hardie 78
Kellogg-Briand Pact 112, 246
Kerensky 170
Keynes 97, 99, 111, 244
Khrushchev 253, 268–70, 280–1, 283–4
Kohl 261, 263
Korean War 279
Kornilov affair 170–1
Kulturkampf 187

Labour Party and governments 78–9, 95–6, 99–100, 120, 130, 133–4, 139, 142–5
League of Nations 111, 202, 244–9
Lenin 166–7, 170–1, 224–7
Liberal Party and governments 32–6, 67, 69–73, 80, 122, 130, 133, 139, 141–2, 146
Liberal reforms (1906–14) 71–2
Liberal Tories 20
Lloyd George 71–2, 80–1, 87, 90, 94–5, 110, 142, 242
Locarno Treaties 111, 209, 246
Lord Liverpool 18–20
Louis Philippe 155–6
Louis XVIII 153–4

MacDonald 78–9, 95–6, 99–100, 111
Macmillan 99, 123–4
Major 133, 136, 146
Manchuria 113, 166, 247–8, 250–1
Marshall Plan 255, 278
Mazzini 157, 174–5
Mensheviks 166, 170
Metternich 174, 180
Morocco crises 64–5, 74, 237
Munich Conference 105, 114, 203, 250
Mussolini 196–203, 248

Napoleon III 156–9, 175–6, 184–5
National Government 99–102, 143
National Health Service 120
National Insurance 71, 94, 121
Nationalisation 121, 148
Naval race (1898–1914) 64, 74, 236
Navy League 191
Nazi Party 210–22
Nazi-Soviet Pact (1939) 114, 232, 250
New Economic Policy (USSR) 226–7
Newspapers, British 150
Nicholas II 165–70
North Atlantic Treaty Organization (NATO) 258, 278–9
North German Confederation 184
Northern Ireland 135-6
November Revolution (Germany) 206
Nuclear Arms 279–83, 286

O'Connell 20, 26, 85
O'Connor 24, 45–6
Octobrists 167
Orange Order 88
Ostpolitik 261–2, 282

Palmerston 29, 56–7, 59, 155
Pan-German League 190
Papacy 174, 176, 199
Papen 212–3
Paris Commune 160
Parliament Act (1911) 72–3, 139, 147
Parliamentary reform 21–3, 33, 42–3, 77, 138–9
Parnell 35–6, 86
Partition of Ireland 87, 90
Pearl Harbour 106, 116, 251
Peel 20, 25–7, 43, 89–90
Peelites 27, 29
Pitt 17–18, 84
Pobedonostsev 165
Poland 114, 222, 226, 242–4, 246, 250, 253, 262, 267, 276–7, 285–6
Poor Law 23–4, 47–8, 72, 96

Populists 164
Potsdam Conference 107, 253, 276
Prime Minister 147–8
Privatisation 131
Prussia 179–83, 186
Prussian army 182, 184
Prussian economy 181–2
Public Health 39, 48–9
Purges 230–1, 268

Radio in Britain 96, 117, 150
Red Terror 224
Reform and Redistribution Acts (1884–5) 33, 42, 139
Reform Act (1832) 21–3, 42,
Reform Act (1867) 31, 42, 138
Reparations 111, 207–8, 243
Reunification of Germany 262–3, 286
Revolution, France (1848) 156–7, 174–5, 180–1
Revolution, Germany (1848) 180–1
Revolution, Italy (1848–9) 174–5
Rhineland, remilitarisation 114, 249
Rhodes 61–2
Roosevelt 106-7, 253, 276
Russia 163–71, 224–33, 265–74
Russian Civil War (1918–20) 225–6
Russian Dumas 167–8
Russian economy 165–6, 229–30, 266–7, 271
Russian Revolution (1905) 166–7
Russian Revolution (1917) 170–1
Russian secret police 224, 226, 231, 268–9
Russo-Japanese War 166

Schleswig-Holstein 183
Schlieffen Plan 239–40
Schutzstaffel (SS) 214–6
Second World War (Britain) 105–7, 115–8,
Second World War (Italy) 203
Serbia 237–8
Seven Weeks War 176, 183
Sinn Fein 73, 87, 95
Six Acts (1819) 19
Solidarity 285–6
South Africa 34, 38, 61–2
Spanish Civil War 112, 202, 232
Speenhamland system 19, 47
Splendid isolation 62–3
Stalin 114, 116, 171, 228–33, 253, 258, 265–8, 276
Stalingrad 116, 265
Stolypin 167–8
Stresa Front 113, 202, 248
Stresemann 208–9
Sudan 34, 61
Sudetenland 114, 243, 250
Suffragettes 76–7, 140

Tamworth Manifesto 25, 42
Thatcher 129–32, 136, 145–6
Trade unions 18, 20, 33, 39, 43, 71, 78–9, 95, 97–8, 121, 126–9, 131, 148–50
Transformism 193, 195
Triple Entente 63–4, 74, 235–6
Trotsky 171, 226, 228–29
Truman Doctrine 277
Tsarist Russia 163–70
Turkey 56–60, 237–8, 240, 243

Ulster Unionists 73, 88–9
Ulster Volunteer Force 73, 89
Unemployment in Britain 19, 94, 98–9, 101

USA 106–7, 116–7, 134, 241–2, 245, 251, 253, 255, 263, 276–83
USSR 225–33 265–74

Versailles Settlement 110–1, 195, 207, 242–4
Vienna Settlement 54, 180

Walesa, Lech 285–6
War Communism 224, 226
Warsaw Pact 260, 269, 278–9, 284
Washington Naval Treaty (1922) 112, 247
Weimar Republic 206–9, 212–3
Welfare State 72, 120–1, 148
Wellington 20, 22
Weltpolitik 189–91, 236
West Germany 256–61, 278–80, 282
Whigs 23–4, 29
William II, Kaiser 63–4, 188–91, 236–9
Wilson 125–7, 128, 135, 144
Witte 165–8
Women in Britain 75–7, 117, 140
Women's suffrage 76–7, 140
Woodrow Wilson 242
Workhouses 23, 47–8

Yalta Conference 107, 253, 276
Yeltsin 273–4, 287
Young Ireland 26, 85
Yugoslavia 277, 287–8

Zollverein 181–2